図表を多用し、フォームを用いて分かりやすく解説

米国特許手続ハンドブック

―第2版―

弁理士 **大坂 雅浩** 著

発明推進協会

推薦のことば

　近年の米国における産業構造の変化から、米国議会への影響に関する産業界のパワーバランスが崩れ、ついに、歴史的な特許法改正が2011年9月に可決された。企業のグローバル化を背景に、従前のような個人発明家や国内企業の保護から、より大企業の利益保護にシフトした改正であったといえる。日本企業やその代理人は、その利益を享受するため、改正内容を十分検討する必要がある。今回の改正内容は多岐に渡るが、現在ではそれら総てが施行され、規則もほぼ出揃ったと言える。

　本書は、ワシントンＤＣに10年以上の長きにわたり在住し、より密接に特許出願手続きに接してきた著者が、実務やセミナー開催等で蓄積した情報やノウハウをまとめたものである。また、豊富な米国特許庁発行のフォームを用いて各種制度の概要から、実際の書類提出時の詳細な注意点まで解説がなされているので、実務経験者はもとより、これから米国特許法に携わる初学者にも理解し易いという点が特徴である。

　米国特許法の歴史的改正後、規則が出揃った段階で米国特許法の最新知識の習得には最適な一冊であり、ご推薦申し上げたい。

　　　　　　　　　　　　　　　　　　　　　　2013年7月
　　　　　　　　　　　　　　　　　　　　　　三好内外国特許事務所
　　　　　　　　　　　　　　　　　　　　　　　会長　弁理士　三好　秀和

はじめに

　米国特許商標庁（The United States Patent and Trademark Office：U.S.P.T.O.）への手続きの理解は、判例を第1次的な法源とする英米法体系を採用する特許法（35USC）の趣旨を理解することが重要です。規則はもちろん守らなければなりませんが、それと同時に道理に適わない規則（37CFR）や審査官マニュアル（MPEP）は、「破るためにある」という一面もあります。すなわち、規則や審査マニュアルは、時としてU.S.P.T.O.に都合よく解釈して編纂され、特許法やその趣旨に適合していないことも少なからず見受けられます。米国特許弁護士は、クライアントの利益を優先し、規則に問題がある場合には戦うことも辞さない、という姿勢を取っています。2007年にバージニア州連邦地裁が、施行目前の規則を特許法に違反する恐れがあるとして、その施行に差止めの仮処分命令をしたことは、日本特許業界にも大きな波紋を広げたことと思います。

　その一方で、大陸法体系を採用する日本法では、特許法においても方式審査便覧や審査基準等詳細な規定が存在し、特許庁への手続きもこの規定に基づいて手続きを行えば、最もよい手続きが行えると言えます。また、日本弁理士にとっては規則通り手続きを行うことが、クライアントの信頼を勝ち得ることにもつながります。従って、米国実務と比較して、日本実務においては、特許庁から提供されるフォームをいかに正確に記入するかという点に重点をおいて手続きを行っている傾向にあるかと思います。

　このように特許手続きに対して日米ではその考え方、取り組み方に大きな隔たりがあるように思えます。その隔たりが、日本の特許実務者が米国特許法の難しさを感じる要因になっているのかもしれません。

　本書では、米国特許法の特に手続きにフォーカスし、可能な限りU.S.P.T.O.が提供する実際のフォームを多用し、米国法律事務所ならではの観点から特許出願手続きを解説しています。また、日常的に発生し得る問題や注意点等も可能な限り指摘しました。日本の特許実務者にとっては、日頃から米国特許出願関連書類に接している方が多いかと存じますが、じっくりレビューする時間がない方も多いかと思います。この機会に是非ご一読頂き、知識の整理に役立てて頂ければ幸いに存じます。

また、2011年9月16日に成立した米国改正特許法において、特許手続面も大幅に改正されました。この改正によってどのように変わったのか？出願人としてはどのような対応を取ればよいのか？についても解説を行っています。

　米国出願するクライアントを担当する弁理士の方々はもちろん、企業の外国特許担当者の方、または、外国特許事務を担当される方まで広く米国特許法理解の一助になるものと考えております。

　ここで、本書の制作においては、MOTSLAW事務所内の出願管理チームにフォームの記入方法等U.S.P.T.O.への確認や各種情報収集をして頂きました。特にチームリーダの伊藤孝代さんには、本書内の説明図等の作成にも関与して頂きました。この場をお借りしてMOTSLAW事務所出願管理チームに感謝の意を表したいと思います。

　なお、本書は教育的観点から作成されたものであり、法的アドバイスの提供を目的としたものではありません。また、本内容は、2013年5月31日時点での法律や規則に基づいて編著されたものであり、その正確性や最新性の確保に努めておりますが、いかなる保証をするものではありませんことをご了承ください。

2013年7月
ワシントンD.C.にて
弁理士　大坂　雅浩

第2版の刊行にあたって

　2011年9月16日発効のLeahy-Smith America Invents Act（AIA）に基づく特許法の改正が成立して6年が経ちました。発行される特許の50％以上が、AIA改正法に基づくものだということが最近の調査で分かりました。

　この6年間の様々な変化の中で、米国特許業界、特に手続き面からは、以下に特徴的な変化があったと感じています。

発明の主題（35U.S.C.101）拒絶の増加

　所謂ビジネス方法関連発明は、2000年初頭に数多く出願され、現在は活用のフェーズとなっています。ビジネス方法関連発明の特色として、突然脚光を浴び、あるときから多くの出願がされたため、それ以前の先行技術文献が不足していました。業界では知られた技術であっても、先行技術文献を用いた無効主張が困難な側面があったのです。

　そこで、ビジネス方法関連発明に係る侵害訴訟の被告は、当該特許は、抽象的であり法上の発明ではない、米国特許法101条を理由に無効の主張をするようになりました。パテントトロールを含むNPE（Non Practicing Entity）が原告のケースも多く、裁判所も被告の主張を認める傾向があったのかもしれません。これにより、徐々に同法101条の判断基準が引き上げられ、結果として、同法101条の拒絶が増加するに至っています。

　これに関する特許出願手続きの影響として、同法101条の拒絶が増えたことから、オフィスアクションの枚数も増えたと実感しています。出願人としては、拒絶理由が増えた事により、応答する事項が増えるため、その分オフィスアクションの応答の負荷が増加したと言えます。

U.S.P.T.O.提出書類の電子提出システムの進展

　U.S.P.T.O.では、従前から出願人からの書類の提出をPDFファイルで受理しています。PDFの生成方法によっては、電子提出時にU.S.P.T.O.のシステムが受理できない場合がありました。特に、非英語（例えば日本語）のコンピュータで生成されたPDFは、フォントや言語設定によって問題が生じることが少なくありません。

近年では、出願人からの書類の提出を、ウェブページのフォームに入力させて完成するものが増えてきました。

NPE（Non Practicing Entity）による訴訟の減少

　AIAにて付与後レビュー（Post Grant Review）や、当事者系レビュー（Inter Parte Review）等の特許無効審判制度が創設され、従前と比較して、申立人の関与が認められつつ、審判官のより専門的な判断により、特許の有効性が判断されることになりました。またAIAにて、訴訟における当事者の併合の制限規定（35U.S.C.299）が創設されました。これにより、複数の被告のケースを１つに併合することに制限が加えられ、実質的に異なる会社の訴訟を併合することが、事実上不可能になりました。

　2011年以降、NPE（Non Practicing Entity）による提訴数は、減少傾向にありますが、これらを含む改正が影響しているように思います。

　さて、初版の発行から４年が経ち、上述の様な変化に対応した構成が必要になってきました。また、U.S.P.T.O.は頻繁にフォームを変更しており、本書の内容も変更する必要性が出てきました。

　そこで第２版では、各フォームを最新のものに変更して説明を追加し、特許の主題（同法101条）、新規性（同法102条）やミーンズプラスファンクションの規定を含む記載要件（同法112条）に関し、重要判決を交えながら説明しています。さらに、電子ターミナルディスクレーマの提出等のオンラインベースの書類提出や、付与後レビュー（Post Grant Review）や当事者系レビュー（Inter Parte Review）等の説明を追加しました。

　最後に、改訂作業に関してMETROLEXIS LAW GROUPの坂井愛子氏には、図表の作成や校閲に関与して頂きました。また、一般社団法人発明推進協会の神林宏美氏には、度重なる原稿の追加修正に応じて頂き、詳細な校正作業をして頂きました。

　ここで、改めて感謝の意を表したいと思います。

2017年12月

大坂　雅浩

目　　次

推薦のことば……………………………………………………………… i
はじめに …………………………………………………………………… ii
第2版の刊行にあたって………………………………………………… iv
凡例 ……………………………………………………………………… xvii

第1章　米国特許概要……………………………………………… 1

米国特許概要………………………………………………………………… 1
　増加する出願件数……………………………………………………… 1
　特許出願件数…………………………………………………………… 1
　国又は地域別特許取得件数…………………………………………… 2
　法令等の表記…………………………………………………………… 2
特許出願から取得まで…………………………………………………… 4
　特許出願………………………………………………………………… 4
　形式審査………………………………………………………………… 4
　出願公開………………………………………………………………… 4
　選択／限定指令………………………………………………………… 4
　実体審査………………………………………………………………… 5
　審判請求………………………………………………………………… 6
　ワンポイント解説：優先日？出願日？……………………………… 6

第2章　特許出願……………………………………………………… 9

特許出願の種類…………………………………………………………… 9
　本出願（Non-provisional Application）…………………………… 9
　パリルート出願…………………………………………………………10
　PCT米国国内移行出願 …………………………………………………10
　PCTバイパス出願（M.P.E.P.1895）…………………………………10
　PCT国内移行出願とPCTバイパス出願との比較 ……………………11
　日本語出願（非英語出願）……………………………………………12
　仮出願（Provisional Application）…………………………………12

目　　次

意匠出願（Design Patent Application）……………………………………15
特許出願の方法…………………………………………………………………16
　電子出願システム（EFS-Web）を活用しよう ……………………………16
　ワンポイント解説：仮出願制度の有効活用…………………………………16
　電子出願の受理証………………………………………………………………18
　電子出願以外の提出方法………………………………………………………20
出願書類を準備しよう…………………………………………………………21
　送付状（PTO/AIA/15）………………………………………………………21
　ワンポイント解説：PCTバイパス出願時の送付状の注意点 ……………21
　PCT国内移行時の送付（PTO-1390）………………………………………23
　明細書の準備例…………………………………………………………………30
　クレーム（35U.S.C.112, 37C.F.R.1.75, M.P.E.P.608.1(n)）……………32
　要約（37C.F.R.1.72(b), M.P.E.P.608.01(b)）……………………………34
　必要な図面の作成例……………………………………………………………35
　出願データシート（Application Data Sheet：ADS）……………………37
　ワンポイント解説：法人を出願人として出願する場合の注意点…………38
　優先権書類の電子取寄せ申請書（Request to Retrieve Electronic Priority
　　Applications）（PTO/SB/38）……………………………………………45
　予備的補正書（Preliminary Amendment）………………………………46
出願人等のサインが必要な書類………………………………………………47
　宣誓書（Oath or Declaration）………………………………………………47
　ワンポイント解説：極小規模事業体…………………………………………49
　ワンポイント解説：ResidenceとMailing Address………………………54
　譲渡証（Assignment）…………………………………………………………59
　ワンポイント解説：*Stanford v. Roche*　………………………………………60
　U.S.P.T.O.の譲渡書登録データベース ……………………………………64
　委任状（Power of Attorney）…………………………………………………65
　ワンポイント解説：現地代理人事務所を変えたいとき(移管)に必要な書類…65
情報開示義務とIDS……………………………………………………………68
　ワンポイント解説：情報開示義務は特許法の規定ではない！……………72
　ワンポイント解説：包袋（File Wrapper）とは……………………………79
庁手数料及び手数料の軽減……………………………………………………82

出願手数料は出願人の規模によって異なります（小規模事業体、
　　極小規模事業体）……………………………………………………82
　出願人の規模が変わったら？……………………………………………83
出願費用の節約術……………………………………………………………84
　ワンポイント解説：返金請求……………………………………………85
出願日の認定要件及び救済措置……………………………………………86
　パリ優先権期間を徒過してしまった場合の救済措置…………………86
出願のステータスをチェックしよう………………………………………87
　ワンポイント解説：カスタマー番号……………………………………87

第3章　特許要件 …………………………………………………………91

新規性　Novelty ……………………………………………………………91
　新規性の解説………………………………………………………………91
　新規性の例外の解説………………………………………………………93
　新規性に関するその他の条文の解説……………………………………98
純粋な先願主義と米国の先願主義との相違のポイント …………………100
新規性審査における経過措置………………………………………………102
非自明性　Unobviousness …………………………………………………104
　出願後に公知になった文献でも非自明性拒絶の引用例になり得る……104
　ワンポイント解説：非自明性……………………………………………105
明細書の記載要件　Specification …………………………………………106
　ワンポイント解説：ベストモード要件（35U.S.C.112(a)）……………107
　ワンポイント解説：*Williamson v. Citrix Online, LLC* 事件
　　　　　　　　　　連邦高裁大法廷判決………………………………110
法定主題　Inventions Patentable …………………………………………111
　法定主題か否かの判断（Mayo/Alice Test）……………………………111
　ワンポイント解説：*Enfish, LLC v. Microsoft* 事件（5/12/2016）
　　　　　　　　　　連邦高裁判決 ………………………………………113
二重特許　Double Patent …………………………………………………114
　同一タイプの二重特許（35U.S.C.101）…………………………………114
　自明タイプの二重特許……………………………………………………114
　ターミナルディスクレーマ………………………………………………114

目 次

　　ワンポイント解説：同一タイプの二重特許 …………………………………115
　　ワンポイント解説：eTDの結果 ……………………………………………119

第4章　審査 …………………………………………………………………121

出願受領証 ……………………………………………………………………121
　外国出願ライセンス（Foreign Filing License）…………………………121
　出願受領証の例 ……………………………………………………………123
形式審査とその応答 …………………………………………………………124
　欠落部分提出通知（Notice to File Missing Parts）………………………124
　ワンポイント解説：延長手続き ……………………………………………125
　ワンポイント解説：宣誓書の提出時期 ……………………………………127
　修正書面提出通知（Notice to File Corrected Application Papers）………127
　不完全出願通知（Notice to Incomplete Application）……………………129
　ワンポイント解説：不完全出願通知への応答 ……………………………129
　選択／限定要求とその応答 ………………………………………………130
　ワンポイント解説："クレーム・アップ"という言葉 ……………………130
　ワンポイント解説：Office Action on the Meritsとは ……………………137
局指令（Office Action：OA）………………………………………………138
　局指令とは …………………………………………………………………138
　局指令を受けた時の対応 …………………………………………………138
　延長費用について …………………………………………………………138
　図面に関する局指令への応答 ……………………………………………139
　審査官面談（Interview）について ………………………………………140
　Ex Parte Quayle Actionとは ………………………………………………142
　ワンポイント解説：先行技術文献とは ……………………………………142
最終局指令（Final Office Action）…………………………………………143
　最終局指令とは ……………………………………………………………143
　最終局指令応答時の補正の制限 …………………………………………143
　最終局指令を回避するためには …………………………………………143
　最終局指令後の審査官面談 ………………………………………………143
　最終局指令を受けたときの対応 …………………………………………144
　意見書・補正書の提出 ……………………………………………………147

アドバイザリアクション（Advisory Action：AA） …………148
　ワンポイント解説：審査官の上司、スーパーバイザとは？ …………148
　最終局指令に応答しただけでは、時計は止まらない！ …………150
　最終局指令後の期間の計算について …………150
継続審査請求（RCE） …………152
継続的出願 …………155
　ワンポイント解説：CIP出願の注意点 …………156
　継続的出願とRCEの相違点 …………158
放置 …………160

第5章　審判 …………163

審判請求：Notice of Appeal（37C.F.R.41.31） …………163
　審判費用 …………163
審判理由補充書：Appeal Brief（37C.F.R.41.37） …………165
　審判請求理由補充書の例 …………166
審査官による答弁書：Examiner's Answer（37C.F.R.41.39） …………172
　審査が再開される場合〜U.S.P.T.O.の審判制度の問題点 …………172
応答書：Reply Brief（37C.F.R.41.41） …………175
　特許審判控訴部（PTAB）による審理に進んだ旨の通知 …………176
口頭審尋：Oral Hearing（37C.F.R.41.47） …………177
　口頭審尋請求書の記入例（PTO/AIA/32） …………177
　口頭審尋期日指定通知書 …………178
審判官合議体による審理及び審決：Board Review and Decision
（37C.F.R.41.50） …………179
　審決に不服がある場合 …………179
　ワンポイント解説：審決不服時の提訴先 …………179
プレアピールブリーフ（Preappeal Brief） …………180
　プレアピールブリーフの記入例（PTO/AIA/33） …………181

第6章　早期権利化のために　—早期審査— …………183

出願人の年齢・健康状態により受けられる早期審査 …………183
特定の発明内容により受けられる早期審査 …………185

目　次

　優先権を主張する対応外国出願により受けられる早期審査 ················188
　　日本出願の審査結果を利用した特許ハイウエイ施行プログラム
　　（Global/IP5 Patent Prosecution Highway：PPH）···············188
　割増し料金を支払うことによる優先審査 ·······························192
　意匠出願の早期審査 ···194
　　ワンポイント解説：早期審査のパイロットプログラム ··············194

第7章　発明者決定手続 ··197

発明者決定手続とは ···197
　　冒認出願への真発明者の手続き（35U.S.C.135）·····················197
　　発明者決定手続の請願（37C.F.R.42.405）···························197
　　請願者の手続き ···198
　　特許審判控訴部（PTAB）の決定 ······································198
　　冒認特許への真発明者の手続き（35U.S.C.291）·····················199
　　冒認出願への手続きと冒認特許への手続きとの比較 ··············199
　　ワンポイント解説：発明者決定手続の導入、
　　　　　　　　　　　　インターフェアレンス手続の廃止 ··············199
　　ワンポイント解説：発明者決定手続き ·······························199

第8章　許可通知及び特許の維持 ·······································201

許可通知の発行 ···201
　　許可通知 ···201
　　許可通知後の補正 ··201
　　許可通知の例（PTOL-85）···202
　　許可可能通知の例（PTOL-37）······································206
特許発行料の支払 ···209
　　特許発行料支払い送付状の例 ·······································210
　　特許発行料支払前に確認すべきこと ································212
特許発行料支払から特許発行まで ·······································213
　　特許発行通知の例 ··214
　　特許発行の延期（37C.F.R.1.314）··································215
　　特許発行の取下げ（37C.F.R.1.313）································215

特許の維持年金 ……………………………………………………………216
　維持年金の支払い期間を徒過した場合 ………………………………216
　上記猶予期間をも徒過した場合の取得る措置 ………………………216
　ワンポイント解説：手続きの遅延が不意図（Unintentional）な場合 ……217

第9章　特許の修正 ……………………………………………………219

訂正証明書の請求（Certificate of Correction）……………………………219
　訂正証明書の請求制度とは ……………………………………………219
　訂正証明書の請求の手続 ………………………………………………220
　訂正証明書請求の手数料 ………………………………………………220
　訂正証明書の記入例（PTO/SB/44）……………………………………221
再発行特許制度（Reissue Patent）…………………………………………222
　再発行特許制度とは ……………………………………………………222
　再発行特許出願の提出書類 ……………………………………………222
　再発行特許出願手数料（37C.F.R.1.16(e)(h)(i)(s)）…………………223
　再発行特許出願の手続 …………………………………………………223
　再発行特許の送付状（PTO/AIA/50）…………………………………224
　再発行特許の発明者宣誓書（PTO/AIA/05）…………………………225
査定系再審査制度（Ex Parte-Reexamination）……………………………226
　査定系再審査制度とは …………………………………………………226
　査定系再審査の提出書類 ………………………………………………226
　査定系再審査請求料（37C.F.R.1.20(c)）………………………………226
　査定系再審査の手続 ……………………………………………………227
　ワンポイント解説：特許が無効（Invalid）と
　　　　　　　　　　行使不能（Unenforceable）とはどこが違う？ ………227
補充審査（Supplemental Examination）……………………………………228
　補充審査とは ……………………………………………………………228
　補充審査の提出物 ………………………………………………………228
　補充審査請求手数料（37C.F.R.1.20(k)）………………………………228
　補充審査の手続き及び効果 ……………………………………………229
　ワンポイント解説：詐欺の意図と認められる場合 …………………229
　補充審査請求送付状の記入例（PTO/SB/59）………………………230

目　次

第10章　特許の攻撃 …………………………………………… 235

第三者文献提出（Preissurance Submissions by Third Parties）……… 236
　第三者文献提出制度とは ……………………………………… 236
　時期的要件 ……………………………………………………… 236
　第三者文献提出の要件 ………………………………………… 237
　提出された文献はIDSと同じように取り扱われる ………… 238
　第三者文献提出の記入例（PTO/SB/429）…………………… 239
当事者系審判の規則体系 ………………………………………… 241
付与後レビュー（Post Grant Review：PGR）制度…………… 242
　付与後レビュー制度とは ……………………………………… 242
　PGR申立要件 …………………………………………………… 242
　PGR申立ができる出願（経過措置）………………………… 242
　PGR申立の手続き ……………………………………………… 243
　ワンポイント解説：WANTED ― 先行文献！……………… 246
当事者系レビュー（Inter Partes Review：IPR）制度 ………… 247
　当事者系レビュー制度とは（35U.S.C.311）………………… 247
　IPR申立要件（35U.S.C.312）………………………………… 247
　IPR申立の手続き ……………………………………………… 248
　和解（35U.S.C.317、37C.F.R.42.74）……………………… 250
　PTABによる最終審決（35U.S.C.318、37C.F.R.42.71）…… 250
　審決に不服の場合 ……………………………………………… 250
PGRとIPRとの主な相違点 ……………………………………… 250
　費用 ……………………………………………………………… 250
　申立の時期 ……………………………………………………… 250
　申立の理由 ……………………………………………………… 251
　審理手続きに進むための基準 ………………………………… 251
　ディスカバリ …………………………………………………… 251
　一事不再理 ……………………………………………………… 251
金融系ビジネス方法特許レビュー
（Covered Business Method Patent Review：CBMPR）……… 252
特許の攻撃はU.S.P.T.O.か裁判所か …………………………… 253

クレーム解釈における相違 ……………………………………253
　時間的な相違 ……………………………………………………253
　費用的な相違 ……………………………………………………253
　判断の相違 ………………………………………………………253
　補正の可能性の相違 ……………………………………………254
　審理開始可能性の相違 …………………………………………254
　ワンポイント解説："ロケット・ドケット"裁判所とは？……………254

資料 ……………………………………………………………………255
U.S.P.T.O.料金表 ……………………………………………………321
索引 ……………………………………………………………………329

凡　例

A		
AA	Advisory Action	アドバイザリ・アクション
ADS	Application Data Sheet	アプリケーションデータシート
AFCP 2.0	After Final Consideration Pilot 2.0	最終局指令後応答の審査パイロットプログラム2.0
AIA	Leahy-Smith America Invents Act	リーヒ・スミス米国発明法
Amendment		補正（書）
Appeal Brief		審判理由補充書
Assignee		譲受人
Assignment		譲渡証
Assignor		譲渡人
B		
Bypass Application (PCT bypass application)		バイパス出願
Board Decision		審判官会議体による審決
Board Review		審判官会議体による審理
C		
CAFC	Court of Appeals for the Federal Circuit	連邦巡回控訴裁判所
CBMPR	Covered Business Method Patent Review	ビジネス方法特許レビュー（金融系）
Certificate of Correction		訂正証明書
Certificate of Mailing		郵送証明書付郵便
CIP Application	Continuation-In-Part Application	一部継続出願
Continuation Application		継続出願
Continuing Application		継続的出願
37C.F.R.	The Code of Federal Regulations (Title 37)	米国特許規則

D		
Declaration		宣誓書
Derivation Proceedings		発明者決定手続
Design Patent Application		意匠出願
District Court for the Eastern District of Virginia		バージニア州東部連邦地方裁判所
Divisional Application		分割出願
Drawings		図面

E		
EFS-web	Eleccrtic Filing System-web	インターネット電子出願システム
Election/Restriction Requirement		選択／限定要求
Electronic Acknowledgement Receipt		電子受理証
eTD	electronic Terminal Disclaimer	電子ターミナルディスクレーマ
Examiners Answer		審査官による答弁（書）
Exparte Quayle Action		一方的方式オフィスアクション
Express Abandonment		放棄表明（書）
Express Mail		速達郵便

F		
Final Office Action		最終局指令　ファイナルオフィスアクション
Foreign Filing Lisence		外国出願ライセンス

I		
IBR	Incorporation By Reference	参照による編入
IDS	Information Disclosure Statement	情報開示陳述書
Interview		審査官面談
International Application		国際出願
Interview Summary		インタビューサマリ
IPER	International Prelimimnary Examination Report	国際予備審査報告
IPR	Inter Partes Review	当事者系レビュー
ISA	International Search Authority	国際調査機関
ITC	International Trade Commission	国際貿易委員会

xviii

J		
JPO	Japan Patent Office	日本特許庁

L		
Lapse		放置

M		
M.P.E.P.	Manual of Patent Examining Procedure	特許審査マニュアル

N		
New Issue		新たな争点（ファイナルOA応答時の不適正な補正等）
New Matter		新規事項（明細書記載範囲外の補正等）
Non-final Office Action		非最終局指令
Non-provisional Application		本出願（通常出願）
Notice of Abandonment		放棄通知書
Notice of Allowance		許可可能通知（書）
Notice of Appeal		審判請求（書）
Notice of Publication		出願公開公報発行通知（書）
Notice to File Corrected Application Papers		修正書面提出通知（書）
Notice to File Missing Parts		出願の欠落部分提出通知（書）
Novelty		新規性

O		
OA	Office Action	局指令　オフィスアクション
OEE	Office of Earlier Examination	先に審査を行った特許庁
Office Action on the Merits		実体的オフィスアクション
OLE	Office of Later Examination	後に審査を行った特許庁
Oral Hearing		口頭審尋

P		
PCT	Patent Cooperation Treaty	特許協力条約
PDF	Portable Document Format	米国アドビシステムが開発したファイル形式
PGR	Post Grant Review	付与後レビュー
Plant Patent Application		植物特許出願
Power of Attorney		委任状
PPH	Patent Prosecution Highway	特許審査ハイウエイ
Preappeal Brief		プレアピールブリーフ
Preissurance Submissions by Third Parties		第三者文献提出
Preliminary Amendment		予備的補正（書）
Provisional Application		仮出願
PTA	Patent Term Adjustment	特許期間調整
PTAB	Patent Trial and Appeal Board	特許審判控訴部

R		
RCE	Request for Continued Examination	継続審査請求
Real party-in-interest		利害関係人
Recapture		再発行特許審査にて放棄したクレームを再発行特許にて取り戻すこと
Reissue Patent		再発行特許
Remarks		意見書
Reopen		審査再開（通知）

S		
Settlement		和解
Small Entity		小規模事業体
SNQ	Substantial New Question of Patentability	特許性に関する新たな問題
Specification		明細書
SPE	Supervisory Patent Examiner	審査官の上司(スーパーバイザー)
SSP	Shortened Statutory Period	短縮された法定期限
Statement		陳述書
Submission		提出物
Substutute Statement		代用陳述書
Supplemental Examination		補充審査

T		
Terminal Disclaimer		ターミナルディスクレーマ
Transmittal		送付状

U		
Unavoidable		不可避
Unintentional		不意図
Unobviousness		非自明性
Utility patent		(実用)特許出願
Utility Patent Application Transmittal Form		(実用)特許出願送付状
U.S.P.T.O.	United States Patent and Trademark Office	米国特許商標庁
35U.S.C.	United States Code (Title 35)	米国特許法

第1章

米国特許概要

米国特許概要

増加する出願件数

米国特許出願件数は増加の一途を辿っています。機械、電気、化学等を含む特許出願件数は、2015年のデータで約59万件です。特に外国企業からの出願の増加が顕著になっています。また、物品の装飾的デザインを保護対象とする意匠出願は、同データで約3.9万件です。植物特許出願は、同データで約1千件となっています。次に、国別特許取得件数ですが、米国、日本、ドイツ共に微減となっています。一方、韓国、中国は増加傾向にあります。これらを含めたU.S.P.T.O.の詳細な統計情報は下記リンクから参照できます。

https://www.uspto.gov/learning-and-resources/statistics

特許出願件数

Year	Utility Patent Applications, U.S. Origin	Utility Patent Applications, Foreign Origin	Design Patent Applications	Plant Patent Applications	Total Patent Applications
2015	288,335	301,075	39,097	1,140	629,647
2014	285,096	293,706	35,378	1,063	615,243
2013	287,831	283,781	36,034	1,406	609,052
2012	268,782	274,033	32,799	1,149	576,763

第1章　米国特許概要

2011	247,750	255,832	30,467	1,139	535,188
2010	241,977	248,249	29,059	992	520,277
2009	224,912	231,194	25,806	959	482,871
2008	231,588	224,733	27,782	1,209	485,312
2007	241,347	214,807	27,752	1,049	484,955
2006	221,784	204,183	25,515	1,151	452,633

国又は地域別特許取得件数

Origin	2008	2009	2010	2011	2012	2013	2014	2015
U.S.A.	77,502	82,382	107,791	108,622	121,026	133,593	144,621	140,969
JAPAN	33,682	35,501	44,813	46,139	50,677	51,919	53,848	52,409
GERMANY	8,914	9,000	12,363	11,919	13,835	15,498	16,550	16,549
U.K.	3,085	3,173	4,298	4,292	5,211	5,806	6,488	6,417
FRANCE	3,163	3,140	4,450	4,532	5,386	6,083	6,691	6,565
SOUTH KOREA	7,548	8,762	11,671	12,262	13,233	14,548	16,469	17,924
TAIWAN	6,341	6,642	8,239	8,781	10,646	11,071	11,333	11,690
CANADA	3,393	3,655	4,852	5,014	5,775	6,547	7,042	6,802
CHINA	1,223	1,654	2,655	3,174	4,637	5,928	7,236	8,116

法令等の表記

米国特許出願は米国連邦政府の商務省に属する米国特許商標庁（U.S.P.T.O.）で審査され、出願人に特許権が付与されます。米国特許手続きの理解に下記の3つが欠かせません。本書でも頻繁に参照します。

- **Title 35 of the United States Code（35U.S.C.）　米国特許法**[1]

  米国の法律には連邦法、及び州法がありますが、特許法は連邦法にて規定されています。米国連邦議会の承認により改正等がなされます。例えば、米国特許法102条(b)項は35U.S.C.102(b)と表記します。

- **Title 37 of the Code of Federal Regulations（37C.F.R.）　米国特許連邦規則**[2]

  特許等の規則が定められています。連邦政府により連邦官報（Federal

1　米国特許法35U.S.C.
　　https://www.uspto.gov/web/offices/pac/mpep/consolidated_laws.pdf
2　米国特許連邦規則37C.F.R.
　　https://www.uspto.gov/web/offices/pac/mpep/consolidated_rules.pdf

Register：FR）にて公布されます。例えば、米国特許連邦規則1.56(a)項は37C.F.R.1.56(a)と表記します。

- Manual of Patent Examining Procedure（M.P.E.P.） **特許審査マニュアル**[3]

  U.S.P.T.O.が審査官向けに発行しています。例えば、M.P.E.P.2181と表記します。

3 　特許審査マニュアルM.P.E.P.
　　https://www.uspto.gov/web/offices/pac/mpep/index.html

第1章　米国特許概要

特許出願から取得まで

　米国特許商標庁（U.S.P.T.O.）へ特許出願を行う際の手続きの主な流れについて、図1（P.7）を参照しながら見てみましょう。

特許出願
　米国特許出願を行う際、同一発明者のなした同一発明に関する先の出願の優先権を主張することができます。先の出願には、①米国仮出願（U.S. Provisional Application）、②パリ条約締約国でなされた外国出願、及び③PCTに基づく国際出願（International Application）が含まれます。これらの出願に基づいて優先権主張を行い、④米国本出願（Non-provisional Application）を行うことで、先の出願の出願日を基準に新規性や非自明性等の審査が行われます。

形式審査
　出願後、出願書類に不足があった場合には、U.S.P.T.O.より⑤出願の欠落部分提出通知（Notice to File Missing Parts）が送達されます。出願人は、送達日から原則2月（5月間延長可能）以内に、通知で指摘された書類の追加提出を行うことで⑥欠落部分提出通知に対する応答を行います。なお、欠落部分提出通知と似た性質の通知として、出願書類の形式的な修正を通知する修正書面提出通知（Notice to File Corrected Application Paper）が送達される場合もあります。応答期間は同様に送達日から原則2月（5月間延長可能）です。

出願公開
　原則総ての出願は優先日から18月後にその内容を公衆に知らしめるべく出願公開されます。公開時にはU.S.P.T.O.から⑦出願公開通知（Notice of Publication）が送付されます。特許出願は公開後、一定の要件を満たす場合に、無断実施者に対して実施料相当額の賠償請求が可能になります（35U.S.C.154(d)）。

選択／限定指令
　出願に2つ以上の発明が含まれていると認定された場合には、⑧選択／限定

指令（Election/Restriction Requirement）が発せられます。指令日から原則2月（4月間延長可能）以内に⑨応答します。なお、この指令は、書面ではなく審査官からの電話連絡による場合があります。

実体審査

　審査官が特許出願に係る発明の実体審査を行い、拒絶理由を発見しない場合には★許可通知が発せられます。拒絶理由を発見した場合には、⑩非最終局指令（Non-final Office Action）が発せられます。出願人は、この局指令に対し、クレームの補正（補正書）や反論（意見書）等を含む⑪応答書（Response to the Office Action）を提出することができます。補正は出願当初の明細書の記載内容の範囲内で行うことができます。局指令に対する応答は、局指令から原則3月（3月間延長可能）以内に行います。

　審査官は、提出された補正書（Amendment）及び意見書（Remarks）を考慮して再度審査を行います。これらの書類で拒絶理由が解消された場合には★許可通知が発せられます。解消されない場合には、⑫最終局指令（Final Office action）が発せられます。

　⑫最終局指令が発せられると、出願審査は最終状態になります。出願人は、⑬応答書を再提出、⑭継続審査請求（Request for Continued Examination）、若しくは、⑮審判請求（Notice of Appeal）をする必要があります。⑬応答書を提出する場合には、出願が最終状態であるため補正の範囲に大きな制約があります。審査官が同意する内容で応答し、拒絶理由が解消された場合には★許可通知が発せられます。解消されない場合には、⑯アドバイザリ・アクション（Advisory Action: AA）が発せられます。その場合、出願人は⑭継続審査請求または⑮審判請求を行わなければ、出願が放棄扱いとされてしまいます。これらは最終局指令から3月（3月間延長可能）以内に行います。

　なお、⑭継続審査請求をする際には、補正書と意見書等の提出物（Submission）を請求と一緒に提出します。これにより、出願の最終状態が解かれ、審査官が拒絶理由を発見しない場合には★許可通知が発せられます。拒絶理由が解消されない場合には再度⑫最終局指令が発せられます。また、審査官がそれでもなお拒絶を維持する場合、若しくは、新たな拒絶理由を発見した場合には、通常⑩非最終局指令が発せられます。

第1章　米国特許概要

審判請求

　審査官の拒絶に承服しない場合には⑮審判請求を行う事ができます。審判の争点は審査官の行った局指令の適否です。争点は審査官の局指令の適否ですので、日本の特許法と異なり、審判中に補正を行うことができません。出願人は、審判請求後所定期間内に審判理由補充書を提出します。その後、審査官による答弁書の提出がなされ、出願人及び審査官の意見が出揃った場合に、審判官合議体による審決がなされます。

ワンポイント解説：優先日？出願日？
　米国で出願する前の一定期間中にパリ条約に加盟する国や国際出願の機関に同一発明者が同一の発明について先の出願を行い、その特許出願の優先権を主張して米国出願を行った場合、その国等で出願した日は「優先日」と言います。一方、出願日とは、米国に実際に出願した日を言います。従って、優先権を主張した場合には、優先日と出願日とは異なる場合があります。

特許出願から取得まで

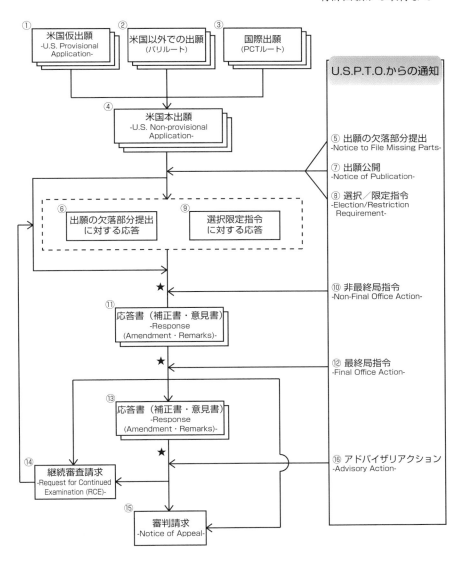

★… 許可通知 -Notice of Allowamce- のタイミングを示す

図1　米国特許出願審査手続の主な流れ

第2章

特許出願

特許出願の種類

本出願（Non-provisional Application）

　本出願の「本」は、仮出願（Provisional Application）との対比で付してあり、通常の出願を意味します。

　本出願の種類として、特許出願（Utility Patent Application）、植物特許出願（Plant Patent Application）、及び、意匠出願（Design Patent Application）があります。これら、特許出願、植物特許出願、及び、意匠出願は共に特許法（35U.S.C.）で保護がなされています。

	Utility Patent	Plant Patent	Design Patent
保護対象	物、方法	植物	物品の装飾的デザイン
存続期間	出願から20年	出願から20年	登録から14年
優先権	1年	1年	6月
年金制度	あり	なし	なし
出願公開制度	あり	あり	なし
出願件数（2015年）	約59万件	約1千件	約3.9万件

第2章　特許出願

パリルート出願

　パリ条約締約国で最初の特許出願を行い、当該特許出願に係る発明について、同条約に基づく優先権を主張して1年（意匠特許は6月）以内に米国特許出願を行います。これにより、原則として先の出願日を基準として新規性等の審査がなされます（35U.S.C.119(a)）。これをパリ優先権出願、若しくは、パリルート出願と言います。

PCT米国国内移行出願

　特許協力条約（Patent Cooperation Treaty：PCT）に基づく国際出願を行い、所定期間内に米国に国内移行手続きを行います（35U.S.C.371）。これにより、国内移行手続きを経た出願は、原則として国際出願日を基準として新規性等の審査がなされます。

　国際出願を行うと、国際調査報告書（ISR：International Search Report (PCT/ISA/210)）等を入手することができます。国際調査報告書等から当該発明の先行技術文献を知ることができ、また、国際調査機関の審査官の見解も得ることができます。これにより、各国移行前に特許取得の可能性を確認することができます。

　国際出願の米国への国内移行出願の期限は、最先の優先日から30月です。これは、最先の優先日から1年以内に出願しなければならないパリルート出願と比較して時間的な余裕があります。特に明細書の翻訳文が必要な場合には時間的、費用的な負担が大きいですが、国際調査報告と相まって、出願国の技術動向を見据えた上で、厳選した出願のみ移行する等、出願戦略を立てることができます。翻訳文は国際出願の明細書の逐語訳でなければなりません。

PCTバイパス出願（M.P.E.P.1895）

　PCTに基づく国際出願は、PCTに加盟する各国の国内出願の束として考えることができます。このPCT出願を米国出願の先の出願とみなして、当該PCT出願に基づく継続的出願を行うことができます（35U.S.C.120, 37C.F.R.1.56(b)）。このような出願をいわゆるバイパス出願とよばれています。バイパス出願の明細書や図面は、必ずしも国際出願の逐語訳である必要はなく、国際出願の開示の範囲内で比較的自由に記載することができます。これは米国内では継続出願と扱われるためです。ここで、通常のPCT国内移行出願の場合には、

U.S.P.T.O.はPCTの発明の単一性の規定に基づいて判断します。バイパス出願の場合には米国特許法に基づいて判断がなされます。一方、一部継続出願としても出願できますので、国際出願時の明細書等に新規事項を追加した出願を行うこともできます。

PCT国内移行出願とPCTバイパス出願との比較

PCT国内移行出願	バイパス出願
国内移行時の翻訳文は逐語訳（ミラー翻訳）の提出が必要です。	厳密な逐語訳が求められないため、PCT出願を一言一句厳密に翻訳する必要がありません。このため、PCT出願の開示範囲にて米国の判例法に基づいた修正も可能です。
誤記、クレームの追加、クレーム複数従属項の補正は予備的補正書の提出が必要です。	厳密な逐語訳が求められないため、明白な誤記は明細書中で修正が可能です。また、PCT出願の開示範囲でのクレームの追加／修正も可能です。
発明の単一性の基準はPCT規則（PCT規則13）です。	発明の単一性の基準は米国特許法です。（PCT規則よりも狭いと考えられています）
審査着手が通常出願より遅い傾向にあります。	審査着手がPCT国内移行出願に比して早い傾向があります。
予備的補正書の提出により出願経過禁反言リスクがあります。	予備的補正書を提出しないことで出願経過禁反言のリスクが低減します。

PCTバイパス出願の注意点

ここで、バイパス出願時の明細書等の修正は、あくまでもPCT出願明細書の範囲で行うべき、という点に注意が必要です。理論上は、CIP出願（一部継続出願）も行い、PCT出願明細書の範囲外の新規事項をバイパス出願時に追加することもできます。しかしながら、当該新規事項を含むクレームは、バイパス出願日が審査の基準日となり、当該PCT国際出願の国際公報が引用例となってしまうリスクがあります。そこで、修正はあくまでもPCT国際出願の開示範囲で行うことが肝要です。

旧法との関係

なお、旧特許法の下では、非英語で国際公開された国際出願に係る国内移行出願については、35U.S.C.102(e)に基づく後願排除効が得られませんでした。

この点、バイパス出願を行うことで、バイパス出願日から後願排除効を得ることができるため、バイパス出願を行う利点がありました。しかしながら、現行特許法においては、35U.S.C.102(a)(2)によって、後願排除効が発生する基準日は、言語の種類に関係無く、一律に最先の優先日となりました。従って、国内移行出願とバイパス出願とにおいて、後願排除効の有無の差異はなくなりました。

日本語出願　(非英語出願)

U.S.P.T.O.に英語以外の言語で特許出願を行い、出願日を確保することができます(37C.F.R.1.52(d))。非英語出願を行った場合には、U.S.P.T.O.より欠落部分提出通知が送達され、所定の応答期間(送達日より2月、5月延長可能)内に、下記を提出します。
- 当該非英語出願の英語翻訳文
- 当該翻訳が正確である旨の翻訳者の翻訳証明書
- 手数料(37C.F.R.1.17(i))

日本語出願時の注意点

優先期限等の問題で英文明細書が準備できない場合に、緊急処置として日本語のまま出願して、出願日を確保することができます。ここで注意すべきなのは、後に出す英訳文は、提出した非英語出願の逐語訳でなければならない、ということです。従って、日本語明細書を準備するときにある程度米国出願用のフォーマットに変更し、米国実務に沿った明細書に変更してから出願する事が好ましいと言えます。

仮出願 (Provisional Application)

仮出願制度は、外国出願に基づく優先権を主張した出願と存続期間に関する同等の利益を国内出願に与える趣旨で1995年に導入されました。仮出願は、発明の内容を出願形式にとらわれずに出願し、より早く先願権を得たい場合には有利です。本出願(Non-provisional Application)とは異なり、仮出願は審査がされないため、より安価で提出書類は必要最小限で済みます。

仮出願の特徴、注意点
- 仮出願時には仮出願である旨の主張、明細書、必要な図面、および料金が必要です。クレーム、宣誓書、IDSは不要です(35U.S.C.111(b))。

- しかし、仮出願に基づく外国出願を行う場合、国によっては、パリ条約上の「正規の出願」であるためには、少なくとも1つのクレームが要求される場合があります。そこで、仮出願にクレームを含めると後に出願経過禁反言のリスクが考えられますが、仮出願に基づく外国出願を予定している場合には、クレームを含め、ある程度明細書の形にして出願する方が無難です。
- 仮出願は出願日から12月以内に仮出願に基づく優先権を主張して本出願をするか、または、当該仮出願から本出願への変更を行う必要があります（37C.F.R.1.53(c)(3)）。仮出願自体は出願から12月後に放棄されたものとみなされます（37C.F.R.1.53(c)(3)）。
- 仮出願は優先権主張の基礎となることはできますが、優先権主張を行う事ができません（35U.S.C.111(b)(7)）。
- 仮出願庁費用は本出願庁費用と比べて安価です（37C.F.R.1.16(d)）。
- 明細書や図面の書式に関して規定は特にありません。従って、学会発表用の論文自体や研究ノートをそのまま出願可能と解されますが、本出願が仮出願の優先権を得るためには、明細書としての記載要件（35U.S.C.112）を満たす必要があります（35U.S.C.111(b)(1)）。
- 言語についても制限はありません。ただし、非英語の仮出願を行った場合には、本出願の出願日までに仮出願の翻訳文および翻訳者の翻訳証明書を提出するのが安全です。非英語仮出願に基づく優先権を主張して本出願を行う場合には、下記の書類の提出が必要です。
  - 当該非英語仮出願の英語翻訳文
  - 当該翻訳が正確である旨の翻訳者の翻訳証明書

    上記書類を提出しなかった場合には、通常U.S.P.T.O.から提出通知が発せられます。この通知に応じて所定期限内に仮出願に対して上記書類提出することができます。つまり、仮出願の翻訳文及び翻訳証明書は仮出願から12月経過後であっても提出することができます。一方、本出願に対しては、仮出願に翻訳文及び翻訳証明書を提出した旨か、仮出願の利益の取下げた旨の連絡を行う必要があります。上記翻訳文及び翻訳証明書を提出しなかった場合には本出願は放棄されたものとみなされてしまいますので、注意が必要です（37C.F.R.1.78(a)(5)）。
- 仮出願に基づく優先権主張した本出願の特許性判断の基準日は、仮出願日

第2章　特許出願

となります。
- 仮出願は原則として公開されませんが、優先権の基礎となった場合には閲覧可能です。
- 仮出願に基づく優先権主張を行った本出願の特許権存続期間は、当該本出願の出願日が起算点となります（35U.S.C.154(a)(2)（図2参照））。一方、仮出願後に本出願へ変更した場合の特許権存続期間は、仮出願の出願日が起算点となる点に注意が必要です。(37C.F.R.1.53(c)(3))。なお、外国出願に基づくパリ優先を主張した米国出願は、特許権存続期間は米国出願の出願日が起算日となります。PCT出願に基づく国内移行出願では、特許権存続期間はPCT出願日が起算日となります。(M.P.E.P.2701)。

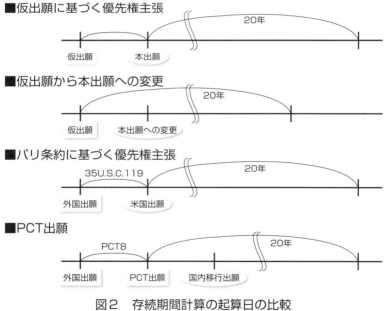

図2　存続期間計算の起算日の比較

意匠出願（Design Patent Application）

　物品の装飾的デザインを創作した者は意匠権（デザイン特許）を受ける事ができます。米国においては、意匠についても特許法にて保護規定がなされています。技術的創作である特許と比較して以下の特徴があります。

- 存続期間は登録から14年
- 特許維持年金制度なし
- IDS義務あり
- クレームは1つのみ
- PCT国内移行不可
- パリ条約の優先権期間は6月
- 仮出願に基づく優先権の主張不可
- 出願公開制度なし
- U.S.P.T.O.とJPOとの優先権書類の電子的取寄せは未だ実現されていません。そのため、日本出願の優先権主張をする場合は、出願人は優先権書類をJPOから取寄せ、U.S.P.T.O.に提出する必要があります。

第2章　特許出願

特許出願の方法

電子出願システム（EFS-Web）を活用しよう

電子出願システム（EFS-Web）は、インターネットを介して電子データ（PDFファイル）を用い特許出願を行うシステムです。従前の紙による出願方法と比較して下記の特徴があります。

電子出願の特徴
- インターネット出願を行うことができるので、どこからでも（米国外でも）米国特許出願を行うことができます。
- 出願完了後すぐに出願番号を取得できます。
- 同日に提出した書面は、同時に提出処理しなくても出願の一部として取り扱われます。
- 提出基準時は米国東海岸時間です。
- EFS-Webは、基本的に年中無休です。

ワンポイント解説：仮出願制度の有効活用

　技術内容や発明者によっては、1つの発明から関連/改良発明が後に生まれる場合があります。このような状況の場合の対応として仮出願制度を利用すると良い場合があります。すなわち、各々発明が生まれた時点で仮出願を行い、先願権を確保します。その後、発明の単一性要件を考慮しつつ、複数の仮出願の優先権に基づく本出願をします。これにより、先願権を確保しつつ、全体として出願庁費用の削減を図ることができます。

特許出願の方法

EFSの初期画面

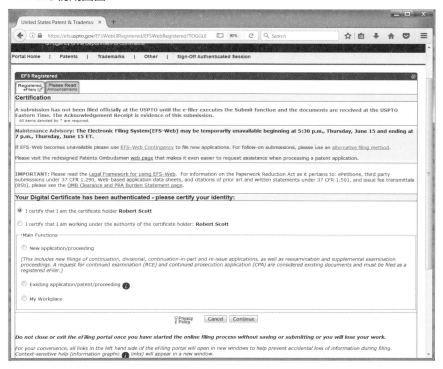

第2章　特許出願

電子出願の受理証

　電子出願が完了すると、U.S.P.T.O.より電子受理証（Electronic Acknowledgement Receipt）が発行されます。この電子受理証には、出願番号、確認番号の他、書誌的事項や提出した書類を確認することができます。

図面の電子出願と特許証にまつわるこぼれ話
～U.S.P.T.O.の電子出願用ビューアの解像度について～
　出願後の出願書類は出願の代理人であれば公開を待たずにU.S.P.T.O.のウェブサイトで出願直後から閲覧できます。文書をPDFファイルでダウンロードすることができ簡便ではありますが、出願時に出願書類をアップロードする時の解像度が低く、アップロード後は細かい点に注意して作成した図面も細い線などが黒く塗り潰されていたり、グレーのグラデーションが判別がつかないほど黒くなってしまうことが多々あります。特許証もそれをデータとして作成され、時には各図の縮尺がランダムに変えられて発行されます。今のところ対処法には、図面をなるべく大きく、細部の陰影等はなるべく粗めにするなどしかなく、U.S.P.T.O.側には早期に改善してほしいものです。

電子出願受理証の例

Electronic Acknowledgement Receipt	
EFS ID:	98765432
Application Number:	13123654
International Application Number:	
Confirmation Number:	2586
Title of Invention:	ELECTRIC METAL POLISHER
First Named Inventor/Applicant Name:	
Customer Number:	65181
Filer:	
Filer Authorized By:	
Attorney Docket Number:	MOT.085.0012.NP
Receipt Date:	04-JUL-2012
Filing Date:	
Time Stamp:	12:24:28
Application Type:	Utility under 35 USC 111(a)

> 電子出願の場合は出願手続き完了直後に願番を得ることができる

Payment information:

Submitted with Payment	yes
Payment Type	Credit Card
Payment was successfully received in RAM	$1250
RAM confirmation Number	12096
Deposit Account	
Authorized User	

File Listing:

Document Number	Document Description	File Name	File Size(Bytes)/ Message Digest	Multi Part /.zip	Pages (if appl.)

第2章　特許出願

電子出願以外の提出方法

U.S.P.T.O.へ書類提出するには下記の方法があります。

- 持参（M.P.E.P 501）

　　直接書類をU.S.P.T.O.（バージニア州アレキサンドリア市）へ持参して提出することができます。書類を提出すると受理証を受け取ることができ、その受理証は提出の証明となります。なお、受理証は受取る事ができますが、その時点では出願番号は確定せず、提出書類の確認後に出願番号が付与されます。

- ファクシミリ

　　所定の書面を除き、ファクシミリ送信された場合は、U.S.P.T.O.における受信完了時に提出されたものとして扱われます（37C.F.R.1.6(d)）。下記郵送証明付郵便が適用されないものは原則としてファクシミリによる提出も認められません（37C.F.R.1.6(d)(3)(f)）。従って、特許出願をファクシミリで提出することはできません。

- 郵送証明書付郵便（Certificate of Mailing）

　　期限がある応答については、郵送証明書に刻印された発信日が期限内であれば期限内に提出されたものとみなされます（37C.F.R.1.8(a)(1)(ii)）。ただし特許出願には適用されず、出願書類の場合は到達日に提出されたものとして扱われます（37C.F.R.1.8(a)(2)(i)(A)）。

- 速達郵便（Express Mail）

　　米国郵政公社（United States Postal Service: USPS）による"Express Mail"により米国内から発信された場合には、特許出願書類を含む全ての書類は発信日に提出されたものとみなされます（37C.F.R.1.10(a)）。従って特許出願書類をUSPSの速達で送る場合にはUSPSの受領スタンプの日付が出願日となります。その証明のため、USPSで発行された受理証を保管します。

出願書類を準備しよう

米国に特許出願を行う際には、原則として以下の書類を提出します。
- 送付状（Utility Patent Application Transmittal Form）
- 出願データシート（Application Data Sheet：ADS）
- 宣誓書（Declaration）
- 譲渡証（Assignment）
- 委任状（Power of Attorney）
- 明細書（Specification）
- 図面（Drawings）
- 情報開示陳述書（Information Disclosure Statement：IDS）

送付状（PTO/AIA/15）

送付状とは、出願時にどの書類を送付したかを特定するためのもので、各種出願書類のチェックリストの役割を果たします。通常は、U.S.P.T.O.から提供されたフォームを利用します。

本出願の送付状を準備する

本出願の送付状にはPTO/AIA/15を用います。

ワンポイント解説：PCTバイパス出願時の送付状の注意点

　PCT国内移行に際し、いわゆるバイパス出願の場合には、継続出願として出願を行いますので、PTO/AIA/15を用い、先の出願として、国際出願をADSで指定します。一方、PCT国内移行出願の場合にはPTO-1390を用います。

第2章　特許出願

本出願の送付状（PTO/AIA/15）

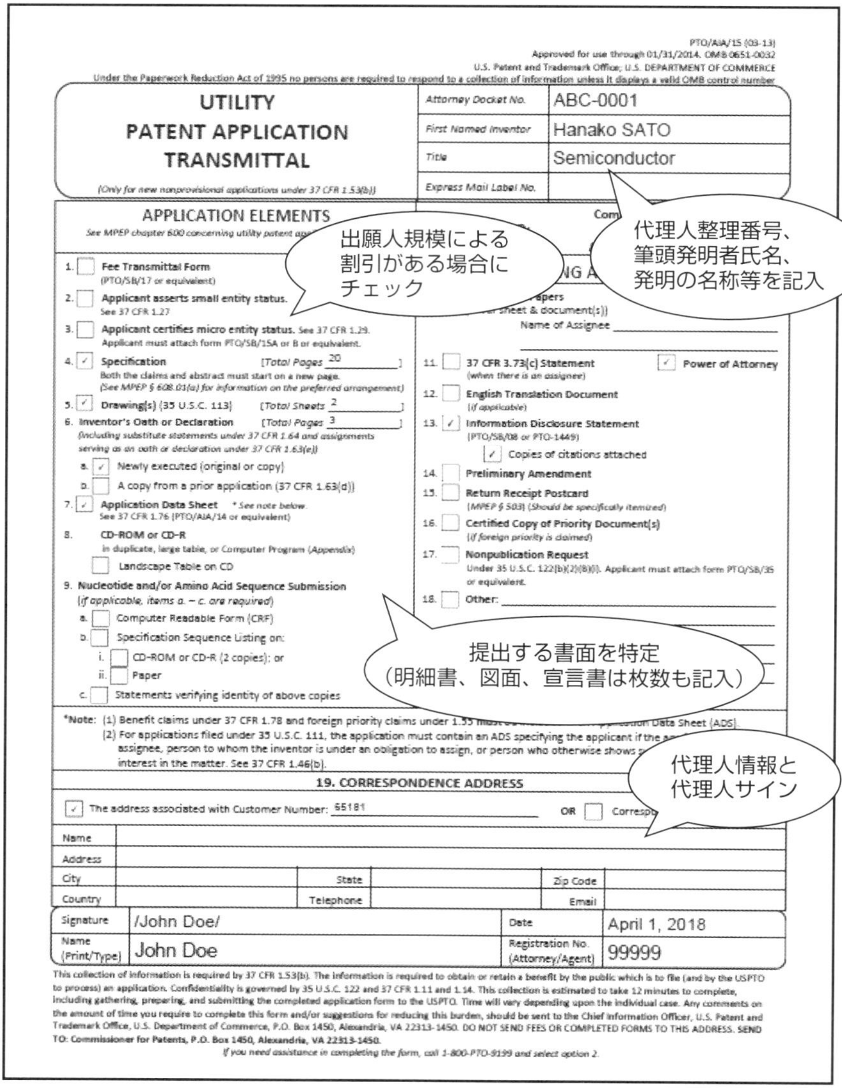

Attorney Docket No.	ABC-0001
First Named Inventor	Hanako SATO
Title	Semiconductor

UTILITY PATENT APPLICATION TRANSMITTAL
(Only for new nonprovisional applications under 37 CFR 1.53(b))

APPLICATION ELEMENTS
See MPEP chapter 600 concerning utility patent application contents.

1. ☐ Fee Transmittal Form (PTO/SB/17 or equivalent)
2. ☐ Applicant asserts small entity status. See 37 CFR 1.27
3. ☐ Applicant certifies micro entity status. See 37 CFR 1.29. Applicant must attach form PTO/SB/15A or B or equivalent.
4. ☑ Specification [Total Pages 20] Both the claims and abstract must start on a new page. (See MPEP § 608.01(a) for information on the preferred arrangement)
5. ☑ Drawing(s) (35 U.S.C. 113) [Total Sheets 2]
6. ☑ Inventor's Oath or Declaration [Total Pages 3] (including substitute statements under 37 CFR 1.64 and assignments serving as an oath or declaration under 37 CFR 1.63(e))
   a. ☑ Newly executed (original or copy)
   b. ☐ A copy from a prior application (37 CFR 1.63(d))
7. ☑ Application Data Sheet * See note below. See 37 CFR 1.76 (PTO/AIA/14 or equivalent)
8. ☐ CD-ROM or CD-R in duplicate, large table, or Computer Program (Appendix)
   ☐ Landscape Table on CD
9. Nucleotide and/or Amino Acid Sequence Submission (if applicable, items a. – c. are required)
   a. ☐ Computer Readable Form (CRF)
   b. ☐ Specification Sequence Listing on:
      i. ☐ CD-ROM or CD-R (2 copies); or
      ii. ☐ Paper
   c. ☐ Statements verifying identity of above copies

ACCOMPANYING APPLICATION PAPERS
(Sheet & document(s))
10. ☐ Name of Assignee
11. ☑ 37 CFR 3.73(c) Statement (when there is an assignee) ☑ Power of Attorney
12. ☐ English Translation Document (if applicable)
13. ☑ Information Disclosure Statement (PTO/SB/08 or PTO-1449)
   ☑ Copies of citations attached
14. ☐ Preliminary Amendment
15. ☐ Return Receipt Postcard (MPEP § 503) (Should be specifically itemized)
16. ☐ Certified Copy of Priority Document(s) (if foreign priority is claimed)
17. ☐ Nonpublication Request Under 35 U.S.C. 122(b)(2)(B)(i). Applicant must attach form PTO/SB/35 or equivalent.
18. ☐ Other:

*Note: (1) Benefit claims under 37 CFR 1.78 and foreign priority claims under 1.55 must be identified in an Application Data Sheet (ADS). (2) For applications filed under 35 U.S.C. 111, the application must contain an ADS specifying the applicant if the applicant is an assignee, person to whom the inventor is under an obligation to assign, or person who otherwise shows sufficient proprietary interest in the matter. See 37 CFR 1.46(b).

19. CORRESPONDENCE ADDRESS

☑ The address associated with Customer Number: 65181　　OR　☐ Correspondence address below

Name	
Address	
City	State	Zip Code
Country	Telephone	Email
Signature	/John Doe/	Date	April 1, 2018
Name (Print/Type)	John Doe	Registration No. (Attorney/Agent)	99999

（吹き出し注釈）
- 出願人規模による割引がある場合にチェック
- 代理人整理番号、筆頭発明者氏名、発明の名称等を記入
- 提出する書面を特定（明細書、図面、宣言書は枚数も記入）
- 代理人情報と代理人サイン

PCT国内移行時の送付（PTO-1390）

　PCT国内移行出願時には、通常出願とは異なるフォームを用います。このフォームは、PCT国内移行に特化したものであり、PCT国内移行時に必要な情報を含めます。

審査着手請求（Express Request）

　指定官庁は、PCT国内移行期間の満了前に、国際出願の処理または審査を行ってはならない旨が規定されています（PCT第23条(1)）。このチェックボックスにチェックすることで、U.S.P.T.O.は出願人の明示の請求と解して審査手続きを進めます（PCT第23条(2)）。ただし、審査を進めるためには、1）国内移行費用、2）国際出願のコピー、3）国際出願が非英語の場合には、英語の翻訳文、及び4）宣誓書の提出が必要です。

国際段階で19条、34条補正

　国際段階で19条、34条補正を行った場合、これらの補正を米国出願に適用させたい場合には、該当するチェックボックスにチェックします。国際段階での補正を米国出願に適用させたくない場合には、該当するチェックボックスをチェックします。

　ここで、米国特許法においては、多項従属クレームの費用が高額という理由から、米国出願時に多項従属クレームを回避する補正が行われることが多いです。この場合、国際段階の補正をそのまま適用せずに、米国用のクレームを作成して、予備的補正書（Preliminary Amendment）として提出することができます。

第2章　特許出願

PCT国内移行出願の送付状を準備する（PTO-1390）

> 代理人整理番号、国際出願番号、筆頭発明者氏名、発明の名称等を記入

TRANSMITTAL LETTER TO THE UNITED STATES DESIGNATED/ELECTED OFFICE (DO/EO/US) CONCERNING A SUBMISSION UNDER 35 U.S.C. 371

International Application No.	International Filing Date	Priority Date Claimed
PCT/JP2019/999999	April 1, 2017	April 1, 2016

Title of Invention: Semiconductor
First Named Inventor: Hanako SATO

Applicant herewith submits to the United States Designated/Elected Office (DO/EO/US) the following items:

1. [✓] This is an express request to begin national examination procedures (35 U.S.C. 371(f)). 35 U.S.C. 371(f) will not be effective unless the requirements under 35 U.S.C. 371(c)(1), the national fee, copy of the International Application and English translation thereof (if required), inventor(s) have been received.

> 審査着手請求する場合はチェック

2. [✓] A copy of the International Application (35 U.S.C. 371(c)(2)) is attached hereto (not required if previously communicated by the International Bureau or was filed in the United States Receiving Office).

> 国際出願の写しを添付（国際公報の写しでも可）

3. An English language translation of the International Application (35 U.S.C. 371(c)(2))
   a. [✓] is attached hereto.
   b. [ ] has been previously submitted under 35 U.S.C. 154(d)(4).

4. An oath or declaration of the inventor(s) (35 U.S.C. 371(c)(4))
   a. [✓] is attached.
   b. [ ] was previously filed in the international phase under PCT Rule 4.17.

Items 5 to 8 below concern amendments made in the international phase.

PCT Article 19 and 34 amendments

5. [ ] Amendments to the claims under PCT Article 19 are attached (not required) (35 U.S.C. 371(c)(3)).
6. [ ] English translation of the PCT Article 19 amendment is attached (35 U.S.C. 371(c)(3)).
7. [ ] English translation of annexes (Article 19 and/or 34 amendments only) of the International Preliminary Examination Report is attached (35 U.S.C. 371(c)(5)).

> PCT19条、34条補正を添付する場合、及びその補正書を審査対象にするか否かに関する項目

Cancellation of amendments made in the international phase

8a. [ ] Do not enter the amendment made in the international phase under PCT Article 19.
8b. [ ] Do not enter the amendment made in the international phase under PCT Article 34.

NOTE: A proper amendment made in English under Article 19 or 34 will be entered in the U.S. national phase unless instruction from applicant not to enter the amendment(s).

The following items 9 to 17 concern a document(s) or information included.

9. [✓] An Information Disclosure Statement under 37 CFR 1.97 and 1.98.
10. [✓] A preliminary amendment.
11. [✓] An Application Data Sheet under 37 CFR 1.76.
12. [ ] A substitute specification. NOTE: A substitute specification cannot include claims. See 37 CFR 1.125(b).
13. [✓] A power of attorney and/or change of address letter.
14. [ ] A computer-readable form of the sequence listing in accordance with PCT Rule 13ter.3 and 37 CFR 1.821-1.825.
15. [ ] Assignment papers (cover sheet and document(s)). Name of Assignee: _____
16. [ ] 37 CFR 3.73(c) Statement (when there is an Assignee).

> IDSや予備補正等の添付書類に関する項目

This collection of information is required by 37 CFR 1.414 and 1.491-1.492. The information is required to obtain or retain a benefit by the public, which is to file (and by the USPTO to process) an application. Confidentiality is governed by 35 U.S.C. 122 and 37 CFR 1.11 and 1.14. This collection is estimated to take 15 minutes to complete, including gathering, preparing, and submitting the completed application form to the USPTO. Time will vary depending upon the individual case. Any comments on the amount of time you require to complete this form and/or suggestions for reducing this burden should be sent to the Chief Information Officer, U.S. Patent and Trademark Office, U.S. Department of Commerce, P.O. Box 1450, Alexandria, VA 22313-1450. DO NOT SEND FEES OR COMPLETED FORMS TO THIS ADDRESS. SEND TO: Mail Stop PCT, Commissioner for Patents, P.O. Box 1450, Alexandria, VA 22313-1450.

出願書類を準備しよう

PCT国内移行出願の送付状を準備する（PTO-1390）の続き

17. Other items or information: International Search Report	その他の添付書類（国際調査報告等）

支払料金に関する項目

The following fees have been submitted.	CALCULATIONS	PTO USE ONLY
18. ☑ Basic national fee (37 CFR 1.492(a)) $280	$ 280	
19. ☑ Examination fee (37 CFR 1.492(c)) If the written opinion prepared by ISA/US or the international preliminary examination report prepared by IPEA/US indicates all claims satisfy provisions of PCT Article 33(1)-(4) .... $0 All other situations $720	$ 720	
20. ☑ Search fee (37 CFR 1.492(b)) If the written opinion prepared by ISA/US or the international preliminary examination report prepared by IPEA/US indicates all claims satisfy provisions of PCT Article 33(1)-(4) .... $0 Search fee (37 CFR 1.445(a)(2)) has been paid on the international application to the USPTO as an International Searching Authority .... $120 International Search Report prepared by an ISA other than the US and provided to the Office or previously communicated to the US by the IB .... $480 All other situations $600	$ 480	
TOTAL OF 18, 19, and 20 =	$ 1480	

特許サーチ費用は国際調査報告書提出により割引が受けられる

☐ Additional fee for specification and drawings filed in paper over 100 sheets (excluding sequence listing in compliance with 37 CFR 1.821(c) or (e) in an electronic medium or computer program listing in an electronic medium) (37 CFR 1.492(j)). Fee for each additional 50 sheets of paper or fraction thereof $400			
Total Sheets	Extra Sheets	Number of each addition 50 or fraction thereof (round up to a whole number)	RATE
15 - 100 =	/ 50 =		x $400	$

明細書及び図面の合計が規定枚数を超える場合には超過料金

Surcharge of $140.00 for furnishing any of the search fee, examination fee, or the oath or declaration after the date of commencement of the national stage (37 CFR 1.492(h)).

CLAIMS	NUMBER FILED	NUMBER EXTRA	RATE	
Total claims	1	- 20 =	x $80	$
Independent claims	3	- 3 =	x $420	$
MULTIPLE DEPENDENT CLAIM(S) (if applicable)			+ $780	$

クレーム数が基本料金を超える場合には超過料金

Processing fee of $140.00 for furnishing the English translation later than 30 months from the earliest claimed priority date (37 CFR 1.492(i)). +

TOTAL OF ABOVE CALCULATIONS = $

☐ Applicant asserts small entity status. See 37 CFR 1.27. Fees above are reduced by ½.
☐ Applicant certifies micro entity status. See 37 CFR 1.29. Fees above are reduced by ％. Applicant must attach form PTO/SB/15A or B or equivalent.

出願人規模による割引がある場合にチェック

TOTAL NATIONAL FEE = $ 1480

Fee for recording the enclosed assignment (37 CFR 1.21(h)). The assignment must be accompanied by an appropriate cover sheet (37 CFR 3.28, 3.31). $40.00 per property. + $

TOTAL FEES ENCLOSED = $ 1480

合計金額を記入

Amount to be refunded:	$
Amount to be charged:	$

[Page 2 of 3]

第2章 特許出願

PCT国内移行出願の送付状を準備する（PTO-1390）の続き

支払い方法の特定

代理人情報と代理人サイン

意匠出願の送付状を準備する（PTO/AIA/18）

PTO/AIA/18 (03-13)
Approved for use through 01/31/2014. OMB 0651-0032
U.S. Patent and Trademark Office; U.S. DEPARTMENT OF COMMERCE
Under the Paperwork Reduction Act of 1995 no persons are required to respond to a collection of information unless it displays a valid OMB control number

DESIGN PATENT APPLICATION TRANSMITTAL

(Only for new nonprovisional applications under 37 CFR 1.53(b))

Attorney Docket No.	ABC-0002
First Named Inventor	Taro SATO
Title	Electric Fan
Express Mail Label No.	

代理人整理番号、
筆頭発明者氏名、
発明の名称等を記入

ADDRESS TO:
Commissioner for Patents
P.O. Box 1450
Alexandria, VA 22313-1450

DESIGN V. UTILITY: A "design patent" protects an article's or... way an article looks) (35 U.S.C. 171), while a "utility patent"... and works (35 U.S.C. 101). The ornamental appearance of a... shape/configuration or surface ornamentation upon the artic... utility patent may be obtained on an article if invention resides bo... appearance and its utility. For more information, see MPEP § 1502.01.

APPLICATION ELEMENTS
See MPEP chapter 1500 concerning design patent application contents.

1. ☐ **Fee Transmittal Form** (PTO/SB/17 or equivalent)
2. ☐ **Applicant asserts small entity status.** See 37 CFR 1.27
3. ☐ **Applicant certifies micro entity status.** See 37 CFR 1.29. Applicant must attach form PTO/SB/15A or B or equivalent.
4. ☑ **Specification** [*Total Pages* 1]
   (*preferred arrangement set forth below, MPEP § 1503.01*)
   - Preamble
   - Cross References to Related Applications
   - Statement Regarding Fed sponsored R & D
   - Description of the figure(s) of the drawings
   - Feature description
   - Claim (only one (1) claim permitted, MPEP § 1503.03)
5. ☑ **Drawing(s)** [*Total Sheets* 5]
   See 37 CFR 1.152
6. **Inventor's Oath or Declaration** [*Total Pages* 3]
   (*including substitute statements under 37 CFR 1.64 and assignments serving as an oath or declaration under 37 CFR 1.63(e)*)
   a. ☑ Newly executed (original or copy)
   b. ☐ A copy from a prior application (37 CFR 1.63(d))
7. ☑ **Application Data Sheet** ** See note below.*
   See 37 CFR 1.76 (PTO/AIA/14 or equivalent)

ACCOMPANYING APPLICATION PARTS

8. ☐ **Assignment Papers** (cover sheet & document(s))
9. ☐ **37 CFR 3.73(c) Statement** (*when there is an assignee*) ☑ **Power of Attorney**
10. ☐ **English Translation Document** (*if applicable*)
11. ☐ **Information Disclosure Statement (IDS)** (PTO/SB/08 or PTO-1449)
    ☐ Copies of foreign patent documents, publications, and other information
12. ☐ **Preliminary Amendment**
13. ☐ **Return Receipt Postcard** (*MPEP § 503*) (*Should be specifically itemized*)
14. ☐ **Certified Copy of Priority Document(s)** (*if foreign priority is claimed*)
15. ☐ **Request for Expedited Examination of a Design Application** (37 CFR 1.155) (NOTE: Use "Mail Stop Expedited Design")
16. ☐ Ot...

提出する書面を特定
（明細書、図面、宣言書は枚数も記入）

*Note: (1) Benefit claims under 37 CFR 1.78 and foreign priority clai... (ADS).
(2) For applications filed under 35 U.S.C. 111, the application must contain an ADS ... if the applica... assignee, person to whom the inventor is under an obligation to assign, or person who otherwise shows suff... interest in the matter. See 37 CFR 1.46(b).

17. CORRESPONDENCE ADDRESS

代理人情報と
代理人サイン

☑ The address associated with Customer Number: 65181 OR ☐ Correspon...

Name					
Address					
City		State		Zip Code	
Country		Telephone		Email	

Signature	/John Doe/	Date	April 1, 2018
Name (Print/Type)	John Doe	Registration No. (Attorney/Agent)	99999

This collection of information is required by 37 CFR 1.53(b). The information is required to obtain or retain a benefit by the public which is to file (and by the USPTO to process) an application. Confidentiality is governed by 35 U.S.C. 122 and 37 CFR 1.11 and 1.14. This collection is estimated to take 12 minutes to complete, including gathering, preparing, and submitting the completed application form to the USPTO. Time will vary depending upon the individual case. Any comments on the amount of time you require to complete this form and/or suggestions for reducing this burden, should be sent to the Chief Information Officer, U.S. Patent and Trademark Office, U.S. Department of Commerce, P.O. Box 1450, Alexandria, VA 22313-1450. DO NOT SEND FEES OR COMPLETED FORMS TO THIS ADDRESS. **SEND TO: Commissioner for Patents, P.O. Box 1450, Alexandria, VA 22313-1450.**

If you need assistance in completing the form, call 1-800-PTO-9199 and select option 2.

第2章 特許出願

仮出願用のカバーシートを準備する（PTO/SB/16）

発明者の氏名と居住地の市と国（もしくは州）を記入

発明の名称

代理人情報

提出する明細書等書類の特定

出願人の規模の特定

出願書類を準備しよう

仮出願用のカバーシートを準備する（PTO/SB/16）の続き

PTO/SB/16 (03-13)
Approved for use through 01/31/2014. OMB 0651-0032
U.S. Patent and Trademark Office; U.S. DEPARTMENT OF COMMERCE
Under the Paperwork Reduction Act of 1995 no persons are required to respond to a collection of information unless it displays a valid OMB control number

PROVISIONAL APPLICATION FOR PATENT COVER SHEET – Page 2 of 2

The invention was made by an agency of the United States Government or under a contract with an agency of the United States Government.

[✓] No.

[ ] Yes, the invention was made by an agency of the U.S. Government. The U.S. Government agency name is: _____

[ ] Yes, the invention was made under a contract with an agency of the U.S. Government. The name of the U.S. Government agency and Government contract number are: _____

（米国政府関連の発明か否かの特定）

WARNING:

Petitioner/applicant is cautioned to avoid submitting personal information in documents filed in a patent application that may contribute to identity theft. Personal information such as social security numbers, bank account numbers, or credit card numbers (other than a check or credit card authorization form PTO-2038 submitted for payment purposes) is never required by the USPTO to support a petition or an application. If this type of personal information is included in documents submitted to the USPTO, petitioners/applicants should consider redacting such personal information from the documents before submitting them to the USPTO. Petitioner/applicant is advised that the record of a patent application is available to the public after publication of the application (unless a non-publication request in compliance with 37 CFR 1.213(a) is made in the application) or issuance of a patent. Furthermore, the record from an abandoned application may also be available to the public if the application is referenced in a published application or an issued patent (see 37 CFR 1.14). Checks and credit card authorization forms PTO-2038 submitted for payment purposes are not retained in the application file and therefore are not publicly available.

SIGNATURE _____ DATE _____

（代理人サイン）

TYPED OR PRINTED NAME _____ REGISTRATION NO. _____
(*if appropriate*)

TELEPHONE _____ DOCKET NUMBER _____

（代理人整理番号）

第2章　特許出願

明細書の準備例

　明細書には、特許出願人が発明の詳細内容を開示します。明細書は、明細書本文、少なくとも１つのクレーム、そして、150ワード以内の要約を含めます。これら明細書本文、クレーム、要約は用紙を分けます。

明細書の書式（37C.F.R.1.52, M.P.E.P.608.01）

　用紙は、Ａ４またはレターサイズで、用紙の上部、下部、及び、右側マージンは最低２cm（３/４インチ）と規定され、用紙の左側マージンは最低2.5cm（１インチ）と規定されています。

　テキストのフォントは、筆記体フォントでないもの、例えば、Arial、Times New Roman、Courier等です。フォントの大きさは12ptが好ましいとされています。

明細書中の見出し例

　発明の名称
　関連出願の表示（Cross Reference to Related Applications）
　従来技術（Background）
　発明の概要（Summary）
　図面の簡単な説明（Brief Description of The Drawings）
　実施例（Detailed Description）
　クレーム（Claims）
　要約（Abstract）

出願書類を準備しよう

明細書書式例

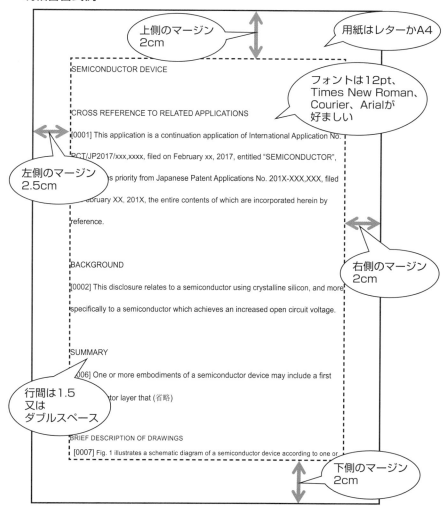

第2章　特許出願

明細書記載例（実施形態）

```
more embodiments.

DETAILED DESCRIPTION
[0006] Embodiments are explained with referring to drawings. In the respective drawings referenced herein, the same constituents are designated by the same reference numerals and duplicate explanation concerning the same constituents is basically omitted. All of the drawings are provided to illustrate the respective examples only. No dimensional proportions in the drawings shall impose a restriction on the embodiments. For this reason, specific dimensions and the like should be interpreted with the following descriptions taken into consideration. In addition, the drawings include parts whose dimensional relationship and ratios are different from one drawing to another.
[0007] Fig. 1 illustrates a schematic diagram of a semiconductor device according to one or more embodiments.
(省略)
．
．
．
```

クレーム（35U.S.C.112, 37C.F.R.1.75, M.P.E.P.608.1(n)）

　明細書は、出願人が自己の発明とみなす主題を特定し、明瞭に請求する1以上のクレームで完結させます（35U.S.C.112(b)）。

　クレームは明細書本文とは別用紙で記載します。クレームは複数記載することができ、クレーム毎に番号を振ります。手続き中は同一のクレーム番号を使用します。補正によりクレームが削除された場合であっても、番号の振り直しはできません。

多項従属クレームとクレーム数の計算

クレームの数によって出願時の費用が異なります。総クレーム数が20個までの場合には、追加費用は発生しませんが、20個を越える場合、クレーム1つ毎に追加費用が発生します。クレームは複数のクレームに従属させることができます。この多項従属クレーム（Multiple Dependent Claim）の場合には、従属させた数のクレームとカウントされます。例えば、3つに従属させたクレームは、クレーム数の計算上、その多項従属クレームは3つとカウントされます。多項従属クレームを多項従属クレームに従属させる事は出来ません（37C.F.R. 1.75(c)）。なお、誤って多項従属クレームに従属する多項従属クレームをクレームした場合には、クレーム数の計算上、1つとカウントされます。

ここで、多項従属クレームを含む場合、出願時に高額な追加費用が発生します。さらに、上述のようなクレームの計算方法を採りますので、米国出願時には、多項従属クレームが必要か否かを今一度検討する必要があります。また、多項従属クレームに従属する多項従属クレームは不適法となりますので、出願時にチェックして、単数従属クレームに修正する等する必要があります。

適切な多項従属クレームの例

Claim 5. A gadget according to claims 3 or 4, further comprising ---

Claim 5. A gadget as in any one of the preceding claims, in which ---

Claim 5. A gadget as in any one of claims 1, 2, and 3, in which ---

Claim 3. A gadget as in either claim 1 or claim 2, further comprising ---

Claim 4. A gadget as in claim 2 or 3, further comprising ? ---

Claim 16. A gadget as in claims 1, 7, 12, or 15, further comprising ---

不適切な多項従属クレームの例

Claim 5. A gadget according to claim 3 and 4, further comprising ---
択一的に従属するクレームを列挙していない。

Claim 8. A gadget as in claim 5（claim 5は多項従属クレーム）or claim 7, in which ---
多項従属クレームに従属するクレームが多項従属クレームとなっている。

第2章　特許出願

クレームの記載例

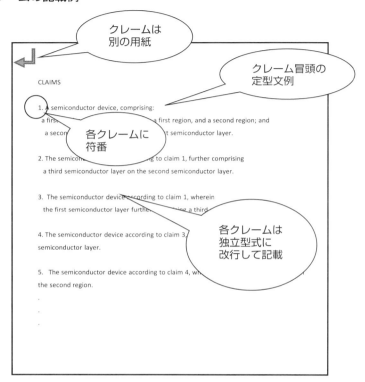

要約 (37C.F.R.1.72(b), M.P.E.P.608.01(b))

　要約は別用紙で、クレームの後に準備します。要約は、明細書の開示の範囲で完結に記載する必要があり、好ましくは、150ワード以内でまとめます。要約書の目的は、U.S.P.T.O.や公衆が開示技術の要旨を手早く判断できる事を目的としています。要約は、符号や means や said 等のクレームで使われるような法律用語を回避して作成します。ここで、日本等と異なり、要約はクレーム解釈に影響する判例[1]が存在することから、最も広いクレームを利用して作成し、問題点や効果の記載を避けるのが無難です。

1　HILL-ROM COMPANY, INC., v. KINETIC CONCEPTS, INC. 209 F.3d 1337（Fed Cir 2000), Lucent Technologies, Inc. v. Gateway, Inc., 525 F.3d 1200（Fed. Cir. 2008)

要約の記載例（37C.F.R.1.72(b)、M.P.E.P.608.01(b)）

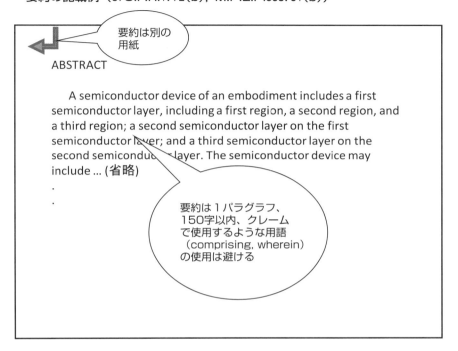

必要な図面の作成例

　図面は、発明理解のため必要に応じて提出する事になっていますが、殆どのケースで図面が提出されています。図面は規則に定められたマージンで作成します。ここで、図面に関する規則違反として指摘される場合があるのが、文字の大きさです。特に、PCに表示するウインドウを図面にする場合、そのウインドウ内の文字を小さくしなければ枠に入らない場合があります。図面内の文字の大きさは高さ0.32センチ以上とされているため、原則として10pt以上で作成すべきです。また、クレームに示した要素は図面に記載されていなければなりません。図面の符号で示された要素は明細書中で説明されなければなりません。

第2章 特許出願

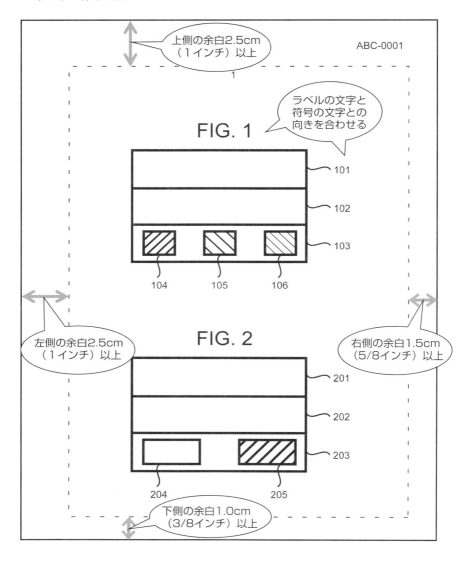

出願データシート（Application Data Sheet：ADS）

　出願データシート（ADS）とは、出願に関する書誌的情報をまとめたもので、発明者、連絡先、代理人、優先権情報、発明の譲受人などの情報を含めます。旧法では任意の提出物でしたが、U.S.P.T.O.での転記ミスを未然に防ぐ観点から提出することが望ましいと考えられていました。特に、日本人発明者の場合には、U.S.P.T.O.による発明者氏名等の転記ミスの可能性が比較的高くなるため、日本企業はADSを提出することが多いようでした。

ADSは任意の提出書類ですが……

　ADSは任意の提出書類です。以下の場合にはADSの提出が必須となります。
- 発明者以外を出願人とする場合（法人を出願人とする場合）
- 出願時に発明者の宣誓書の提出が行われない場合
- 優先権主張を行う場合

　日本企業は第1国出願を日本に行う事が多いこと、現行法では法人を出願人とする日本企業が多いと考えられることから、日本企業が出願を行う際にはADSは実質的に提出必須の書類と言えます。

ADSの取扱い

　ADSは出願の一部となります（37C.F.R.1.76(a)）。ADS、宣誓書を補正／再提出する場合には、登録費用の支払いまでに補充出願データシートを提出することができます（37C.F.R.1.76(c)）。なお、優先権の主張（37C.F.R.1.55および37C.F.R.1.78）の記載において、他の書類と齟齬があった場合、最新の出願データシートが効力を有します。また、発明者名については、最新の宣誓書が効力を有します（37C.F.R.1.76(d)）。

ADSの提出

　ADSは、U.S.P.T.O.のウェブページからダウンロードが可能であり、情報を追加可能なPDF型式のフォームに必要事項を記入してインターネット経由で提出します。ADSには、代理人整理番号、出願番号、発明の名称の他、発明者情報や書類送付先情報等を記入します。現行法では法人名を出願人として記入することができます。出願時には、実際に発明者から出願人への譲渡証の提出を行わなくても法人名で出願を行うことができます。その理由は、法人名で出願を行う際には、発明者から予め特許を受ける権利の譲渡を受けた場合のみならず、譲渡の約束をしている場合であっても法人名で出願を行う事ができるためです（35U.S.C.118）。譲渡の約束とは、たとえば、業務中になした発明は

第 2 章　特許出願

法人に帰属する旨の雇用契約(典型的には入社時に契約される)が含まれます。出願時にはこのような雇用契約等の譲渡の約束についての立証を要求されないことから、結果として、法人出願を行う場合でも出願時に譲渡証の提出は必要ありません。譲渡証は、特許発行料納付前までに提出します（37C.F.R.1.46(b)(1)）。

ここで、法人出願の場合には、このADSは代理人のみがサインすることができます（37C.F.R.1.33(b)）。従って、出願人といえどもADSにはサインをすることができません。これはすなわち、法人出願を行う際には必ず代理人経由で特許出願がなされなければならない事を意味します。

継続的出願を行う場合や、外国優先権主張を行う場合は、ADSでその主張と共に先の出願を特定する必要があります。

ワンポイント解説：法人を出願人として出願する場合の注意点

　法人出願の場合には、ADSは代理人のみがサインすることができます。これはすなわち、法人名を出願人とする場合には、必ず代理人を選任しなければ出願できない事になります。サインがなされていない場合には、ADSは単なる送付状（Transmittal Letter）とみなされます（37C.F.R.1.76(e)）。

出願書類を準備しよう

ADS (PTO/AIA/14)

Application Data Sheet 37 CFR 1.76

- Secrecy Order 37 CFR 5.2
- Inventor Information: 発明者情報
- Correspondence Information: 書類送付先（通常は代理人情報）
- Application Information: 出願情報

第2章 特許出願

ADS（PTO/AIA/14）の続き

```
                                                            PTO/AIA/14 (11-15)
                                              Approved for use through 04/30/2017. OMB 0651-0032
                                     U.S. Patent and Trademark Office; U.S. DEPARTMENT OF COMMERCE
Under the Paperwork Reduction Act of 1995, no persons are required to respond to a collection of information unless it contains a valid OMB control number.
```

Application Data Sheet 37 CFR 1.76	Attorney Docket Number	
	Application Number	
Title of Invention		

Filing By Reference:

Only complete this section when filing an application by reference under 35 U.S.C. 111(c) and 37 CFR 1.57(a). Do not complete this section if application papers including a specification and any drawings are being filed. Any domestic benefit or foreign priority information must be provided in the appropriate section(s) below (i.e., "Domestic Benefit/National Stage Information" and "Foreign Priority Information").

For the purposes of a filing date under 37 CFR 1.53(b), the description and any drawings of the present application are replaced by this reference to the previously filed application, subject to conditions and requirements of 37 CFR 1.57(a).

Application number of the previously filed application	Filing date (YYYY-MM-DD)	Intellectual Property Authority or Country

（早期公開や非公開を希望する場合にはチェック）

Publication Information:

☐ Request Early Publication (Fee required at time of Request 37 CFR 1.219)

☐ **Request Not to Publish.** I hereby request that the attached application not be published under 35 U.S.C. 122(b) and certify that the invention disclosed in the attached application **has not and will not be the subject** of an application filed in another country, or under a multilateral international agreement, that requires publication at eighteen months after filing.

Representative Information: （代理人情報）

Representative information should be provided for all practitioners having a power of attorney in the application. Providing this information in the Application Data Sheet does not constitute a power of attorney in the application (see 37 CFR 1.32). Either enter Customer Number or complete the Representative Name section below. If both sections are completed the customer Number will be used for the Representative Information during processing.

Please Select One:	● Customer Number	○ US Patent Practitioner	○ Limited Recognition (37 CFR 11.9)
Customer Number			

Domestic Benefit/National Stage Information: （米国の先の出願情報）

This section allows for the applicant to either claim benefit under 35 U.S.C. 119(e), 120, 121, 365(c), or 386(c) or indicate National Stage entry from a PCT application. Providing benefit claim information in the Application Data Sheet constitutes the specific reference required by 35 U.S.C. 119(e) or 120, and 37 CFR 1.78.
When referring to the current application, please leave the "Application Number" field blank.

Prior Application Status				Remove
Application Number	Continuity Type	Prior Application Number	Filing or 371(c) Date (YYYY-MM-DD)	

Additional Domestic Benefit/National Stage Data may be generated within this form by selecting the **Add** button. [Add]

EFS Web 2.2.12

40

出願書類を準備しよう

ADS（PTO/AIA/14）の続き

```
                                                              PTO/AIA/14 (11-15)
                                  Approved for use through 04/30/2017. OMB 0651-0032
                                  U.S. Patent and Trademark Office; U.S. DEPARTMENT OF COMMERCE
Under the Paperwork Reduction Act of 1995, no persons are required to respond to a collection of information unless it contains a valid OMB control number.
```

Application Data Sheet 37 CFR 1.76	Attorney Docket Number	
	Application Number	
Title of Invention		

Foreign Priority Information: 〔外国優先権情報〕

This section allows for the applicant to claim priority to a foreign application. Providing this information in the application data sheet constitutes the claim for priority as required by 35 U.S.C. 119(b) and 37 CFR 1.55. When priority is claimed to a foreign application that is eligible for retrieval under the priority document exchange program (PDX)[i] the information will be used by the Office to automatically attempt retrieval pursuant to 37 CFR 1.55(i)(1) and (2). Under the PDX program, applicant bears the ultimate responsibility for ensuring that a copy of the foreign application is received by the Office from the participating foreign intellectual property office, or a certified copy of the foreign priority application is filed, within the time period specified in 37 CFR 1.55(g)(1).

			Remove
Application Number	Country[i]	Filing Date (YYYY-MM-DD)	Access Code[i] (if applicable)

Additional Foreign Priority Data may be generated within this form by selecting the Add button. [Add]

Statement under 37 CFR 1.55 or 1.78 for AIA (First Inventor to File) Transition Applications

☐ This application (1) claims priority to or the benefit of an application filed before March 16, 2013 and (2) also contains, or contained at any time, a claim to a claimed invention that has an effective filing date on or after March 16, 2013.
NOTE: By providing this statement under 37 CFR 1.55 or 1.78, this application, with a filing date on or after March 16, 2013, will be examined under the first inventor to file provisions of the AIA.

EFS Web 2.2.12

第2章 特許出願

ADS (PTO/AIA/14) の続き

```
                                                                    PTO/AIA/14 (11-15)
                                                Approved for use through 04/30/2017. OMB 0651-0032
                                              U.S. Patent and Trademark Office; U.S. DEPARTMENT OF COMMERCE
Under the Paperwork Reduction Act of 1995, no persons are required to respond to a collection of information unless it contains a valid OMB control number.
```

Application Data Sheet 37 CFR 1.76	Attorney Docket Number	
	Application Number	
Title of Invention		

Authorization or Opt-Out of Authorization to Permit Access:

When this Application Data Sheet is properly signed and filed with the application, applicant has provided written authority to permit a participating foreign intellectual property (IP) office access to the instant application-as-filed (see paragraph A in subsection 1 below) and the European Patent Office (EPO) access to any search results from the instant application (see paragraph B in subsection 1 below).

Should applicant choose not to provide an authorization identified in subsection 1 below, applicant **must opt-out** of the authorization by checking the corresponding box A or B or both in subsection 2 below.

NOTE: This section of the Application Data Sheet is **ONLY** reviewed and processed with the **INITIAL** filing of an application. After the initial filing of an application, an Application Data Sheet cannot be used to provide or rescind authorization for access by a foreign IP office(s). Instead, Form PTO/SB/39 or PTO/SB/69 must be used as appropriate.

1. Authorization to Permit Access by a Foreign Intellectual Property Office(s)

A. **Priority Document Exchange (PDX)** - Unless box A in subsection 2 (opt-out of authorization) is checked, the undersigned hereby **grants the USPTO authority** to provide the European Patent Office (EPO), the Japan Patent Office (JPO), the Korean Intellectual Property Office (KIPO), the State Intellectual Property Office of the People's Republic of China (SIPO), the World Intellectual Property Organization (WIPO), and any other foreign intellectual property office participating with the USPTO in a bilateral or multilateral priority document exchange agreement in which a foreign application claiming priority to the instant patent application is filed, access to: (1) the instant patent application-as-filed and its related bibliographic data, (2) any foreign or domestic application to which priority or benefit is claimed by the instant application and its related bibliographic data, and (3) the date of filing of this Authorization. See 37 CFR 1.14(h)(1).

B. **Search Results from U.S. Application to EPO** - Unless box B in subsection 2 (opt-out of authorization) is checked, the undersigned hereby **grants the USPTO authority** to provide the EPO access to the bibliographic data and search results from the instant patent application when a European patent application claiming priority to the instant patent application is filed. See 37 CFR 1.14(h)(2).

The applicant is reminded that the EPO's Rule 141(1) EPC (European Patent Convention) requires applicants to submit a copy of search results from the instant application without delay in a European patent application that claims priority to the instant application.

2. Opt-Out of Authorizations to Permit Access by a Foreign Intellectual Property Office(s)

☐ A. Applicant **DOES NOT** authorize the USPTO to permit a participating foreign IP office access to the instant application-as-filed. If this box is checked, the USPTO will not be providing a participating foreign IP office with any documents and information identified in subsection 1A above.

☐ B. Applicant **DOES NOT** authorize the USPTO to transmit to the EPO any search results from the instant patent application. If this box is checked, the USPTO will not be providing the EPO with search results from the instant application.

NOTE: Once the application has published or is otherwise publicly available, the USPTO may provide access to the application in accordance with 37 CFR 1.14.

〔JPO等他国の特許庁からのアクセスを認めない場合はチェック〕

EFS Web 2.2.12

出願書類を準備しよう

ADS（PTO/AIA/14）の続き

```
PTO/AIA/14 (11-15)
Approved for use through 04/30/2017. OMB 0651-0032
U.S. Patent and Trademark Office; U.S. DEPARTMENT OF COMMERCE
Under the Paperwork Reduction Act of 1995, no persons are required to respond to a collection of information unless it contains a valid OMB control number.
```

Application Data Sheet 37 CFR 1.76	Attorney Docket Number	
	Application Number	
Title of Invention		

出願人情報
（発明者が出願人の場合は空欄）

Applicant Information:

Providing assignment information in this section does not substitute for compliance with any requirement of part 3 of Title 37 of CFR to have an assignment recorded by the Office.

| Applicant | 1 | | | Remove |

If the applicant is the inventor (or the remaining joint inventor or inventors under 37 CFR 1.45), this section should not be completed. The information to be provided in this section is the name and address of the legal representative who is the applicant under 37 CFR 1.43; or the name and address of the assignee, person to whom the inventor is under an obligation to assign the invention, or person who otherwise shows sufficient proprietary interest in the matter who is the applicant under 37 CFR 1.46. If the applicant is an applicant under 37 CFR 1.46 (assignee, person to whom the inventor is obligated to assign, or person who otherwise shows sufficient proprietary interest) together with one or more joint inventors, then the joint inventor or inventors who are also the applicant should be identified in this section.

Clear

○ Assignee	○ Legal Representative under 35 U.S.C. 117	○ Joint Inventor
○ Person to whom the inventor is obligated to assign.	○ Person who shows sufficient proprietary interest	

If applicant is the legal representative, indicate the authority to file the patent application, the inventor is:

Name of the Deceased or Legally Incapacitated Inventor:

If the Applicant is an Organization check here. ☒

| Organization Name | |

Mailing Address Information For Applicant:

Address 1	
Address 2	
City		State/Province	
Country		Postal Code	
Phone Number		Fax Number	
Email Address	

Additional Applicant Data may be generated within this form by selecting the Add button. [Add]

Assignee Information including Non-Applicant Assignee Information:

Providing assignment information in this section does not substitute for compliance with any requirement of part 3 of Title 37 of CFR to have an assignment recorded by the Office.

EFS Web 2.2.12

第2章 特許出願

ADS (PTO/AIA/14) の続き

[Form PTO/AIA/14 (11-15) — Application Data Sheet 37 CFR 1.76]

- Attorney Docket Number
- Application Number
- Title of Invention

Assignee 1

Complete this section if assignee information, including non-applicant assignee information, is desired to be included on the patent application publication. An assignee-applicant identified in the "Applicant Information" section will appear on the patent application publication as an applicant. For an assignee-applicant, complete this section only if identification as an assignee is also desired on the patent application publication.

If the Assignee or Non-Applicant Assignee is an Organization check here. ☒

Organization Name

Mailing Address Information For Assignee including Non-Applicant Assignee:

Address 1	
Address 2	
City	
Country i	
State/Province	
Postal Code	
Phone Number	
Fax Number	
Email Address	

Additional Assignee or Non-Applicant Assignee Data may be generated within this form by selecting the Add button.

Signature:

NOTE: This Application Data Sheet must be signed in accordance with 37 CFR 1.33(b). However, if this Application Data Sheet is submitted with the INITIAL filing of the application and either box A or B is not checked in subsection 2 of the "Authorization or Opt-Out of Authorization to Permit Access" section, then this form must also be signed in accordance with 37 CFR 1.14(c).

This Application Data Sheet **must** be signed by a patent practitioner if one or more of the applicants is a juristic entity (e.g., corporation or association). If the applicant is two or more joint inventors, this form must be signed by a patent practitioner, all joint inventors who are the applicant, or one or more joint inventor-applicants who have been given power of attorney (e.g., see USPTO Form PTO/AIA/81) on behalf of all joint inventor-applicants.

See 37 CFR 1.4(d) for the manner of making signatures and certifications.

Signature		Date (YYYY-MM-DD)	
First Name		Last Name		Registration Number	

Additional Signature may be generated within this form by selecting the Add button.

（代理人サイン）

EFS Web 2.2.12

出願書類を準備しよう

優先権書類の電子取寄せ申請書（Request to Retrieve Electronic Priority Applications）（PTO/SB/38）

　出願人は、U.S.P.T.O.に対して、電子的に優先権書類を入手するよう申請をすることができます。現在U.S.P.T.O.は日本出願の優先権書類を自動的に入手を試みます。ただし、意匠特許出願、PCT国際出願は対象外です。

https://www.uspto.gov/sites/default/files/patents/process/file/pdx/moreinfosb38.pdf

第2章　特許出願

予備的補正書（Preliminary Amendment）

　出願人は、最初の拒絶通知を受ける前に予備的補正書を提出して明細書または図面の補正を行うことができます。(37C.F.R.1.115)。予備的補正書が出願書類と同日に提出された場合には、出願書類の一部とされます。出願日以降に提出する際には、出願当初の明細書に記載のない新規事項の追加は認められません。よく使われる例として、費用的な観点から、国際出願の移行時に国際出願に含まれるクレームの複数従属項の削除を行う際に、この予備的補正書を提出します。

IN THE UNITED STATES PATENT AND TRADEMARK OFFICE

In re application of: Taro YAMADA	Art Unit: To be assigned
Application No.: To be assigned	Examiner: To be assigned
Based on PCT/JP2009/0xxxxx	Confirmation No.: To be assigned
Filed: May x, 2011	Attorney Docket No.: MOT.002.0011
For: SEARCH DEVICE AND SEARCH PROGRAM	

PRELIMINARY AMENDMENT UNDER 37 C.F.R. § 1.115

Mail Stop PCT
Commissioner for Patents
P.O. Box 1450
Alexandria, VA 22313-1450

Dear Sir:

　Prior to examination, please enter the following specification and claim amendments for the above-identified PCT application.

　It is not believed that a fee is required for filing of this paper. However, the Commissioner is hereby authorized to charge any fee deficiency or credit any fee payment to Deposit Account xx-xxxx.

出願人等のサインが必要な書類

　米国出願時に出願人側でサインが必要な書類（サイン書類）は、宣誓書、譲渡証、及び委任状が含まれます。これらのサイン書類は、発明者や出願人がサインを行いますが、書類の種類や出願形態によりサインする人が異なるため、注意が必要です。

サイン書類は原本でなくても提出可能
　U.S.P.T.O.に提出する多くのサイン書類は、電子出願時にスキャン等でPDF化してU.S.P.T.O.のサーバへアップロードします。従って、現地代理人に原本を郵送する必要はありません。電子メールでサイン書類のPDFデータを現地代理人に送付し、原本は出願人が保管することができます。

宣誓書（Oath or Declaration）
　米国特許法では、発明者に自らが発明者であることを宣誓することを求めています。特許法において、Oathとは、自己が真の発明者であることを証人の面前でサインする書面をいいます。一方、Declarationとは、宣誓の代わりに自己が真の発明者である陳述に対してサインする書面です。Declarationは証人の面前でサインする必要はありません。米国特許法においては、発明者サインの負担軽減の観点からDeclarationでの宣誓が認められています。

宣誓書？宣言書？
　ここで、辞書を見るとOathの対訳として「宣誓書」、そして、Declarationの対訳として「宣言書」となっているものが多いように思います。負担軽減の観点から実質的に殆どの発明者がDeclarationにサインしていると思いますが、日本国内において、発明者サイン書類は一般に「宣誓書」と呼ばれる方が多いように思います。これは、"Oath or Declaration" の対訳とする広い概念として「宣誓書」という言葉で対訳されたためと考えられます。本稿でも "Oath or Declaration" の広い概念として「宣誓書」として説明したいと思います。

　宣誓書は、発明者がその明細書に記載された発明の内容について、自らが発明者であることを宣誓する書面です（35U.S.C.115）。宣誓書は宣誓文及び出願を特定するための情報を含めます。

第2章　特許出願

宣誓書に含める3つの宣誓文（35U.S.C.115, 37C.F.R.1.63）
- 発明者の信じる限りにおいて、独自の発明である旨
- 出願は発明者によって、または発明者の許可を得て作成された旨
- 故意の誤陳述は刑法上の処罰があることを理解した旨

宣誓書に含める出願を特定するための情報
- 発明者のサイン
- 発明者の氏名（フルネーム）
- 発明者の居住地及び書類郵送先
- 特許出願の特定

宣誓書は補正できない

宣誓書は補正を行うことができません。補正が必要な事態が生じた場合には再提出する必要があります。ADSと一緒に宣誓書を提出する場合には、宣誓書には発明者のフルネーム及び居住地等の記載は省略することができます（37 C.F.R.1.62(b)）。

宣誓書の提出時期

提出時期は登録料納付日までです（35U.S.C.115(f)）。ただし、出願時に後充費用（Late Filing Fee）の支払いを行わなかった場合には、欠落部分提出通知（Notice to File Missing Parts）が発行されます。宣誓書を出願時に提出しない場合には、出願時にADSにて発明者の氏名と住所に関する情報を提供します（37C.F.R.1.41(d)）。ここで、宣誓書の提出時期は登録料納付日ですが、出願日に提出できなかった場合には、後充費用の支払いが発生すること、時間が経てば発明者からサインを入手することが困難になる可能性があることを考慮すれば、従前の通り出願時に提出することが望ましいと言えます。

新旧宣誓文の比較
- 旧法下の宣誓文では、発明者は、出願のクレームを含む書類の内容をレビューし、理解する旨宣誓する必要がありました。従って、発明者は最終の出願書類をレビューした上で宣誓書にサインする必要があると解されていました。現行法下の宣誓文では、単に、出願を自分で行うか、他人に出願を認めた旨を宣誓すれば足りるようになりました。
- 旧法下の宣誓書では、発明者は、信じる限りにおいて、<u>独自かつ最先</u>に発明した旨を宣誓する必要がありました。現行法下の宣誓書では、単に、発明者は、信じる限りにおいて、<u>独自</u>に発明した旨を宣誓すれば足りるようになりま

した。これは、先発明主義から修正先願主義に変更されたためと解されます。
- 旧法下の宣誓書では、発明者は、情報開示義務を有する事を理解している旨を宣誓する必要がありましたが、現行法では宣誓書において宣誓を行う必要がなくなりました。しかしながら、情報開示義務は、37C.F.R.1.63(c)になお規定がなされている点に留意する必要があります。
- 旧法下の宣誓書では、発明者は、故意に行った虚偽陳述があった場合には、刑事罰の他、当該特許出願や特許の有効性に関して問題となる事がある旨に宣誓する必要がありましたが、現行法下において、この宣誓文は削除されました。
- しかしながら、発明者は、故意に行った虚偽陳述があった場合には刑事罰の対象となる旨の宣誓は現行法下でも必要です。

ワンポイント解説：極小規模事業体

極小規模事業体と認定されるためには、収入が前年度の米国平均世帯年収の3倍を超える者等へ譲渡や譲渡契約等をしていないことが必要です。極小規模事業体と認定されるか否かは世帯年収＄169,548が目安となります。
https://www.uspto.gov/patent/laws-and-regulations/micro-entity-status-gross-income-limit

第2章 特許出願

新旧宣誓文の比較

	旧 宣 誓 文	現 宣 誓 文
1	I hereby state that I have reviewed and understand the contents of the above identified application, including the claims, as amended by any amendment specifically referred to above.	The above-identified application was made or authorized to be made by me.
2	I believe the inventor(s) named below to be the original and first inventor(s) of the subject matter which is claimed and for which a patent is sought ton the invention titled.	I believe I am the original inventor or an original joint inventor of a claimed invention in the application.
3	I acknowledge the duty to disclose information which is material to patentability as defined in 37CFR1.56, including for continuation-in-part applications, material information which became available between the filing date of the prior application and the national or PCT international filing date of the continuation-in-part application.	削除
4	I hereby declare that all statements made herein of my own knowledge are true and that all statements made on information and belief are believed to be true; and further that these statements were made with the knowledge that willful false statements and the like so made are punishable by fine or imprisonment, or both, under 18 U.S.C. 1001 and that such willful false statements may jeopardize the validity of the application or any patent issued thereon.	削除
5	I hereby acknowledge that any willful false statement made in this declaration is punishable under 18 U.S.C. 1001 by fine or imprisonment of not more than five (5) years, or both.	I hereby acknowledge that any willful false statement made in this declaration is punishable under 18 U.S.C. 1001 by fine or imprisonment of not more than five (5) years, or both.

出願人等のサインが必要な書類

宣誓書の記入例① (PTO/AIA/01)

```
                                                        PTO/AIA/01 (06-12)
                                       Approved for use through 01/31/2014. OMB 0651-0032
                                       U.S. Patent and Trademark Office; U.S. DEPARTMENT OF COMMERCE
Under the Paperwork Reduction Act of 1995, no persons are required to respond to a collection of information unless it displays a valid OMB control number.
```

DECLARATION (37 CFR 1.63) FOR UTILITY OR DESIGN APPLICATION USING AN APPLICATION DATA SHEET (37 CFR 1.76)

Title of ... : SEMICONDUCTOR DEVICE ← 発明の名称の記入

（出願と同時提出の場合にチェック）■ The attached application, or

（後充提出の場合にチェック）□ United States application or PCT international application number _____ ← 後充提出の場合：願番と出願日の記入
filed on _____

...ntified application was made or authorized to be made by me.

I believe that I am the original inventor or an original joint inventor of a claimed invention in the application.

I hereby acknowledge that any willful false statement made in this declaration is punishable under 18 U.S.C. 1001 by fine or imprisonment of not more than five (5) years, or both.

WARNING:

Petitioner/applicant is cautioned to avoid submitting personal information in documents filed in a patent application that may contribute to identity theft. Personal information such as social security numbers, bank account numbers, or credit card numbers (other than a check or credit card authorization form PTO-2038 submitted for payment purposes) is never required by the USPTO to support a petition or an application. If this type of personal information is included in documents submitted to the USPTO, petitioners/applicants should consider redacting such personal information from the documents before submitting them to the USPTO. Petitioner/applicant is advised that the record of a patent application is available to the public after publication of the application ... an abandoned application may also be available to the public ... an issued patent (see 37 CFR 1.14). Checks and credit ... es are not retained in the application file and therefor...

LEGAL NAME ...

Inventor: Taro YAMADA   Date (Optional): _____ ← サイン日付の記入（＊任意＊）
Signature: *Taro Yamada*

← 発明者氏名の記入とサイン

Note: An application data sheet (PTO/SB/14 or equivalent), including naming the entire inventive entity, must accompany this form or must have been previously filed. Use an additional PTO/AIA/01 form for each additional inventor.

This collection of information is required by 35 U.S.C. 115 and 37 CFR 1.63. The information is required to obtain or retain a benefit by the public which is to file (and by the USPTO to process) an application. Confidentiality is governed by 35 U.S.C. 122 and 37 CFR 1.11 and 1.14. This collection is estimated to take 1 minute to complete, including gathering, preparing, and submitting the completed application form to the USPTO. Time will vary depending upon the individual case. Any comments on the amount of time you require to complete this form and/or suggestions for reducing this burden, should be sent to the Chief Information Officer, U.S. Patent and Trademark Office, U.S. Department of Commerce, P.O. Box 1450, Alexandria, VA 22313-1450. DO NOT SEND FEES OR COMPLETED FORMS TO THIS ADDRESS. **SEND TO: Commissioner for Patents, P.O. Box 1450, Alexandria, VA 22313-1450.**

If you need assistance in completing the form, call 1-800-PTO-9199 and select option 2.

第2章　特許出願

宣誓書の記入例② (PTO/AIA/08)

出願人等のサインが必要な書類

宣誓書の記入例②（PTO/AIA/08）の続き

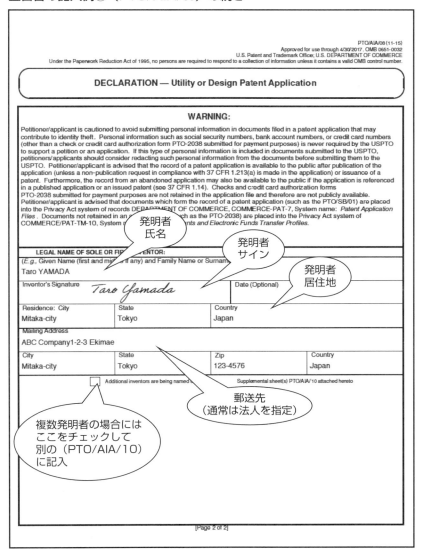

第2章　特許出願

代用陳述書　Substitute Statement

宣誓書は通常発明者が署名しますが、以下の場合には、特許出願人が代用陳述書を提出することができます（35U.S.C.115(d)）。

- 発明者が死亡した場合
- 発明者が法的無能力者の場合
- 勤勉な努力の後においても発明者を発見できなかった場合
- 発明者が署名を拒否した場合

代用陳述書には、以下の内容を含めます（35U.S.C.115(d)）。

- どの発明者が該当するかの特定
- 代用陳述書の提出が必要になった状況の説明
- その他、法上要求される必要な情報

ワンポイント解説：ResidenceとMailing Address

　宣誓書には発明者のResidence及びMailing Addressを記入する必要があります。なぜ、この2つを記入する必要があるのでしょうか？米国では、歴史的に人を特定する際に氏名のみではなく、居住地を含めて個人を特定するようにしていたという背景と関係があると思います。Residenceには発明者が実際に居住している地を特定します。宣誓書には、居住地の市（町村）、州（都道府県）、国を特定すれば足り、番地等の記入は必要がありません。一方、Mailing Addressは実際にU.S.P.T.O.からの書類を送付して欲しい場所を記入します。米国代理人を使用している場合には代理人へ送付されますが、代理人を指名していない等の場合には宣誓書に記載されたアドレスへ送付される場合があります。なお、U.S.P.T.O.からの書類が届いた場合に、その書類が理解できる人がいることが望ましいとの観点から、企業の場合には、知的財産部をMailing Addressにすることが多いようです。

出願人等のサインが必要な書類

宣誓書の代用陳述書（PTO/AIA/02）

Doc code: Oath
Document Description: Oath or declaration filed

PTO/AIA/02 (06-12)
Approved for use through 01/31/2014. OMB 0651-0032
U.S. Patent and Trademark Office; U.S. DEPARTMENT OF COMMERCE
Under the Paperwork Reduction Act of 1995, no persons are required to respond to a collection of information unless it displays a valid OMB control number.

SUBSTITUTE STATEMENT IN LIEU OF AN OATH OR DECLARATION FOR UTILITY OR DESIGN PATENT APPLICATION (35 U.S.C. 115(d) AND 37 CFR 1.64)

（出願と同時提出の場合にチェック）

This statement is directed to:

☐ The attached application,

OR

☐ United States application or PCT international application number _____ filed on _____

（発明の名称の記入）

LEGAL NAME of inventor to whom this substitute statement applies:

(E___) Given Name (first and middle (if any)) and Family Name or Surname

___ot for a deceased or legally incapacitated inventor):

| | State | Country |

（後充提出の場合にチェック）

___ot for a deceased or legally incapacitated inventor):

| City | State | Zip | Country |

（該当する発明者情報の記入）

I believe the above-named inventor or joint inventor to be the original inventor or an original joint inventor of a claimed invention in the application.

The above-identified application was made or authorized to be made by me.

I hereby acknowledge that any willful false statement made in this statement is punishable under 18 U.S.C. 1001 by fine or imprisonment of not more than five (5) years, or both.

Relationship to the inventor to whom this substitute statement applies:

☐ Legal Representative (for deceased or legally incapacitated inventor only),
☐ Assignee,
☐ Person to whom the inventor is under an obligation to assign,
☐ Person who otherwise shows a sufficient proprietary interest in the matter (petition under 37 ___), or
☐ Joint Inventor.

（サイン者と発明者との関係をチェック）

[Page 1 of 2]

This collection of information is required by 35 U.S.C. 115 and 37 CFR 1.63. The information is required to obtain or retain a benefit by the public which is to file (and by the USPTO to process) an application. Confidentiality is governed by 35 U.S.C. 122 and 37 CFR 1.11 and 1.14. This collection is estimated to take 1 minute to complete, including gathering, preparing, and submitting the completed application form to the USPTO. Time will vary depending upon the individual case. Any comments on the amount of time you require to complete this form and/or suggestions for reducing this burden, should be sent to the Chief Information Officer, U.S. Patent and Trademark Office, U.S. Department of Commerce, P.O. Box 1450, Alexandria, VA 22313-1450. DO NOT SEND FEES OR COMPLETED FORMS TO THIS ADDRESS. **SEND TO: Commissioner for Patents, P.O. Box 1450, Alexandria, VA 22313-1450.**

If you need assistance in completing the form, call 1-800-PTO-9199 and select option 2.

第2章 特許出願

宣誓書の代用陳述書（PTO／AIA／02）の続き

```
                                                        PTO/SB/AIA02 (06-12)
                                        Approved for use through 01/31/2014. OMB 0651-0032
                                        U.S. Patent and Trademark Office; U.S. DEPARTMENT OF COMMERCE
Under the Paperwork Reduction Act of 1995, no persons are required to respond to a collection of information unless it displays a valid OMB control number.
```

SUBSTITUTE STATEMENT

Circumstances permitting execution of this substitute statement:
- [ ] Inventor is deceased,
- [ ] Inventor is under legal incapacity,
- [ ] Inventor cannot be found or reached after diligent effort, or
- [ ] Inventor has refused to execute the oath or declaration under 37 CFR 1.63.

→ 発明者がサインできない理由をチェック

If there are joint inventors, please check the appropriate box below:
- [ ] An application data sheet under 37 CFR 1.76 (PTO/AIA/14 or equivalent) naming the entire inventive entity has been or is currently submitted.

OR

- [ ] An application data sheet under 37 CFR 1.76 (PTO/AIA/14 or equivalent) has not been submitted. Thus, a Substitute Statement Supplemental Sheet (PTO/AIA/11 or equivalent) naming the entire inventive entity and providing inventor information is attached. See 37 CFR 1.64(b).

WARNING:

Petitioner/applicant is cautioned to avoid submitting personal information in documents filed in a patent application that may contribute to identity theft. Personal information such as social security numbers, bank account numbers, or credit card numbers (other than a check or credit card authorization form PTO-2038 submitted for payment purposes) is never required by the USPTO to support a petition or an application. If this type of personal information is included in documents submitted to the USPTO, petitioners/applicants should consider redacting such personal information from the documents before submitting them to the USPTO. Petitioner/applicant is advised that the record of a patent application is available to the public after publication of the application (unless a non-publication request in compliance with 37 CFR 1.213(a) is made in the application) or issuance of a patent. Furthermore, the record from an abandoned application may also be available to the public if the application is referenced in a published application or an issued patent (see 37 CFR 1.14). Checks and credit card authorization forms PTO-2038 submitted for payment purposes are not retained in the application file and therefore are not publicly available.

PERSON EXECUTING THIS SUBSTITUTE STATEMENT:

Name: _____ Date (Optional): _____

Signature: _____

Residence (unless provided in an application data sheet, PTO/AIA/14 or equivalent):

City	State	Country

Mailing Address (unless provided in an application data sheet, PTO/AIA/14 or equivalent):

City	State	Zip	Country

→ サイン者の情報の記入及び署名

Note: Use an additional PTO/AIA/02 form for each inventor who is deceased, legally incapacitated, cannot be found or reached after diligent effort, or has refused to execute the oath or declaration under 37 CFR 1.63.

[Page 2 of 2]

出願人等のサインが必要な書類

宣誓文が含まれた譲渡証

　譲受人は、譲渡証にて宣誓文を含めることができます（35U.S.C.115(e)）。旧法下での宣誓書は出願時の必須提出書類であり、譲渡証は必須書類ではありませんでした。現行法下において、譲受人が出願する場合には、これら宣誓書中の3つの宣誓文（P.48参照）を譲渡証に含めることができます。従来発明者は宣誓書と譲渡証の2種類の書類にサインする必要がありましたが、上述の3つの宣誓文を譲渡証に含めることで1つの書類にサインのみで手続きを完了させる事ができるようになりました。

　宣誓書のステートメントを含む譲渡証は、法律施行日時点（2012年9月16日）でU.S.P.T.O.から正式なフォームは発行されておりません。今後も発行されない可能性があります。従って、現状では、米国法律事務所が独自に提供するフォームを用いることが多いようです。

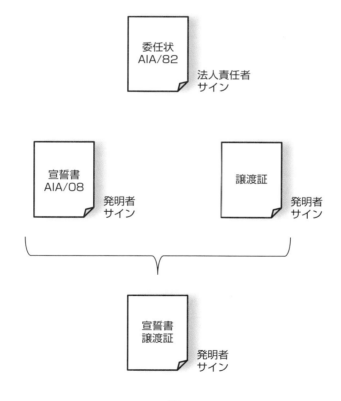

第2章　特許出願

宣誓文が含まれた譲渡証の例

Our Ref: ABC-0001

DECLARATION AND ASSIGNMENT

Whereas, the undersigned individual(s) (referred to herein as the INVENTOR(S)) of the invention described in:

☐ The attached application to be filed as a United States application or PCT international application, or

■ United States application or PCT international application number _12/345,678_ filed on _April 1, 2018_; and, entitled: _Semiconductor_.

Regarding that application, each of the INVENTOR(S) declares the following:

- The above-identified application was made or authorized to be made by me.
- I believe that I am the original inventor or an original joint inventor of a claimed invention in the application.
- I hereby acknowledge that any willful false statement made in this declaration is punishable under 18 u.s.c.1001 by fine or imprisonment of not more than five(5) years, or both.

For good and valuable consideration, the receipt and sufficiency of which are hereby acknowledged, INVENTOR(S) hereby assign, transfer, and set over to:

Company Name: AABBCC CORPORATION

Having the following business address: 1-2, Hon-cho, Chuo-ku, Tokyo, 345-0067 JAPAN

(referred to herein as "COMPANY"), its successors, and assigns, the entire right, title, and interest for the United States of America(including without limitation its possessions) in and to the invention described in the patent application identified above (referred to herein as INVENTION), together with said patent application, all divisions, continuations, continuations-in-part, reissues, and extensions thereof, and all United States Letters Patent which may be granted therefor. Such interest represents the entire ownership of said applications and Letters Patent when granted and is to be owned by COMPANY, its successors, and assigns, or their legal representatives, for the full and entire term for which such Letters Patent may be granted or extended, as fully and entirely as the same would have been enjoyed by the INVENTOR(S) if this assignment had not been made.

In addition, the undersigned INVENTOR(S) each hereby agrees:

1. To sign and execute any further document that may be necessary or desirable, lawful, and proper in connection with the prosecution of all applications for patent(s) on the INVENTION in the United States, including without limitation said application and all divisions, continuations, continuations-in-part, amendment thereof, and all interference or derivation proceedings associated therewith, or otherwise necessary or desirable to secure the title thereto to COMPANY;

2. To execute all papers and documents and to perform all lawful acts that may be necessary in connection with claims to priority or otherwise under the International Convention for the Protection of Industrial Property or similar treaties or agreements;

3. To perform all lawful affirmative acts that may be necessary to obtain the grant of valid and enforceable patents to COMPANY.

The undersigned INVENTOR(S) each hereby authorizes and requests the Commissioner of Patents and Trademarks in the United States to issue any and all Letters Patent resulting from said application, including without limitation any division, continuation, continuation-in-part, or reissue thereof to COMPANY.

The undersigned INVENTOR(S) each hereby grants to the firm of XYZ firm the power to insert into this Declaration and Assignment any further identification that may be necessary or desirable in order to comply with the rules of the United States Patent Trademark Office for the recordation of this document.

IN WITNESS WHEREOF, this Declaration and Assignment has been executed by each of the below individuals on the date appearing by such individual's signature:

Print or type Name: _Hanako SATO_ Date: _April 1, 2018_ 1st Inventor Signature: _Hanako Sato_

(注記:
- 事務所作成にはPTO番号を付さない
- 3つの宣言文
- 譲渡証部分
- 発明者サイン)

譲渡証（Assignment）

　発明をなした者は、原始的に特許を受ける権利を有します。発明者は特許を受ける権利を第三者に譲渡することができます。この場合には譲渡証（Assignment）にその旨を記載してU.S.P.T.O.に提出します。

　譲渡書（Assignment）は譲渡人（Assinor）と譲受人（Assignee）との間の契約書であるので、譲渡の条件等は各譲渡書によって異なります。

発明者以外による出願

　発明者から発明の譲渡または譲渡を受ける権利を有する者は、特許出願をすることができ、また、特許を得ることができます（35U.S.C.118）。譲受人が法人等の場合には、代理人により手続きを行う必要があります（37C.F.R.1.33(d)）。譲受人が特許出願を行った場合であって、その後に所有権の変更があった場合には、登録料納付までにU.S.P.T.O.に通知する必要があります。通知が無かった場合には所有権の変更が無かったものとして特許証が発行されます（37C.F.R.1.3.81）。

譲渡証の提出はコピー可

　譲渡証はオンラインで提出することができ、その場合には、サイン書類をスキャンしてPDF化した上で登録を行います。従って、譲渡証の提出は原本である必要はありません。現地代理人にはPDF等の電子データを送付し、原本は出願人が保管することをお勧めします。

企業から企業への移転、合併、社名変更のときの手続き

　U.S.P.T.O.には出願の審査部門とは別に譲渡証管理部門があります。譲渡証管理部門では、特許若しくは特許出願たる財産権の保護の立場から登録情報データベースを管理・公開しています。通常、特許出願と共に出願の所有権者が発明者から企業に移転する譲渡書が提出されますが、登録内容はそれに限らず、社名変更や合併、企業から企業への所有権の移転、質権設定、ライセンス契約等、出願に係る財産権に制約が発生したときや、所有権者の名前が変更されたとき等にも利用します。これにより、第三者への公示がなされ、二重譲渡等の不測の事態を未然に防ぐことが可能となります。また、代理人を任命する場合に任命権のある所有権者であることを示すのに出願が譲渡証管理部門に登録されていることが要求されます。

所有権の連鎖（Chain of Title）

　特許の所有権を明確に公示するため、所有権者が変わる毎にU.S.P.T.O.の譲

第2章 特許出願

渡証管理部門に登録するのが好ましいのですが、実際には所有権の移転が行われても未登録のままにされている特許や特許出願があります。特に、特許権を譲渡／譲受する場合は、真の権利者を特定するために、過去の所有権の移転が連鎖的に登録されてきているかをチェックする必要があります。例えば、発明者Aから企業Bへ譲渡され、企業Bから企業Cへ譲渡され、……の如くです。連鎖が途切れて所有権者が不明な空白期間がある場合には、別途、所有権の調査が必要でしょう。

ワンポイント解説：*Stanford v. Roche*
〜譲渡契約書の記載が問題になったケース〜

　発明者Aが大学Sに譲渡契約をし、数年後、法人Cと譲渡契約を行いました。その後連邦基金を受けて発明者Aは発明を行い、その所有権が問題となりました。問題になったのは、契約書の文言でした。裁判所は下記のように判断しました。大学Sの契約書の文言 "agree to assign" は単に将来譲渡する約束に過ぎない、と判示し、未だ譲渡は行われていないと認定しました。また、法人Cの契約書の文言 "will assign and do hereby assign" は即座の権利移転を意味する、と判示しました。そして、法人Cの契約書のサインの時点で当該発明の譲渡が行われていた事になり、法人Cが所有権を有することになりました。雇用契約書の発明譲渡に関する文言をチェックしてみてはいかがでしょうか？

出願人等のサインが必要な書類

譲渡証の例

下記の例は、発明者から雇用主である企業に社内発明を譲渡する際に用いられる典型的な譲渡書です。

MOT.085.0017.NP

ASSIGNMENT

For good and valuable consideration, the receipt and sufficiency of which are hereby acknowledged, each undersigned inventor has sold and assigned, and by presents hereby sells and assigns, unto

Name and address of assignee:

KAMAKURA CORPORATION

1234 Tokimasa-cho, Genpei Bldg. 3F, Kamakura-shi, Kanagawa, Japan

(hereinafter ASSIGNEE) all right, title and interest for the United States, its territories and possessions in and to the invention relating to

Title of invention:

ELECTRIC METAL POLISHER

as set forth in the United States Patent Application

check one
☐ executed concurrently herewith
☐ executed on _____
☒ Serial No. 13/123,789 Filed May 23, 2012

in and to said United States Patent Application including any and all divisions, continuations, or continuations-in-part there of and in and to any and all Letters Patent of the United States which may issue on any such application or for said invention, including any and all reissues or extensions thereof, to be held and enjoyed by said ASSIGNEE, its successors, legal representatives and assigns to the full end of the term or terms for which Letters Patent on may be granted as fully and entirely as the same would have been held by the undersigned had this Assignment not been made;

[inventor] hereby authorizes and requests the Director of U.S. [Patent Office to issue] any and all such Letters Patent to said ASSIGNEE, [executed concurrently] herewith;

[inventor] warrants and covenants that he has the full and [right to] assign the interests herein sold and assigned and that he [will] not execute any document or instrument and conflict herewith;

Page - 1 - of 2

吹き出し注釈:
- 譲受人を法人正式名称と所在地で特定
- 発明の名称や願番等で譲渡する対象を特定
- この譲渡証の効力が上記出願だけでなく、この出願から派生する全ての継続的出願や再発行特許出願にも及ぶ旨の文言

第2章　特許出願

譲渡証の例の続き

MOT.085.0017.NP

Each of the undersigned further covenants and agrees he will communicate to said ASSIGNEE, its successors, legal representatives or assigns all information known to him relating to said invention or patent application and that he will execute and deliver any papers, make all rightful oaths, testify in any legal proceedings and perform all other lawful acts deemed necessary or desirable by said ASSIGNEE, its successors, legal representatives or assigns to perfect title to said invention, to said application including divisions, continuations and continuations-in-part thereof and to any and all Letters Patent which may be granted therefore or thereon, including reissues or extensions, in said ASSIGNEE, its successors, or assigns or to assist said ASSIGNEE, its successors, legal representatives or assigns in obtaining, reissuing or enforcing Letters Patent of the United States for said invention;

Each of the undersigned hereby grants the attorneys and PLLC the power to insert in this Assignment any further necessary or desirable to comply with the rules of Trademark office for recordation of this Assignment.

（発明者（譲渡人）の署名と署名日の記入）

NAMES AND SIGNATURES OF INVENTORS

Name:	Signature:	Date:
Yoshitsune MINAMOTO	Yoshitsune	5 - 11 - 2012
Name:	Signature:	Date:
Name:	Signature:	Date:
Name:	Signature:	Date:
Name:	Signature:	Date:

NAMES AND SIGNATURES OF WITNESSES (Optional)

Name:	Signature:	Date:
Name:	Signature:	Date:
Name:	Signature:	Date:
Name:	Signature:	Date:
Name:	Signature:	Date:

Note: *Prima facie* evidence of execution optionally may be obtained by execution of this document before a United States Consul or before a local officer authorized to administer oaths whose authority is proved by a certificate from a United States Consul.

Page - 2 - of 2

出願人等のサインが必要な書類

譲渡書登録通知の見本

譲渡証の提出が完了すると、譲渡証の登録完了通知が届きます。譲渡証の検索は、リール／フレーム番号で行います。

```
                    UNITED STATES PATENT AND TRADEMARK OFFICE
                       UNDER SECRETARY OF COMMERCE FOR INTELLECTUAL PROPERTY AND
                       DIRECTOR OF THE UNITED STATES PATENT AND TRADEMARK OFFICE

MAY 24, 2012                    PTAS
                                                     987654321
MOTS LAW, PLLC
1629 K STREET N.W.
SUITE 200
WASHINGTON, DC 20006-1635


                  UNITED STATES PATENT AND TRADEMARK OFFICE
                  NOTICE OF RECORDATION OF ASSIGNMENT DOCUMENT

THE ENCLOSED DOCUMENT HAS BEEN RECORDED BY THE ASSIGNMENT RECORDATION BRANCH
OF THE U.S. PATENT AND TRADEMARK OFFICE. A COMPLETE COPY IS AVAILABLE AT THE
ASSIGNMENT SEARCH ROOM ON THE REEL AND FRAME NUMBER REFERENCED BELOW.

PLEASE REVIEW ALL INFORMATION CONTAINED ON THIS NOTICE. THE INFORMATION
CONTAINED ON THIS RECORDATION NOTICE REFLECTS THE DATA PRESENT IN THE PATENT
AND TRADEMARK ASSIGNMENT SYSTEM. IF YOU SHOULD FIND ANY ERRORS OR HAVE
QUESTIONS CONCERNING THIS NOTICE, YOU MAY CONTACT THE ASSIGNMENT RECORDATION
BRANCH AT 571-272-3350. PLEASE SEND REQUEST FOR C
AND TRADEMARK OFFICE, MAIL STOP: ASSIGNMENT RE       リール/フレーム番号
1450, ALEXANDRIA, VA 22313.

RECORDATION DATE: 05/23/2012        REEL/FRAME: 0123/4567
                                    NUMBER OF PAGES: 3

BRIEF: ASSIGNMENT OF ASSIGNORS INTEREST (SEE DOCUMENT FOR DETAILS).

DOCKET NUMBER: MOT.085.0017.NP

ASSIGNOR:
    YOSHITSUNE MINAMOTO              DOC DATE: 05/11/2012

ASSIGNEE:
    KAMAKURA CORPORATION
    1234 TOKIMASA-CHO, GENPEI BLDG. 3F
    KAMAKURA-SHI, JAPAN

APPLICATION NUMBER: 13/123,789       FILING DATE: MAY 23, 2012
PATENT NUMBER:                       ISSUE DATE:
TITLE: ELECTRIC METAL POLISHER


ASSIGNMENT RECORDATION BRANCH
PUBLIC RECORDS DIVISION



              P.O. Box 1450, Alexandria, Virginia 22313-1450 · WWW.USPTO.GOV
```

第2章　特許出願

U.S.P.T.O.の譲渡書登録データベース

　U.S.P.T.O.に登録された譲渡証の情報はU.S.P.T.O.ウェブサイトから検索することができます。但し、未公開の出願に係る譲渡証の情報は閲覧することができません。また、提出された譲渡書自体は一般公開されません。提出文書の写しを請求する際には庁料金及び出願人の許諾書が必要です。

http://assignments.uspto.gov/assignments/?db=pat

United States Patent and Trademark Office
Home | Site Index | Search | Guides | Contacts | eBusiness | eBiz alerts | News | Help

Assignments on the Web > **Patent Query**

Patent Assignment Abstract of Title

NOTE:Results display only for issued patents and published applications.
For pending or abandoned applications please consult USPTO staff.

Total Assignments: 1
Patent #:　　　　　　　Issue Dt:　　　　　　Application #: 13/123,789　　Filing Dt: 05/23/2012
Publication #: 20140098721　　Pub Dt: 11/23/2014
Inventors: Yoshitsune MINAMOTO
Title: ELECTRIC METAL POLISHER

Assignment: 1
Reel/Frame: 0123/4567　　　　Recorded: 05/23/2012　　　　　　　　Pages: 3
Conveyance: ASSIGNMENT OF ASSIGNORS INTEREST (SEE DOCUMENT FOR DETAILS).
Assignors: YOSHITSUNE MINAMOTO　　　　　　　　Exec Dt: 05/11/2012
Assignee: KAMAKURA CORPORATION
　　　　　　1234 TOKIMASA-CHO, GENPEI BLDG. 3F
　　　　　　KAMAKURA-SHI, JAPAN
Correspondent: MOTS LAW, PLLC
　　　　　　　1629 K STREET, NW
　　　　　　　SUITE 200
　　　　　　　WASHINGTON, DC 20006

Search Results as of: 06/08/2012 02:44 PM
If you have any comments or questions concerning the data displayed, contact PRD / Assignments at 571-272-3350. v.2.3.1
Web interface last modified: Jan 26, 2012 v.2.3.1

| .HOME | INDEX | SEARCH | eBUSINESS | CONTACT US | PRIVACY STATEMENT |

委任状（Power of Attorney）

　特許出願人は自分自身で出願手続きを行うことができますが、代理人に出願の手続きを依頼することもできます。代理人にその出願の手続きを依頼する際には委任状（Power of Attorney）を提出します。この委任状をU.S.P.T.O.へ提出することにより、委任された代理人が出願人の代わりに手続きを行う事ができます。

委任状のサインは誰がするか？

　旧法下においては、宣誓書と委任状とが一緒のフォームになっていたので、発明者が宣誓書にサインすれば代理人の委任も行えるようになっていました。現行法下では、法人も出願人となることができ、この場合は法人のどのような立場の人がサインするかが問題になります。ここで、委任状のサインは出願を行う権限を法人から与えられた方であれば良いと解され、法人の代表者（例えば社長）でなければならないという訳ではありません。ただし、サイン者は、少なくともManager（管理職）という肩書きを要すると解されます。

委任状を準備する（PTO/AIA/82）

　U.S.P.T.O.は様々な状況を考慮して複数の委任状のフォームを準備しています。本稿ではPTO/AIA/82の委任状を説明します。PTO/AIA/82は82Aと82Bとからなり、82Aには出願情報を記入し、82Bに出願人がサインを行います。この82BはPDFでの提出可能ですので、再利用することができます。82Aに出願毎の書誌的事項を記入し、82Bを再利用して2つのフォームを一緒に提出することで、実質的に包括委任状のように使用することができます。委任状にはU.S.P.T.O.に登録されたカスタマー番号で代理を委任する特許弁護士／特許エージェントを特定します。また、直接特許弁護士／特許エージェントの氏名を記入して特定することもできます。

ワンポイント解説：現地代理人事務所を変えたいとき（移管）に必要な書類
　現地代理人事務所を変更したい場合には、出願人はU.S.P.T.O.に対して特定の案件につき、今までの弁護士に対する委任状を破棄して、新たな弁護士を委任する旨を記載した書面（PTO/AIA/80等）を提出する必要があります。それと同時に出願人が委任権を有する真の所有者であることを示す書類（PTO/SB/96）も添付します。

第2章　特許出願

委任状の記入例　PTO/AIA/82A

Doc Code: PA..
Document Description: Power of Attorney

PTO/AIA/82A (07-13)
Approved for use through 01/31/2018. OMB 0651-0035
U.S. Patent and Trademark Office; U.S. DEPARTMENT OF COMMERCE
Under the Paperwork Reduction Act of 1995, no persons are required to respond to a collection of information unless it displays a valid OMB control number.

TRANSMITTAL FOR POWER OF ATTORNEY TO ONE OR MORE REGISTERED PRACTITIONERS

NOTE: This form is to be submitted with the Power of Attorney by Applicant form (PTO/AIA/82B) to identify the application to which the Power of Attorney is directed, in accordance with 37 CFR 1.5, unless the application number and filing date are identified in the Power of Attorney by Applicant form. If neither form PTO/AIA/82A nor form PTO/AIA82B identifies the application to which the Power of Attorney is directed, the Power of Attorney will not be recognized in the application.

Application Number	14/xxx,xxxx
Filing Date	04/04/2011
First Named Inventor	YAMADA, Taro
Title	SOLAR CELL MODULE
Art Unit	xxxx
Examiner Name	DOE, John
Attorney Docket Number	MLG.001.0001.NP

（出願情報の記入）

SIGNATURE of Applicant or Patent Practitioner

Signature		Date (Optional)	
Name		Registration Number	xx,xxxx
Title (if Applicant is a juristic entity)			
Applicant Name (if Applicant is a juristic entity)			

NOTE: This form must be signed in accordance with 37 CFR 1.33. See 37 CFR 1.4(d) for signature requirements and certifications. If more than one applicant, use multiple forms.

☐ *Total of _____ forms are submitted.

This collection of information is required by 37 CFR 1.131, 1.32, and 1.33. The information is required to obtain or retain a benefit by the public which is to file (and by the USPTO to process) an application. Confidentiality is governed by 35 U.S.C. 122 and 37 CFR 1.11 and 1.14. This collection is estimated to take 3 minutes to complete, including gathering, preparing, and submitting the completed application form to the USPTO. Time will vary depending upon the individual case. Any comments on the amount of time you require to complete this form and/or suggestions for reducing this burden, should be sent to the Chief Information Officer, U.S. Patent and Trademark Office, U.S. Department of Commerce, P.O. Box 1450, Alexandria, VA 22313-1450. DO NOT SEND FEES OR COMPLETED FORMS TO THIS ADDRESS. **SEND TO: Commissioner for Patents, P.O. Box 1450, Alexandria, VA 22313-1450.**

If you need assistance in completing the form, call 1-800-PTO-9199 and select option 2.

出願人等のサインが必要な書類

委任状の記入例　PTO/AIA/82B

Doc Code: PA..
Document Description: Power of Attorney

PTO/AIA/82B (07-13)
Approved for use through 01/31/2018. OMB 0651-0035
U.S. Patent and Trademark Office; U.S. DEPARTMENT OF COMMERCE
Under the Paperwork Reduction Act of 1995, no persons are required to respond to a collection of information unless it displays a valid OMB control number

POWER OF ATTORNEY BY APPLICANT

I hereby revoke all previous powers of attorney given in the application identified in either the attached tr...

> もし前に委任状を提出した場合にはその委任状は破棄する旨の文言

Number	Filing Date
/xxx,xxxx	04/04/2011

...may be left blank if information is provided on form PTO/AIA/82A).

> U.S.P.T.O.に登録されたカスタマー番号に関連づけられた代理人に委任する旨の文言

...ctitioner(s) associated with the following Customer Number as my/our attor... United States Patent and Trademark Office connected therewith for the applica... (form PTO/AIA/82A) or identified above:

65181

☐ I hereby appoint Practitioner(s) named in the attached list (form PTO/AIA/82C) as... all business in the United States Patent and Trademark Office... attached transmittal letter (form PTO/AIA/82A) or identified abo...

> 添付署名の氏名及び登録番号で特定された代理人に委任する旨の文言

Please recognize or change the correspondence address for th... letter or the boxes above to:

☐ The address associated with the above-mentioned Customer Number
  OR
☑ The address associated with Customer Number: 65181
  OR
☐ Firm or Individual Name

Address			
City	State		Zip
Country			
Telephone	Email		

I am the Applicant (if the Applicant is a juristic entity, list the Applicant name in th...

> 出願人の種別を記載チェック

☐ Inventor or Joint Inventor (title not required below)
☐ Legal Representative of a Deceased or Legally Incapacitated Inventor (title not required below)
☑ Assignee or Person to Whom the Inventor is Under an Obligation to Assign (provide signer's title if applicant is a juristic entity)
☐ Person Who Otherwise Shows Sufficient Proprietary Interest (e.g., a petition under 37 CFR 1.46(b)(2) was granted in the application or is concurrently being filed with this document) (provide signer's title if applicant is a juristic entity)

SIGNATURE of Applicant for Patent

The undersigned (whose title is supplied below) is authorized to act on behalf of the applicant (e.g., where the applicant is a juristic entity).

Signature	*T.Nakamura*	Date (Optional)	
Name	NAKAMURA, Takashi		
Title	Senior Director, ABC company		

> サインはここへ

NOTE: Signature - This form must be signed by the applicant in accorda... R 1.4 for signature requirements and certifications. If more than one applicant, use multiple forms.

☐ Total of _____ forms are submitted.

This collection of information is required by 37 CFR 1.131, 1.32, and 1.33. The information is required to obtain or retain a benefit by the public which is to file (and by the USPTO to process) an application. Confidentiality is governed by 35 U.S.C. 122 and 37 CFR 1.11 and 1.14. This collection is estimated to take 3 minutes to complete, including gathering, preparing, and submitting the completed application form to the USPTO. Time will vary depending upon the individual case. Any comments on the amount of time you require to complete this form and/or suggestions for reducing this burden, should be sent to the Chief Information Officer, U.S. Patent and Trademark Office, U.S. Department of Commerce, P.O. Box 1450, Alexandria, VA 22313-1450. DO NOT SEND FEES OR COMPLETED FORMS TO THIS ADDRESS. **SEND TO: Commissioner for Patents, P.O. Box 1450, Alexandria, VA 22313-1450.**

If you need assistance in completing the form, call 1-800-PTO-9199 and select option 2.

第2章　特許出願

情報開示義務とIDS

　出願関係者は、特許性に関する重要な情報について、公正かつ誠実にU.S.P.T.O.にその情報を提出する義務を有します。これらの情報を提出する際には情報開示陳述書（Information Disclosure Statement：IDS）に添えて提出します。対象となる重要な情報には、対応外国出願のサーチレポートや拒絶理由書で挙げられた先行技術が含まれます。審査の進展によって情報開示陳述書と共に提出する書類は異なり、審査手続きがより進めば、提出する書類や手続きが増加します。許可通知が来た後も登録料を納めて特許証の発行を待っている状態でも情報開示義務はありますので注意が必要です。

不衡平行為とは

　そもそもなぜU.S.P.T.O.は出願人に情報開示義務を課したのでしょうか？これは、裁判所は不衡平行為により得られた特許権の行使を拒否することができる、という過去の裁判例[1]が根拠になっています。この裁判例から、特許権を得て第三者に権利行使する場合には、衡平の観点から、権利行使者は潔白でなければならず、欺瞞の意図で得た権利に対してはその行使を認めない、ということになっています。従って、U.S.P.T.O.への手続きに対しても出願人は潔白である必要があり、出願人は特許にならない理由を知りながら、それを隠匿して特許を得たと認定された場合には、その行為は不衡平行為であり、特許権の行使を拒否され、権利行使不能とされます。

不衡平行為の判断

　不衡平行為か否かは、2つの要因で判断されます。第1の要因は、情報の重要性（Materiality）です。具体的には、提出しなかった文献が当該特許性に関して影響があるか否かで判断されます。不均衡行為の主張は、例えば特許侵害訴訟において、被告の抗弁としてなされます。従って、立証責任は、被告にあるのですが、どの程度までその重要性を立証する必要があるかが問題となります。すなわち、外国特許庁で引用された文献であれば即重要と判断されるか、さらに立証が必要なのか？という点です。この点、被告はその文献をU.S.P.T.O.

1　Precision Inst. Mfg. Co. v. Auto Maint. Mach, 324 US 806（1945）

に提出していたならば、当該特許は許可されなかった旨を立証する必要があります（Therasense v. Becton (Fed. Cir. May 25, 2011)）。従って、単に外国特許庁で引用された文献であるというのみでは足らず、その文献でU.S.P.T.Oは当該特許出願を特許しなかったであろう旨を立証する必要があります。

重要であると考えられるものについては、以下のような規定がなされています（37C.F.R.1.56(b)）。
- 単独または組み合わせにより特許性の否定を疎明できるもの
- U.S.P.T.O.の非特許性に対する反論と反対の立場にたつもの
- 特許性があるとする立場に対する反論、もしくは矛盾するもの
- 対応外国出願のOAに記載された先行技術文献などは重要であると考えられる

ただし、これらはU.S.P.T.O.が規定したものであり、後のTherasense事件が判示する内容と齟齬が生じています。U.S.P.T.O.と裁判所の判断に齟齬が生じている例はこれ以外にもありますので、37C.F.R.1.56(b)の規定は、「これらを提出しておけば安全である目安」と解釈でき、「これらを提出しなければ、即不衡平行為と認定される」訳ではない、と理解しておけば良いかと思います。

第2の要因は、詐欺の意図（Intent to Deceive）です。どの程度悪意の意図があったのか、うっかりして提出し忘れたのか、意図的に隠匿したのかが判断されます。原則として、この2つの要件を満たした場合に不衡平行為と認定されます。

不衡平行為か否かは、原則裁判所で判断されます。裁判所では、この2つの要因に関して様々な事実を考慮して当該行為（典型的には文献を提出しなかった行為）が不衡平行為に該当するか否かを総合的に判断します。

この「総合的に」をもう少し解説します。例えば、「日本公開公報を情報開示するのに要約部分のみの翻訳文を提出した。」としましょう。上記手続きを同様にしていたとしても不衡平行為に該当する場合としない場合があるとように思います。例えば、上記事実の他に「当該日本公開公報はあまり重要ではなく、その関連部分は要約の部分にあった」事実が判明したとしましょう。これら2つの事実のみでは、不衡平行為と認定されることは殆ど考えにくいです。その一方、上記の「日本公開公報を情報開示するのに要約部分のみの翻訳文を提出した。」の事実の他に、もし当該日本公開公報が提出されていたら、審査官は許可しなかったであろう程「当該日本公開公報は非常に重要な影響を与え

第2章　特許出願

るものであった。」、「その重要部分が要約部分以外の部分にあり、それを発明者が意図的に隠匿する目的で要約部分のみの翻訳文を提出した。」という事実が判明したとしましょう。これらの事実が裁判で明らかになった場合には、かなり特許権者には不利な証拠になり、不衡平行為と判断される可能性が上がってしまいます。このような理由から、安全を考慮して全文翻訳を提出するのが好ましいとされています。

　上記の事実が出揃った後に、裁判所で複数の人間が各々判断します。これは、ビーカーの中の牛乳に墨汁をスポイトで落とし、それを複数の人に「ビーカーの中の色は白色でしょうか？黒色でしょうか？」と聞くのに似ています。元々ビーカーの中は牛乳ですので、誰が見ても白色をしています。そして、裁判の中で、特許権者にとって不利な事実が出てくる毎に墨汁がスポイトからビーカーへ垂らされます。不利な事実の度合によっては、垂らされる墨汁はほんの少しかもしれませんし、一気にビーカー内が真っ黒になる量かもしれません。真っ白や真っ黒ならば、判断は統一されますが、「灰色」の場合、ある人は「白色」と判断し、ある人は「黒色」と判断するかもしれません。

　しかし、裁判では正に白黒はっきりさせる必要があります。100％安全な真っ白のままを保つには、費用や時間が掛かってしまいます。IDSにかける費用や時間を考慮し、「常識的な範囲で白に見える」ようにしておく必要があります。この辺にIDS手続きの難しさがあり、実務者がいつも悩む部分であるかと思います。

　IDS手続きにおいては、個々の手続きに拘泥することなく、法の趣旨に基づいて大局的な観点から、費用や時間等妥当な範囲で行うことが肝要と言えます。

情報開示義務は誰にあるか？
　情報開示義務は、発明者は勿論のこと、その出願を担当する代理人等実質的に出願に関わる総ての人に義務があります。従って、出願手続きに責任を有

し、米国代理人を通じて手続きに関わる外国の代理人も含まれると解されます（M.P.E.P.2001, 2002）。

情報開示義務はいつまであるのか？

情報開示義務は出願後、特許が発行されるまで続きます。具体的には米国特許証に記載された日付まで情報開示義務が続きます。従って、特許発行費用支払後も情報開示義務はあることに注意が必要です。特許が発行された後は情報開示義務は解消されます。

非衡平行為は後の手続きで治癒できるか？

一旦不衡平行為を行ってしまった場合には、その後の手続きで治癒できるか？という問題があります。具体的には、ある時点で提出し忘れた文献について所定期間が過ぎてしまったら提出は可能であるか？という点です。これに関しては、同一審査手続き中であれば、提出し忘れた文献についての提出は可能です。場合によっては、継続審査請求（RCE）が必要になることもあります。一旦特許になった後は、今回の法改正で新設された補充審査制度を用いて治癒が可能な場合があります。

同時係属出願があるときの注意点

継続的出願等で近似した発明について複数の出願手続きが同時に進行している場合には注意が必要です。すなわち、一方の特許出願に許可が出て登録料を納めて待っている段階で、他方の出願に新たな引用例が記載されたOAが発せられた場合には、一方の出願の許可取り下げの後にRCEと共に当該引用例を提出する必要があります。この無駄なステップは、関連出願が多くなると生じる可能性が高くなることに留意が必要です。

情報開示陳述書（Information Disclosure Statement：IDS）

提出する書類は以下の通りです。出願の審査段階により提出する書類が異なります。審査が進めば、換言すれば、提出が遅れれば、提出する書類も増えます。

1）出願から3月または実体的第1回局指令まで
提出物
- PTO/SB/08
- 文献のコピー（U.S.P.T.O.文献の場合は不要）

2）1）の後であって、最終局指令または許可通知まで
提出物
- PTO/SB/08
- 文献のコピー（U.S.P.T.O.文献の場合は不要）
- 下記のいずれか1つ
  - ➢提出文献は対応外国出願に対して送達されたOA／調査報告書等に初めて引用され、送達から3月以内に提出している旨のステートメント
  - ➢提出文献は対応外国出願に送達された通知にも今まで引用されたことがなく、IDS提出の義務がある者が3月以内に初めて知った情報である旨のステートメント
  - ➢37C.F.R.1.17(p)のペティションフィー

3）2）の後であって、特許証発行費用支払い時まで
提出物
- PTO/SB/08
- 文献のコピー（U.S.P.T.O.文献の場合は不要）
- 下記のいずれか1つ
  - ➢提出文献は対応外国出願に対して送達されたOA／調査報告書等に初めて引用され、送達から3月以内に提出している旨のステートメント
  - ➢提出文献は対応外国出願に送達された通知にも今まで引用されたことがなく、IDS提出の義務がある者が3月以内に初めて知った情報である旨のステートメント
- 37C.F.R.1.17(p)のペティションフィー

ワンポイント解説：情報開示義務は特許法の規定ではない！
　情報開示義務は特許法上の規定はありません。また、不衡平行為による特許不行使も特許法上の規定ではなく、衡平法（equity）上の救済です。

情報開示義務とIDS

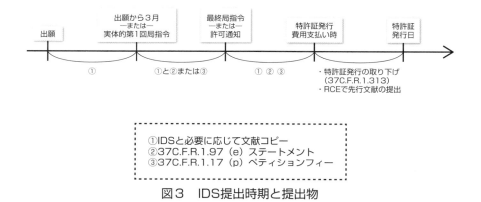

図3　IDS提出時期と提出物

IDSに関する注意点

- IDSの提出期間に関しては延長することができません（37C.F.R.1.97(f)）。
- IDSの提出に際して、先行技術文献調査を行う必要はありません（37C.F.R.1.97(g)）。従って、出願関係者が知っている範囲で提出すれば良いということになります。
- 提出により文献は重要であるとの自認の推定は働きません（37C.F.R.1.97(h)）。
- 37C.F.R.1.97の規定以外で提出の場合には包袋には入るが考慮されません（37C.F.R.1.97(i), M.P.E.P.609.05(a)）
- 提出したPTO/SB/08は、通常、次の局指令で考慮され、各先行技術の欄に考慮された証明である審査官のサインがなされ、そのコピーが局指令と共に送付されます。PTO/SB/08を受領後には、これら審査官の考慮済みである旨のサインを確認するとよいでしょう。

第2章 特許出願

IDS文献リストの記入例（PTO/SB/08a）

Doc code: IDS		PTO/SB/08a (03-15)
Doc description: Information Disclosure Statement (IDS) Filed		Approved for use through 07/31/2016. OMB 0651-0031
		U.S. Patent and Trademark Office; U.S. DEPARTMENT OF COMMERCE

Under the Paperwork Reduction Act of 1995, no persons are required to respond to a collection of information unless it contains a valid OMB control number.

INFORMATION DISCLOSURE STATEMENT BY APPLICANT (Not for submission under 37 CFR 1.99)	Application Number	14123456
	Filing Date	2017-12-22
	First Named Inventor	YAMADA, Taro
	Art Unit	xxxxxx
	Examiner Name	DOE, John
	Attorney Docket Number	MLG.001.00001.NP

→ 願番等で出願を特定

U.S.PATENTS

→ 米国特許、米国公開公報の場合には願番等のみ

Examiner Initial*	Cite No	Patent Number	Kind Code¹	Issue Date	Name of Patentee or Applicant of cited Document	Pages,Columns,Lines where Relevant Passages or Relevant Figures Appear
	1	12345678	B1	2011-06-05	Suzuki et al.	(Cited in ISR; Corresponding to JP2010-123456A)

If you wish to add additional U.S. Patent citation information please click the Add button.

U.S.PATENT APPLICATION PUBLICATIONS

Examiner Initial*	Cite No	Publication Number	Kind Code¹	Publication Date	Name of Patentee or Applicant of cited Document	Pages,Columns,Lines where Relevant Passages or Relevant Figures Appear
	1	20131234343	A1	2013-04-04	Smith et al.	

If you wish to add additional U.S. Published Application citation information please click the Add button

→ 外国特許文献の場合には願番等の情報の他、文献のコピーも添付

FOREIGN PATENT DOCUMENTS

Examiner Initial*	Cite No	Foreign Document Number³	Country Code² i	Kind Code⁴	Publication Date	Name of Patentee or Applicant of cited Document	Pages,Columns,Lines where Relevant Passages or Relevant Figures Appear	T⁵
	1	2011-234567	JP	A1	2011-02-21	ABC Company	(Corresponding to US 20131234343)	☒

If you wish to add additional Foreign Patent Document citation information please click the Add button

NON-PATENT LITERATURE DOCUMENTS

Examiner Initials*	Cite No	Include name of the author (in CAPITAL LETTERS), title of the article (when appropriate), title of the (book, magazine, journal, serial, symposium, catalog, etc), date, pages(s), volume-issue number(s), publisher, city and/or country where published.

EFS Web 2.1.17

→ 各文献が審査官に考慮されると、審査官のイニシャルが記入される

→ 非英語文献で翻訳文提出の場合にはここをチェック

→ 非特許文献を特定

IDS文献リストの記入例（PTO/SB/08a）の続き

INFORMATION DISCLOSURE STATEMENT BY APPLICANT (Not for submission under 37 CFR 1.99)	Application Number: 14123456 Filing Date: 2017-12-22 First Named Inventor: YAMADA, Taro Art Unit: xxxxxx Examiner Name: DOE, John Attorney Docket Number: MLG.001.00001.NP

1. B Smith et al. "Method of collecting electricity using giant kite," Washington Science Journal; Vol. 7 No. 5; pp 125-149; Movember 7, 2009

If you wish to add additional non-patent literature document citation information please click the Add button

EXAMINER SIGNATURE

Examiner Signature		Date Considered	

*EXAMINER: Initial if reference considered whether or not citation is in conformance with MPEP 609. Draw line through a citation if not in conformance and not considered. Include copy of this form with next communication to applicant.

[1] See Kind Codes of USPTO Patent Documents at www.USPTO.GOV or MPEP 901.04. [2] Enter office that issued the document, by the two-letter code (WIPO Standard ST.3). [3] For Japanese patent documents, the indication of the year of the reign of the Emperor must precede the serial number of the patent document. [4] Kind of document by the appropriate symbols as indicated on the document under WIPO Standard ST.16 if possible. [5] Applicant is to place a check mark here if English language translation is attached.

EFS Web 2.1.17

（吹き出し1：文献1を指して）
文献の著者名、題名、学会誌名、出版日、掲載ページ、掲載巻、出版会社、出版された場所、国名等で文献を特定し、文献のコピーを添付する

（吹き出し2：EXAMINER SIGNATURE欄を指して）
提出した文献が考慮されると、審査官はサインして出願人にフォームを返送する

第2章 特許出願

IDS文献リストの記入例（PTO/SB/08a）の続き

INFORMATION DISCLOSURE STATEMENT BY APPLICANT (Not for submission under 37 CFR 1.99)	Application Number: 14123456 Filing Date: 2017 First Named Inventor: YAMADA Art Unit: xx Examiner Name: DOE, Jo Attorney Docket Number: ML

CERTIFICATION STATEMENT

Please see 37 CFR 1.97 and 1.98 to make the appropriate selection(s):

☐ That each item of information contained in the information disclosure statement was first cited in any communication from a foreign patent office in a counterpart foreign application not more than three months prior to the filing of the information disclosure statement. See 37 CFR 1.97(e)(1).

> 提出文献は対応外国出願に対して送達されたOA/調査報告書等に初めて引用され、送達から3月以内に提出している旨のステートメント。

OR

☐ That no item of information contained in the information disclosure statement was cited in a communication from a foreign patent office in a counterpart foreign application, and, to the knowledge of the person signing the certification after making reasonable inquiry, no item of information contained in the information disclosure statement was known to any individual designated in 37 CFR 1.56(c) more than three months prior to the filing of the information disclosure statement. See 37 CFR 1.97(e)(2).

> 提出文献は、外国対応出願に送達された通知にも今まで引例されたことがなく、IDS提出の義務のある者が3月以内に初めて知った情報である旨のステートメント

☐ See attached certification statement.
☐ The fee set forth in 37 CFR 1.17 (p) has been submitted herewith.
☒ A certification statement is not submitted herewith.

> 料金を支払う場合にはここをチェック

SIGNATURE
A signature is required in accordance with...
form of the...

Signature: ___ Date (YYYY...)
Name/Print: ___ Registration N...

This collection of information is required by 37 CFR 1.97 and 1.98. The information is required to obtain or retain a benefit by the public which is to file (and by the USPTO to process) an application. Confidentiality is governed by 35 U.S.C. 122 and 37 CFR 1.14. This collection is estimated to take 1 hour to complete, including gathering, preparing and submitting the completed application form to the USPTO. Time will vary depending upon the individual case. Any comments on the amount of time you require to complete this form and/or suggestions for reducing this burden, should be sent to the Chief Information Officer, U.S. Patent and Trademark Office, U.S. Department of Commerce, P.O. Box 1450, Alexandria, VA 22313-1450. DO NOT SEND FEES OR COMPLETED FORMS TO THIS ADDRESS. **SEND TO: Commissioner for Patents, P.O. Box 1450, Alexandria, VA 22313-1450.**

EFS Web 2.1.17

文献が非英語の場合

文献が非英語の場合には、英語の説明文を提出する必要があります（37C.F.R.1.98(a)(3)）。この説明文として当該文献の翻訳文の提出を行うことができます。先行技術文献の部分訳を提出したため、特許が権利行使不可と認定されたケース[1]がありますので、全文翻訳の提出が安全と言えます。下記のリンク[2]から機械翻訳を入手することができます。

また、英語の説明文として、外国特許庁のOA中の引用例の説明でも提出の義務を果たす場合があります（37C.F.R.1.98(a)(3)）。

対応外国特許庁の局指令自体は提出すべきか？

外国特許庁の局指令自体は引用例ではありませんので、他国の特許庁で発せられた局指令自体が米国特許に重大な影響を及ぼす事は希であると言えます。前掲のTherasense事件では外国特許庁の局指令が問題になりましたが、外国特許庁へ出願人の主張とU.S.P.T.O.へのそれに矛盾があり、その矛盾した主張が不衡平行為と認定されました。従って、局指令自体の重要性が問題になった訳ではありません。また、今回の法改正により、補充審査で瑕疵が治癒できる点を考慮して局指令自体のIDS提出の必要性は低いと解されます。なお、上述の非英語文献の説明として局指令の該当部分の翻訳文の提出は可能です。

技術背景を示す文献（A文献）を提出すべきか？

PCTや欧州特許庁から受領したサーチレポート等に引用された文献には、その関連性に応じてX文献、Y文献、A文献等に分類されます。ここで、X及びY文献は、関連性が高い、若しくは関連性がある文献であると認定されたものですので、提出すべきです。その一方、対象特許に関して技術的背景が記載される参考程度の文献であるAに分類される文献（A文献）について、提出すべきか否かが問題になります。

ここで、昨今のサーチレポート等を見ると、A文献と認定しているにも関わらず、見解書部分に当該A文献を引用している場合があります。そして、審査官は当該A文献をY文献のような、すなわち、関連性があるような見解をして

1　SEL v. Samsung 54 USPQ2d 1001
2　https://worldwide.espacenet.com/
　https://www4.j-platpat.inpit.go.jp/eng/tokujitsu/tkbs_en/TKBS_EN_GM101_Top.action
　https://patents.google.com/

第2章　特許出願

いる場合があります。このような可能性を考慮すれば、「A文献は提出不要」と一律に処理するのはリスクがあります。規則上、出願人等が情報提供すべきは、「特許性に関する重要な情報」を提出すべきであって、参考程度の文献を除外しているわけではない点に注意が必要です。

IDSに関する試行プログラム〜Quick Path IDS Program〜

　上述の通り、情報開示義務は特許発行日まで続きます。特許発行費用支払後特許発行前に情報開示すべき文献が発見された場合には、特許発行取り下げの誓願を行い（37C.F.R.1.313）、継続審査請求（RCE）を当該文献と一緒に提出する必要がありました。特許が発行されるのを待っていた出願人にとって、再度の継続審査請求は、特許発行の期日が遅れる等出願人にとっての負担が大きいものでした。

　この試行プログラムは、既に特許発行費用を支払った後に提出すべき先行技術文献が発見された場合に、特許発行を仮取り下げして、当該文献を提出するものです。仮取り下げの際にRCE料金を仮払いしますが、文献の開示内容が特に本願の特許性に影響がなければ、取り下げはなかったことにしてそのまま特許発行に至りRCE料金は返金されます。提出後、文献の開示内容が本願の特許性に影響があると審査官が判断する場合には、RCEがそのまま有効となり審査が再開されます。このプログラムによって特許発行料支払い後のIDSにかかる費用と時間が削減できるようになります。現時点では本試行プログラムは、2018年9月30日まで有効となっています。

QPIDSの要件

- 特許発行費用支払後特許発行前であること
- 提出する文献は外国OAに引用されてから3月以内、または関係者が知りえてから3月以内のものであること
- 特許発行費用支払後のIDS考慮誓願書（PTO/SB/09）の提出
- RCE（PTO/SB/30）の提出
- IDS（PTO/SB/08）の提出（37C.F.R.1.97(e)）
- 文献の提出
- 費用の支払い（特許発行取下げ請願費用（37C.F.R.1.17(h)）、RCE費用（37C.F.R.1.17(e)）、及び、IDSに関する費用（37C.F.R.1.17(p)））

審査官の考慮の結果、下記のような取り扱いになります。

- 文献の開示内容が本願発明の特許性に影響がないと判断された場合には、

許可可能通知(PTOL-37)が発せられます。また、前払いしたRCE料金は返金されます。
- 文献の開示内容が本願発明の特許性と影響があると判断された場合には、審査再開通知(PTO-2300)が発せられ、審査が再開されます。IDSに関する費用は返金されます。

ワンポイント解説:包袋(File Wrapper)とは
　「ファイル」や「ファイルラッパー」とも呼ばれます。特許事務所では、特許庁とのやり取りや、クライアントとのやり取りを時系列的に綴じておく書類の束です。特許庁内にも出願人やその代理人とのやり取りが同様に保管されています。U.S.P.T.O.では「イメージ・ファイルラッパー」という電子的な包袋がウェブサイトに掲示され、公開後の出願であれば誰でも閲覧できるようになっています。

第2章 特許出願

特許発行費用支払後のIDS考慮申請書の記入例　PTO/SB/09

Doc Code: QPIDS.REQ
Document Description: Quick Path Information Disclosure Statement

CERTIFICATION AND REQUEST FOR CONSIDERATION OF AN INFOR
STATEMENT FILED AFTER PAYMENT OF THE ISSUE FEE UNDER THE

| Non-Provisional Application Number: 13/123456 | Filing Date: 12/23/20 |
| First Named Inventor: YAMADA, Taro | Title of Invention: Metho |

THE UNDERSIGNED HEREBY CERTIFIES AND REQUESTS THE FOLLOWING FO
IDENTIFIED APPLICATION.

1. Consideration is requested of the information disclosure statement (IDS) submitted herewith ... filed after payment of the issue fee.

2. Check the box next to the appropriate selection:

   ☑ Each item of information contained in the IDS was first cited in any communication from a foreign patent office in a counterpart foreign application not more than three months prior to the filing of the IDS. See 37 CFR 1.97(e)(1).

   OR

   ☐ No item of information contained in the IDS was cited in a communication from a foreign patent office in a counterpart foreign application, and, to the knowledge of the person signing the certification after making reasonable inquiry, no item of information contained in the IDS was known to any individual designated in 37 CFR 1.56(c) more than three months prior to the filing of the IDS. See 37 CFR 1.97(e)(2).

   OR

   ☐ See attached certification statement in compliance with 37 CFR 1.97

3. Please charge the IDS fee set forth in 37 CFR 1.17(p) to Deposit Acc

4. A Petition to Withdraw from Issue After Payment of the Issue Fee ... petition fee set forth in 37 CFR 1.17(h), is submitted herewith a ... **WARNING**: Do not submit the petition as a follow-on paper v ... based ePetition by signing on to EFS-Web as a registered us ... application/patent," and then selecting the radio button next t ... immediate grant, if all petitions requirements are met)." Failur ... result in automatic entry of the RCE.

5. A request for continued examination (RCE) under 37 CFR 1.11 ... submitted herewith.

6. The RCE will be treated as a "conditional" RCE. In the event the exam ... information contained in the IDS necessitates the reopening of prosecution ... undersigned understands that (i) the RCE will be processed and treated as an RCE under 37 CFR 1.114 and therefore (ii) the IDS fee under 37 CFR 1.17(p) will be returned in accordance with 37 CFR 1.97(b)(4). In the event that no item of information in the IDS necessitates reopening prosecution, the undersigned understands that the RCE will not be processed and the RCE fee under 37 CFR 1.17(e) will be returned.

7. This certification and request is being filed as a **Web-based ePetition** and is not accompanied by an amendment to the application. Inclusion of an amendment will result in automatic entry of the RCE.

| Signature | Date 12/22/2017 |
| Name (Print/Typed) | Practitioner Registration Number XXXXXX (If applicable) |

Note: Signatures of all the inventors or assignees of record of the entire interest or their representative(s) are required in accordance with 37 CFR 1.33 and 11.18. Please see 37 CFR 1.4(d) for the form of the signature. If necessary, submit multiple forms for more than one signature, see below.*

☐　*Total of _____ forms are submitted.

If you need assistance in completing the form, call 1-800-PTO-9199 and select option 2.

（吹き出し1）提出文献は対応外国出願に対して送達されたOA/調査報告書等に初めて引用され、送達から3月以内に提出している旨のステートメント

（吹き出し2）提出文献は、外国対応出願に送達された通知にも今まで引例されたことがなく、IDS提出の義務のある者が3月以内に初めて知った情報である旨のステートメント

情報開示義務とIDS

特許発行費用支払後のIDS考慮誓願書が許可された通知の例

UNITED STATES PATENT AND TRADEMARK OFFICE

Commissioner for Patents
United States Patent and Trademark Office
P.O. Box 1450
Alexandria, VA 22313-1450
www.uspto.gov

Decision Date : September 5, 2012
In re Application of :

（吹き出し：誓願が認められた旨の表示）

DECISION ON PETITION
37 CFR 1.313(c)(2)

Application No : 11
Filed : 09
Attorney Docket No :

This is an electronic decision on petition under 37 CFR 1.313(c)(2), filed September 5, 2012 to withdraw the above-identified application from issue after payment of the issue fee.

The petition is **GRANTED**.

The above-identified application is withdrawn from issue for consideration of a submission under 37 CFR 1.114 (request for continued examination). See 37 CFR 1.313(c)(2).

Petitioner is advised that the issue fee paid in this application cannot be refunded. If, however, this application is again allowed, petitioner may request that it be applied towards the issue fee required by the new Notice of Allowance.

Telephone inquiries concerning this decision should be directed to the Patent Electronic Business Center (EBC) at 866-217-9197.

This application file is being referred to Technology Center AU 2611 for processing of the request for continuing examination under 37 CFR 1.114 .

Office of Petitions

第2章　特許出願

庁手数料及び手数料の軽減

　U.S.P.T.O.へ支払う出願料金は、基本料金、サーチ料金、審査料金が含まれます。また、明細書中の独立クレーム、複数従属クレームの有無、クレーム全体数（独立クレームと従属クレームの総数）が一定数を超えると超過料金が発生します。
　U.S.P.T.O.への手数料は、出願人の規模によって異なり、小規模事業体、極小規模事業体には減額措置があります。

出願手数料は出願人の規模によって異なります（小規模事業体、極小規模事業体）
　出願人や譲受人の規模によってU.S.P.T.O.の手数料が異なります。
１．大規模事業体（Large Entity）
　　下記の２、３に該当しない法人等をいいます。U.S.P.T.O.の手数料の減額はありません。
２．小規模事業体（Small Entity: 37C.F.R.1.27）
　　小規模法人等とは、１）個人、２）小規模企業体、及び３）非営利団体が含まれます。小規模事業体の場合にはU.S.P.T.O.の一定の手数料が50％減額されます。
　１）個人
　　　発明者又は他の個人（例えば譲受人）であって、発明に関するいかなる権利も譲渡、譲与、移転又はライセンスしておらず、かつ、契約上又は法律上、譲渡、譲与、移転又はライセンスする義務を負っていない者をいいます。ここで、発明に関する権利の譲渡を受けた場合にはその全員が37C.F.R.1.27の規定上の個人、小規模企業体又は非営利団体の何れかである必要があります。
　２）小規模企業体
　　　ⅰ）発明に関する権利を37C.F.R.1.27の規定上の個人、小規模企業体又は非営利団体以外に譲渡等しておらず、かつ契約上又は法律上の譲渡等の義務を負っておらず、ⅱ）関連法人を含めても500人を越えない従業員で

ある必要があります。

  3）非営利団体

　　ⅰ）発明に関する権利を37C.F.R.1.27の規定上の個人、小規模企業体又は非営利団体以外に譲渡等しておらず、かつ契約上又は法律上の譲渡等の義務を負っておらず、ⅱ）（A）いずれの国の大学等、（B）26U.S.C.501(c)(3)に規定され、26U.S.C.501(a)に基づく課税免除を受けている団体、（C）科学又は教育に関する非営利団体であって、米国の何れかの州の非営利団体法に基づく資格を有するもの、又は、（D）外国に所在する非営利団体であって、当該団体が米国に所在しているとすれば、本規定の非営利団体としての資格を有することになるもの、のいずれかである必要があります。

3．極小規模事業体（Micro Entity: 35U.S.C.123）

　極小規模事業体に該当する場合には、U.S.P.T.O.の一定の手数料が75％減額されます。この極小規模事業体に該当するためには、ⅰ）上記の小規模事業体（37C.F.R.1.27）に該当し、ⅱ）過去の発明者としての米国出願が4件以下であり、ⅲ）収入が米国平均世帯年収の3倍を超えていないこと、及び、ⅳ）収入が米国平均世帯年収の3倍を超える者等へ譲渡や譲渡契約等をしていないこと、である必要があります。本規定は、AIA法改正により新設され、2011年9月16日より施行されています。

出願人の規模が変わったら？

　上記の出願人の規模に関しては、通常出願時のフォームに該当箇所をチェックするのみ[1]で、そのステータスを得ることができます。その後の手続きにおいては、そのステータスは引き継がれます。出願人の規模が変わった場合には、特許発行料支払い時にその旨の通知を行う必要があります（37C.F.R.1.27(g)(2)）。ステータスに関する虚偽の申告は、特許を得たとしても特許不行使の状態になる場合があります（37C.F.R.1.27(h)）ので、注意が必要です。

1　極小規模事業体の場合には、別途フォームの提出が必要です。

第2章　特許出願

出願費用の節約術

- クレームの総数は20以内にとどめる。

  クレームの総数が20を越えると追加1クレーム毎に追加料金が発生します。
- 独立クレームの総数は3以内にとどめる。

  独立クレームの総数が3を越えると、追加1クレーム毎に追加料金が発生します。
- 複数従属クレームは単数従属クレームに修正する。

  複数従属クレームが1または複数含まれていると、追加料金が発生します。さらに、複数従属クレームをばらしたクレーム数としてカウントされるので、いずれにしても割高になります。

  複数従属クレームの料金計算の例（M.P.E.P.608.01(n)）

1. An apparatus comprising：
   A；and
   B.
2. The apparatus of claim 1, wherein A comprises C
   ……
3. The apparatus of claim 1 or 2 wherein A is X.
4. The apparatus of one of claims 1 to 3 wherein B is Y.

  ➤複数従属クレーム3は、クレーム1及び2に従属しています。従って、クレーム3は2つのクレームとして料金計算されます。
  ➤複数従属クレーム4の従属先は複数従属クレームなため違反クレームです。この場合補正により従属関係を変更するか、単数従属項にするか、クレームを削除する必要があります。ただし、クレーム4は、1つとして料金計算されます。
  ➤上記のクレームセットの場合には、クレーム総数5としてカウントされ、複数従属クレームが存在するので、複数従属に係る追加料金が発生します。

- 英文明細書を提出する

  日本語明細書で出願した場合には、翻訳文の提出の際に追加料金（37C.F.R. 1.17(i)）が必要になるとともに、現地事務所の費用も発生するためです。

● PCT国内移行出願の場合には予備的補正を利用する

　国際段階では、米国以外の国を考慮して複数従属項を多用して出願することが多いと思います。しかし、そのままのクレームセットで米国に国内移行した場合には、U.S.P.T.O.の手数料が多大になるばかりか、規則違反のクレームを提出してしまう可能性もあります。そこで、PCT国内移行出願の場合には、複数従属項クレームをばらしてクレームを追加するか、最上位概念のみを残して複数従属を解除するような予備的補正書の提出を行うことで、上記のような問題点を回避することができます。

ワンポイント解説：返金請求

　小規模出願人なのに割引料金でなく正規料金を払ってしまった場合や、審査前に出願放棄する場合、誤って二重払いしてしまった場合など、U.S.P.T.O.に対して過剰にお金を支払った場合には、支払いから2年以内であれば返金請求することができます。返金請求には、なぜ返金されるべきかの理由を記載したカバーレターに証拠となる書類を添付して提出します。通常、数週間以内に請求に対する庁側の決定が送付され、請求が受け入れられると返金されます。

第2章　特許出願

出願日の認定要件及び救済措置

　特許出願をする際に特に重要な事は、特許出願日を確定することです。この特許出願日を確定するためには、少なくとも下記の書類が含まれている事を要します（37C.F.R.1.53(b)）。
- 明細書
- 少なくとも1つのクレーム
- 必要な図面

　また、出願を完了するためには、上記37C.F.R.1.53(b)の3つの書類の他、下記を満たす必要があります（37C.F.R.1.51(b)）
- 宣誓書
- U.S.P.T.O.の手数料

パリ優先権期間を徒過してしまった場合の救済措置
　期せずしてパリ優先権期間を徒過してしまった場合、一定の要件の下に優先期間を延長することはできます（35U.S.C.119(a)）。要件は以下の通りです。
- 最先の優先日から14月以内の出願であること
- パリ優先権の基礎となる外国出願を特定した優先権主張
- 遅延は意図的ではない旨のステートメント
- 37C.F.R.1.17(m)の請願費用

　上記の通り、パリ優先権期間を徒過してしまっても、優先権期間（12月）から2月に限り優先権の延長が認められる場合があります。出願の遅延は意図的ではないことを要しますので、例えば、事前に出願取りやめ等の決定がなされた場合には、本要件を満たさない事になります。

出願のステータスをチェックしよう

　米国出願のステータスをチェックするには、U.S.P.T.O.のウェブサイトの特許出願情報検索サイト（Patent Application Information Retrieval：PAIR）を利用します。このステータスチェックは自社や法律事務所が代理権を有する特許出願のみならず、公開公報が発行された他社の特許出願についても情報を検索することができます。
https://www.uspto.gov/patents-application-process/checking-application-status/check-filing-status-your-patent-application

- Public PAIR

　公開済みの特許出願および特許が閲覧できます。一般の利用者も使用可能です。

- Private PAIR

　公開済みの特許出願および特許に加え、代理権を有する公開前の係属中の出願が閲覧できる。主に代理人用であって、アクセスするには専用の電子公開キーとパスワードが必要です。

　PAIRの画面を実際に見てみましょう。

ワンポイント解説：カスタマー番号
　U.S.P.T.O.カスタマー番号は、通常法律事務所に固有に割り当てられます。特許弁護士／特許エージェントは自身が所属する法律事務所のカスタマー番号に関連付けられます。
　特許弁護士／特許エージェントは複数のカスタマー番号に登録することができます。

第2章　特許出願

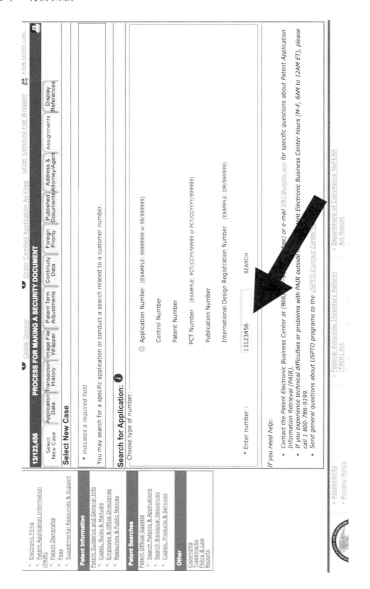

"Select New Case" タブで調べたい案件の出願番号、公開番号、特許番号等を入力します。

出願基本情報が掲載されているメインの画面

出願のステータスをチェックしよう

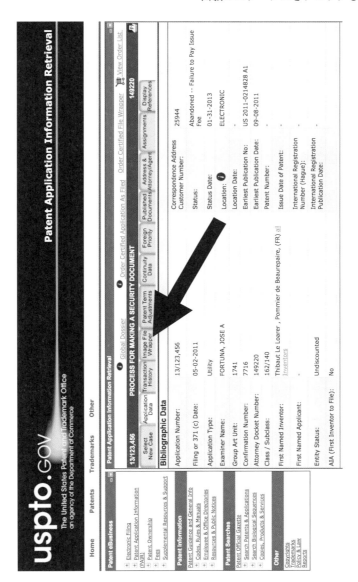

　タブをクリックして、この案件の審査経過、ファミリー出願、公開出願情報（テキストで入手可能）、や譲渡人情報等を閲覧することができます。

第2章　特許出願

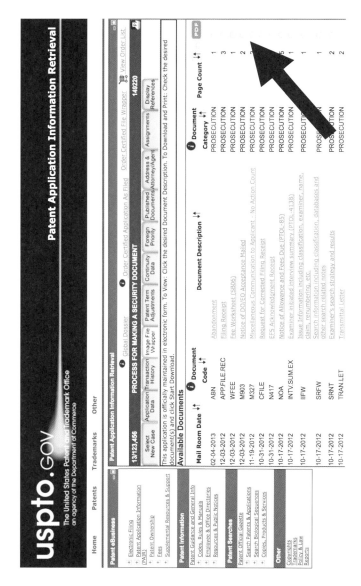

"Image File Wrapper"タブをクリックすると、包袋に含まれる書類のタイトルが閲覧できます。必要な書類について右側のボックスをクリックすると、各書類のPDFファイルを得ることができます。

第3章

特許要件

新規性　Novelty

　特許を得るには発明の新規性が要求されます。新規性欠如としてクレームされた発明を拒絶する場合、原則審査官は、<u>1つの引例中にクレームされた発明の全ての構成要件</u>が開示されていることを示さなければなりません。

　現行法では、それまで旧法で採用されていた、最先に発明した人に特許を付与する主義である先発明主義から、原則として、最先に発明を出願した者に特許を付与する主義である修正先願主義に移行しました。これに伴い、原則として出願日を基準として新規性や非自明性、先後願が判断されます。

　なお、修正先願主義は、2013年3月16日以降の有効出願日を有する出願に適用されます。従って、優先権主張出願やPCT国内移行出願の場合には、実際の米国の出願日が2013年3月16日以降であっても旧法が適用される場合があります。

新規性の解説

35U.S.C.102(a)　新規性：先行技術
　以下の場合を除いて特許を得ることができる。
(1)　クレームされた発明の有効出願日以前に、米国または他国において、特許され、刊行物に記載され、公然と使用され、販売された場

第 3 章　特許要件

> 合、または公衆が入手可能な場合
> (2) クレームされた発明が特許法151条に従って発行された特許に記載され、または、同法122条(b)項に基づいて公開されたか公開とみなされる出願に記載され、その特許若しくは公開出願に他の発明者の名前が示され、そのクレームされた発明の有効出願日以前に有効に出願された場合

(1) 35U.S.C.102(a)(1)は、日本特許法第29条第1項（新規性）と類似します。まず、「有効出願日」を基準に新規性が判断され、「発明日」基準の新規性判断の規定が現行法で条文から無くなりました。ここで、「有効出願日」とは、優先日と同義です。従って、日本特許出願に基づくパリ優先権主張を行って米国に出願を行った場合には、日本特許出願日が有効出願日になります。また、PCTに基づく国際出願を行った場合には国際出願日が有効出願日となります。

「米国または他国で、」とありますので、米国国内だけでなく、外国での行為が含まれます。また、前段の「特許され、刊行物に記載され、公然と使用され、販売された場合、」は具体例で、「公衆が入手可能な場合」はこれら具体例以外において、公衆が入手可能（Available to Public）な状態となった発明は、新規性を喪失する趣旨です。旧法102(b)では、米国出願から1年以内の開示についてはグレースピリオドがありましたが、現行法では総て有効出願日が基準日になりました。

(2) 35U.S.C.102(a)(2)は、日本特許法第29条の2に類似し、先出願であって、自分の出願の後に公開の他人の出願（先願未公開出願）に拡大された先願の地位を与える趣旨です。本条文は、先後願関係は出願日基準である点で、発明日基準である旧法35U.S.C.102(e)と異なります。

旧法下では、英語で国際公表された国際出願に係る国内移行出願のみ、当該国際出願日から後願排除効を有していました。また、非英語で国際公開された国際出願には後願排除効を有していませんでした。現行法下では、言語を問わずに国際出願日から後願排除効を有することになり、国際出願の言語による不平等が是正されました。

図4の35U.S.C.102(a)(1)の例につき、出願1は有効出願日以前に、米国または他国において、特許され、刊行物に記載され、公然と使用され、販売され

た場合、または公衆が入手可能な開示があったので、当該開示を理由に新規性が阻却されます。

また、図4の35U.S.C.102(a)(2)の例につき、出願2は有効出願日以降に他人の出願が公開されたとしても、当該他人の特許出願が先に出願された場合には、当該開示を理由に新規性が阻却されます。

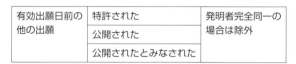

図4　35U.S.C.102(a)の説明

新規性の例外の解説

35U.S.C.102(b)　新規性の例外
(1)　102条(a)(1)に該当する行為であっても、以下の開示から1年以内に出願をした場合には、当該開示は先行技術とはみなさない

第3章　特許要件

> (A)　発明者、共同発明者が開示した場合、もしくは、発明者又は共同発明者から直接または間接的に発明主題の知見を得た第三者が開示した場合
> (B)　当該開示前に、発明者、共同発明者、もしくは、発明者又は共同発明者から直接または間接的に発明主題の知見を得た第三者が公表した場合

　35U.S.C.102(b)(1)は引用例適格の例外を規定したものです。
　(A)は、発明者等の開示から1年以内に出願した場合には、当該開示は先行技術とはならない旨の規定です。「発明者、共同発明者が開示した場合、もしくは、発明者又は共同発明者から直接または間接的に発明主題の知見を得た第三者」は、発明者等のなした発明に関連した開示のみを含む趣旨であり、他人が独自になした発明は含まない趣旨です。すなわち、開示は発明者等の発明が起因している必要があります。
　(B)は、発明者等の公表があった後、他人の開示前から1年以内にした出願は、当該開示は先行技術とはならない旨の規定です。「他人の開示」は他人が独自になした発明に関する開示です。
　なお、これらの例外規定は、U.S.P.T.O.に適用申請等を行わなくても適用を受けることができます。
　図5の35U.S.C.102(b)(1)(A)の例につき、出願1は有効出願日から1年以内の発明者等の開示なので、当該開示は新規性阻却事由にはなりません。出願2は有効出願日から1年以上前の発明者等の開示なので、当該開示は新規性阻却事由になります。出願3は有効出願日から1年以内の開示ですが、発明者等以外の開示は、35U.S.C.102(b)(1)(B)の適用を受けることができず、当該開示は新規性阻却事由にはなります。
　図5の35U.S.C.102(b)(1)(B)の例につき、出願4は有効出願日から1年以内の発明者等以外の開示があったとしても、さらにその開示前に発明者等の公表があったので、当該発明者等以外の開示は新規性阻却事由にはなりません。出願5は、有効出願日から1年以上前の発明者等以外の開示があったので、さらにその開示前に発明者等の公表があったとしても、当該発明者等以外の開示は35U.S.C.102(b)(1)(B)の適用を受けることができず、新規性阻却事由になります。

新規性 Novelty

35U.S.C.102 (b)(1)

35U.S.C.102(b)(1)（35U.S.C.102(a)(1)の例外規定）

(A) 発明者、共同発明者、知見した第三者	開示	有効出願日から1年以内	開示は先行技術とはみなされない
(B) 他人（(A)とは無関係）		有効出願日から1年以内 発明者、共同発明者、知見した第三者の公表後	

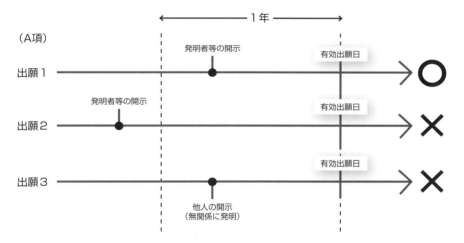

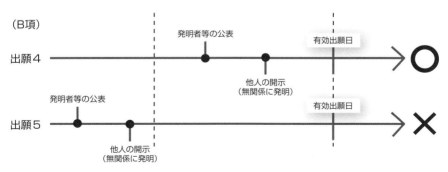

図5　35U.S.C.102(b)(1)の説明

第3章　特許要件

> 35U.S.C.102(b)　新規性の例外
> （2）　102条(a)(2)に該当する特許または出願であっても、以下の場合には先行技術とはみなさない。
> （A）　発明者又は共同発明者から直接または間接的に発明主題の知見を得た第三者が開示した場合
> （B）　当該出願前に、発明者、共同発明者、もしくは、発明者又は共同発明者から直接または間接的に発明主題の知見を得た第三者が公表した場合
> （C）　開示された発明主題とクレームされた発明とが、有効出願日より前に同一人に所有され、もしくは同一人に所有するとする譲渡の約束があった場合

35U.S.C.102(b)(2)項は、先願未公開出願の先願の地位の例外を規定したものです。

（A）は、発明者等がなした発明に起因してなされた他人の出願は、拡大された先願の地位を有さない旨の規定です。すなわち、第三者が冒認出願を行った場合に拡大された先願の地位の例外を認めたものです。

（B）は、発明者等の公表があった後、第三者が独自になした発明が出願された場合には、当該出願は拡大された先願の地位を有さない旨の規定です。すなわち、第三者が独自になした発明に関する出願の場合であっても、その他人の出願以前に発明者等による開示があった場合には、拡大された先願の地位の例外を認めたものです。

（C）は、出願日までに同一人が所有もしくは譲渡の約束をしていた場合には、拡大された先願の地位を有さない旨の規定です。出願前に何らかの理由で先出願を発見した場合には、当該先出願を後の出願までに譲渡を受けるか、譲渡の約束をしている必要があります。従って、出願前に調査を行い先出願がある場合には、譲渡交渉を行い、当該先出願を購入またはその約束をすることで、引用例ではなくなります。ただし、本願規定は102条(a)(2)、即ち拡大された先願の例外規定ですので、公開がなされていない特許出願が対象になります。従って、通常は未公開出願の先願は知ることができない点に留意する必要があります。

新規性 Novelty

　図6の35U.S.C.102(b)(2)(A)の例につき、真の発明者であるAさんから知見したBさんの冒認出願がなされ、その後にAさんが出願し、さらにその後にBさんの特許出願が公開された場合、Bさんの冒認出願が先願未公開出願ではありますが冒認出願であるため、それを理由にAさんの出願は特許性が阻却されることはありません。

　図6の35U.S.C.102(b)(2)(B)の例につき、Aさんが発明の内容を公表し、その後、Aさんとは無関係に独自になした発明に関してBさんが特許出願をしました。その後、Aさんが特許出願を行い、Bさんの特許出願が公開されました。ここで、Bさんの出願はAさんの出願からみると先願未公開出願ですが、Bさんの出願の前にAさんが発明の内容を開示しているので、この場合には、Bさんの出願を理由にAさんの出願は特許性が阻却されることはありません。

　図6の35U.S.C.102(b)(2)(C)の例につき、Aさんが出願①をし、Bさんの出願②の前に出願①をBさんに譲渡しました。その後出願①が公開となった場合に、出願①は出願②からみて先願未公開出願ですが、出願②の前に出願①の権利をBさんに譲渡し同一人の所有となったので、出願②は出願①を理由に新規性に関する特許性が阻却されることはありません。

第3章　特許要件

35U.S.C.102 (b)(2)

35U.S.C.102(b)(2)
35U.S.C.102(a)(2)の例外規定

(A) 発明者、共同発明者から知見した第三者 (B) 他人（(A)とは無関係）	出願	発明者、共同発明者、知見した第三者の公表後	開示は先行技術とはみなされない
(C) 他人		有効出願日までに、譲渡により出願人同一、または譲渡契約	

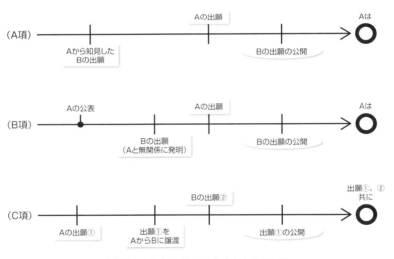

図6　35U.S.C.102(b)(2)の説明

新規性に関するその他の条文の解説

> 35U.S.C.102(c)　共同研究契約における共有
> 　開示された発明主題とクレームされた発明とは、下記の場合に102条(b)(2)(C)の適用において、同一人に所有され、若しくは同一人に所有されるとする譲渡の約束があるものとみなす。

新規性 Novelty

> (1) クレームされた発明の有効出願日かそれ以前に効力を有する共同研究契約の一またはそれ以上の者、若しくは、この者の代理者により、開示された発明主題が開発され、そして、発明がなされ、
> (2) 共同研究契約の範囲内においてなされた活動の成果として、クレームされた発明がなされ、そして、
> (3) クレームされた発明の特許出願が、共同研究契約の当事者氏名を開示若しくは補正して開示された場合

35U.S.C.102(c)は、一定の共同研究契約があった場合に、先願後公開出願の後願排除効に制限を設けたものです。この先願後公開出願の後願排除効に制限を得るためには、35U.S.C.102(c)(1)乃至(3)の総ての条件を満たす必要があります。

> 35U.S.C.102(d)　先行技術として有効な特許、公開公報
> 102条(a)(2)の規定において、特許又は特許出願が先行技術となるか否かの判断において、当該特許又は特許出願に記載された発明主題は、以下の日に有効に出願されたものとみなす。
> (1) 特許若しくは公開された特許出願の実際の出願日
> (2) 1以上の先の特許出願に基づく、119条、365条(a)(b)の優先権主張を行う場合、あるいは、120条、121条、365条(c)の先の出願の利益を主張する場合には、当該発明主題が記載された最先の出願の出願日

35U.S.C.102(d)は、35U.S.C.102(a)(2)の先願の地位として後願排除効の基準日に関する規定です。本規定では、国の内外を問わずに最先に開示された出願の出願日を一律に後願排除効の基準日としています。よって、従前のヒルマードクトリンやPCT出願の公開言語によって後願排除効が異なる、という事態に終止符を打ったことになります。

第3章　特許要件

純粋な先願主義と米国の先願主義との相違のポイント

　日欧など純粋な先願主義を採用する国や地域では、一般に出願前の学会発表等の開示行為については一定の制限を設け、例外的に新規性を認めています。一方、米国においては、上述の通り、出願前の開示については時期的な制限のみであり、さらに、その開示行為について一定の条件下に有利な取り扱いを定めています。

　この相違点について、図7を用いて具体例で考えてみましょう。この例では、AさんとBさんが独自に同じ発明を行ったとします。Aさんの発明開示AはBさんの発明開示Bより先に行いました。Aさんは自身の発明開示Aより1年以内に特許出願Aを行い、Bさんは自分の発明開示Bより1年以内、且つAさんより先に特許出願Bを行いました。この事実関係の場合、Aさん、Bさんの特許取得の可能性について検討してみましょう。

Aさんの特許出願

　Aさんの特許出願Aの審査において、発明開示A、発明開示B、及び、特許出願Bが引用例となるかを検討しましょう。まず、Aさんの発明開示Aは、35 U.S.C.102(b)(1)(A)の例外適用を受けることができます。また、Bさんの発明開示Bは、35U.S.C.102(b)(1)(B)の例外適用を受けることができます。さらに、Bさんの出願Bは、35U.S.C.102(b)(2)(B)の例外適用を受けることができます。従って、他の理由が無ければAさんの特許出願Aは特許を受けることができます。

Bさんの特許出願

　一方、Bさんの特許出願Bを検討してみましょう。Bさんの発明開示Bは、35U.S.C.102(b)(1)(A)の例外適用を受けることができます。しかし、Aさんの発明開示AはBさんの開示よりも前なので、35U.S.C.102(b)(1)(B)の例外適用を受けることができません。従って、Bさんは特許を得ることができない事になります。

　上記の例では、BさんはAさんよりも先に特許出願を行ったにも関わらず、後に特許出願したAさんが特許を得ることができます。このように、先願主義の下、基本的には先に出願を行った者に権利を与えるものの、一定の条件の下

に先に開示した者に権利を与えるような制度になっています。これこそが日欧のような先願主義とは異なる点であり、先願主義ではなく、先公表主義、若しくは、先願主義と先公表主義の二面性があることからハイブリッド先願主義などと呼ばれる所以になっています。

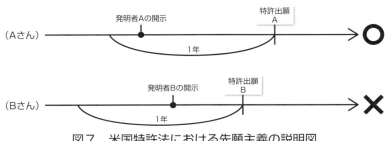

図7　米国特許法における先願主義の説明図

　以上から、一見、できるだけ早く発明について公表を行い、その後に特許出願を行った方が有利なようにも見えます。特許出願の準備にはそれ相当の時間が掛かるためです。出願前の公表を行うのは、米国にのみ出願する場合は良いかもしれませんが、他の国や地域の法制度ではこのように広範な新規性喪失の例外規定がある国は希です。従って、その公表が米国では例外適用を受けることができても、他国では受けられない可能性があります。これにより得べかりし権利をみすみす逃すことにもなりかねません。そこで、通常は出願前の不要な公表は控えるべきであり、もし、出願前の発明を公表する場合には、どの国に出願するか、そして、出願国の新規性喪失の例外規定をよく調査して慎重に行う必要があると言えます。

第3章 特許要件

新規性審査における経過措置

〜基準日以降に追加された事項を含む、基準日前の有効出願日を有する出願について〜

　上述のとおり、有効出願日が2013年3月16日の基準日以前の出願は、旧法が適用され、基準日以降の出願は、現行法が適用されます。ここで、基準日以前の出願日を有する先の外国特許出願に基づく優先権主張を行った基準日以降の後の特許出願について、当該先の出願に開示されていない追加事項が当該後の特許出願に追加された場合には問題になります。この経過措置として、当該追加事項がクレームされていない場合には、当該出願は旧法が適用され、旧法に係る新規性要件で審査されます。その一方、当該追加事項がクレームされた場合には、当該出願現行法が適用され、現行法に係る新規性要件で審査されます。追加事項がクレームされた場合とは、1つでも、一度でもクレームに追加された場合を含みます。従って、一旦クレームされた追加事項を削除したとしても現行法が適用されます。また、現行法適用の親出願に基づいて継続的出願を行い、この継続的出願には当該基準日以前に開示された事項のみを含む場合であっても、現行法が適用されます。このように、旧法／現行法の適用は出願毎に判断され、クレーム毎には判断されない点に注意が必要です。

　このような、基準日以前の有効出願日に係る出願に基づく優先権主張を行うが、現行法が適用される出願については、陳述書（Statement）の提出が必要です。

陳述書の提出（37C.F.R.1.55(j)）

　陳述書は、1）米国出願日から4月、2）PCT国内移行日から4月、3）優先権の基礎となる外国出願日から16月、若しくは、4）追加事項が最初にクレームされた日、のいずれか遅い日までに提出する必要があります。陳述書には、基準日以前の出願に基づく優先権主張を行うが、本出願のクレームには、当該基準日以降の有効出願日を有する事項を含む旨を陳述します。この陳述書は、別途書面を準備して提出するか、または、ADS（AIA/14）の該当部分にチェックして、サインすることで、陳述書が提出されたものとみなされます。

陳述書提出の効果

陳述書を提出した場合には、基準日前の有効出願日を有する出願であっても、現行法が適用されます。旧法／現行法の適用の別は、局指令やPAIRで確認することができます。

陳述書提出の注意点

上記基準日以降に追加された事項を含むクレームがあると認識しながら、上記陳述書の提出を怠った場合には、特許になったとしても権利不行使状態になる可能性がある点に注意が必要です。

陳述書の提出はクレームに関する事項のみであり、明細書への追加のみの場合には陳述書の提出は不要です。

出願人の戦略

出願時はクレームに追加事項が含まれていないとしても、後のクレーム補正により意図せず含まれてしまう可能性があるかと思います。そこで、追加事項を予め明確にしておき、その情報を現地代理人と共有しておく事が良いと思います。現地代理人に予め追加された部分を知らせておき、その部分については補正による追加は行わないように指示しておくのも一案です。

第3章　特許要件

非自明性　Unobviousness

> 35U.S.C.103　自明でない主題
> (a)　発明が、第102条に規定するのと同様に開示又は記載がされていない場合であっても、特許を受けようとするその主題と先行技術との間の差異が、クレーム発明の有効出願日前に、その主題が全体として、当該主題が属する技術の分野において通常の知識を有する者にとって自明であるようなものであるときは、特許を受けることができない。特許性は、発明の行われ方によっては否定されない。

　35U.S.C.103は、クレームされた発明が102条に掲げる開示と同一でなくとも、当該技術分野の通常の知識を有する者が、その有効出願日前に、クレームされた発明全体として先行技術との相違が自明である場合には特許を受けることはできない、と規定されています。

出願後に公知になった文献でも非自明性拒絶の引用例になり得る

　米国特許法における先行技術（Prior art）とは、35U.S.C.102に該当するものを言います。35U.S.C.102には、公知、公用等の先行技術（35U.S.C.102(a)(1)）の他、いわゆる拡大された先願の地位を有する特許出願に記載された技術も含まれます（35U.S.C.102(a)(2)）。ここで、拡大された先願の地位とは、ある特許出願の有効出願日後に出願公開され、当該特許出願よりも先に特許出願された場合に与えられる先願の地位を言います。換言すれば、ある特許出願の出願時点では公開されていない先願特許出願（先願未公開特許出願）に先願の地位を与え、当該先願未公開特許出願に記載された技術を先行技術とするものであります。35U.S.C.103は、「第102条に規定するのと同様に開示又は記載がされていない場合であっても、特許を受けようとするその主題と先行技術との間の差異が（略）自明である時」と規定されていますので、「先行技術」には、いわゆる拡大された先願の地位を有する特許出願に記載された技術も含まれます。

　その一方、日本特許法第29条第2項、いわゆる進歩性の要件では、「特許出

非自明性　Unobviousness

願前にその発明の属する技術の分野における通常の知識を有する者が<u>前項各号に掲げる発明に基いて</u>容易に発明をすることができたときは、その発明については、同項の規定にかかわらず、特許を受けることができない。」と規定されています。ここで、「前項各号」とは、日本特許法第29条第1項の各号、即ち新規性の要件の事であり、いわゆる拡大された先願の地位に関する特許法第29条の2が含まれておりません。従って、日本特許法においては、いわゆる拡大された先願の地位を有する特許出願に記載された技術に基づいて進歩性欠如を理由に特許出願を拒絶することができない、と言う事になります。換言すれば、日本特許法においては、先願未公開特許出願は進歩性欠如の引用例になり得ない、と言えます。

以上から、非自明性（進歩性）に関する先願未公開出願の引用例としての取り扱いについて、日米では異なることに留意する必要があります。

現行法では非自明性の判断時が「発明時」から「有効出願日」に変更されました。

ワンポイント解説：非自明性

　KSR最高裁判決[1]では、TSMテスト（Teaching-Suggestion-Motivation test）を厳格適用した連邦高裁の判断を否定し、グラハム判決[2]における柔軟なアプローチ、即ち、当業者の一般常識等を考慮して非自明性を否定することができる、と判示しました。

1　KSR Int'l Co. v. Teleflex Inc., 550 U.S. 398（2007）
2　Graham v. John Deere, 383 U.S. 1, 17-18, 148 USPQ 459, 467（1966）

第3章　特許要件

明細書の記載要件　Specification

35U.S.C.112　明細書
(a)　一般
　明細書は、その発明の属する技術分野又はその発明と極めて近い関係にある技術分野において知識を有する者が、その発明を製造、使用することができるような完全、明瞭、簡潔、かつ正確な用語によって発明並びにその発明を製造、使用する手法及び方法の説明を含まなければならず、また、発明者又は共同発明者が考える発明実施のベストモードを記載していなければならない。
(b)　結び
　明細書は、発明者又は共同発明者が発明とみなす主題を特定し、明白にクレームする1又は2以上のクレームで終わらなければならない。
(c)　形式
　クレームは、独立形式又は事件の内容上適切な場合は、従属形式若しくは多項従属形式で記載することができる。
(d)　従属形式における引用
　(e)に従うことを条件として、従属形式のクレームは、先に記載された1のクレームを引用し、それに続けてクレームされている主題についての更なる限定を明示しなければならない。従属形式のクレームは、それが引用するクレームに係るすべての限定事項を含んでいると解釈される。
(e)　多項従属形式における引用
　多項従属形式のクレームは、先に記載された2以上のクレームを択一的にのみ引用し、それに続けてクレームされている主題についての更なる限定を明示しなければならない。多項従属形式のクレームは、他の多項従属クレームの基礎とすることができない。多項従属形式のクレームは、引用により、それが関係していると考えられる特定のクレームのすべての限定事項を含んでいると解釈される。

(f) 組合せに係るクレームの要素

　組合せに係るクレームの要素は、その構造、材料又はそれを支える作用を詳述することなく、特定の機能を遂行するための手段又は工程として記載することができ、当該クレームは、明細書に記載された対応する構造、材料又は作用及びそれらの均等物を対象としているものと解釈される。

　クレームされた発明に新規性等の特許性を具備していたとしても、明細書や図面等が不明瞭では第三者がそれを読んで発明を再現することができません。そこで、クレームされた発明が特許を得るためには、明細書が、1）当業者が発明を実施しうる程度に（実施可能要件）、2）発明を十分、明確、簡潔、且つ正確な用語を用いて記載し（記載要件）、3）発明者が最善と考える発明の態様を記載すること（ベストモード要件）を要件としています（35U.S.C.112(a)）。

　また、クレーム（特許請求の範囲）は、発明の主題を明白に特定する必要があります。米国においても複数従属クレームは認められていますが、庁費用が高額となるため、あまりお勧めできません。また、多項従属クレームに従属するクレームを複数従属にすることができません（37C.F.R.1.75）。

　ワンポイント解説：ベストモード要件（35U.S.C.112(a)）
　ベストモード要件は審査の際には満たす必要がありますが、一旦特許になったあとは、無効理由から除外されます。

第3章 特許要件

ミーンズプラスファンクション（MPF）（35U.S.C112(f)）

クレームの要素は、特定の機能を遂行するための手段（means）又は工程（step）として記載することができます。その場合のクレームは、明細書に記載された対応する構造等やそれらの均等物を対象としているものと解釈されます（35U.S.C.112(f)）。これは、機能的表現をクレームとして認めると共に、その機能的表現に含まれる総てについて権利を与えてしまうのは不公平との観点から、発明者の認識限度と考えられる明細書に開示した構造範囲等にのみ権利を与えてバランスを取る趣旨です。

ここで、MPFクレームと認定されると以下の2つのリスクがあります。

1）クレームの解釈が限定されてしまうリスク

MPFクレームは、クレーム中の文言の範囲ではなく、明細書中の開示範囲等に限定されてしまうため、クレームの範囲が狭く解釈される可能性があります。

2）特許が無効になるリスク

裁判所において、MPFクレームと認定されると、次に、明細書の開示から対応する構造等を認定してクレームの範囲を画定します。このとき明細書中に対応する構造等に関する記述がない場合には、35U.S.C.112(b)違反として特許が無効になってしまう可能性があります。

MPFクレームと認定されないために

以上の2つのリスクを鑑み、米国実務においてMPFクレームと認定されないようにするクレームドラフティングがされる事が多いように思います。機能を要素とするクレームドラフティングWilliamson v. Citrix Online, LLC事件CAFC大法廷判決（Williamson事件）以降、MPFクレームと認定を回避するためのクレームドラフティングの際には注意が必要です。

Williamson事件では、単語meansを用いていなくても実質的に機能表現をしている場合には、MPFクレームと認定する旨が判示されました。

U.S.P.T.OのMPFクレームの審査基準（M.P.E.P.§2181）

U.S.P.T.O.では、MPFクレームに関する審査基準を公表しています。この審査基準では、審査対象クレームが以下の3つの要件を満たすか否かのテストを行い、この3つの要件を満たした場合には、MPFクレームの条項を適用し、明細書中に開示された対応する構造物等の範囲で審査を行う、としています。一方、上記3つの要件を満たさない場合には、合理的に最も広い解釈の範囲で

明細書の記載要件　Specification

審査を行う、としています。

要件1　クレームにmeansなる用語、または、meansの代用語（placeholder）が使われていること
　第1の要件では、クレームの構成要素に単語meansまたは代用語が用いられているか否かが判断されます。ここで、注意すべきは、単語meansのみならずその代用語が用いられている場合でもこの要件を満たす点です。U.S.P.T.O.による代用語の具体例は以下の通りです。
　"mechanism for," "module for," "device for," "unit for," "component for," "element for," "member for," "apparatus for," "machine for," or "system for"

要件2　Meansや代用語が機能的用語に修飾されていること
　第2の要件では、単語meansや代用語が機能的用語に修飾されているか否かが判断されます。典型的には、means forの後に機能的な表現があるか否かを判断します。ここで、"means"や代用語と機能的用語を繋ぐ用語（リンキングワード）について、"for"のほか、"configured to"、"so that"も含まれます。M.P.E.P.§2181によれば、クレーム中の要素に"means"を用いているにも関わらず、十分な構造が修飾されている場合には、同法第112条(b)項で拒絶される可能性がある点に注意が必要です。

要件3　meansや代用語が構造、物質、または特定の機能を達成するための作用に修飾されていないこと
　第3の要件では、"means"や代用語が構造等で修飾されているか否かが判断されます。すなわち、クレーム中の構造要素がその機能を実現する構成等で修飾されている場合には、少なくともU.S.P.T.O.ではMPFクレームの条項の適用を受けないと言えます。

過去に構造と認定された要素名
　一方、当業者がその要素名を構造物と認識する場合には、たとえ、その要素名が複数の構造を想起させるようなものであっても要件1に該当しないものとしています。U.S.P.T.O.による構造物の具体例としては以下の通りです。
　"filters," "brakes," "clamp," "screwdriver," and "locks," "circuit," "detent mechanism," "digital detector," "reciprocating member," "connector assem-

第3章 特許要件

bly," "perforation," "sealingly connected joints," and "eyeglass hanger member."

> ワンポイント解説：*Williamson v. Citrix Online, LLC*事件 連邦高裁大法廷判決[1]
> 　単語"means"を含まない機能的要件を含むクレームについて、米国特許法第112条(f)項（MPFクレームの条項）の適用可否が争われました。従前から"means"を含まないクレームは「強い推定」が働き、反証がない限りMPFクレームの条項を適用しない傾向がありました。同判決では「強い推定」が破棄され、たとえ"means"を使用していないクレームであっても、クレームの記載からMPFクレームの条項を適用する判断がされました。また、同判決では、MPFクレームの条項が適用されたクレームの機能を実施するための十分なアルゴリズムが明細書に開示されていないとして同法112条に違反するとして特許が無効となりました。この事件以降、機能的表現に関するクレームドラフティングの方針が大幅に変わる事になりました。

1　Williamson v. Citrix Online, LLC, 792 F.3d 1339（Fed. Cir. June 16, 2015）

法定主題　Inventions Patentable

> 35U.S.C.101
> 　新規且つ有用な工程、機械、製造物、物質の組成物を発明または発見し、またはそれらに関する新しく便利な改良をした者は、本法の条件及び要件に従い特許を得ることができる。

35U.S.C.101は法上の特許可能な発明主題を定義します。法上の発明主題には、工程／方法（Process）、機械（Machine）、製造物（Manufacture）、物質の組成物（Composition of Matter）、または、これらに関する新しく有益な改良（Any New and Useful Improvement Thereof）と規定されています。

法定主題か否かの判断（Mayo/Alice Test）

クレームが法定主題か否かは以下のステップで判断されます。

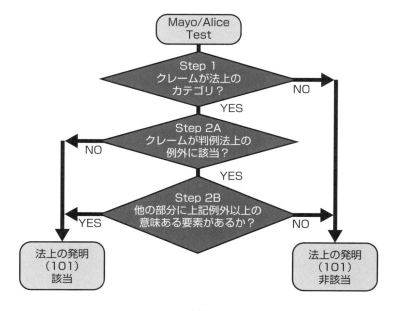

第3章　特許要件

Step 1　クレームが法上のカテゴリか否か

法上のカテゴリとは、工程／方法（Process）、機械（Machine）、製造物（Manufacture）、物質の組成物（Composition of Matter）、または、これらに関する新しく有益な改良（Any New and Useful Improvement Thereof）です。従って、クレームはこれらのいずれかのカテゴリに属する必要があります。

Step 2A　クレームが判例法上の例外に該当するか否か

判例法上の例外（Judicial Exception）とは以下が該当します。
- 自然法則
- 自然現象
- 抽象的なアイディア

    抽象的なアイディアとは以下が含まれます。
    - 数学的な関係／数式
    - アイディア自体
    - 基本的な経済的慣行
    - 人間の活動を組織化する特定の方法

Step 2B　他の部分に上記例外以上の意味のある要素があるか

Step 2Aにて判例法上の例外と認定された場合には、判例法上の例外（自然法則、自然現象、または抽象的アイディア）よりも意味のある要素（Significantly More）があるか否かが判断されます。

この要素としては以下が含まれます。
- 他の技術や技術分野への改良
- コンピュータ自身の機能の改良
- 特定の機械で、または、特定の機械を利用した、判例法上の例外の適用
- 特定の物を異なる状態や物への変形、変換
- その分野でよく知られたもの、ルーチン的なもの、ありふれたもの以外の特定の限定の追加、または、従来にはないステップを加え、クレームを特定の有用な適用への限定した従来にはないステップの追加
- その他、特定の技術環境に判例法上の例外を用いた一般的な関連付けを超えた有意ある限定

一方、以下は"Significantly More"には不十分な例です。
- 単に判例法上の例外を適用（またはこれと等価な用語）をしただけもの、または、コンピュータに抽象的アイディアを実施するための命令

法定主題　Inventions Patentable

- 業界で従来に知られ、よく理解されているルーチン、および従来の活動である汎用コンピュータ機能を実行するために一般的なコンピュータのみを必要とする抽象的アイディアに関するクレーム
- 判例法上の例外に些細な解決案を追加
- 判例法上の例外の使用と特定の技術とのリンク

ワンポイント解説：*Enfish, LLC v. Microsoft*事件（5/12/2016）　連邦高裁判決[1]
　自己参照型の論理モデルデータベースに関する特許が法定主題を満たすか否かが争われました。連邦高裁は、汎用PCで実行可能という理由のみでは必ずしも抽象的なアイディアとは言えず、本特許はコンピュータの機能の改良であり、抽象的アイディアとは言えない、と判示しました。それまで、ソフトウエア関連発明に否定的な判決が重なっていたところに一筋の光明が差した判決と言えます。

1　Enfish, LLC v. Microsoft Corp.（Fed Cir. May 12, 2016）

第3章　特許要件

二重特許　Double Patent

　一発明一特許の原則及び実質的存続期間の延長防止に観点から、二重特許は拒絶理由となっています。二重特許には下記の概ね二種類があります。

同一タイプの二重特許（35U.S.C.101）
　同一の発明者や所有者が有する、互いに文言侵害の関係にある特許の状況を言い、法定二重特許とも言います。このタイプの拒絶がなされた場合には、クレームの補正以外、どちらかのクレームを削除すること以外に拒絶を回避する方策はありません。（後述のターミナルディスクレーマでは拒絶回避不可能）

自明タイプの二重特許
　少なくとも一方から見て他方の特許が自明である2つの特許の状況を言います。このタイプの拒絶がなされた場合には、クレームの補正以外では、1）どちらかのクレームの削除、2）ターミナルディスクレーマ（Terminal Disclaimer）の提出、のどちらかを行う事になります。

ターミナルディスクレーマ
　ターミナルディスクレーマとは、特許権者が、特許存続期間の一部を放棄する旨を表明する書面を言います。ターミナルディスクレーマには、以下の陳述を含めます。
- 他の1つ以上の特許や特許出願を特定し、それらの中で最先の特許満了日以降の特許存続期間を放棄する旨の陳述
- 上記特定された特許や特許出願と共通の所有者である場合に限り権利行使可能である旨の陳述

ターミナルディスクレーマのフォーム
　ターミナルディスクレーマのフォームは下記の2種類あります。
- 出願と特許との二重特許

　対象の特許出願と、二重特許となる特許：出願と特許との二重特許（PTO/SB/26）

二重特許　Double Patent

●出願と出願との二重特許

対象の特許出願と、二重特許となり得る特許出願：出願と出願との二重特許この場合には、出願段階故クレームは確定していないため、予備的なターミナルディスクレーマのフォームを提出します（PTO/SB/25）。

ターミナルディスクレーマ提出のみでは局指令に応答したことにならない

提出されたターミナルディスクレーマは、担当の審査官が審査を行うのではなく、U.S.P.T.O.内のターミナルディスクレーマを管理するグループで精査されます。精査後にその内容に不備を発見しない場合には、ターミナルディスクレーマが承認されます。承認または非承認の結果はPAIRの情報で確認できます。

しかしながら、その提出情報や結果情報は、審査官に通知がされない場合があるようです。出願人がそのまま何もしないと、最悪の場合に出願が放棄したものと見なされてしまう場合もあります。そこで、出願人は二重特許以外に拒絶理由がない場合であっても、審査官に電話連絡等を行うか、局指令の応答書を提出する方が安全です。

ワンポイント解説：同一タイプの二重特許

　同一タイプの二重特許拒絶の根拠は、特許法101条にて "Whoever invents or discovers any new and useful process,... may obtain a patent therefor,..." と規定されているため、と解されています。

第3章　特許要件

出願と特許との二重特許の場合の記入例（PTO/SB/26）

- 願番等で出願を特定
- 所有者及び所有者の持分に関する陳述
- 二重特許と指摘された特許の特定
- 最先の特許満了日以降の特許存続期間を放棄する旨、共通の所有者である場合に限り権利行使可能である旨陳述
- 代理人のサイン

二重特許　Double Patent

出願と出願との二重特許の場合の記入例（PTO/SB/25）

- 願番等で出願を特定
- 所有者及び所有者の持分に関する陳述
- 二重特許の可能性のある特許出願の特定
- 最先の特許満了日以降の特許存続期間を放棄する旨、共通の所有者である場合に限り権利行使可能である旨陳述
- 代理人のサイン

117

第3章　特許要件

eTD〜ターミナルディスクレーマの電子提出〜

　ターミナルディスクレーマは書面で提出する場合には、それが認められるまで数日を要していました。特に、書類の性質上、ある程度審査が進んだ後に提出する場合が多いため、ターミナルディスクレーマが認められるまで出願人はやきもきすることが多いのも事実です。

　eTDでは、PCで作成したPDFを提出するのではなく、U.S.P.T.O.が提供するオンラインベースのフォームを埋めていくことにより書面を作成します。合計100（対出願50＋対特許50）までのターミナルディスクレーマ申請を1回分の申請費用で提出することができます。

　eTDの入力画面1　出願の特定します。
　eTDではウェブ上のフォームに情報を入力し、提出することができます。

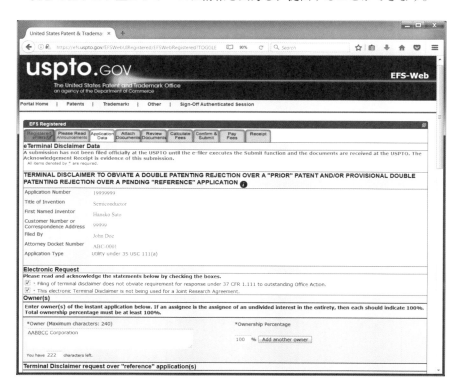

二重特許　Double Patent

　eTDの入力画面２　ターミナルディスクレーマの対象となる出願／特許を特定します。

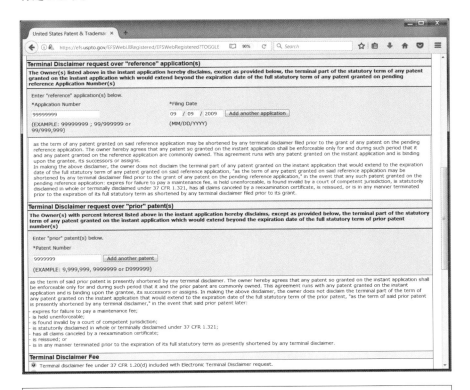

> ワンポイント解説：eTDの結果
> 　PDFで提出したTDはその結果を得るまでに数日を要していましたが、eTDは提出した後、すぐにその結果を得ることができるようになりました。

第4章

審査

　U.S.P.T.O.に提出された特許出願は、まず、特許出願に含まれる書類について型式的な事項を確認する形式審査に供され、その後に特許性の有無を判断する実体審査へと進みます。米国特許法には審査請求制度は存在せず、出願された総てのケースについて審査がなされます。

出願受領証

　電子出願の場合、出願から通常1月程度で出願受領証が送付されます。この出願受領証には、出願日や願番等の書誌的事項の他、外国出願ライセンスが表示されます。

外国出願ライセンス（Foreign Filing License）
　米国で生れた発明はまず米国に出願する必要があります。また、その出願に基づいて外国出願する場合、U.S.P.T.O.から外国出願をしても良い旨のライセンスを得なければなりません（35U.S.C.184）。ライセンスを得ずに他国に特許出願を行ったり、行わせたり、承認した場合には、原則特許を得ることができません（35U.S.C.185）。また、故意に違反した場合には、罰則規定があります（35U.S.C.186）。

　このライセンスは、米国出願日から6月経過後に自動的に付与されます（35U.S.C.184）。通常は、出願後にU.S.P.T.O.から送付される出願受領証にライセンス可否が表示されます。ここで、ライセンスが認められなかった場合には、請

第4章　審査

願費用を付して請願書を提出することができます（37C.F.R.5.12）。

また、米国に出願することなく外国に出願してしまった場合には以下を含めた請願書を提出します。この請願が認められた場合には、遡及的にライセンスが認められます。
- 出願した外国の国名リスト
- 出願した外国の出願日
- 発明の内容が機密命令に該当しない旨の説明
- 外国出願行為が詐欺的意図なしで行なわれたことの説明
- 請願費用

外国出願ライセンス～そもそも外国の第1国出願がある場合は？
　U.S.P.T.O.では、米国内で発明され出願された特許出願は大量破壊兵器など米国国防関係に関連する技術が含まれていないか一律にチェックするため、外国出願ライセンスを得ずに出願から45日以内に米国以外の外国でも出願することが禁じられています。しかし、日本企業から提出される特許出願の多くは日本で発明・出願され、その出願に基づく優先権を主張して米国出願されています。このような既に米国以外で出願されている特許出願についても一律にチェックされ、出願受領書にライセンス承認日が記載されます。しかし、45日間の出願禁止期間は適用されません。

出願受領証

出願受領証の例

UNITED STATES PATENT AND TRADEMARK OFFICE

UNITED STATES DEPARTMENT OF COMMERCE
United States Patent and Trademark Office
Address: COMMISSIONER FOR PATENTS
P.O. Box 1450
Alexandria, Virginia 22313-1450
www.uspto.gov

APPLICATION NUMBER	FILING or 371(c) DATE	GRP ART UNIT	FIL FEE REC'D	ATTY.DOCKET.NO	TOT CLAIMS	IND CLAIMS
13/123,654	07/04/2012	1733	1120	MOT.085.0012.NP	4	1

CONFIRMATION NO. 5196

65181
MOTS LAW, PLLC
1629 K STREET N.W.
SUITE 200
WASHINGTON, DC 20006-1635

FILING RECEIPT

（願番等の書誌的事項）

Date Mailed: 07/10/2012

Receipt is acknowledged of this non-provisional patent application. The application will be taken up for examination in due course. Applicant will be notified as to the results of the examination. Any correspondence concerning the application must include the following identification information: the U.S. APPLICATION NUMBER, FILING DATE, NAME OF APPLICANT, and TITLE OF INVENTION. Fees transmitted by check or draft are subject to collection. Please verify the accuracy of the data presented on this receipt. **If an error is noted on this Filing Receipt, please submit a written request for a Filing Receipt Correction. Please provide a copy of this Filing Receipt with the changes noted thereon. If you received a "Notice to File Missing Parts" for this application, please submit any corrections to this Filing Receipt with your reply to the Notice. When the USPTO processes the reply to the Notice, the USPTO will generate another Filing Receipt incorporating the requested corrections.**

Applicant(s)   Yoritomo MINAMOTO, Kamakura-shi, JAPAN;
　　　　　　　　　Masako HOJYO, Izu-shi, JAPAN;

（発明者氏名等の表示）

Assignment For Published Patent Application
　　KAMAKURA CORPORATION　Kamakura-shi
Power of Attorney: The patent practitioners associated with Customer Number 65181

Domestic Priority data as claimed by applicant
　　This application is a 371 of PCT/JP/2011/012345　05/27/2011

Foreign Applications (You may be eligible to benefit from the **Patent Prosecution Highway** program at the USPTO. Please see http://www.uspto.gov for more information.)
JAPAN 2010-654321　06/18/2010

If Required, Foreign Filing License Granted:　07/23/2012

（外国出願ライセンスの表示）

The country code and number of your priority application, to be used for filing abroad under the Paris Convention, is **US 13/123,654**

Projected Publication Date: 01/04/2014

Non-Publication Request: No

Early Publication Request: No

page 1 of 3

第4章 審査

形式審査とその応答

　形式審査では、提出された出願書類の書誌的事項の他、提出すべき書類の有無、文書のフォントやフォーマットの確認、提出書類のレイアウトや印刷の明瞭さ等が審査されます。U.S.P.T.O.が出願書類の形式に問題があると判断した場合には、以下のような通知がなされ、出願人は定められた期限内に対応が求められます。定められた期限内に応答しない場合には、当該出願は放棄されたものとみなされます。

欠落部分提出通知（Notice to File Missing Parts）
　出願日認定のために最低限必要な書類（明細書、クレーム、図面）は提出されているが、その他の必要な書類が出願時に欠如している場合等に出願人に欠落部分の提出を求める旨が通知（Notice to File Missing Parts）されます。欠落部分の通知には、その他にも、提出済みの文書が不明瞭である場合や、出願庁費用を支払っていなかった場合にも発せられます。
　欠落部分提出通知の応答
　出願人はこの送達日から2月以内に応答を行う必要があります。なお、この期限は、5月間延長が可能です。すなわち、送達日から最長7月まで応答が可能となります。欠損部分提出通知で指摘された書類等を提出します（図8参照）。
　欠落部分提出通知の応答費用
　U.S.P.T.O.料金についてですが、宣誓書を出願後に提出する際は遅延料金（37

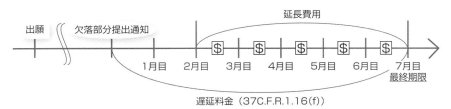

図8　出願の欠落部分提出通知への応答のタイミング

C.F.R.1.16(f))を支払います。この遅延料金は欠落部分提出通知が送達される前に提出する場合であっても、出願と同時に提出しない限り支払う必要があります。但し、PCT国内移行出願については、最先の優先日から30月以内であれば遅延料は発生しません。

延長費用について

欠落部分提出通知の送達から2月以内は無料で応答書を提出できます。それ以降は延長費用が発生し、1月経過毎に費用が増加します。

ワンポイント解説：延長手続き

　欠落部分提出通知やOAの応答で期限内に提出ができない場合であっても所定期間内であれば、延長手続きの上、応答書を提出することができます。延長手続きは、応答書の提出の際に手続きを行うことができ、事前に延長申請を行う必要はありません。とはいえ、延長費用は高額なので、期限内の提出を心がけたいものです。

第4章　審査

欠落部分提出通知の例

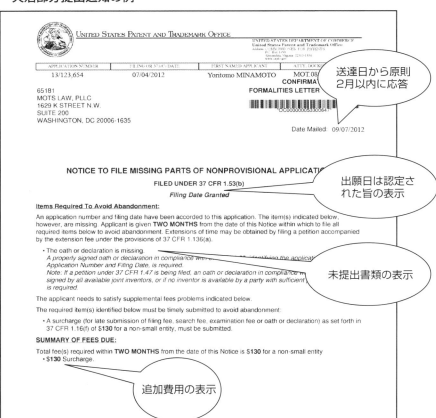

宣誓書の未提出による通知の対応方法

　宣誓書を後充する場合には発明者の署名、署名の日付、出願番号が記入された宣誓書を提出します。従って、出願人は出願番号の通知が行われた後に、宣誓書に当該出願番号を記入の上、発明者に署名してもらいます。この点で、出願番号の記入が不要な出願時提出の宣誓書の記入方法と異なります。

　ここで、出願と同時に宣誓書を提出することを前提にして出願番号が記入されていない宣誓書フォームにサイン準備し、出願時に間に合わずに当該宣誓書フォームを欠落部分提出の応答で後充したい場合があります。上述の通り、宣誓書は一旦発明者が署名を行った後は第三者が修正をすることができないため、宣誓書に出願番号を追加する修正は認められません。このような場合には、出願書類（出願時に提出した明細書および図面）のコピーをその宣誓書に添付した宣誓書による提出により、認められる場合があります。

ワンポイント解説：宣誓書の提出時期
　宣誓書は、特許発行費用支払いまでに提出することができます（35U.S.C.115(f)）。

明細書の不備による通知の対応方法

明細書の不備により、欠落部分提出通知は発せられる事があります。
例えば、以下の場合です。
- 英文明細書が出願時に提出されていない
- 要約が出願時に提出されていない

この場合の対処法としては、以下が考えられます。
- 英文明細書および翻訳者の翻訳証明を提出する。PCT国内移行出願である場合、最先の優先日から30月以上経過している場合は遅延料が発生する。）
- 150ワード以内の要約を作成して提出する。

修正書面提出通知（Notice to File Corrected Application Papers）

　出願時に提出した書面の形式に誤りがあった場合や、書面が不鮮明である場合には、修正書面提出通知が発せられます。出願人はそれらの書面の不備を是

第4章　審査

正して一定期間内に提出する必要があります。
不備の例
　修正書面提出通知で通知される例としては、下記の事項があります。
　明細書関連
　(修正明細書提出通知例1)　マージン、フォントなどの書式が正しくない
　(修正明細書提出通知例2)　明細書中に表や図が含まれている
　図面関連
　(修正図面提出通知例1)　マージンが規則違反
　(修正図面提出通知例2)　グレイトーンのグラデーションが、真っ黒になっているかグラデーションが見えないほど低画質である(これはU.S.P.T.O.が受領するPDFファイルの画素が非常に粗い場合に発生する場合がある)
　(修正図面提出通知例3)　図中の文字のフォントサイズが規則違反
　(修正図面提出通知例4)　図番Fig. 1、Fig. 2…の向きが図面の縦横の向き(図面の文字の向き)と合っていない
修正書面提出通知の対応方法
　明細書関連
　(修正明細書提出通知例1の対応)　明細書のマージンは最低でも上と下と右は各2.0cm、左は2.5cm空けるようにします。フォントスタイルはArial、Times New Roman、Courierのうちどれかでサイズは12ptが好ましい、とされています。行間は1.5またはダブルスペースとし、正しい書式で作成しなおした明細書は右肩のマージン内にSubstitute Specificationと記載して提出します。
　(修正明細書提出通知例2の対応)　明細書中の表や図を明細書から削除し、別個の図面として作成しなおす。このとき明細書中の表・図面を示す文言も適宜補正する必要があります。
　図面関連
　(修正図面提出通知例1の対応)　正しいマージンの図面を再提出します。図面のマージンは、最低でも上と左は2.5cm、右は1.5cm、下は1.0cm空けます。
　(修正図面提出通知例2の対応)　グレイトーンに代えて、ハッチング等、スキャンされても図面の画質があまり変わらない方法を使用します。また、PDFファイルの解像度を調整することで対応することができることがあります。

（修正図面提出通知例3の対応）図中の文字のフォントサイズは最低でも高さ0.32センチのフォントを使用します。

（修正図面提出通知例4の対応）Fig. 1、Fig. 2…の図示の向きは、図面の縦横の向きと合せます。

なお、修正した各図面の上側のマージン内にReplacement Sheet及び出願番号を記載します。

不完全出願通知（Notice to Incomplete Application）

不完全出願通知（Notice to Incomplete Application）は、出願時に提出した書類に、出願日が認定されるために最低限必要な書類（明細書、クレーム、図面）の全部または一部が欠落している場合に通知されます。例えば、出願時に明細書のページが脱落していた場合が該当します。その出願が優先権主張を行うものの場合、出願人は、欠落部分が出願時に存在した他のページや図面の内容、優先権書類によって支持されていること等を主張する請願書および手数料（37C.F.R.1.17(f)）（大規模事業体の場合）を支払います。この請願が認められた場合には、出願日を回復することができます。一方、請願が認められなかった場合には出願日は実際に欠落部分を提出した日に繰り下がってしまいます。

ワンポイント解説：不完全出願通知への応答

不完全出願通知に対する応答に関し、当該出願が優先権を主張している場合、米国出願明細書中のIBR（Incorporation By Reference）を根拠に日本出願の明細書の内容を追加し、欠落した内容を実質的に回復させることができる場合があります。

第4章　審査

選択／限定要求とその応答

限定要求（Restriction Requirement）

1出願中に「2以上の別個独立な発明」が含まれている場合には、審査官は、1発明に限定するよう要求することができます（35U.S.C.121）。2つのクレームされた発明に関係が開示されていない場合や、または、関係は開示されているが、別々に製造、使用、若しくは、販売が可能で、互いに非自明である場合に限定要求が発せられます（M.P.E.P.802.01）。限定要求は、例えば、カテゴリが異なる場合（装置とその製造方法）、複数の実施例の場合（第1実施例と第2実施例）、複数の実施例が図面に表されている場合（図1と図2）で限定されることがあります。

選択要求（Election Requirement）

1つの出願に属クレームとその属クレームに包含される概念の複数の種クレームとが含まれている場合に、審査官は、後の審査で属クレームが許可されない場合を考慮して、出願人に下位の種クレームを予め選択することを要求します。これを選択要求と言います（37C.F.R.1.146）。

ワンポイント解説："クレーム・アップ"という言葉

　日本特許業界において"クレーム・アップ"という言葉が"クレームの範囲に追加する"といった意味で慣用的に使用されていますが、この言葉は国内実務者の間で作られた造語で英語ではありません。従って、米国代理人に理解してもらえない可能性があります。従って、現地代理人に指示を出すとき等に"クレーム・アップしてください"、という表現は避け、"include xx in a new claim"などの適切な表現を使用すべきです。

形式審査とその応答

選択/限定要求の例（PTOL-326）

（実体OAと同様の書面）

	Application No.	Applicant(s)
Office Action Summary	13/123,654	MINAMOTO ET AL.
	Examiner	Art Unit
	JOHN DOE	1733

-- The MAILING DATE of this communication appears on the cover sheet with the correspondence address --

Period for Reply

A SHORTENED STATUTORY PERIOD FOR REPLY IS SET TO EXPIRE $\underline{1}$ MONTH(S) OR THIRTY (30) DAYS, WHICHEVER IS LONGER, FROM THE MAILING DATE OF THIS COMMUNICATION.
- Extensions of time may be available under the provisions of 37 CFR 1.136(a). In no event, however, may a reply be timely filed after SIX (6) MONTHS from the mailing date of this communication.
- If NO period for reply is specified above, the maximum statutory period will apply and will expire SIX (6) MONTHS from the mailing date of this communication.
- Failure to reply within the set or extended period for reply will, by statute, cause the application to become ABANDONED (35 U.S.C. § 133).
- Any reply received by the Office later than three months after the mailing date of this communication, even if timely filed, may reduce any earned patent term adjustment. See 37 CFR 1.704(b).

Status

1) ☐ Responsive to communication(s) filed on _____.
2a) ☐ This action is **FINAL**.   2b) ☒ This action is non-final.
3) ☐ An election was made by the applicant in response to a restriction requirement set forth during the interview on _____; the restriction requirement and election have been incorporated into this action.
4) ☐ Since this application is in condition for allowance except for formal matters, prosecution as to the merits is closed in accordance with the practice under Ex parte Quayle, 1935 C.D. 11, 453 O.G. 213.

Disposition of Claims

5) ☒ Claim(s) _1-11_ is/are pending in the application.
　　5a) Of the above claim(s) _____ is/are withdrawn from consideration.
6) ☐ Claim(s) _____ is/are allowed.
7) ☐ Claim(s) _____ is/are rejected.
8) ☐ Claim(s) _____ is/are objected to.
9) ☒ Claim(s) _1-11_ are subject to restriction and/or election requirement.

Application Papers

10) ☐ The specification is objected to by the Examiner.
11) ☐ The drawing(s) filed on _____ is/are: a) ☐ accepted or b) ☐ objected to by the Examiner.
　　Applicant may not request that any objection to the drawing(s) be held in abeyance. See 37 CFR 1.85(a).
　　Replacement drawing sheet(s) including the correction is required if the drawing(s) is objected to. See 37 CFR 1.121(d).
12) ☐ The oath or declaration is objected to by the Examiner. Note the attached Office Action or form PTO-152.

（選択/限定要求に係る旨の表示）

Priority under 35 U.S.C. § 119

13) ☐ Acknowledgment is made of a claim for foreign priority under 35 U.S.C. § 119(a)-(d) or (f).
　　a) ☐ All   b) ☐ Some *   c) ☐ None of:
　　　1. ☐ Certified copies of the priority documents have been received.
　　　2. ☐ Certified copies of the priority documents have been received in Application No. _____.
　　　3. ☐ Copies of the certified copies of the priority documents have been received in this National Stage application from the International Bureau (PCT Rule 17.2(a)).
　　* See the attached detailed Office action for a list of the certified copies not received.

Attachment(s)

1) ☐ Notice of References Cited (PTO-892)
2) ☐ Notice of Draftsperson's Patent Drawing Review (PTO-948)
3) ☐ Information Disclosure Statement(s) (PTO/SB/08) Paper No(s)/Mail Date _____.
4) ☐ Interview Summary (PTO-413) Paper No(s)/Mail Date. _____.
5) ☐ Notice of Informal Patent Application
6) ☐ Other: _____.

U.S. Patent and Trademark Office
PTOL-326 (Rev. 03-11)　　　Office Action Summary　　　Part of Paper No./Mail Date 20120319

第4章 審査

選択/限定要求の例

Application/Control Number: 13/123,654　　　　　　　　　　　　　　Page 2
Art Unit: 1733

DETAILED ACTION

Election/Restrictions

（この場合、審査官は出願に発明が2つ含まれると主張）

...on to one of the following inventions is required under 35 U.S.C. 121:

　　Claims 1 – 4, 9 and 10, drawn to a metal polisher , classified in class 310, subclass 254.1.

　II.　Claims 5 – 8 and 11, drawn to a turbine unit , classified in class 310, subclass 43.

The inventions are distinct, each from the other because of the following reasons:

　　Inventions I and II are related as combination and subcombination. Inventions in this relationship are distinct if it can be shown that (1) the combination as claimed does not require the particulars of the subcombination as claimed for patentability, and (2) that the subcombination has utility by itself or in other combinations (MPEP § 806.05(c)). In the instant case, the combination as claimed does not require the particulars of the subcombination as claimed because the turbine unit does not require the particulars of the subcombination claimed in claim 1 (e.g. polisher and stem). The subcombination has separate utility such as turbines for use in a tunnel drilling.

　　The examiner has required restriction between combination and subcombination inventions. Where applicant elects a subcombination, and claims thereto are subsequently found allowable, any claim(s) depending from or otherwise requiring all the limitations of the allowable subcombination will be examined for patentability in

選択／限定要求への応答

出願人は、審査官の選択／限定要求の反論の有無にかかわらず、期限内にいずれのグループを選択する必要があります。すなわち、出願人は審査官の限定要求に同意できない場合でも選択が必要となります（M.P.E.P.818.01(b)）。この場合、出願人は限定要求に否認（traverse）した上で仮選択します（37C.F.R.1.143）。グループを選択し、必要に応じてそのグループの概念に含まれるクレームを選択します。若しくは否認しない場合には、限定要求を自認したことになり、その後に限定要求が不服である旨の請願書を提出できなくなります（37C.F.R.1.144）。

以上から選択／限定要求に応答する場合には、応答書に以下を含めます。
- 選択したグループ／種
- そのグループ／種に含まれるクレーム
- 否認の有無とその理由

クレームの選び方

選択／限定要求の応答の際には、グループを選択すると共に、そのグループの概念に属するクレームを総て選びます。例えば、図1を選択した場合には図1に含まれる概念の総てのクレームを選びます。ここで、例えば図1と図2で限定指令が出た場合を考えます。図1の図2の相違は非常に小さく、上位クレーム、中位クレームでは図面の相違が現れず、下位クレームでその図面の相違が現れているとします。この場合に、図1を選び、その対応するクレームとしては、上位クレームはもちろん、中位クレームそして図1に対応する下位クレームを総て選びます。また、他の中位クレームも図1に現れているかを検討し、可能であれば当該他のクレームも選ぶようにします。審査官は、審査の負荷を考慮して、できるだけ審査するクレームを減らすために選択／限定要求をすることがあります。そこで、出願人は、審査官の選択／限定要求の意図を考慮せずにクレームができるだけ多く含まれるグループを選択すると良いでしょう。選択したグループにクレームした総てが含まれるのであれば、総てのクレームが対応する、と主張しても問題ありません。

否認の方法

審査官の発した選択／限定要求否認する理由として、以下が考えられます。
- 選択／限定要求が細かすぎる
  例）図面1と図面2に表された発明は、特徴を有するサブコンビネーショ

ンとそれを含むコンビネーションである。
- 選択／限定要求の分け方がおかしい
  例）発明の概念から第2実施例は第1実施例と同じではなく、第3実施例と同じグループのはずである。
- 別発明であったとしても、審査に深刻な負担が掛かる、というほどの内容ではない
  例）装置クレームは19個あり、その製法クレームは1つであり、クレームの要素はほぼ同一なので、負荷は少ないはず。

選択／限定要求の応答期間

書面による選択／限定要求の場合は、応答期限は選択／限定要求の発行日から2月（4月の延長可能）です。期限徒過の場合には、放棄したものとみなされます。

選択／限定要求の応答の効果

出願人が否認した場合、審査官はその否認の内容を確認し、出願人の否認内容に同意する場合には、選択／限定要求を取り下げ、または、修正を行い、審査に進みます。一方、否認に同意しない場合には、次の局指令でその理由が付され、出願人が仮選択したクレームに基づいて審査します。非選択クレームは審査の範囲外（withdrawn）となります（37C.F.R.1.142(b)）。実務では、審査官の裁量が非常に大きく、出願人の主張が認められるケースは少ないようです。

否認するべきか否か

出願人が考える以上に発明の単一性を狭く判断されることがあります。特に、米国の発明の単一性実務は日本のそれと比較しても狭いように感じている方も多いと思います。発明の単一性を細かく判断されれば、それに伴い分割出願を行う必要性が生じ、また、権利化後の維持年金もその分増えることになります。従って、安易に審査官の選択／限定要求を認めずに否認したいところです。

しかしながら、例えば、「グループ1とグループ2とは同じ発明である。」を要旨とする否認は後から不利益が生じる可能性があります。すなわち、上記の例で説明すると、出願人はグループ1とグループ2とは別個独立ではなく、互いに自明ではない旨を主張することになります。換言すれば、グループ1とグループ2に係る発明は特徴に相違はなく、ほぼ同一であるとの主張を行うこと

になります。この主張がU.S.P.T.O.に提出されると包袋に入り内部証拠になります。その後、その否認は結局認められず、分割出願を行い、グループ１及びグループ２のクレームをそれぞれ含む２つの特許が発行されたとしましょう。後の訴訟等で、グループ１に係る特許が新規性、非自明性違反で無効になってしまった場合、グループ２に係る特許も比較的容易に無効になってしまう可能性があります。すなわち、出願人が行った選択／限定要求の応答での自明ではない旨の主張等が証拠となって、それを自認とみなして無効になる可能性があります。選択／限定要求の応答時の否認は、特許無効の証拠を特許出願人自らU.S.P.T.O.に提出してしまう、というリスクがあることに注意する必要があります。

それでは、どのようにすべきでしょうか？上述の通り否認は、選択／限定要求に係る発明は特徴に相違はなく、ほぼ同一であるとの主張をするとリスクがあるのはご説明しました。そこで、このリスクを回避しつつ、後に請願書の提出の可能性を残すために、発明の単一性に関する議論を行わず、「別発明であったとしても、審査に深刻な負担が掛かる、というほどの内容ではない」との否認のみを行う、という対応も一考に値するかと思います。

選択範囲外になったクレームはキャンセルすべきか？

選択の範囲外になったクレームは審査の考慮から一旦除外（withdrawn）されます。その後の審査で上位クレームが許可になった場合等には再加入（re-join）の可能性があります（M.P.E.P.821.04）。しかし、選択の範囲外になったクレームをキャンセル（cancel）してしまうと、その機会を逸してしまいます。その一方、審査除外の状態ですと、U.S.P.T.O.の手数料の観点からのクレーム数にカウントされてしまい（M.P.E.P.607）、その後の補正によるクレームの追加でU.S.P.T.O.の手数料が発生する場合があります。従って、後の審査手続きで再加入の可能性とクレーム追加によるU.S.P.T.O.の追加料金の要否を考慮してクレームをキャンセルするか審査除外のままにするかを判断します。

局指令応答時の補正書を準備するときには、審査除外になったクレームは後の再加入の時に備えてクレームの補正を行っておくべきです。具体的には、上位概念のクレームを書き直してクレームの番号が変更になる場合には、それに合わせて従属先を変更します。また、記載不備等の拒絶理由が当該審査除外クレームにも及ぶ場合には、それに合わせて補正を行います。審査官によっては許可通知を送る際に代理人に確認の上、職権補正を行ってくれる場合もありま

すが、審査官の裁量であるため、審査官に頼ることなく出願人が行うべきです（M.P.E.P.821.04）。

なお、クレームを審査除外にする場合には、補正書のクレーム番号の後に（withdrawn）のラベルを付し、クレームの文言（テキスト）は削除せずにそのままにします。その一方、クレームをキャンセルする場合には、補正書のクレーム番号の後（canceled）のラベルを付して、クレームのテキストは削除する必要があります（37C.F.R.1.121(c)(4)）。

そもそも単一性違反が明白な時にクレームすべきではない？

多角的な権利取得の観点から、出願人は様々な可能性を考え、クレームのカテゴリや形態を検討します。これは非常に重要なことでありますが、その一方で、独立クレームが3つを超えると超過1クレーム毎に追加料金（37C.F.R.1.16(h)）が加算されます。独立クレーム及び従属クレームを合計した総数が20個を超えると1クレーム毎に追加料金（37C.F.R.1.16(i)）が加算されます。また、独立クレームが多いと審査官の負荷がそれだけ多くなるため、選択／限定要求の可能性が上がる傾向にあるようです。

ここで、選択／限定要求や後の手続きでクレームを審査除外、またはキャンセルしても、一旦支払ったU.S.P.T.O.の手数料は、出願の放棄を行う以外払い戻しされません（M.P.E.P.607, 37C.F.R.1.138(d)）。特に、超過独立クレームは高額であり、再加入の可能性が従属項と比較して低い場合が多いようです。そこで、単一性違反が明白な場合には独立クレームは3つに留め、必要に応じて、他のカテゴリや形態に係るクレームを追加した継続的出願で対応することも検討すべきでしょう。

電話による選択／限定要求

審査官は、電話による選択／限定要求の通知をすることができます（M.P.E.P.812.01）。典型的には、審査官は代理人に通知を行います。審査官としては即座の代理人からの応答を期待でき、すぐに出願に着手することができます。また、審査官は、選択／限定要求を起草する手間も省けるため、電話による選択／限定要求が好まれているようです。この場合の応答は、期限が3営業日以内、1週間以内等かなり短い期間が設定されます。出願人が書面による選択／限定要求を希望した場合や、応答しない場合には、審査官は通常通り、選択／限定要求を起草し、通知します。一方、応答した場合には、応答内容に基づいて審査官は着手します。出願人が応答した内容（出願人が選んだクレームセッ

ト）は次の局指令に表示され、その内容が局指令を通じて公示されることになります。

> ワンポイント解説：Office Action on the Meritsとは
> 　局指令のうち、新規性や非自明性等の実体的な特許要件を審査した後に発する局指令（実体的OA）をOffice Action on the Merits と言います。実体的な特許要件を審査した後であれば、非最終局指令（Non-final OA）、最終局指令（Final OA）の別は問いません。しかし、選択／限定指令はこのOffice Action on the Meritsには含まれません（M.P.E.P.810）。

第4章　審査

局指令（Office Action：OA）

局指令とは
　審査官が特許出願の新規性や非自明性等の特許要件を審査し、特許性が欠如すると認定した場合には、局指令を発してその拒絶理由を通知します。通常、1回目の局指令は「非最終の局指令（Non-final Office Action）」になります。また、2回目以降は「最終の拒局指令（Final Office Action）となり得ます。「非最終」か「最終」かによって、補正ができる範囲など出願人の応答できる内容が変わります。

局指令を受けた時の対応
　局指令を受けた出願人は所定期間内にその応答を行うことができます（37C.F.R.1.111(a)）。応答書には補正書（Amendment）と意見書（Remarks）等を含めることができます。応答書の提出自体にはU.S.P.T.O.の手数料は発生しません。応答期間は局指令が発せられた日から6月の法定期間が認められ、その期間に応答書を提出します。なお、最終日が土曜日、日曜日、またはワシントンD.C. の祝日である場合は、翌実働日に応答書の提出が可能です（37C.F.R.1.7）。所定期間内に応答しない場合には、その出願は放棄されたものとみなされます（37C.F.R.1.135）。

延長費用について
　上記6月の法定期間のうち、局指令から3月の短縮された法定期間（Shortened Statutory Period：SSP）内であれば、無料で応答書を提出することができます（37C.F.R.1.134）。SSP経過後は、応答書提出の際に延長費用が発生します（37C.F.R.1.136）。延長費用は1月経過毎に費用が異なり、提出時期が遅れるほど高くなります。

局指令(Office Action:OA)

図面に関する局指令への応答

提出した図面に関して規則上の違反があった場合、再提出が求められる場合があります。この場合には、差し替え図面を提出します。

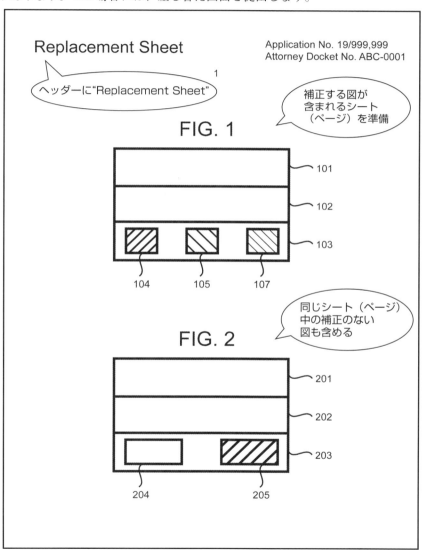

第4章　審査

審査官面談（Interview）について

　出願人は、技術的な理解を得たり、引用例との相違を説明したりする目的で審査官に面談を申し込むことができます（37C.F.R.1.133）。面談はU.S.P.T.O.にて面前、または電話で行います。通常、第1回局指令の後から面談を行うことができます（37C.F.R.1.133(a)(2)）。審査官面談の申し込みは通常代理人による電話で行われます。簡単な内容であれば、その時すぐに面談を行うことを認める審査官もいますが、通常は日時を指定して改めて面談を行います（37C.F.R.1.133(a)(3)）。審査官面談には審査官から面談内容（Agenda）を要求されることがあります。この場合、クレーム補正案や意見書案を前もって送付します。

　審査官面談には以下の特徴があります。

- 審査官と代理人とが会話することにより書面のみよりもスムーズな意志の疎通が図れます。
- 面談をするにより、出願人は、より局指令の審査官の意図を理解することができます。
- 技術内容が複雑な場合や引用例との相違が書面では説明しにくい場合等は、特に審査官面談は重要です。
- 口頭で説明することができますので、書面に残したくないような内容の場合には有効です。
- 面談で審査官からその補正案に対してコメントをもらった上で、そのコメントの内容を考慮して正式な補正書を提出することができます。この場合には実質的に2種類のクレームセットの判断をもらうことができます。ただし、様々なクレームセットを準備し「このクレームはどうか？こっちはどうか？」のような態度は慎んだ方が良いでしょう。

　審査官面談が完了後に審査官はインタビューサマリーを発行します。インタビューサマリーには、参加した人の氏名やインタビューの内容が記載されます。

局指令 (Office Action：OA)

インタビューサマリの例 (PTOL-413)

	Application No.	Applicant(s)
Applicant-Initiated Interview Summary	13/123,654	MINAMOTO ET AL.
	Examiner	Art Unit
	DOE, JOHN M.	1733

インタビュー参加者の表示

(applicant, applicant's representative, PTO personnel):

(1) John M. Doe (3) _____
(2) _____ (4) _____

Date of Interview: *30 April 2012*

Type: ☒ Telephonic ☐ Video Conference
       ☐ Personal [copy given to: ☐ applicant ☐ applicant's representative]

Exhibit shown or demonstration conducted: ☐ Yes ☒ No.
If Yes, brief description: _____

インタビュー形態の表示

Issue Discussed ☐101 ☐112 ☐102 ☒103 ☐Others
(For each of the checked box(es) above, please describe below the issue and detailed description of the discussion)

Claim(s) discussed: *rejected - claims 1-2, 4*.

Identification of prior art discussed: *US 3,210,654 US 9,876,543*

Substance of Interview
(For each issue discussed, provide a detailed description and indicate if agreement was reached. Some topics may include: identification or clarification of a reference or a portion thereof, claim interpretation, proposed amendments, arguments of any applied references etc...)

Discussed rejection of record. Discussed possible amendment to overcome the rejection of record.

13

インタビューで議論した内容の表示

Applicant recordation instructions: The formal written reply to the last Office action must include the substance of the interview. (See MPEP section 713.04). If a reply to the last Office action has already been filed, applicant is given a non-extendable period of the longer of one month or thirty days from this interview date, or the mailing date of this interview summary form, whichever is later, to file a statement of the substance of the interview.

Examiner recordation instructions: Examiners must summarize the substance of any interview of record. A complete and proper recordation of the substance of an interview should include the items listed in MPEP 713.04 for complete and proper recordation including the identification of the general thrust of each argument or issue discussed, a general indication of any other pertinent matters discussed regarding patentability and the general results or outcome of the interview, to include an indication as to whether or not agreement was reached on the issues raised.

☐ Attachment

/Eric Thomas/
Primary Examiner, Art Unit 2835

U.S. Patent and Trademark Office
PTOL-413 (Rev. 8/11/2010)   Interview Summary   Paper No. 20120430

第4章 審査

Ex Parte Quayle Actionとは

　クレームされた発明は許可される状態にあるが、軽微な補正が必要な場合があります。また、形式審査で看過された軽微な瑕疵が審査段階で発見される場合があります。この場合には、Ex Parte Quayle Actionが発せられ、出願人は原則として当該送達から2月以内（4月延長可能）に審査官に指摘された部分を修正した書面を提出します。

ワンポイント解説：先行技術文献とは
　審査官が出願審査時に先行技術文献調査を行います。この際に、当該出願の発明を開示し、有効出願日以前に公開等された文献であって、局指令に引用されたものを先行技術文献と呼びます。この先行技術文献には、特許文献の他、学会誌、専門書等、公にアクセス可能な文献が含まれます。

最終局指令(Final Office Action)

最終局指令とは
　審査官は2回目以降の局指令を一定の条件の下に最終局指令(Final Office action)とすることができます(37C.F.R.1.113(a))。例えば、出願人の補正により生じた拒絶理由や、非最終局指令以降に提出したIDSに基づいて拒絶理由が発生した場合には、最終局指令となりえます(M.P.E.P.706.07(a))。最終局指令と認定された場合には、出願手続きは一旦閉じられますので、出願人が行う補正の範囲に大きな制限が課されます。

最終局指令応答時の補正の制限
　最終局指令が発せられた後、出願手続きは一旦閉じられますので、引用例のサーチ等審査官が新たな作業とするような補正は行うことができません。具体的には、下記の補正に制限されます(37C.F.R.1.116(b))。
- クレームのキャンセル
- 審査官の要求に則した補正
- 審判請求を考慮した補正

最終局指令を回避するためには
　最終局指令が発せられると補正の制限が厳しくなり、有効な補正が殆どできなくなります。従って、最終局指令が発せられる前に許可通知を得ることが重要です。そのためには、下記の点に留意する必要があります。
- 第1回OAの際に総ての拒絶理由通知を解消する
- IDSは早めに提出する
- 継続審査請求(RCE)を行う際にはクレーム補正を行う(補正を行わないとFirst Final OAが来る可能性)

最終局指令後の審査官面談
　審査官面談は審査官に技術内容の理解を得るのに非常に有益です。しかし、最終局指令後は出願手続きが一旦閉じられますので、以前主張した反論を再度

第 4 章 審査

行う事や、新たな審査が発生するような議論を行う面談は、審査官によっては断られる事もあります。ただし、その後のRCEや継続的審査での補正を前提した面談は認められる可能性が高くなると言えます。いずれにしても、面談前には、議論のポイントを書面にまとめて事前に審査官に提出することが望まれます（M.P.E.P.713.09）。

最終局指令を受けたときの対応

最終局指令を受けた後、出願人の取り得る措置は複数あります。出願の状況によって、どのように手続きを進めるかによって、権利化のスピードや費用に大きく差がでる場合があります。手続きの概略フローを図9及び図10に示します。

1．意見書／補正書の提出

OAの審査官の意見に不服の場合、または、最終局指令の認定自体に不服の場合には、意見書にて反論します。補正には一定の制限があります。

2．継続審査請求（RCE）

出願が最終状態（最終局指令を受取った後）の場合には、RCEをすることができます。RCEを行うと最終状態は解除され、非最終状態になります。

3．継続的出願（Continuing Application）

最終局指令を受けた出願を基礎に新たに出願を行うことができます。継続的出願には、継続出願、分割出願、一部継続出願が含まれます。

4．放棄／放置する（Abandonment/Lapse）

局指令に承服する場合には、これ以上審査手続きを進めないようにすることができます。

5．審判請求する（Notice of Appeal）

最終局指令の審査官の判断に不服の場合には、審判請求をすることができます。

最終局指令（Final Office Action）

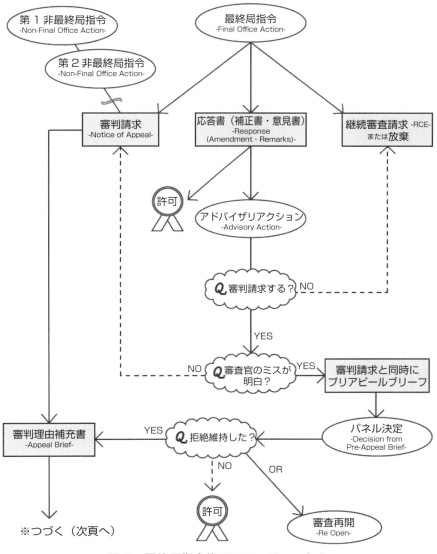

図9　最終局指令後のフローチャート1

第4章　審査

※つづき（前頁から）

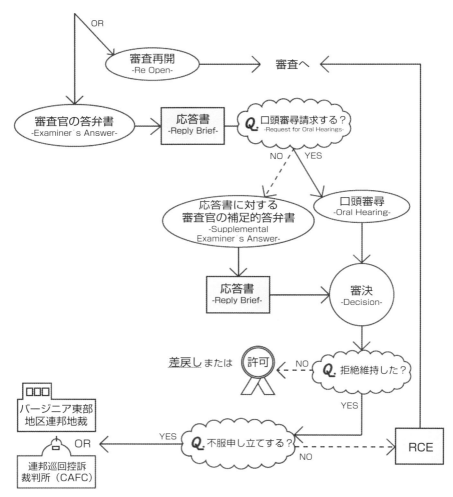

図10　最終局指令後のフローチャート2

最終局指令（Final Office Action）

意見書・補正書の提出

　審査官の主張に反論を行う余地がある場合には、意見書で反論を主張することができます。また、クレーム等の補正を行う場合には、補正書を提出することができます。最終局指令に対する応答によっても、なお拒絶が解消されないと認定された場合には、審査官からアドバイザリアクション（Advisory Action）が発せられます。応答書は37C.F.R.1.116に基づいて作成します。

最終局指令後応答の審査パイロットプログラム（AFCP 2.0）

　上述の通り、最終局指令を受け取った出願人は、クレームのキャンセル等補正出来る範囲に大きな制限があり、些細な補正であってもRCE等を行う必要がありました。U.S.P.T.O.は、試行プログラムとして、最終局指令後に審査官は必要に応じて3時間以内で審査可能と判断する場合には、審査を行い許可すべきか否かを判断します。ここで、許可すべきでないと判断する場合には、審査官は、出願人（代理人）にコンタクトをしてインタビューの依頼をします。ここで、出願人がインタビューを拒否したり、10日以内にインタビューが出来ない場合には、審査官は、通常の最終局指令通知後の手続き、即ち、アドバイザリアクションを発します。

　ガイドラインによると、下記の応答は審査が認められます。このパイロットプログラムに対するU.S.P.T.O.の手数料は無料です。

　なお、本試行プログラムは2018年9月30日（本稿作成時点の情報）までとなっております。

- クレームのキャンセル、または、最終局指令に応答した方式的な記載不備に関する補正
- 拒絶クレームに従属している故オブジェクションを有する従属クレームを独立クレームにする補正
- 許可クレームの構成要素を拒絶クレームに追加する補正。この場合には限定的な量の審査で済むような新たなクレームの追加も認められる。
- 限定的な量の審査で済むような補正。この場合には、最終拒絶を受けたクレームをキャンセルせずにクレームの追加が認められる。
- 限定的な量の審査で済むような新たな要素を追加する補正
- 先の発明日の立証や、新たな証拠を提出するための宣誓書の提出

第4章　審査

アドバイザリアクション（Advisory Action：AA）

　最終局指令に対する応答によっても、なお拒絶が解消されないと認定された場合には、審査官からアドバイザリアクションが発せられます。具体的には、上記補正の制限の範囲内の補正と認められた場合には、新たな争点の提起（New Issue）を含むとして補正が審査対象にされない旨が通知されます（37 C.F.R.1.116(c)）。すなわち、補正が却下されたような状態となります。ここで、補正によって新たなサーチや審査が必要となったと判断された場合に新たな争点の提起と認定されます。実務では、かなり些細な補正でも新たな争点の提起であるとして、補正が認められない場合が多いようです。最終局指令に対する応答は補正範囲の制限もあり、この時点で許可を得ることができるのは困難である、と言えます。

ワンポイント解説：審査官の上司、スーパーバイザとは？
　応答や面接などのU.S.P.T.O.とのやり取りにおいて、時として担当審査官の主張がどうしても腑に落ちない、審査官が誤解していて埒があかない、いつも留守で連絡がつかない、といった場合があります。そのような時には、審査官の上司であるスーパーバイザ（SPE：Supervisory Patent Examiner）と話し合うことができます。スーパーバイザは知識・能力ともに優れた経験豊富な審査官であって、特定の技術部門における審査官の訓練、評価、実績管理する責任を負っているので、審査官の明白な誤解やミスを正してくれることも少なくありません。

アドバイザリアクションの例（PTOL-303）

Advisory Action Before the Filing of an Appeal Brief	**Application No.** 13/123,654	**Applicant(s)** Yoritomo MINAMOTO
	Examiner JOHN DOE	**Art Unit** 1733

--The MAILING DATE of this communication appears on the cover sheet with the correspondence address --

…ILED July 30, 2016 FAILS TO PLACE THIS APPLICATION IN CONDITION FOR ALLOWANCE.

…PEAL FILED

…after a final rejection. No Notice of Appeal has been filed. To avoid abandonment of this application, applicant must timely file …eplies: (1) an amendment, affidavit, or other evidence, which places the application in condition for allowance; … (with appeal fee) in compliance with 37 CFR 41.31; or (3) a Request for Continued Examination (RCE) in compliance with … a utility or plant application. Note that RCEs are not permitted in design applications. The reply must be filed within one of …ods:

…reply expires ______months from the mailing date of the final rejection.

…r reply expires on: (1) the mailing date of this Advisory Action; or (2) the date set forth in the final rejection, whichever is later. …ent, however, will the statutory period for reply expire later than SIX MONTHS from the mailing date of the final rejection.

c) ☐ A prior Advisory Action was mailed more than 3 months after the mailing date of the final rejection in response to a first after-final reply filed within 2 months of the mailing date of the final rejection. The current period for reply expires months from the mailing date of *the prior Advisory Action* or SIX MONTHS from the mailing date of the final rejection, whichever is earlier.

Examiner Note: If box 1 is checked, check either box (a), (b) or (c). ONLY CHECK BOX (b) WHEN THIS ADVISORY ACTION IS THE FIRST RESPONSE TO APPLICANT'S FIRST AFTER-FINAL REPLY WHICH WAS FILED WITHIN TWO MONTHS OF THE FINAL REJECTION. ONLY CHECK BOX (c) IN THE LIMITED SITUATION SET FORTH UNDER BOX (c). See MPEP 706.07(f).

Extensions of time may be obtained under 37 CFR 1.136(a). The date on which the petition under 37 CFR 1.136(a) and the appropriate extension fee have been filed is the date for purposes of determining the period of extension and the corresponding amount of the fee. The appropriate extension fee under 37 CFR 1.17(a) is calculated from: (1) the expiration date of the shortened statutory period for reply originally set in the final Office action; or (2) as set forth in (b) or (c) above, if checked. Any reply received by the Office later than three months after the mailing date of the final rejection, even if timely filed, may reduce any earned patent term adjustment. See 37 CFR 1.704(b).

NOTICE OF APPEAL

2. ☐ The Notice of Appeal was filed on __________ A brief in compliance with 37 CFR 41.37 must be filed within two months of the date of filing the Notice of Appeal (37 CFR 41.37(a)), or any extension thereof (37 CFR 41.37(e)), to avoid dismissal of the appeal. Since a Notice of Appeal has been filed, any reply must be filed within the time period set forth in 37 CFR 41.37(a).

AMENDMENTS

3. ☒ The proposed amendments filed after a final rejection, but prior to the date of filing a brief, will not be entered because
   a) ☒ They raise new issues that would require further consideration and/or search (see NOTE below);
   b) ☐ They raise the issue of new matter (see NOTE below);
   c) ☒ They are not deemed to place the application in better form for appeal by materially reducing or simplifying the issues for appeal; and/or
   d) ☐ They present additional claims without canceling a corresponding number of finally rejected claims.
   …OTE: *See Continuation Sheet*. (See 37 CFR 1.116 and 41.33(a)).

…s are not in compliance with 37 CFR 1.121. See attached Notice of Non-Compliant Amendment (PTOL-324).

… overcome the following rejection(s): _____.

…nded claim(s) _____ would be allowable if submitted in a separate, timely filed amendment canceling the non-…

…e proposed amendment(s): (a) ☒ will not be entered, or (b) ☐ will be entered, and an explanation of how the …uld be rejected is provided below or appended.

…CE

…ce filed after final action, but before or on the date of filing a Notice of Appeal will not be entered because …a showing of good and sufficient reasons why the affidavit or other evidence is necessary and was not earlier …1.116(e).

…dence filed after the date of filing the Notice of Appeal, but prior to the date of filing a brief, will not be entered …or other evidence failed to overcome all rejections under appeal and/or appellant fails to provide a showing of good …sons why it is necessary and was not earlier presented. See 37 CFR 41.33(d)(1).

…it or other evidence is entered. An explanation of the status of the claims after entry is below or attached.

REQUEST FOR RECONSIDERATION/OTHER

11. ☒ The request for reconsideration has been considered but does NOT place the application in condition for allowance because: _____.

12. ☐ Note the attached Information *Disclosure Statement*(s). (PTO/SB/08) Paper No(s). _____

13. ☐ Other: _____.

STATUS OF CLAIMS

14. The status of the claim(s) is (or will be) as follows:
   Claim(s) allowed: .
   Claim(s) objected to: .
   Claim(s) rejected: .
   Claim(s) withdrawn from consideration: .

/Jane M. SMITH/
Supervisory Patent Examiner, Art Unit 1733

U.S. Patent and Trademark Office
PTOL-303 (Rev. 09-2010) **Advisory Action Before the Filing of an Appeal Brief** Part of Paper No. 20120417

ファイナルOAの応答によっても許可されない旨の表示

補正によって新たな争点が提起され、更なるサーチが必要なので、当該補正は考慮されない旨の表示

第4章　審査

最終局指令に応答しただけでは、時計は止まらない！

一旦最終局指令が発せられた後は、出願人は最終局指令から6月以内に当該出願を下記の状態にする必要があります。従って、最終局指令に応答しただけでは、期限の時計が止まらない事に注意が必要です。この点が非最終局指令での応答と大きく異なる点です。最終局指令から6月以内に下記の状態とならなかった出願は放棄されたとみなされます（37C.F.R.1.135, M.P.E.P.710.02(e)）。

- 許可通知の発行
- RCEで最終局指令の取下げ
- 審判請求にて審判段階への移行

たとえ何らかの事情でアドバイザリアクションが発せられない場合であっても、最終局指令の送達日から6月（3月延長期限日）までに下記RCEや継続出願を行なわないと出願が放棄されることになるため注意が必要です。

最終局指令後の期間の計算について

最終局指令から2月以内に出願人が応答を行った場合には、延長費用の計算は、最終局指令から3月もしくはアドバイザリアクションの何れか遅い日から開始されます（M.P.E.P.706.07(f)）。すなわち、審査官がアドバイザリアクションを発するのが遅くなった場合には、その時点が延長費用の支払いの基準になりますので、延長費用が軽減される可能性があります（図11参照）。

ここで、注意したいのは、上記は延長費用計算の上の措置であり、応答期限はなお最終局指令から6月であり、この期限は延長されない、ということです。従って、何らかの理由でアドバイザリアクションが発せられなくても、出願人は、最終局指令から6月までに当該出願を許可通知の発行、RCEを行うことで最終局指令の取下げ、審判請求にて審判段階への移行のいずれかの状態にする必要がある点に注意が必要です。

アドバイザリアクション (Advisory Action：AA)

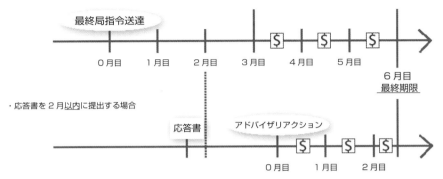

図11　最終局指令送達後の期間の計算について

第4章　審査

継続審査請求（RCE）

　最終局指令での審査官の主張にある程度同意し、出願人が更なる補正を希望する場合には、継続審査請求（RCE）を行うことができます。このRCEにより、最終局指令で一旦閉じられた出願手続きは再開されます（37C.F.R.1. 114(d)）。その後に許可通知若しくは通常は非最終局指令が発せられます。

RCEの手続き
RCEを行う際には下記を提出する必要があります。
- 継続審査請求書（PTO/SB/30）
- RCE費用37C.F.R.1. 17(e) ＋ 延長費用（37C.F.R.1. 17(a)）（最終局指令より3月経過後）
- 提出物（必要に応じて、補正書、意見書、宣誓書、先行技術文献等）

　補正書等の提出物はRCEと同時に行う必要がある点に注意が必要です。ここで、RCEは最終局指令が発せられた後でも、最終局指令に応答し、アドバイザリアクションが発せられた後でもすることができます。

　最終局指令の応答で提出した補正書が、新たな争点の提起（New Issue）を含むとして審査対象にされなかった場合、RCEを行うことで、その補正書を審査対象にする事を請求することができます。RCEで実質的に前回受けた最終局指令と同じクレームが審査対象になる場合、換言すれば、最終局指令を受けたクレームの補正を行わずにRCEをする場合には、RCE後の局指令が最終（First Final OA）になることがあるので、注意が必要です（M.P.E.P.706. 07 (b)）。また、前の審査で提出期限を逃した先行技術文献のIDS提出を行う目的でRCEを行う場合があります。審判継続中にRCEを行った場合には審判取り下げと見なされ（37C.F.R.1. 114(d)）、審査段階に戻ります。

RCEの費用
　規則改正により、2013年3月19日以降は、RCEはその請求回数によって費用が異なり、2回目以降は高額となります。

継続審査請求（RCE）

RCEの送付状の例

PATENT

IN THE UNITED STATES PATENT AND TRADEMARK OFFICE

In re application of:
Yoritomo MINAMOTO et al.
Application No.: 13/123,654
Filing Date: July 4, 2012
For: ELECTRIC METAL POLISHER

Art Unit: 1733
Examiner: DOE, John M.
Confirmation No.: 2586
Attorney Docket No.: MOT.085.0012.NP

（出願情報の表示）

**REQUEST FOR CONTINUED EXAMINATION UNDER 37 CFR 1.114
AND AMENDMENT**

（RCEである旨の表示）

Mail Stop RCE
Commissioner for Patents
P.O. Box 1450
Alexandria, VA 22313-1450

Dear Sir:

This request for continued examination continues prosecution following the office action mailed on August 10, 2012 for the above-identified application. Please reconsider based on the following claim amendments and remarks.

Please charge any shortage in fees related to the filing of this document to Deposit Account No. 50-4257. Please credit any excess fees paid to this account.

第4章 審査

RCEの送付状の例（電子出願用フォーム）PTO/SB/30EFS

継続的出願

　RCE以外の審査を継続する方法として、継続的出願を行うことができます（37C.F.R.1.53(b)）。継続的出願には、継続出願、分割出願、一部継続出願が含まれます。

Continuing Application　継続的出願
- ➢Continuation Application（37C.F.R.1.53(b)(1)）継続出願：同じカテゴリのクレームについて審査を希望する場合。現在の出願とは別に出願を行って権利化を図りたい場合。現段階で許可になっているクレームについては特許し、拒絶クレームに関して別途権利化を図りたい場合
- ➢Divisional Application（37C.F.R.1.53(b)(1)）分割出願：限定指令等で審査の対象外になったクレームの審査を希望する場合
- ➢Continuation-In-Part（37C.F.R.1.53(b)(2)）一部継続出願（CIP）：新規事項を追加して権利化を図りたい場合。ただし、新規に追加された事項を含むクレームは新規性等の基準日が繰り下がるため、親出願で拒絶される可能性があり注意が必要です。

継続的出願の手続き

継続出願は、親出願の利益を享受する新規出願ですので、親出願の表示を行う以外は新規出願と同様の手続きをおこないます。

- 送付状（Transmittal）
- 出願データシートADS（Application Data Sheet）
- 宣誓書（Declaration）
- 譲渡証（Assignment）＊必要に応じて
- 委任状（Power of Attorney）
- 明細書（Specification）
- 図面（Drawings）
- 情報開示陳述書(Information Disclosure Statement：IDS)＊必要に応じて
- 予備的補正書（Preliminary Amendment）

第4章　審査

　ここで、宣誓書は親出願のものを原則援用可能です[1]。譲渡証や情報開示陳述書は必要に応じて提出します。明細書及び図面は親出願のコピーを使うことができます。クレーム等明細書中の必要な補正は、予備的補正書にて行います。予備的補正書では、少なくとも下記を補正します。

親出願に関する情報の追加

　親出願の利益を得るために親出願を特定します。親出願の特定は、願番、出願日、発明の名称等複数の情報で特定します。また、親出願等はIBR（Incorporation By Reference）することで、後の補正で親出願等の内容を編入の可能性を含めておきます。

クレームの補正

　親出願の明細書等のコピーを利用して継続的出願を行う場合、クレームは親出願と同一になっています。そこで、予備的補正書にて、親出願のクレームをキャンセルして、新たに継続出願用のクレームを追加します。従って、新たなクレームの番号は親出願のクレーム数の次の番号からになります。新たなクレームの追加ですが、補正の扱いですので、追加するクレームには（New）のラベルを付します。

　その他、明細書中のSummary of the InventionやAbstractの記載内容について必要に応じて補正を行います。注意する点としては、補正は出願当初の明細書等の開示の範囲内で行うべきです。当初明細書の開示の範囲外の新規事項が追加された場合にはCIP出願となり、新規性等の判断基準日が繰り下がる可能性があります。判断基準日が繰り下がってしまいますと、親出願の公開公報で拒絶されてしまう可能性があります。

ワンポイント解説：CIP出願の注意点

　CIP出願は、クレーム要素が当初明細書に記載がある故、審査基準日が繰り下がらない事を出願人が立証する必要があります（Poweroasis v. T-Mobile（Fed. Cir. April 11, 2008））。

1　親出願が2012年9月16日以前の出願（旧法適用出願）で、子出願がそれ以降の出願（現行法適用出願）には、現行法下の宣誓書を提出する必要があります。

継続的出願

予備的補正書例

PATENT

IN THE UNITED STATES PATENT AND TRADEMARK OFFICE

In re Application of Taro YAMADA et al. : Art Unit: 1725 (*expected*)
:
Application No.: *to be assigned* : Confirmation No.: *to be assigned*
:
Filing Date: October XX, 2012 : Examiner: DOE, John
: (*expected*)
For SOLAR CELL MODULE :
: Attorney Docket No.: MOT.002.0001

（出願の特定）

PRELIMINARY AMENDMENT UNDER 37 C.F.R. § 1.115

（予備的補正である旨の表示）

Commissioner for Patents
P.O. Box 1450
Alexandria, VA 22313-1450

Dear Sir:

Prior to examination, please enter the following amendments for the above-identified application.

It is not believed that a fee is required for filing of this paper. However, the Commissioner is hereby authorized to charge any fee deficiency or credit any fee payment to Deposit Account XX-XXXX.

Amendments to the Specification

Replace the first full paragraph on page 1, beneath the title of the invention and before the "BACKGROUND OF THE INVENTION" with the following:

CROSS REFERENCE TO RELATED APPLICATION
This application is a continuation of application Serial No. 11/946,XXX, filed November XX, 2007, which claims priority based on 35 USC 119 from Japanese Patent Application No. 20XX-XXXXX filed on November XX, 2006, the entire contents of which are incorporated herein by reference.

（親出願の情報を追加）

第4章　審査

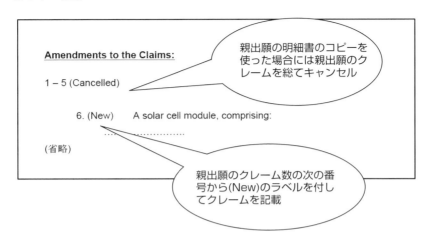

継続的出願とRCEの相違点

　RCEの効果は、前の審査手続きでの最終性が取り下げられ、審査が再開されます。すなわち、同一出願についての審査の再開といえます。従って、RCE後は出願番号が一緒であり、明細書等のコピーの提出は不要です。以前は、審査官はRCEから2月以内に応答する目標がありましたが、2009年11月のU.S.P.T.O.内部処理の改正によりこれが無くなりました。しかしながら、RCEは未だ継続的出願と比較すると早く局指令が発せられる傾向にあります。
　以上から、RCEは継続的出願と比較して、下記の場合に利用することが考

えられます。
- 早いOAを希望する場合
- コストを抑えたい場合

図12　RCEの模式図

一方、継続的出願は、新たな出願を行う事になり、U.S.P.T.O.でも新たなケースとして包袋が作られます。従って、元出願とは別の出願になりますので、異なる出願番号、明細書等のコピーの提出が必要になります。以上から継続的出願はRCEと比較して、下記の場合に利用することが考えられます。

- 遅いOAを希望する場合
- 審査官を変えたい場合（変わらない場合もあります）
- 親出願を残したい場合
- 許可クレームのみを親に残して許可を得て、拒絶クレームを別出願で審査を希望する場合

図13　継続的出願の模式図

第4章 審査

放置

最終局指令に応答しない場合には、最終局指令から6月で出願が放棄されたものとみなされます。また、放棄書を提出することにより出願を放棄することができます。放棄となった場合には、放棄通知書（Notice of Abandonment）が発行されます。

権利化を断念 ～「放棄」と「放置」の違い～

審査結果や技術の開発方針の変更等により発明の権利化を断念するには、「放棄表明」と「放置」との2つの方法があります。「放棄表明（Express Abandonment）」は、特許庁に対し書面（PTO/AIA/24）を提出し、これ以上の権利化を追求しない旨を表明するものです。提出直後、出願は放棄扱いにされ、その後、放棄通知（Notice of Abandonment）が送付されます。一方、「放置（Lapse）」は、放棄表明を提出せず、かつ庁指令が送達されてもそれに応答しないことで期限切れさせることです。放棄表明しますと、その後は庁指令が出ず、新たな先行文献も引用されないので、係属中の関連出願に対してをIDSを提出する必要がなくなるため、戦略的に放棄表明を提出する出願人もいます。また、審査がまだ始まっていない段階で放棄表明及び返金請求をすると、出願時に支払ったサーチ料金と超過クレーム料金を全額返金してもらえます。但し、放棄表明することにより、後々に出願の復活可能性がなくなることにも注意が必要です。

放棄表明書を提出する場合の特徴

- 出願公開前の場合には、公開公報の発行を回避できます。
- 審査着手前の場合には、U.S.P.T.O.に支払ったサーチ費用及び超過クレームに関する追加費用の返金を請求することができます。
- 局指令の前であれば、審査がなされませんので、局指令の発行が止まります。他の類似出願がある場合にはIDSの提出が回避できる可能性があります。
- 放棄表明書を提出した後に、権利化したい事が判明した場合、復活させるのは困難となります。

放置

放棄表明書のサンプル（PTO/AIA/24）

（出願の特定）

（公開公報発行の停止や返金請求を行う場合には他のフォームを用いる旨の表示）

（代理人等サイン）

第4章　審査

放棄通知書の例　PTOL-1432

Notice of Abandonment	Application No.	Applicant(s)
	13/321,987	Shizuka GOZEN
	Examiner	Art Unit
	Jaine M. DOE	1733

-- The MAILING DATE of this communication appears on the cover sheet with the correspondence address--

This application is abandoned in view of:

1. ☒ Applicant's failure to timely file a proper reply to the Office letter mailed on _26 August 2011_.
   (a) ☐ A reply was received on _____ (with a Certificate of Mailing or Transmission dated _____), which is after the expiration of the period for reply (including a total extension of time of _____ month(s)) which expired on _____.
   (b) ☐ A proposed reply was received on _____, but it does not constitute a proper reply under 37 CFR 1.113 (a) to the final rejection. A proper reply under 37 CFR 1.113 to a final rejection consists only of: (1) a timely filed amendment which places the application in condition for allowance; (2) a timely filed Notice of Appeal (with appeal fee); or (3) a timely filed Request for Continued Examination (RCE) in compliance with 37 CFR 1.114).
   (c) ☐ A reply was received on _____ but it does not constitute a proper reply, or a bona fide attempt at a proper reply, to the non-final rejection. See 37 CFR 1.85(a) and 1.111. (See explanation in box 7 below).
   (d) ☐ No reply has been received.

2. ☐ Applicant's failure to timely pay the required issue fee and publication fee, if applicable, within the statutory period of three months from the mailing date of the Notice of Allowance (PTOL-85).
   (a) ☐ The issue fee and publication fee, if applicable, was received on _____ (with a Certificate of Mailing or Transmission dated _____), which is after the expiration of the statutory period for payment of the issue fee (and publication fee) set in the Notice of Allowance (PTOL-85).
   (b) ☐ The submitted fee of $_____ is insufficient. A balance of $_____ is due.
   The issue fee required by 37 CFR 1.18 is $_____. The publication fee, if required by 37 CFR 1.18(d), is $_____.
   (c) ☐ The issue fee and publication fee, if applicable, has not been received.

3. ☐ Applicant's failure to timely file corrected drawings as required by, and within the three-month period set in, the Notice of Allowability (PTO-37).
   (a) ☐ Proposed corrected drawings were received on _____ (with a Certificate of Mailing or Transmission dated _____), which is after the expiration of the period for reply.
   (b) ☐ No corrected drawings have been received.

4. ☐ The letter of express abandonment which is signed by the attorney or agent of record, the assignee of the entire interest, or all of the applicants.

5. ☐ The letter of express abandonment which is signed by an attorney or agent (acting in a representative capacity under 37 CFR 1.34(a)) upon the filing of a continuing application.

6. ☐ The decision by the Board of Patent Appeals and Interference rendered on _____ and because the period for seeking court review of the decision has expired and there are no allowed claims.

7. ☒ The reason(s) below:

Marvin Motsenbocker confirmed 03/02/2012 that no response has been filed in responding the 08/26/2011 office action.

/Jaine M. DOE/
Primary Examiner, Art Unit 1733

Petitions to revive under 37 CFR 1.137(a) or (b), or requests to withdraw the holding of abandonment under 37 CFR 1.181, should be promptly filed to minimize any negative effects on patent term.

U.S. Patent and Trademark Office
PTOL-1432 (Rev. 04-01)　　　Notice of Abandonment　　　Part of Paper No. 20120302

（吹き出し: なぜ特許出願が放棄になったかの理由の表示）

第5章

審判

　最終局指令に不服がある場合には、出願人は、審判請求（Notice of Appeal）を行うことができます（35U.S.C.134, 37C.F.R.41.31(a)）。審判での争点は審査官がなした局指令の是非なので、審判継続中は補正を行うことは殆どできません（37C.F.R.41.33）。この点が日本の特許実務と大きく異なる点です。審判請求を行う時には審判請求書（PTO/AIA/31）に庁費用を提出します。

　審判請求するときは以下の状況が考えられます。
- 数回RCE等をしても審査官の理解が得られない場合
- 審査官に客観的な意見を説明させたい場合

審判請求：Notice of Appeal(37C.F.R.41.31)

　出願人は特許出願が2回拒絶された場合に審判請求を行うことができます（35U.S.C.134）。通常は最終局指令を受け取った後に審判請求を行いますが、これに限られず2回拒絶を受けた段階で審判請求を行うことができます。この点で最終局指令を受け取った後でなければ請求できないRCEとは請求のタイミングが異なります。

審判費用
　以下のタイミングで審判に関する費用が発生します。
- 審判請求時（37C.F.R.41.31(a)(1), 41.20(b)(1)）
- 審査官の答弁書発行から2月以内（37C.F.R.41.45(a), 41.20(b)(4)）

第5章　審判

審判請求書フォーム　PTO/AIA/31

PTO/AIA/31 (03-14)
Approved for use through 07/31/2016. OMB 0651-0031
U.S. Patent and Trademark Office; U.S. DEPARTMENT OF COMMERCE
Under the Paperwork Reduction Act of 1995, no persons are required to respond to a collection of information unless it displays a valid OMB control number.

NOTICE OF APPEAL FROM THE EXAMINER TO THE PATENT TRIAL AND APPEAL BOARD

Docket Number (Optional): MLG.001.0001.NP

I hereby certify that this correspondence is being facsimile transmitted to the USPTO, EFS-Web transmitted to the USPTO, or deposited with the United States Postal Service with sufficient postage as first class mail in an envelope addressed to "Commissioner for Patents, P.O. Box 1450, Alexandria, VA 22313-1450" [37 CFR 1.8(a)]

（審判請求費用の特定）

In re Application of: YAMADA, Taro
Application Number: 13/xxx,xxxx
Filed: MM/DD/YY
For:
Art Unit: XXX
Examiner: DOE, John

（出願の特定）

Typed or printed name _____

Applicant hereby **appeals** to the Patent Trial and Appeal Board from the last decision of the examiner.

The fee for this Notice of Appeal is (37 CFR 41.20(b)(1))　$ 800

☐ Applicant asserts small entity status. See 37 CFR 1.27. Therefore, the fee shown above is reduced by 50%, and the resulting fee is:　$ _____

☐ Applicant certifies micro entity status. See 37 CFR 1.29. Therefore, the fee shown above is reduced by 75%, and the resulting fee is:　$ _____
Form PTO/SB/15A or B or equivalent must either be enclosed or have been submitted previously.

☐ A check in the amount of the fee is enclosed.

☐ Payment by credit card. Form PTO-2038 is attached.

☐ The Director is hereby authorized to charge any fees which may be required, or credit any overpayment to Deposit Account No. _____ .

（審判請求費用支払方法の特定）

☑ Payment made via EFS-Web.

☐ A petition for an extension of time under 37 CFR 1.136(a) (PTO/AIA/22 or equivalent) is enclosed.
For extensions of time in reexamination proceedings, see 37 CFR 1.550.

WARNING: Information on this form may become public. Credit card information should not be included on this form. Provide credit card information and authorization on PTO-2038.

I am the
☐ applicant
☑ attorney or agent of record
　 Registration number XXX,XXX
☐ attorney or agent acting under 37 CFR 1.34
　 Registration number _____

Signature _____
Typed or printed name _____
Telephone Number _____
Date _____

NOTE: This form must be signed in accordance with 37 CFR 1.33. See 37 CFR 1.4 for signature requirements and certifications. Submit multiple forms if more than one signature is required, see below*.

☐ * Total of _____ forms are submitted.

This collection of information is required by 37 CFR 41.20(b)(1) and 41.31. The information is required to obtain or retain a benefit by the public which is to file (and by the USPTO to process) an application. Confidentiality is governed by 35 U.S.C. 122 and 37 CFR 1.11, 1.14 and 41.6. This collection is estimated to take 12 minutes to complete, including gathering, preparing, and submitting the completed application form to the USPTO. Time will vary depending upon the individual case. Any comments on the amount of time you require to complete this form and/or suggestions for reducing this burden, should be sent to the Chief Information Officer, U.S. Patent and Trademark Office, U.S. Department of Commerce, P.O. Box 1450, Alexandria, VA 22313-1450. DO NOT SEND FEES OR COMPLETED FORMS TO THIS ADDRESS. **SEND TO: Commissioner for Patents, P.O. Box 1450, Alexandria, VA 22313-1450.**

If you need assistance in completing the form, call 1-800-PTO-9199 and select option 2.

審判理由補充書：Appeal Brief(37C.F.R.41.37)

　審判請求人は審判請求日から２カ月以内に理由補充書（Appeal Brief）を提出する必要があります。この期間は、５月まで延長可能です(37C.F.R.1.136)。当該期限までに理由補充書の提出が無い場合には審判請求は取り下げたものと見なされます（37C.F.R.41.37(b)）。理由補充書には、なぜ審査官が発した局指令でなされた認定が誤っているのかを記載します。

審判請求して時間稼ぎ？
　最終局指令の送達日より６月以内に許可を受けるか、RCE等をする必要があります。ここで、６月ギリギリになって、許可も受けられず、RCEするにも補正書や意見書を準備していない場合にはどのようにしたら良いでしょうか？
　この場合には、審判請求を行います。これによって、最終局指令から６月期限の時計は止まります。審判請求の日から２月以内（５月延長可能）に理由補充書を提出する代わりにRCEを行います。これにより、審判請求は取り下げられ、審査段階に入ります（37C.F.R.1.114(d)）。審判請求を行う際には、最終局指令から起算した延長費用の支払いが必要です。

第5章 審判

審判請求理由補充書の例

表紙部分には願番等で出願を特定し、書類の種類を特定します。

例）

IN THE UNITED STATES PATENT AND TRADEMARK OFFICE

In re application of: :   Art Unit: 2621
YAMADA, Taro   :   Examiner: DOE, John
Application No.: 13/xxx,xxx :   Confirmation No.: 68xx
Filed: 04/04/2011   :   Attorney Docket No.: MOT.001.0002.RE
                            ::

For: Method of hitting a ball

(出願の特定)

COMMISSIONER FOR PATENTS
P.O. BOX 1450
ALEXANDRIA, VA 22313-1450

(書類の特定)

Appellants' Amended Appeal Brief under 37 C.F.R. § 41.37

Dear Sir:

　　Appellants respectfully submit this "amended brief or other appropriate correction", in response to a "Notification of Non-Compliant Appeal Brief" mailed February x, 20xx.

　　It is not believed that a fee is required for filing of this paper. However, the Commissioner is hereby authorized to charge any fee deficiency or credit any fee payment to deposit account No. 50-xxxx.

審判理由補充書：Appeal Brief（37C.F.R. 41.37）

次ページには目次を準備します。例としては以下のように、TABLE OF CONTENTSとして各項目のページ数を付します。
例）

TABLE OF CONTENTS

I. REAL PARTY IN INTEREST	3
II. RELATED APPEALS AND INTERFERENCES	4
III. STATUS OF CLAIMS	5
IV. STATUS OF AMENDMENTS	6
V. SUMMARY OF CLAIMED SUBJECT MATTER	7
VI. GROUNDS OF REJECTION TO BE REVIEWED ON APPEAL	12
VII. ARGUMENT	13
VIII. CLAIMS APPENDIX	29
IX. EVIDENCE APPENDIX	38
X. RELATED PROCEEDINGS APPENDIX	39

第5章　審判

Ⅰ．REAL PARTY IN INTEREST：利害関係人であることを立証します。
例）

> **I. REAL PARTY IN INTEREST**
>
> The real party in interest is ABC Company of Japan, Ltd., the assignee of this application. ABC Company of Japan, Ltd. is incorporated in Japan.

Ⅱ．RELATED APPEALS AND INTERFERENCES：関連する審判等があれば特定します。
例）

> **II. RELATED APPEALS AND INTERFERENCES**
>
> There are no prior or previous appeals, interferences or judicial proceedings known to Appellants, Appellants' legal representative, or assignee which may be related to, directly affect or be directly affected by or have a bearing on the Board's decision in this pending appeal.

審判理由補充書:Appeal Brief (37C.F.R. 41.37)

Ⅲ. STATUS OF CLAIMS:現段階のクレームの状況を記載します。
例)

> **III. STATUS OF CLAIMS**
>
> Claims 1-19 are pending in this application. Claims 1, 2, 10-17 and 19 have been withdrawn from consideration. Claims 3-9 and 18 were finally rejected in the final office action. The rejections of claims 3-9 and 18 are appealed. Independent claim 3 and claims 4-9 and 18 dependent thereon stand and fall together. The claims are reproduced in the Appendix attached hereto.

Ⅳ. STATUS OF AMENDMENTS:最終局指令以降に補正した場合には、その内容を記載します。
例)

> **IV. STATUS OF AMENDMENTS**
>
> No amendments subsequent to the final office action have been filed.

第5章 審判

V. SUMMARY OF CLAIMED SUBJECT MATTER：審査対象のクレームで、議論上重要なものを選択し、その上でクレームの技術内容を説明します。

例）

> **V. SUMMARY OF CLAIMED SUBJECT MATTER**
>
> Figure numbers, specification columns and line numbers in the following table refer to the specification of U.S. patent application 13/xxx,xxx as filed in this case. Each claim element listed in the table is supported by the specification throughout. Therefore, each entry under "specification support" is exemplary only.
>
> All claims include the contents of independent claim 3, which recites:
>
> "A method of hitting a ball, comprising:
>
> (略)

また、クレームの各要素が明細書中でサポートされている事をチャートにして示します。

例）

CLAIM CHART WITH SPECIFICATION SUPPORT	
Claim 3	Specification Support
A method of hitting a ball, comprising:	Col. 1 lines 25-34 Col. 4 lines 19-27
各構成要素を記入する	記載の根拠となる明細書部分を特定する

審判理由補充書：Appeal Brief（37C.F.R. 41.37）

Ⅵ. GROUNDS OF REJECTION TO BE REVIEWED ON APPEAL：誤っていると考える拒絶理由の根拠を記載します。

例）

VI. GROUNDS OF REJECTION TO BE REVIEWED ON APPEAL

Appellants request review of the rejection of claims 3-6, 8 and 9 under 35 U.S.C. § 102 as anticipated by U.S. Pat. x,xxx,xxx to XXX. Appellants request review of the rejection of claims 17 and 18 under 35 U.S.C. § 103 as obvious by U.S. Pat. x,xxx,xxx to XXX.

Ⅶ. ARGUMENT：なぜ審査官が発した拒絶理由が誤っているかを説明します。その最後には、まとめを記載して総括します。

例）

VII. ARGUMENT

 1. **The Rejection of Claims 3-6, 8 and 9 on anticipation grounds over XXX is improper.**

Summary

   （略）

第5章　審判

Ⅷ. CLAIMS APPENDIX：現在審査対象となっているクレームセットを添付します。
Ⅸ. EVIDENCE APPENDIX：何か示すべき証拠があれば添付します。
Ⅹ. RELATED PROCEEDINGS APPENDIX：何か関連する手続きがあれば添付します。

審査官による答弁書：Examiner's Answer (37C.F.R.41.39)

　審査官は、審判請求人が提出した理由補充書に対する審査官の答弁書の発することができます。この時点で審査官は拒絶を撤回することもできます。また、新たな拒絶理由を発見した場合には、審査の再開（Reopen）を行う事もできます。前者の場合には、許可通知が発せられ、後者の場合には局指令が発せられます。この場合には、審判請求は取り下げたものと見なされます。

審査が再開される場合〜U.S.P.T.O.の審判制度の問題点

　審査官は、審判請求人による理由補充書の提出の後に、答弁書を発するか、許可するか、もしくは、審査再開することができると説明しました。ここで、答弁書の準備は局指令よりも多くの書類を準備する必要がある割には、処理は1件としてカウントされます。即ち、審査官にとっては、「労多くして功少なし」の処理と言えます。また、審査官は何らかの理由で自身が発した拒絶を審判官にレビューしてほしくない場合があります。これらの要因を考慮して、審査官が敢えて他の引用例を探して、審査再開に持ち込むことも少なからず見受けられます。そうすれば、当該出願は特許審判控訴部によるレビューを経ずに審査段階に戻りますので、また自分の所掌範囲になります。審判請求人からすると、せっかく審判請求して審判官に判断を求めたにも関わらず、また審査段階で審査官と議論しなければならない事態に陥ってしまいます。この辺に審判制度の改善の余地がありそうです。

審査官による答弁書：Examiner's Answer（37C.F.R. 41.39）

審査官答弁書の例

答弁書の表紙例）

UNITED STATES PATENT AND TRADEMARK OFFICE

Commissioner for Patents
United States Patent and Trademark Office
P.O. Box 1450
Alexandria, VA 22313-1450
www.uspto.gov

**BEFORE THE BOARD OF PATENT APPEALS
AND INTERFERENCES**

Application Number:
Filing Date:
Appellant(s):

Adam Scott
For Appellant

EXAMINER'S ANSWER

This is in response to the appeal brief filed 3/8/10 appealing from the Office action mailed 5/18/09.

第5章　審判

　審査官答弁書は、理由補充書に沿った形で審判請求人の主張に対して項目毎に応答します。

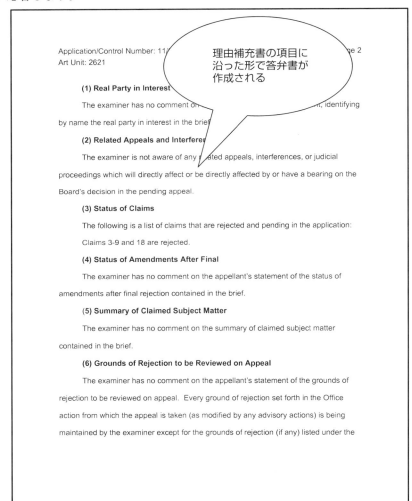

応答書：Reply Brief（37C.F.R. 41. 41）

応答書：Reply Brief（37C.F.R.41.41）

　審判請求人は、審査官答弁書送達日より2月以内に応答書を提出することができます。応答書では、審査官の答弁書に対する反論を行う事ができます。応答書では新たな証拠や補正等は認められません。応答書も理由補充書と同様の項目を立てて審査官の主張に対して反論等を行います。

応答書の受領例

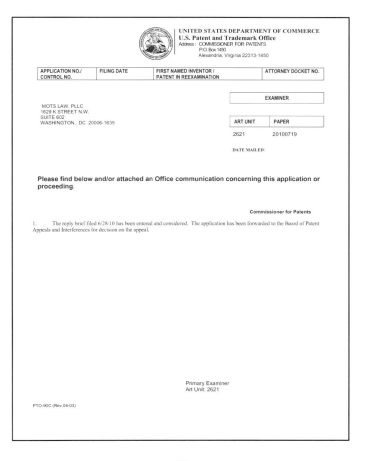

第5章 審判

特許審判控訴部（PTAB）による審理に進んだ旨の通知

出願人から理由補充書が提出され、担当審査官から答弁書が提出された場合には、PTABから審理予定通知が送付されます。注意したいのは、審判請求した直後に審理が開始される訳ではなく、出願人から理由補充書が提出され、担当審査官から答弁書が提出された後、本通知後に審理が開始されます。

Page 1

United States Patent and Trademark Office
Under Secretary of Commerce for Intellectual Property and
Director of the United States Patent and Trademark Office
P.O. Box 1450
Alexandria, Virginia 22313-1450
www.uspto.gov

MOTS LAW, PLLC
1629 K STREET N.W.
SUITE 602
WASHINGTON, DC 20006-1635

Appeal No:
Application:
Appellant:

Board of Patent Appeals and Interferences
Docketing Notice

Application   was received from the Technology Center at the Board on July 26, 2010 and has been assigned Appeal No:

In all future communications regarding this appeal, please include both the application number and the appeal number.

The mailing address for the Board is:

BOARD OF PATENT APPEALS AND INTERFERENCES
UNITED STATES PATENT AND TRADEMARK OFFICE
P.O. BOX 1450
ALEXANDRIA, VIRGINIA 22313-1450

The facsimile number of the Board is 571-273-0052. Because of the heightened security in the Washington D.C. area, facsimile communications are recommended. Telephone inquiries can be made by calling 571-272-9797 and referencing the appeal number listed above.

By order of the Board of Patent Appeals and Interferences.

口頭審尋：Oral Hearing（37C.F.R. 41. 47）

口頭審尋：Oral Hearing（37C.F.R.41. 47）

　審判請求人は審査官答弁書送達日から２月以内（応答書を提出した際には、その審査官答弁書送達日より２月以内）に口頭審尋を請求することができます。その後、期日が設定され、審尋は概ね20分程度の時間が設定されます。

口頭審尋請求書の記入例（PTO/AIA/32）

第5章 審判

口頭審尋期日指定通知書

　口頭審尋請求を行うと、口頭審尋期日指定通知書が送付されます。この通知書には、U.S.P.T.O.審判廷への出頭期日が指定されます。指定期日での口頭審尋を受諾、若しくは、口頭審尋をキャンセルの別を記入し、指定のファクシミリ番号へ返送します。

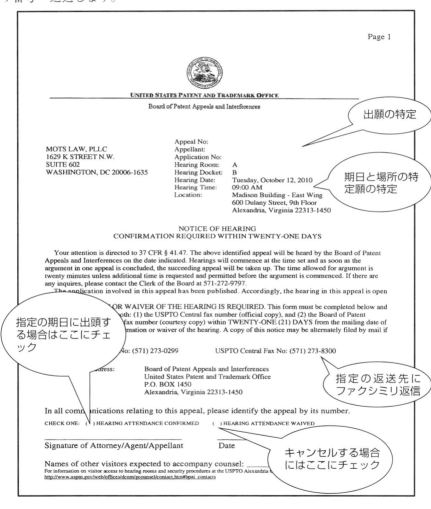

審判官合議体による審理及び審決：Board Review and Decision(37C.F.R. 41. 50)

審判官合議体による審理及び審決：Board Review and Decision(37C.F.R.41.50)

　審判請求人及び審査官の意見が出尽くした後に審判官合議体により審理がなされます。換言すれば、上記書の提出までは審判請求人と審査官との意見の主張であり、審判段階とはいえ、実質的には審判請求人と審査官とのやりとりとなります。審判請求人及び審査官双方の意見が出尽した後に、審判官合議体が口頭審理等で争点を整理し、審決をするのに期が熟したときに審決がなされます。審決には以下が含まれます。

- 請求認容審決（Affirm）
- 請求棄却審決（Reverse）
- 一部認容一部棄却審決（Affirm-in-Part）
- 差し戻し（Remand）

審決に不服がある場合

　審判請求人は、審決に不服がある場合には、バージニア州東部連邦地方裁判所（District Court for the Eastern District of Virginia）または連邦巡回控訴裁判所（Court of Appeals for the Federal Circuit：CAFC）に審決の取消しを求める訴訟を提起することができます。

ワンポイント解説：審決不服時の提訴先
　U.S.P.T.O.の審決に不服の場合、旧法下における提訴先は、ワシントンDC地区連邦地裁（またはCAFC）でした。現行法下では、バージニア州東部連邦地方裁判所（またはCAFC）が管轄となりました（35U.S.C.145）。U.S.P.T.O.及びバージニア州東部連邦地方裁判所は共にアレキサンドリア市内にあり、徒歩圏内です。

第5章　審判

プレアピールブリーフ（Preappeal Brief）

　審査官の局指令の明白な誤りを指摘するために、多大な費用を掛けて審判理由補充書を準備し、それを審理するのは、審判請求人及びU.S.P.T.O.の双方に不利益があることから、プレアピールブリーフ制度が創設されました。プレアピールブリーフは、審判請求と同時に下記の書面を提出する必要があります。プレアピールブリーフの申請自体のU.S.P.T.O.の手数料は掛かりません。プレアピールブリーフは、5ページ以内のまとめ、審査官の明らかな誤りを具体的に記載します。

　プレアピールブリーフは、当該局指令を発した審査官とそのスーパーバイザとその他1名の合計3名のパネルで検討され、プレアピールブリーフ提出から45日以内にパネルの判断がなされます。パネル判断の結論は以下の通りです。

- 審判請求人の主張が認められた場合には許可通知
- 審判請求人の主張が認められない場合には審判の継続
- 審判請求人の主張は認めるが、新たな拒絶理由通知を発見した場合には、審査の再開（Reopen）

　アピールブリーフの理由が認められなかった場合、その後出願人はそのまま審判請求を維持する際には、パネル判断から1月以内（5月延長可能）に理由補充書を提出します。また、この時点で審判請求の維持が難しいと判断した出願人は、補正書を添付したRCEを行うこともできます。RCEを行うと、審判請求は取り下げられたものと見なされ、審査段階に戻ります。

プレアピールブリーフ（Preappeal Brief）

プレアピールブリーフの記入例（PTO/AIA/33）

```
Doc Code: AP.PRE.REQ                                      PTO/AIA/33 (07-09)
                                      Approved for use through 01/31/2013 OMB 0651-0031
                                      U.S. Patent and Trademark Office; U.S. DEPARTMENT OF COMMERCE
Under the Paperwork Reduction Act of 1995, no persons are required to respond to a collection of information unless it displays a valid OMB control number.
```

PRE-APPEAL BRIEF REQUEST FOR REVIEW

Docket Number (Optional)	MOT.001.0001

I hereby certify that this correspondence is being facsimile transmitted to the USPTO, EFS-Web transmitted to the USPTO, or deposited with the United States Postal Service with sufficient postage as first class mail in an envelope addressed to "Mail Stop AF, Commissioner for Patents, P.O. Box 1450, Alexandria, VA 22313-1450" [37 CFR 1.8(a)]
on _____

Signature _____
Typed or printed name _____

Application Number	Filed
13/xxx,xxx	04/xx/2011

First Named Inventor: YAMADA, Taro

Art Unit	Examiner
xxx	DOE, John

（出願の特定）

Applicant requests review of the final rejection in the above-identified application. No amendments are with this request.

This request is being filed with a notice of appeal.

The review is requested for the reason(s) stated on the attached sheet(s).
  Note: No more than five (5) pages may be provided.

（吹き出し）
1) プレアピール提出の際は補正不可
2) プレアピール請求は審判請求と同時に提出
3) プレアピールブリーフは5枚以内

I am the _____
☐ applicant
☑ attorney or agent of record. Registration number xxx,xxx
☐ attorney or agent acting under 37 CFR 1.34. Registration number if acting under 37 CFR 1.34 _____

Signature _____
Typed or printed name _____
Telephone number _____
Date _____

NOTE: This form must be signed in accordance with 37 CFR 1.33. See 37 CFR 1.4 for signature requirements and certifications. Submit multiple forms if more than one signature is required, see below*.

☐ *Total of _____ forms are submitted.

This collection of information is required by 35 U.S.C. 132. The information is required to obtain or retain a benefit by the public which is to file (and by the USPTO to process) an application. Confidentiality is governed by 35 U.S.C. 122 and 37 CFR 1.11, 1.14 and 41.6. This collection is estimated to take 12 minutes to complete, including gathering, preparing, and submitting the completed application form to the USPTO. Time will vary depending upon the individual case. Any comments on the amount of time you require to complete this form and/or suggestions for reducing this burden, should be sent to the Chief Information Officer, U.S. Patent and Trademark Office, U.S. Department of Commerce, P.O. Box 1450, Alexandria, VA 22313-1450. DO NOT SEND FEES OR COMPLETED FORMS TO THIS ADDRESS. **SEND TO: Mail Stop AF, Commissioner for Patents, P.O. Box 1450, Alexandria, VA 22313-1450.**

If you need assistance in completing the form, call 1-800-PTO-9199 and select option 2.

第５章　審判

パネルの決定通知の例（PTO-2297）

- 不適切な請求の場合にはここにチェックされる
- パネルが請求理由なしとの判断の場合にはここにチェックされる
- 出願の特定
- 許可可能な場合にはここにチェックされる
- 審査再開の場合にはここにチェックされる
- パネル参加者名の表示

第6章 早期権利化のために —早期審査—

　U.S.P.T.O.には米国内の法人や発明家のみならず、世界各国から数多くの特許出願がなされ、2015年度は特許出願件数が約59万件となりました。出願件数は毎年増加の一途を辿っています。2017年では出願から第1回局指令が発せられるまで平均16.4月、出願から特許までに平均24.8月を要しています。

　しかし、出願人の事情で早期の審査を望む場合や、技術開発スピードの速い分野の出願等一定の要件を満たした出願については、早期に審査が開始される制度が用意されています。この制度を利用するためには、請願書の提出が必要となります。早期審査制度には以下の常設の制度と、パイロットプログラムとして試験的に導入される期間限定の制度とがあります。

出願人の年齢・健康状態により受けられる早期審査

　制度：早期審査制度（2006年改正前の制度が適用）
　適用条件：出願人の健康状態、または年齢（65才以上）により、出願の審査手続きを効果的に支援できない場合
　提出書類：請願書（PTO/SB/130）および上記条件を証明する書面
　提出時期：初回局指令までに提出
　料金：請願書提出料金は不要
　効果：通常の審査待ちの順番とは異なる特別枠の審査の順番が付与されますが、審査官には、具体的な審査着手や最終決定の期限の義務はありません。

第6章 早期権利化のために―早期審査―

出願人の年齢・健康状態を理由に行う早期審査請願書（PTO／SB／130）

Doc code : PET.OP.AGE
Description : Petition to make special based on Age/Health

PTO/SB/130 (07-09)
Approved for use through 07/31/2012. OMB 0651-0031
U.S. Patent and Trademark Office; U.S. DEPARTMENT OF COMMERCE
Under the Paperwork Reduction Act of 1995, no persons are required to respond to a collection of information unless it contains a valid OMB control number

PETITION TO MAKE SPECIAL BASED ON AGE FOR ADVANCEMENT OF EXAMINATION UNDER 37 CFR 1.102(c)(1)

Application Information

Application Number		Confirmation Number		Filing Date	
Attorney Docket Number (optional)		Art Unit		Examiner	

First Named ...

（出願の特定）

...ion: Office of Petitions

An application may be made special for advancement of examination upon filing of a petition showing that the applicant is 65 years of age, or more. No fee is required with such a petition. See 37 CFR 1.102(c)(1) and MPEP 708.02 (IV).

APPLICANT HEREBY PETITIONS TO MAKE SPECIAL FOR ADVANCEMENT OF EXAMINATION IN THIS APPLICATION UNDER 37 CFR 1.102(c)(1) and MPEP 708.02 (IV) ON THE BASIS OF THE APPLICANT'S AGE.

...quires one of the following items:
...named inventor in the application that he/she is 65 years of age, or more; or
...gistered attorney/agent having evidence such as a birth certificate, passport, driver's license, etc.
...nventor in the application is 65 years of age, or more.

（65歳以上の発明者の特定）

Name of Inventor who is 65 years of age, or older

Given Name	Middle Name	Family Name	Suffix

A signature of the applicant or representative is required in accordance with 37 CFR 1.33 and 10.18.
Please see 37 CFR 1.4(d) for the format of the signature.

Select (1) or (2) :

　(1) I am an inventor in this application and I am 65 years of age, or more.

● (2) I am an attorney or agent registered to practice before the Patent and Trademark Office, and I certify that I am in possession of evidence, and will retain such in the application file record, showing that the inventor listed above is 65 years of age, or more.

Signature		Date (YYYY-MM-DD)	
Name		Registration Number	

184

特定の発明内容により受けられる早期審査

　適用対象：2006年に改正された早期審査制度です。実用特許出願、意匠出願（35U.S.C.111(a)に基づいて提出された出願）であって、下記の発明内容を含むものです。なおPCT米国国内移行出願、再発行特許出願は対象外です。
- 人類の生存環境の質向上につながる発明、代替エネルギーの発見・開発、資源の有効利用・保全を対象とした発明（料金不要）
- テロ対抗に関する発明（料金不要）
- DNAの組み換えの研究における発明（料金要）
- 超伝導技術に関する発明（料金不要）
- HIV/エイズ、癌に関する発明（料金要）

　提出時期：請願書は出願と同時に提出

　適用条件：基本料金以内であることを要します。すなわち、クレームの数は独立クレーム3項以下、クレーム総数20項以下、複数従属クレームを含めることはできません。

提出書類：
- 請願書（PTO/SB/28）
- 提出前に特許調査を行ったことを示す陳述書
- IDSと関連先行技術文献の写し
- 各先行技術文献に開示されたクレームの限定の特定
- 各クレームの特許性に関する詳細な説明
- 35U.S.C.103(c)に基づき除外される引用例の特定
- 明細書中の各クレームを支持する箇所の表示

　効果：提出から最終決定（許可または最終OA）までを12月で完了させることが目標とされ、審査手続きがなされます。本早期審査では、出願人は前もって特許調査を行い、関連する引用文献中にクレームの要素が開示されるかを記載した書類を提出する必要があります。

第6章 早期権利化のために―早期審査―

特定の発明内容を理由に行う早期審査請願書（PTO/SB/28）

```
Doc Code: PET.SPRE.ACX                                              PTO/SB/28 (07-09)
Doc Description: Petition for 12-month Accelerated Exam          Approved for use through 07/31/2014. OMB 0651-0059
                                                                 U.S. Patent and Trademark Office; U.S. DEPARTMENT OF COMMERCE
Under the Paperwork Reduction Act of 1995, no persons are required to respond to a collection of information unless it displays a valid OMB control number.
```

PETITION TO MAKE SPECIAL UNDER ACCELERATED EXAMINATION PROGRAM

Attorney Docket Number		First Named Inventor	出願の特定
Application Number (if Known)			
Title of Invention			

APPLICANT HEREBY PETITIONS TO MAKE THE ABOVE-IDENTIFIED APPLICATION SPECIAL UNDER THE REVISED ACCELERATED EXAMINATION PROGRAM. See Instruction sheet on page 3.

1. **Claims of the application:**
   a. The application must contain three (3) or fewer independent claims and twenty (20) or fewer total claims. The application may not contain any multiple dependent claims.
   b. **Applicant hereby agrees not to separately argue the patentability of any dependent claim during any appeal** in the application. Specifically, the applicant agrees that the dependent claims will be grouped together with and not argued separately from the independent claim from which they depend in any appeal brief filed in the application (37 CFR 41.37(c)(1)(vii)).
   c. The claims must be directed to **a single invention**.

2. **Interviews:**
   Applicant hereby agrees to have (if requested by examiner):
   a. An interview (including an interview before a first Office action) to discuss the prior art and any potential rejections or objections with the intention of clarifying and possibly resolving all issues with respect to patentability at that time, and
   b. A telephonic interview to make an election without traverse if the Office determines that the claims are not obviously directed to a single invention.

3. **Preexamination Search Statement and Accelerated Examination Support Document:**
   With this petition, applicant is providing: a **preexamination search statement**, in compliance with the requirements set forth in item 8 of the instruction sheet; and an **"accelerated examination support document"** that includes:
   a. An **information disclosure statement** in compliance with 37 CFR 1.98 citing each reference deemed most closely related to the subject matter of each of the claims;
   b. For each reference cited, **an identification of all the limitations of the claims** that are disclosed by the reference specifying where the limitation is disclosed in the cited reference;
   c. A **detailed explanation of how each of the claims are patentable** over the references cited with the particularity required by 37 CFR 1.111(b) and (c);
   d. A concise **statement of the utility** of the invention as defined in each of the independent claims (unless the application is a design application);
   e. An identification of any cited references that may be disqualified as prior art under 35 U.S.C. 103(c) as amended by the CREATE act; and
   f. **A showing of where each limitation of the claims finds support under the first paragraph of 35 U.S.C. 112** in the written description of the specification. If applicable, the showing must also identify: (1) each means- (or step-) plus-function claim element that invokes consideration under 35 U.S.C. 112, ¶6; and (2) the structure, material, or acts that correspond to any means- (or step-) plus-function claim element that invokes consideration under 35 U.S.C. 112, ¶6. If the application claims the benefit of one or more applications under title 35, United States Code, the showing must also include where each limitation of the claims finds support under the first paragraph of 35 U.S.C. 112 in each such application in which such support exists.

The information is required to obtain or retain a benefit by the public which is to file (and by the USPTO to process) an application. Confidentiality is governed by 35 U.S.C. 122 and 37 CFR 1.11 and 1.14. This form is estimated to take 12 hours to complete, including gathering, preparing, and submitting the completed application form to the USPTO. Time will vary depending upon the individual case. Any comments on the amount of time you require to complete this form and/or suggestions for reducing this burden, should be sent to the Chief Information Officer, U.S. Patent and Trademark Office, U.S. Department of Commerce, P.O. Box 1450, Alexandria, VA 22313-1450. DO NOT SEND FEES OR COMPLETED FORMS TO THIS ADDRESS. *If you need assistance in completing the form, call 1-800-PTO-9199 and select option 2.*

特定の発明内容により受けられる早期審査

特定の発明内容を理由に行う早期審査請願書(PTO/SB/28)の続き

Doc Code: PET.SPRE.ACX
Doc Description: Petition for 12-month Accelerated Exam

PTO/SB/28 (07-09)
Approved for use through 07/31/2014. OMB 0651-0059
U.S. Patent and Trademark Office; U. S. DEPARTMENT OF COMMERCE
Under the Paperwork Reduction Act of 1995, no persons are required to respond to a collection of information unless it displays a valid OMB control number.

PETITION TO MAKE SPECIAL UNDER ACCELERATED EXAMINATION PROGRAM (Continued)

Attorney Docket		First Named Inventor	

（提出書類の特定）

	Accelerated Examination Support Document (see item 3 above).
	A statement, in compliance with the requirements set forth in item 8 of the instruction sheet, detailing the preexamination search which was conducted.
c.	Information Disclosure Statement.
d.	Other (e.g., a statement that the claimed subject matter is directed to environmental quality, energy, or countering terrorism (37 CFR 1.102(c)(2)).

Fees: The following fees must be filed electronically via EFS or EFS-Web:

a.	The basic filing fee, search fee, examination fee, and application size fee (if required) under 37 CFR 1.16.
b.	Petition fee under 37 CFR 1.17(h) - unless the petition is filed with a showing under 37 CFR 1.102(c)(2).

（代理人サイン）

Remove if you wish to remove this signatory   Remove

Signature		Date	
Name (Print/Typed)		Registration Number	

Click Add if you wish to add additional signatory   Add

Note: Signatures of all the inventors or assignees of record of the entire interest or their representative(s) are required in accordance with 37 CFR 1.33 and 10.18. Please see 37 CFR 1.4(d) for the form of the signature.

第6章　早期権利化のために―早期審査―

優先権を主張する対応外国出願により受けられる早期審査

日本出願の審査結果を利用した特許ハイウエイ施行プログラム
（Global/IP5 Patent Prosecution Highway：PPH）

　2006年にU.S.P.T.O.は日本特許庁（JPO）との間で特許審査ハイウエイ（Patent Prosecution Highway：PPH）を開始しました。PPHは、先の審査を行った特許庁（Office of Earlier Examination：OEE）で行われた審査結果を後の審査を行う特許庁（Office of Later Examination：OLE）が利用して、重複した審査を減らし、質の向上を図ることを目的としています。また、出願人の海外での早期権利化を容易にする目的もあります。2006年の日米特許庁で開始された特許審査ハイウエイは、現在では、多くの国と地域[1]が参加するGlobal PPHと、日、米、欧、中、韓の5カ国が参加するIP5とが併存しています[2]。

　適用対象：パリルート/PCT出願
　適用条件：対応外国出願/国際段階の見解書等にて少なくともひとつのクレームに特許性が認められた場合
　提出時期：実体審査が開始する前までに提出（通常、初回OA前まで）
　提出書面：
　　　●請願書（PTO/SB/20GLBL）を電子提出
　　　●OEEが対応出願において送達した特許査定前の最新のOAの写し
　　　●OAの英訳（必要に応じて）
　　　●IDSおよび関連先行技術文献
　　　●クレーム対応表
　料金：不要

1　2017年9月現在の参加国一覧
　　https://www.jpo.go.jp/ppph-portal-j/Annex_A.pdf
2　https://www.uspto.gov/patents-getting-started/international-protection/patent-prosecution-highway-pph-fast-track

効果：OEEによる審査が有効利用され審査にかかる時間が短縮されます。通常、請願書が提出されると2月以内にPPH適用の可否が判断され、その後2〜3月で審査が開始されます。但し、審査官には、具体的な審査着手や最終決定の期限の義務はありません。

U.S.P.T.O.ウェブページに詳細情報[3]が掲載されています。

---

3 https://www.uspto.gov/patents-getting-started/international-protection/patent-prosecution-highway-pph-fast-track（U.S.P.T.O.ウェブページ）

http://www.jpo.go.jp/ppph-portal/globalpph.htm（JPOウェブページ）

第6章 早期権利化のために―早期審査―

外国特許庁の審査結果を利用したPPH申請フォーム（PTO/SB/20GLBL）

Doc Code:
PPH.PET.652
Document Description: Petition to make special under Patent Pros Hwy

PTO/SB/20GLBL (12-16)
Approved for use through 04/30/2018. OMB 0651-0058
U.S. Patent and Trademark Office; U.S DEPARTMENT OF COMMERCE
Under the Paperwork Reduction Act of 1995, no persons are required to respond to a collection of information unless it displays a valid OMB control number.

（出願の特定）

REQUEST FOR PARTICIPATION IN THE GLOBAL/IP5
PATENT PROSECUTION HIGHWAY (PPH) PILOT PROGRAM IN THE USPTO

Application No.:	13/123,456	First Named Inventor:	Taro YAMADA
Filing Date:	09/09/16	Attorney Docket No.:	YMD12345
Title of the Invention:	Semiconductor		

...ST FOR PARTICIPATION IN THE PPH PILOT PROGRAM ALONG WITH THE REQUIRED DOCUMENTS MUST BE
... EFS-WEB. INFORMATION REGARDING EFS-WEB IS AVAILABLE AT
...PTO.GOV/PATENTS-APPLICATION-PROCESS/APPLYING-ONLINE/ABOUT-EFS-WEB

...EREBY REQUESTS PARTICIPATION IN THE PATENT PROSECUTION HIGHWAY (PPH) PILOT PROGRAM AND
... MAKE THE ABOVE-IDENTIFIED APPLICATION SPECIAL UNDER THE PPH PILOT PROGRAM.

（審査結果を利用する出願の特定）

Office of earlier examination (OEE): Japan (Japan Patent Office)

OEE application number: 2015-1234x

Both the OEE application and the above-identified U.S. application
have the following earliest date (filing or priority date): 09/09/15

Type of OEE work product relied upon: Decision to grant a patent

Mailing date of OEE work product: 08/08/16

Supporting Documents

1. OEE Work Product and Translation

    （特許査定謄本と引用例の提出）

    A copy of the OEE work product and translation if not already in English:

    [x] Attached [ ] Previously submitted [ ] Not required because the decision to grant a patent was the first office action

    [ ] Applicant requests the USPTO to attempt to obtain the OEE work product from the Dossier Access System or PATENTSCOPE

    NOTE: If the applicant requests the USPTO to obtain the OEE work product electronically and such attempt is unsuccessful, the applicant will be required to supply the document. Accordingly, to avoid dismissal of the initial PPH request and potential denial of participation in the PPH program, the applicant should verify that the OEE work product is actually available via the Dossier Access System or PATENTSCOPE before requesting retrieval. If the applicant is unable to verify availability, then the applicant should submit the document with the PPH request.

2. References Cited in OEE Work Product

    An information disclosure statement (IDS) listing the references cited in the OEE work product and document copies (except U.S. patents and U.S. published patent applications):

    [x] Attached [ ] Previously Submitted [ ] Not required because no references were cited in the OEE work product

[Page 1 of 2]

This collection of information is required by 35 U.S.C. 119, 37 CFR 1.55, and 37 CFR 1.102(d). The information is required to obtain or retain a benefit by the public, which is to file (and by the USPTO to process) an application. Confidentiality is governed by 35 U.S.C. 122 and 37 CFR 1.11 and 1.14. This collection is estimated to take 2 hours to complete, including gathering, preparing, and submitting the completed application form to the USPTO. Time will vary depending upon the individual case. Any comments on the amount of time you require to complete this form and/or suggestions for reducing this burden should be sent to the Chief Information Officer, U.S. Patent and Trademark Office, U.S. Department of Commerce, P.O. Box 1450, Alexandria, VA 22313-1450. DO NOT SEND FEES OR COMPLETED FORMS TO THIS ADDRESS.

優先権を主張する対応外国出願により受けられる早期審査

外国特許庁の審査結果を利用したPPH申請フォーム（PTO/SB/20GLBL）の続き

```
PTO/SB/20GLBL (05-16)
Approved for use through 04/30/2018. OMB 0651-0058
U.S. Patent and Trademark Office; U.S DEPARTMENT OF COMMERCE
Under the Paperwork Reduction Act of 1995, no persons are required to respond to a collection of information unless it displays a valid OMB control number.
```

REQUEST FOR PARTICIPATION IN THE GLOBAL/IP5 PPH PILOT PROGRAM IN THE USPTO
(continued)

| Application No.: | 13/123,456 | First Named Inventor: | Taro YAMADA |

3. Claims Correspondence Certification Statement
All of the claims in this application sufficiently correspond to the patentable/allowable claims in the OEE application.

4. Claims Correspondence Table

Claims in U.S. Application	Patentable Claims in OEE Application	Explanation Regarding the Correspondence
1	1	Sufficiently corresponds to claim in OEE application
2	2	Sufficiently corresponds to claim in OEE application
3	3	Sufficiently corresponds to claim in OEE application

- 米国出願クレーム番号の表示
- 審査利用出願クレーム番号の表示
- 米国出願クレームが以下に対応しているかの説明

Signature		Date	
Name (print or type)		Registration Number	

[Page 2 of 2]

第6章　早期権利化のために—早期審査—

割増し料金を支払うことによる優先審査

制度：優先審査制度"TRACK 1"

適用対象：パリ条約経由、バイパス出願等35U.S.C.111(a)に基づいて提出された出願（PCT米国国内移行出願、意匠出願、再発行特許出願等の米国特許出願は対象外。）

適用条件：電子出願（実用特許）、紙出願（植物特許）であり、総クレーム数は30項以内、独立クレームは4項以内、複数従属クレームは不可。

提出時期：出願と同時（RCEと同時でも可）

提出文書：
- 請願書（PTO/AIA/424）を電子提出
- 宣誓書

料金：通常出願料＋追加料金（37C.F.R.1.17(c)）

効果：12月以内に最終処分（特許査定の通知、最終OA）が得られます。割増し料金を支払う代わりに出願人の負荷がほとんど無く早期審査の申請を行うことができます。

優先審査制度に関する詳細情報は、U.S.P.T.O.ウェブページに掲載されています。

http://www.uspto.gov/aia_implementation/track-1-quickstart-guide.pdf

割増し料金を支払うことによる優先審査

TRACK1　請願書記入例（PTO／AIA／424）

```
Doc Code: TRACK1.REQ
Document Description: TrackOne Request
                                                              PTO/AIA/424 (04-14)

        CERTIFICATION AND REQUEST FOR PRIORITIZED EXAMINATION
                    UNDER 37 CFR 1.102(e) (Page 1 of 1)

First Named    Taro YAMADA             Nonprovisional Application Number (If
Inventor:                              known):
Title of       METHOD OF HITTING A BALL
Invention:

APPLICANT HEREBY CERTIFIES THE FOLLOWING AND REQUESTS PRIORITIZED E
THE ABOVE-IDENTIFIED APPLICATION.                    （出願の特定）

 1. The processing fee set forth in 37 CFR 1.17(i)(1) and the prioritized ex...
    37 CFR 1.17(c) have been filed with the request. The publication fee requir...
    because that fee, set forth in 37 CFR 1.18(d), is currently $0. The basic filing fee, search fee,
    and examination fee are filed with the request or have been already been paid. I understand
    that any required excess claims fees or application size fee must be paid for the application.

 2. I under... （新規出願時は　may not contain, or be amended to contain, more than four
    inde...  （ここをチェック）   irty total claims, or any multiple dependent claims, and that
    any ...                     me will cause an outstanding Track I request to be dismissed.

 3. The ap...  ecked below:

    I.  ☑ Original Application (Track One) - Prioritized Examination under § 1.102(e)(1)

    i.  (a) The application is an original nonprovisional utility application filed under 35 U.S.C. 111(a).
            This certification and request is being filed with the utility application via EFS-Web.
                                         ---OR---
        (b) The a...  iginal nonprovisional plant application filed under 35 U.S.C. 111(a).
            T...       t is being filed with the plant application in paper.
           （RCE提出時は）
    ii. An ...  （ここをチェック） claration under 37 CFR 1.63 or 37 CFR 1.64 for each
        inve...              sheet meeting the conditions specified in 37 CFR 1.53(f)(3)(i) is
        filed wi...

    II. ☐ Request for Continued Examination - Prioritized Examination under § 1.102(e)(2)

    i.   A request for continued examination has been filed with, or prior to, this form.
    ii.  If the application is a utility application, this certification and request is being filed via EFS-Web.
    iii. The application is an original nonprovisional utility application filed under 35 U.S.C. 111(a), or is
         a national stage entry under 35 U.S.C. 371.
    iv.  This certification and request is being filed prior to the mailing of a first Offic...
         to the request for continued examination.        （代理人情報と）
    v.   No prior request for continued examination has been granted prioritize  （代理人サイン）
         under 37 CFR 1.102(e)(2).

Signature /John Doe/                           Date April 1, 2018
Name                                           Practitioner
(Print/Typed)  John Doe                        Registration Number  99999

Note:  This form must be signed in accordance with 37 CFR 1.33. See CFR 1.4(d) for signature requirements and certifications.
       Submit multiple forms if more than one signature is required.

       ☐  "Total of _____ forms are submitted.
```

193

第6章　早期権利化のために―早期審査―

意匠出願の早期審査

　意匠出願の早期審査を請求することができます（37C.F.R.1.155）。出願人は意匠調査を行ったうえ先行文献をIDSとして提出し、所定の料金を支払います（37C.F.R.1.17(k)）。出願時に請求する場合は、PTO/SB/27を出願と同時に提出します。出願後に提出する場合は、U.S.P.T.O.にファクシミリを送ることができます。

> ワンポイント解説：早期審査のパイロットプログラム
> 　U.S.P.T.O.では、期間限定で試験的に早期審査を行うパイロットプログラムを導入しています。このパイロットプログラムの中には、外国出願人にとって有利であるプログラムや、先着ｘｘ件の出願のみ、というプログラムもありますので、これらの情報の入手にはアンテナを高くしておく必要があります。

意匠出願の早期審査

意匠出願早期審査請求書の例（PTO/SB/27）

Doc Code: ROCKET
Document Description: Req for Expedited Processing, Design Rocket Docket

→ 出願の特定

Approved for use through 07/31/... OMB 0651-0031
U.S. Patent and Trademark Office, U.S. DEPARTMENT OF COMMERCE
Under the Paperwork Reduction Act of 1995, no persons are required to respond to a collection of information unless it displays a valid OMB control number.

REQUEST FOR EXPEDITED EXAMINATION OF A DESIGN APPLICATION (37 CFR 1.155)

Application Number	29/xxx,xxx
Filing Date	01/05/2017
First Named Inventor	KATO, Jiro
Title	ELECTRIC GUITAR
Atty Docket Number	MLG.002.0002

ADDRESS TO:
MAIL STOP EXPEDITED DESIGN
COMMISSIONER OF PATENTS
P.O. Box 1450
Alexandria, VA 22313-1450

This is a request for expedited examination of a design application under 37 CFR 1.155.

NOTE: If the present form (PTO/SB/27) accompanies a new nonprovisional design application under 37 CFR 1.53(b), include form PTO/SB/18 "Design Patent Application Transmittal" or its equivalent. Do not include the present form (PTO/SB/27) on the date of filing a new international design application. For an international application to qualify for expedited examination, 37 CFR 1.155(a)(1) provides that ... application first must have been published by WIPO pursuant to Hague Agreement ...

→ 調査範囲を特定

... ch was conducted. The field of search was:

→ 関連出願を記入

Related applications: 29/yyy,yyyy

The following items are required under 37 CFR 1.155:
- Drawings in compliance with 37 CFR 1.84, unless the design application is an international design application that designates the United States and was published by WIPO pursuant to Hague Agreement Article 10(3).
- The fee set forth in 37 CFR 1.17(k).
- An information disclosure statement in compliance with 37 CFR 1.98.

Note: The Office will not grant a request for expedited examination if all of the requirements of 37 CFR 1.155 are not satisfied. In addition, the Office will not examine an application that is not in a condition for examination (e.g., missing basic filing fee) ... cant files a request for expedited examination under 37 CFR 1.155.

→ 代理人サイン

_____ _____
Signature   Date

_____ _____
Typed or printed name   Registration Number, if applicable

_____
Telephone Number

Warning: Information on this form may become public. Credit card information should not be included on this form. Provide credit card information and authorization on PTO-2038.

This collection of information is required by 37 CFR 1.48. The information is required to obtain or retain a benefit by the public which is to file (and by the USPTO to process) an application. Confidentiality is governed by 35 U.S.C. 122 and 37 CFR 1.11 and 1.14. This collection is estimated to take 1 hour to complete, including gathering, preparing, and submitting the completed application form to the USPTO. Time will vary depending upon the individual case. Any comments on the amount of time you require to complete this form and/or suggestions for reducing this burden, should be sent to the Chief Information Officer, U.S. Patent and Trademark Office, U.S. Department of Commerce, P.O. Box 1450, Alexandria, VA 22313-1450. DO NOT SEND FEES OR COMPLETED FORMS TO THIS ADDRESS. **SEND TO: Commissioner for Patents, P.O. Box 1450, Alexandria, VA 22313-1450.**

If you need assistance in completing the form, call 1-800-PTO-9199 and select option 2.

第7章 発明者決定手続

発明者決定手続とは

冒認出願への真発明者の手続き（35U.S.C.135）
　真の発明者の許可無しに第三者が真の発明者に係る出願より先の有効出願日を有する出願をした場合に、真の発明者に係る出願人は、発明者決定手続の請願することができます。請願書は第三者の出願の公開又は、特許から1年以内に行う必要があり、宣誓書及び冒認出願たる証拠と共に提出します（35U.S.C.135(a)）。発明者決定手続の請願は後願特許出願人であることを要します（35U.S.C.135(a), 37C.F.R.42.402）。従って、真の発明者であっても、特許出願がなされていない場合には冒認手続きの請願を行うことができません。また、真の発明者の出願は、冒認出願より後願である必要があります。

発明者決定手続の請願（37C.F.R.42.405）
　請願書には、以下の内容を含めます。
- 発明者決定手続き費用（37C.F.R.42.15(c)）
- 関係する出願や特許番号
- 請願者の特許出願の少なくとも1つのクレームが、1）被疑冒認者のクレームと同一または実質同一であり、2）被疑冒認者へ開示した発明と同一または実質同一である旨の説明
- クレームされた発明が、請願者の出願に係る発明者によりなされた発明で

第7章　発明者決定手続

ある旨の説明、及び冒認被疑者の出願は、その発明者の許可無くなされたものである説明
- 被疑冒認者のクレームが冒認被疑者に開示された発明と同一または実質同一である説明
- クレーム解釈に関する説明

請願者の手続き

- 提出された請願書に不備がある場合には、請願者は、不備の通知から1月または、法定期限(公開/特許から1年)以内に提出する必要があります。
- 請願書及び関連書類を冒認被疑者に係る出願の連絡先へ送付する必要があります(37C.F.R.42.406)。双方が合意すれば、電子メール等での送付も可能です。
- 請願書の提出(提出書類の不備が解消された日)、及び、被疑冒認者に係る出願の連絡先への関連書類の送付が完了して提出日が確定します(37C.F.R.42.407)。提出した請願書に不備があることも考慮して、余裕を持って提出する必要があります。

特許審判控訴部(PTAB)の決定

特許審判控訴部(Patent Trial and Appeal Board：PTAB)は、先願に係る発明が、請願人の出願に係る発明から派生したものであり、許可無しに出願がなされたものであるか否かを決定します(35U.S.C.135(b))。PTABは、特許出願若しくは特許の発明者の氏名を訂正することができます。また、PTABは、請願に係る冒認出願の特許発行後3月まで発明者の決定を遅らせることができます。また、先の特許が再審査(第30章)、当事者系レビュー(第31章)、またはPGR申立(第32章)の何れかの手続きに係属中の場合には、PTABは手続きの遅延や中断をすることがきます(35U.S.C.135(c))。ここで、PTABの決定は最終決定であり、特許出願に関しては該当するクレームはU.S.P.T.O.での最終拒絶とみなされます。また、特許に関しては控訴等されない場合には、該当するクレームのキャンセルとみなされ、特許証にその旨が記載されます(35U.S.C.135(d))。

冒認特許への真発明者の手続き（35U.S.C.291）

　真の発明者の許可無しに第三者が真の発明者に係る出願より先の有効出願日を有する出願が特許になった場合に、真の発明者に係る特許権者は、民事訴訟による救済を求めることができます。民事訴訟は第三者の特許から1年以内に行う必要があります（35U.S.C.291）。

冒認出願への手続きと冒認特許への手続きとの比較

　冒認出願／特許への発明者決定手続き（35U.S.C.135）と、冒認特許への発明者決定手続き（35U.S.C.291）とは以下のような相違点や共通点があります。

	35U.S.C.135	35U.S.C.291
対象	特許出願又は特許	特許
期間	出願公開又は特許の何れか早い方から1年以内	特許から1年
基準日	有効出願日	有効出願日
提出先	U.S.P.T.O.	裁判所

ワンポイント解説：発明者決定手続の導入、インターフェアレンス手続の廃止

　上記発明者決定手続制度は今回の改正で導入されました。また、先願主義への移行でインターフェアレンス手続きは廃止になりました。

ワンポイント解説：発明者決定手続き

　英語の正式名称はDerivation Proceedingsです。用語Derivationには「由来、起源」という意味であり、当該発明はどちらの発明者から由来されたものかを決定する手続き、という意味です。

第8章 許可通知及び特許の維持

許可通知の発行

許可通知

審査官が特許すべきと判断した場合には、許可通知 (Notice of Allowance) を発行します。(37C.F.R.1. 311(a), M.P.E.P.1303)。許可通知には出願の書誌的事項の表示の他、登録料納付書が表示されます。また、許可の具体的な内容は、許可可能通知(Notice of Allowability)に記載されます(M.P.E.P.1302.03)。許可可能通知には、許可されたクレームや優先権書類受領の有無等の表示がされます。ここで、この許可可能通知には、審査官は、軽微な誤りを訂正する目的で許可通知に審査官補正 (Examiner's Amendment) を付することがあります (M.P.E.P.1302.04)。また、審査官は、許可可能通知には、許可理由 (Reasons for Allowance) を付することがあります (37C.F.R.1. 104(e), M.P.E.P.1302. 14)。ここで、出願人は許可理由が非常に限定的な記載であった場合などには当該許可通知に承服できない場合が起こり得ます。この場合には、出願人は、陳述書 (Statement) で当該許可理由に対して反論をすることができます (37C.F.R.1. 104(e))。

許可通知後の補正

許可通知後で且つ発行料納付前の出願書類の補正については、出願人にはその権利はありません。許可を取り下げずに補正を認めるか否かは審査官の裁量

第8章　許可通知及び特許の維持

によります（37C.F.R.1.312）。なお、特許発行料納付後に補正する場合は、特許発行を取り下げるための請願書を提出する必要があります（37C.F.R.1.313(a)）。

許可通知の例（PTOL-85）

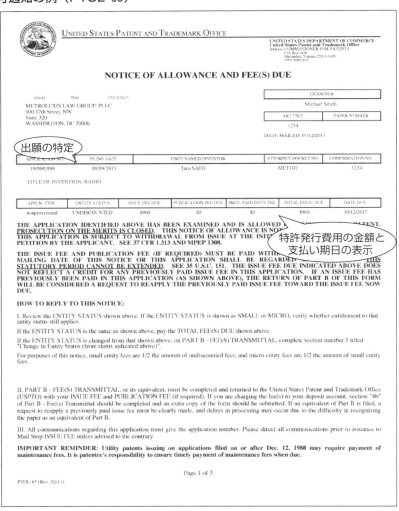

許可通知の例（PTOL–85）の続き

PART B - FEE(S) TRANSMITTAL

Complete and send this form, together with applicable fee(s), to: Mail **Mail Stop ISSUE FEE**
Commissioner for
P.O. Box 1450
Alexandria, Virgi
or Fax (571)-273-2885

２ページ目は特許発行料
支払いの送付状となる

INSTRUCTIONS: This form should be used for transmitting the ISSUE FEE and PUBLICATION FEE (if required). appropriate. All further correspondence including the Patent, advance orders and notification of maintenance fees will b to the current correspondence address as indicated unless corrected below or directed otherwise in Block 1, by (a) specifying a new correspondence address; and/or (b) indicating a separate "FEE ADDRESS" for maintenance fee notifications.

CURRENT CORRESPONDENCE ADDRESS (Note: Use Block 1 for any change of address)

65181 7590 08/16/2017
METROLEXIS LAW GROUP, PLLC
900 17th Street, NW.
Suite 320
WASHINGTON, DC 20006

Note: A certificate of mailing can only be used for domestic mailings of the Fee(s) Transmittal. This certificate cannot be used for any other accompanying papers. Each additional paper, such as an assignment or formal drawing, must have its own certificate of mailing or transmission.

Certificate of Mailing or Transmission
I hereby certify that this Fee(s) Transmittal is being deposited with the United States Postal Service with sufficient postage for first class mail in an envelope addressed to the Mail Stop ISSUE FEE address above, or being facsimile transmitted to the USPTO (571) 273-2885, on the date indicated below.

(Depositor's name)
(Signature)
(Date)

APPLICATION NO.	FILING DATE	FIRST NAMED INVENTOR	ATTORNEY DOCKET NO.	CONFIRMATION NO.
19/999,999	09/09/2015	Taro SATO	MET101	1234

TITLE OF INVENTION: RADIO

APPLN. TYPE	ENTITY STATUS	ISSUE FEE DUE	PUBLICATION FEE DUE	PREV. PAID ISSUE FEE	TOTAL FEE(S) DUE	DATE DUE
nonprovisional	UNDISCOUNTED	$960	$0	$0	$960	11/16/2017

EXAMINER	ART UNIT	CLASS-SUBCLASS
Michael Smith	1234	123-123000

1. Change of correspondence address or indication of "Fee Address" (37 CFR 1.363).
   - ❑ Change of correspondence address (or Change of Correspondence Address form PTO/SB/122) attached.
   - ❑ "Fee Address" indication (or "Fee Address" Indication form PTO/SB/47; Rev 03-02 or more recent) attached. **Use of a Customer Number is required.**

2. For printing on the patent front page, list
   (1) The names of up to 3 registered patent attorneys or agents OR, alternatively,
   (2) The name of a single firm (having as a member a registered attorney or agent) and the names of up to 2 registered patent attorneys or agents. If no name is listed, no name will be printed.
   1 ____
   2 ____
   3 ____

3. ASSIGNEE NAME AND RESIDENCE DATA TO BE PRINTED ON THE PATENT (print or type)
   PLEASE NOTE: Unless an assignee is identified below, no assignee data will appear on the patent. If an assignee is identified below, the document has been filed for recordation as set forth in 37 CFR 3.11. Completion of this form is NOT a substitute for filing an assignment.
   (A) NAME OF ASSIGNEE (B) RESIDENCE: (CITY and STATE OR COUNTRY)

Please check the appropriate assignee category or categories (will not be printed on the patent) : ❑ Individual ❑ Corporation or other private group entity ❑ Government

4a. The following fee(s) are submitted:
- ❑ Issue Fee
- ❑ Publication Fee (No small entity discount permitted)
- ❑ Advance Order - # of Copies ____

4b. Payment of Fee(s): **(Please first reapply any previously paid issue fee shown above)**
- ❑ A check is enclosed.
- ❑ Payment by credit card. Form PTO-2038 is attached.
- ❑ The director is hereby authorized to charge the required fee(s), any deficiency, or credits any overpayment, to Deposit Account Number ____ (enclose an extra copy of this form).

5. **Change in Entity Status** (from status indicated above)
- ❑ Applicant certifying micro entity status. See 37 CFR 1.29 — NOTE: Absent a valid certification of Micro Entity Status (see forms PTO/SB/15A and 15B), issue fee payment in the micro entity amount will not be accepted at the risk of application abandonment.
- ❑ Applicant asserting small entity status. See 37 CFR 1.27 — NOTE: If the application was previously under micro entity status, checking this box will be taken to be a notification of loss of entitlement to micro entity status.
- ❑ Applicant changing to regular undiscounted fee status. — NOTE: Checking this box will be taken to be a notification of loss of entitlement to small or micro entity status, as applicable.

NOTE: This form must be signed in accordance with 37 CFR 1.31 and 1.33. See 37 CFR 1.4 for signature requirements and certifications.

Authorized Signature ____ Date ____

Typed or printed name ____ Registration No. ____

Page 2 of 3

PTOL-85 Part B (10-13) Approved for use through 10/31/2013. OMB 0651-0033 U.S. Patent and Trademark Office; U.S. DEPARTMENT OF COMMERCE

第 8 章　許可通知及び特許の維持

許可通知の例（PTOL-85）の続き

5. Change in Entity Status (from status indicated above)
☐ Applicant certifying micro entity status. See 37 CFR 1.29
☐ Applicant asserting small entity status. See 37 CFR 1.27
☐ Applicant changing to regular undiscounted fee status.

NOTE: Absent a valid certification of Micro Entity Status (see form PTO/SB/15A and 15B), issue fee payment in the micro entity amount will not be accepted at the risk of application abandonment.

NOTE: If the application was previously under micro entity status, checking this box will be taken to be a notification of loss of entitlement to micro entity status.

NOTE: Checking this box will be taken to be a notification of loss of entitlement to small or micro entity status, as applicable.

NOTE: The Issue Fee and Publication Fee (if required) will not be accepted from anyone other than the applicant; a registered attorney or agent; or the assignee or other party in interest as shown by the records of the United States Patent and Trademark Office.

Authorized Signature _____　　Date _____

Typed or printed name _____　　Registration No. _____

This collection of information is required by 37 CFR 1.311. The information is required to obtain or retain a benefit by the public which is to file (and by the USPTO to process) an application. Confidentiality is governed by 35 U.S.C. 122 and 37 CFR 1.14. This collection is estimated to take 12 minutes to complete, including gathering, preparing, and submitting the completed application form to the USPTO. Time will vary depending upon the individual case. Any comments on the amount of time you require to complete this form and/or suggestions for reducing this burden, should be sent to the Chief Information Officer, U.S. Patent and Trademark Office, U.S. Department of Commerce, P.O. Box 1450, Alexandria, Virginia 22313-1450. DO NOT SEND FEES OR COMPLETED FORMS TO THIS ADDRESS. SEND TO: Commissioner for Patents, P.O. Box 1450, Alexandria, Virginia 22313-1450.

Under the Paperwork Reduction Act of 1995, no persons are required to respond to a collection of information unless it displays a valid OMB control number.

Page 3 of 4

PTOL-85 (Rev. 02/11) Approved for use through 08/31/2013.　　OMB 0651-0033　　U.S. Patent and Trademark Office; U.S. DEPARTMENT OF COMMERCE

許可通知の発行

特許期間調整決定の通知（PTOL-85）

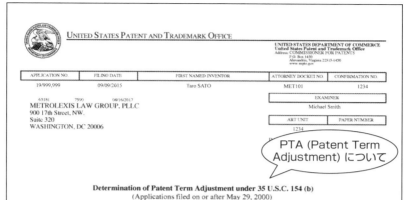

PTA (Patent Term Adjustment) について

Determination of Patent Term Adjustment under 35 U.S.C. 154 (b)
(Applications filed on or after May 29, 2000)

The Office has discontinued providing a Patent Term Adjustment (PTA) calculation with the Notice of Allowance.

Section 1(h)(2) of the AIA Technical Corrections Act amended 35 U.S.C. 154(b)(3)(B)(i) to eliminate the requirement that the Office provide a patent term adjustment determination with the notice of allowance. See Revisions to Patent Term Adjustment, 78 Fed. Reg. 19416, 19417 (Apr. 1, 2013). Therefore, the Office is no longer providing an initial patent term adjustment determination with the notice of allowance. The Office will continue to provide a patent term adjustment determination with the Issue Notification Letter that is mailed to applicant approximately three weeks prior to the issue date of the patent, and will include the patent term adjustment on the patent. Any request for reconsideration of the patent term adjustment determination (or reinstatement of patent term adjustment) should follow the process outlined in 37 CFR 1.705.

Any questions regarding the Patent Term Extension or Adjustment determination should be directed to the Office of Patent Legal Administration at (571)-272-7702. Questions relating to issue and publication fee payments should be directed to the Customer Service Center of the Office of Patent Publication at 1-(888)-786-0101 or (571)-272-4200.

許可可能通知の例（PTOL–37）

Notice of Allowability

Applica… …nt(s)

> 許可されたクレーム、外国優先権書類の受領等の表示

-- *The MAILING DATE of this communication a…* --

All claims being allowable, PROSECUTION ON THE MERITS … herewith (or previously mailed), a Notice of Allowance (PTOL-85) … course. **THIS NOTICE OF ALLOWABILITY IS NOT A GRANT OF PATENT RIGH…** … issue at the initiative of the Office or upon petition by the applicant. See 37 CFR 1.313 and …

1. ☒ This communication is responsive to _02/08/2008_.
2. ☒ The allowed claim(s) is/are _6,9,14-17,22,23,25,31-34,36 … 45_.
3. ☒ Acknowledgment is made of a claim for foreign prio… under 35 U.S.C. § 119(a)-(d) or (f).
   a) ☒ All　b) ☐ Some*　c) ☐ None　of the:
   1. ☒ Certified copies of the priority documents have been received.
   2. ☐ Certified copies of the priority documents have been received in Application No. ______ .
   3. ☐ Copies of the certified copies of the priority documents have been received in this national stage application from the International Bureau (PCT Rule 17.2(a)).

   * Certified copies not received: ______.

Applicant has THREE MONTHS FROM THE "MAILING DATE" of this communication to file a reply complying with the requirements noted below. Failure to timely comply will result in ABANDONMENT of this application.
THIS THREE-MONTH PERIOD IS NOT EXTENDABLE.

4. ☐ A SUBSTITUTE OATH OR DECLARATION must be submitted. Note the attached EXAMINER'S AMENDMENT or NOTICE OF INFORMAL PATENT APPLICATION (PTO-152) which gives reason(s) why the oath or declaration is deficient.
5. ☐ CORRECTED DRAWINGS (as "replacement sheets") must be submitted.
   (a) ☐ including changes required by the Notice of Draftsperson's Patent Drawing Review (PTO-948)
   1) ☐ hereto or 2) ☐ to Paper No./Mail Date ______.
   (b) ☐ including changes required by the attached Examiner's Amendment / Comment or in the … Paper No./Mail Date ______.

   Identifying indicia such as the application number (see 37 CFR 1.84(c)) should be written on the draw… each sheet. Replacement sheet(s) should be labeled as such in the header according to 37 CFR 1.121(…
6. ☐ DEPOSIT OF and/or INFORMATION about the deposit of BIOLOGICAL MATERIAL mus… attached Examiner's comment regarding REQUIREMENT FOR THE DEPOSIT OF BIOLOGICAL …

> 許可可能通知に添付された書類の表示

Attachment(s)

1. ☐ Notice of References Cited (PTO-892)
2. ☐ Notice of Draftperson's Patent Drawing Review (PTO-948)
3. ☐ Information Disclosure Statements (PTO/SB/08), Paper No./Mail Date _____
4. ☐ Examiner's Comment Regarding Requirement for Deposit of Biological Material
5. ☐ Notice of Informal Patent Application
6. ☐ Interview Summary (PTO-413), Paper No./Mail Date _____ .
7. ☒ Examiner's Amendment/Comment
8. ☒ Examiner's Statement of Reasons for Allowance
9. ☐ Other _____.

/Lincoln Donovan/
SPE AU 2837

U.S. Patent and Trademark Office
PTOL-37 (Rev. 08-06)　　**Notice of Allowability**

許可通知の発行

許可可能通知の例（PTOL-37）の続き

Application/Contr○ ... Page 2
Art Unit: 2837

（審査官による職権補正の表示）

EXAMINER'S AMENDMENT

1. An examiner's amendment to the record appears below. Should the changes and/or additions be unacceptable to applicant, an amendment may be filed as provided by 37 CFR 1.312. To ensure consideration of such an amendment, it MUST be submitted no later than the payment of the issue fee.

Authorization for this examiner's amendment was given in a telephone interview with Marvin Motsenbocker on February 21, 2008.

The application has been amended as follows:

Claims

（審査官によるクレームに関する職権補正の表示）

- On page 3 of the claims, Claim 14 line 1, after the number '14.' add – (Previously presented)—
- On page 3 of the claims, Claim 1○ ... (Previously presented)—
- On page 3 of the claims, Claim 16 li○ ... (Previously presented)—
- On page 3 of the claims, Claim 17 line 1, after the number '17.' add – (Previously presented)—
- On page 3 of the claims, Claim 22 line 1, after the number '22.' add – (Previously presented)—

第8章　許可通知及び特許の維持

許可可能通知の例（PTOL-37）の続き

許可可能通知の例（PTOL-37）の続き

> 本件情報については、PAIR (Patent Application Information Retrieval)においても入手可能な旨の表示

```
Application/Contro...                                    Page 5
Art Unit: 2837

    Information regarding the status of an application may be obtained from the
Patent Application Information Retrieval (PAIR) system. Status information for
published applications may be obtained from either Private PAIR or Public PAIR.
Status information for unpublished applications is available through Private PAIR only.
For more information about the PAIR system, see http://pair-direct.uspto.gov. Should
you have questions on access to the Private PAIR system, contact the Electronic
Business Center (EBC) at 866-217-9197 (toll-free). If you would like assistance from a
USPTO Customer Service Representative or access to the automated information
system, call 800-786-9199 (IN USA OR CANADA) or 571-272-1000.


/John M. DOE/
Examiner, Art Unit 2837
August 25, 2012

 /Jane SMITH/
Supervisory Patent Examiner, Art Unit 2837
```

特許発行料の支払

　出願人は、許可通知の日から3月以内に特許発行料（Issue Fee）を支払う必要があります。当該期限内に特許発行料を支払わないと、出願放棄とみなされます（37C.F.R.1.316）。

　ここで、注意したいのは、特許発行料の支払い（3月）は延長することができないという点です。特許発行料の支払いは、許可通知に添付された送付状を用いて行います。

特許発行料支払い送付状の例

PART B - FEE(S) TRANSMITTAL

Complete and send this form, together with applicable fee(s), to: Mail **Mail Stop ISSUE FEE**
Commissioner for Patents
P.O. Box 1450
Alexandria, Virginia 22313-1450
or Fax (571)-273-2885

INSTRUCTIONS: This form should be used for transmitting the ISSUE FEE and PUBLICATION FEE (if required). Blocks 1 through 5 should be completed where appropriate. All further correspondence including the Patent, advance orders and notification of maintenance fees will be mailed to the current correspondence address as indicated unless corrected below or directed otherwise in Block 1, by (a) specifying a new correspondence address; and/or (b) indicating a separate "FEE ADDRESS" for maintenance fee notifications.

CURRENT CORRESPONDENCE ADDRESS (Note: Use Block 1 for any change of address)

65181　7590　06/06/2013
MOTS LAW, PLLC
1629 K STREET N.W.
SUITE 200
WASHINGTON, DC 20006-1635

Note: A certificate of mailing can only be used for domestic mailings of the Fee(s) Transmittal. This certificate cannot be used for any other accompanying papers. Each additional paper, such as an assignment or formal drawing, must have its own certificate of mailing or transmission.

Certificate of Mailing or Transmission
I hereby certify that this Fee(s) Transmittal is being deposited with the United States Postal Service with sufficient postage for first class mail in an envelope addressed to the Mail Stop ISSUE FEE address above, or being facsimile transmitted to the USPTO (571) 273-2885, on the date indicated below.

(Depositor's name)
(Signature)
(Date)

出願の特定

特許証に譲受人情報を掲載したい場合には記入する。大文字／小文字を含めてその通り特許証に掲載される

特許発行費用の金額と期日支払い期日の表示（延長不可）

	FILING DATE	FIRST NAMED INVENTOR	ATTORNEY DO

TITY STATUS	ISSUE FEE DUE	PUBLICATION FEE DUE	PREV. PAID ISSUE FEE	TOTAL FEE(S) D
DISCOUNTED		$0	$0	

R	ART UNIT	CLASS-SUBCLASS

…dence address or indication of "Fee Address" (37 …
…orrespondence address (or Change of Correspondence … TO/SB/122) attached.
☐ "Fe… s" indication (or "Fee Address" Indication form PTO/SB… 03-02 or more recent) attached. Use of a Customer Number … ired.

2. For printing on the patent front page, list
(1) the names of up to 3 registered patent attorneys or agents OR, alternatively,　1________
(2) the name of a single firm (having as a member a registered attorney or agent) and the names of up to 2 registered patent attorneys or agents. If no name is listed, no name will be printed.　2________　3________

3. ASSIGNEE … E AND RESIDENCE DATA TO BE PRINTED ON THE PATENT (print or type)
PLEASE NO… Unless an assignee is identified below, no assignee data will appear on the patent. If an assignee is identified below, the document has been filed for recordation as … forth in 37 CFR 3.11. Completion of this form is NOT a substitute for filing an assignment.
(A) NAME OF … SIGNEE　(B) RESIDENCE: (CITY and STATE OR COUNTRY)

Please check the appropriate assignee category or categories (will not be printed on the patent) : ☐ Individual ☐ Corporation or other private group entity ☐ Government

4a. The following fee(s) are submitted:
☐ Issue Fee
☐ Publication Fee (No small entity discount permitted)
☐ Advance Order - # of Copies ________

4b. Payment of Fee(s): **(Please first reapply any pr… usly paid issue fee shown above)**
☐ A check is enclosed.
☐ Payment by credit card. Form PTO-2038 is attache…
☐ The Director is hereby authorized to charge the requir… any … overpayment, to Deposit Account Number ________

譲受人が法人の場合にはここにチェック

支払費用項目及び支払方法の特定：特許発行料／出願公開料／特許証のソフトコピーの追加注文（@$3）

Page 2 of 4

特許発行料の支払

特許発行料支払い送付状の例の続き

```
5. Change in Entity Status (from status indicated above)
  ☐ Applicant certifying micro entity status. See 37 CFR 1.29      NOTE: Absent a valid certification of Micro Entity Status (see form PTO/SB/15A and 15B), issue
                                                                   fee payment in the micro entity amount will not be accepted at the risk of application abandonment.
  ☐ Applicant asserting small entity status. See 37 CFR 1.27       NOTE: If the application was previously under micro entity status, checking this box will be taken
                                                                   to be a notification of loss of entitlement to micro entity status.
  ☐ Applicant changing to regular undiscounted fee status.         NOTE: Checking this box will be taken to be a notification of loss of entitlement to small or micro
                                                                   entity status, as applicable.
NOTE: The Issue Fee and Publication Fee (if required) will not be accepted from anyone other than the applicant; a registered attorney or agent; or the assignee or other party in
interest as shown by the records of the United States Patent and Trademark Office.

Authorized Signature _____        Date _____

Typed or printed name _____       Registration No. _____

This collection of information is required by 37 CFR 1.311. The information is required to obtain or retain a benefit by the public which is to file (and by the USPTO to process)
an application. Confidentiality is governed by 35 U.S.C. 122 and 37 CFR 1.14. This collection is estimated to take 12 minutes to complete, including gathering, preparing, and
submitting the completed application form to the USPTO. Time will vary depending upon the individual case. Any comments on the amount of time you require to complete
this form and/or suggestions for reducing this burden, should be sent to the Chief Information Officer, U.S. Patent and Trademark Office, U.S. Department of Commerce, P.O.
Box 1450, Alexandria, Virginia 22313-1450. DO NOT SEND FEES OR COMPLETED FORMS TO THIS ADDRESS. SEND TO: Commissioner for Patents, P.O. Box 1450,
Alexandria, Virginia 22313-1450.
Under the Paperwork Reduction Act of 1995, no persons are required to respond to a collection of information unless it displays a valid OMB control number.
```

（吹き出し）出願人の規模に変更があった場合には、ここへチェック

PTOL-85 (Rev. 02/11) Approved for use through 08/31/2013.　　OMB 0651-0033　　U.S. Patent and Trademark Office; U.S. DEPARTMENT OF COMMERCE

第8章　許可通知及び特許の維持

特許発行料支払前に確認すべきこと

　一旦特許発行料を支払ってしまうと安全に行う事ができなくなる可能性がある手続きがあります。以下は特許発行料支払前に確認すべき事項です。

継続的出願の必要の有無の確認

　分割出願を含む継続的出願は、上記特許証の発行前までに手続きを完了しなければなりません。一度特許証が発行されてしまうと、継続的出願を出願できなくなってしまうため、実務では、安全のため、特許発行料の納付時までに継続的出願の出願を完了することが肝要です。確認方法としては、選択／限定指令の有無が一つの指標になります。

未提出先行技術文献の有無の確認

　出願人等の情報開示義務は、特許証が発行されるまで続きます。実務では、安全のため、特許発行料の納付前に未提出の先行技術文献の有無を確認することが肝要です。また、提出済みのIDSも審査官が確認した旨のサインがあるか否かを確認します。具体的には提出済みのPTO／SB／08に掲げた引用例について各々審査官のサインが付されているかを確認します。

譲渡証提出の有無の確認

　発明者から発明者が属する企業への譲渡を証する書面の提出は、特許発行料支払いの前までに行うようにします。

その他、書誌的事項等の確認

　許可通知、許可可能通知に記載された許可理由への反論の有無の確認、発明の名称や、発明者氏名等の書誌的事項の再度の確認、優先権書類は認知されたかの確認等を行います。

```
┌─────────────────────────────────────────────┐
│         特許発行料支払い前のチェックリスト       │
│                                             │
│   ☐  継続的出願の必要の有無の確認              │
│      （限定／選択指令があるか？）              │
│                                             │
│   ☐  未提出先行技術文献の有無の確認            │
│                                             │
│   ☐  譲渡証／宣誓証提出の有無の確認            │
│                                             │
│   ☐  許可通知、許可可能通知に記載された許可理由への │
│      反論の有無の確認                         │
│                                             │
│   ☐  発明の名称や、発明者氏名等の書誌的事項の再度の │
│      確認                                    │
│                                             │
└─────────────────────────────────────────────┘
```

特許発行料支払から特許発行まで

　特許発行料支払いが完了すると、U.S.P.T.O.は特許証の発行の準備を行い、準備が整った場合には、特許証（Letters Patent）発行の約20日前に特許証発行通知（Issue Notification）が発せられます。その後、特許証が発行され、出願人に送付されます。

第8章　許可通知及び特許の維持

特許発行通知の例

特許発行の延期（37C.F.R.1.314）

　U.S.P.T.O.または出願人は、一定の要件の下に特許発行を遅らせることができます（37C.F.R.1.314, M.P.E.P.1306.01）。出願人は特許発行料支払い後、請願書を提出することができます。この請願が認められれば、特許証発行を延期させることができます。特許発行料支払い前に請願書の提出は認められず、特許発行料を支払った後に請願書の提出を要する点に注意が必要です（M.P.E.P.1306.01）。特殊な状況にある場合や規則（e.g., 37C.F.R.1.177）による場合を除き、延期可能な期間は、1月以内です（M.P.E.P.1306.01）。

特許発行の取下げ（37C.F.R.1.313）

　U.S.P.T.O.または出願人は、一定の要件の下に特許発行の取り上げをすることができます（37C.F.R.1.313(a), M.P.E.P.1308）。

　特許発行料支払い前の場合、出願人は、取下げが必要な正当かつ十分な理由を示した請願書の提出が必要になります（37C.F.R.1.313(a)）。ただし、RCEをする場合には、請願書を提出する必要はありません（37C.F.R.1.313(a)）。

　特許発行料支払い後の場合、出願人は請願書を提出の上、下記に掲げる理由の場合にのみ特許発行の取り下げが認められます（37C.F.R.1.313(c)）。

- 許可されたクレームに非特許性事由がある場合。この場合には、以下を提出する必要があります。
  - ➢請願書に、そのクレームは非特許事由がある、と明確な表示
  - ➢補正書
  - ➢補正書によってクレームが特許性がある旨の説明
- RCEを考慮するため
- 出願の放棄を行うため（その前に継続的出願を行う場合の考慮）

　ただし、上記の請願書を適切に提出した場合であっても、特許発行前までに、その請願書が受理され、認められなければならない点に注意が必要です（37C.F.R.1.313(d)）。

第 8 章　許可通知及び特許の維持

特許の維持年金

　特許発行料（37C.F.R.1.18(a)）には、第 1 年分から第 4 年分の特許権の維持費（Maintenance Fee）が含まれます。特許権者がそれ以降も継続して特許権を維持したい場合には、以下の期限内に維持費を支払わなければなりません（37C.F.R.1.362(d), 20(e)-(g)）。

維持年金の支払い期間を徒過した場合
　特許維持年金の支払い期間を徒過した場合の救済措置として、これらの期間経過後であっても、6月の猶予期間以内であれば、追加料金（37C.F.R.1.20(h)）支払の上で維持費の支払いが認められます（37C.F.R.1.362(e)）。

上記猶予期間をも徒過した場合の取得る措置
　更に上記猶予期間をも徒過した場合には、以下の条件を満たした場合にのみ維持年金の支払いが認められます（37C.F.R.1.378）。
維持年金の支払いの遅延が意図しない場合
　意図せず維持年金の支払いが行えなかった場合には、下記の手続きを 2 年以内に行うことが、救済を受ける事ができます（37C.F.R.1.378(c)）。本救済を受ける場合には、維持年金の未払いが意図しないものであったという陳述書を提出すれば足ります。例としては、支払い忘れの場合であってもこの適用を受けることができます。その一方、意図的に支払いを行わなかった場合（例えば、維持年金の支払い時に支払いを行わないと決定があった等）には本適用を受けることができません。一般的には、上記維持年金支払いの遅延が不可避であった場合の救済よりも簡易に認められます。
- 支払うべき維持年金（37C.F.R.1.20(e)-(g)）
- 追加料金（37C.F.R.1.17(m)）
- 維持年金の未支払いが意図しないものであったという陳述

ワンポイント解説：手続きの遅延が不意図（Unintentional）な場合
　維持年金の支払い手続き以外であっても、U.S.P.T.O.への手続きが意図せずに遅延してしまった場合、期間満了後も支払いや提出が認められる場合があります。これはうっかり忘れていた、という場合も含まれます。この場合、遅延が不意図である旨のステートメントを提出すれば足ります。本適用を受けるためには、不意図である必要がありますので、意図的に支払いを行わなかった場合（例えば、局指令に応答しないと決定した旨の証拠が残っていた場合等）には本適用を受けることができません。なお、従前は、遅延が不可避（Unavoidable）な場合の規定もありましたが、2013年12月18日に削除されました。

第9章

特許の修正

　特許証の発行後、特許証に記載された書誌事項が誤っていることに気づいたり、特許クレームの範囲が狭すぎたり等、特許証の記載に修正を加えたい場合が生じます。このようなときには、特許権者等は、修正内容に応じて、以下のような手段で特許証を修正することができます。

訂正証明書の請求 (Certificate of Correction)

訂正証明書の請求制度とは
　特許証中の書誌事項などの些細な誤記を修正する場合には、訂正証明書の請求を行います(35U.S.C.254、255)。この誤記はU.S.P.T.O.の過失による場合と、出願人の軽微な錯誤によって生じた場合とが考えられますが、このどちらも認められます。
　請求主体：特許権者
　修正内容（よくある事例）
　● 発明者や特許権者の名前や住所のタイプミス、スペル間違い、など
　● 明細書中の符号の明らかな間違い
　提出時期：特許証の発行後、随時

U.S.P.T.O.の過失の場合（35U.S.C.254）
　U.S.P.T.O.の過失によって生じた特許証における錯誤がU.S.P.T.O.の記録によって明らかになった場合は、特許の記録に記録されるべき当該錯誤の事実及び内容を記載した訂正証明書に印章を付して<u>無償</u>で発行されます。ここで、訂

正証明書の写しは、そのまま特許証に添付され、当該証明書は、原特許の一部とみなされます。

出願人の錯誤の場合（35U.S.C.255）

事務的若しくは印刷上の錯誤又は軽微な錯誤であって、U.S.P.T.O.の過失でないものが特許証に表示されており、当該錯誤が善意で生じた場合には、特許権者は、手数料を納付した上で訂正証明書の請求を行うことができます。ここで、上記訂正が新規事項を構成するか又は再審査を必要とするような、特許に関する変更を生じさせないことが条件です。

訂正証明書の請求の手続

提出書類：送付状、訂正証明書（PTO/SB/44）

訂正証明書の請求が受入れられると、請求された訂正証明書がそのまま反映されて発行されます。発行された証明書は特許証の一部と見なされ、その特許が初めから訂正された形で発行されていた場合と同一の法律上の効力を有します。

訂正証明書請求の手数料

- U.S.P.T.O.の過失によって生じた特許証における錯誤の場合は無料です。
- 特許権者（出願人）に起因する場合は、費用（37C.F.R.1.20）が発生します。

訂正証明書の請求 (Certificate of Correction)

訂正証明書の記入例 (PTO/SB/44)

PTO/SB/44 (09-07)
Approved for use through 08/31/2013. OMB 0651-0033
U.S. Patent and Trademark Office; U.S. DEPARTMENT OF COMMERCE
Under the Paperwork Reduction Act of 1995, no persons are required to respond to a collection of information unless it displays a valid OMB control number.
(Also Form PTO-1050)

UNITED STATES PATENT AND TRADEMARK OFFICE
CERTIFICATE OF CORRECTION

(特許を特定)

Page __1__ of __1__

PATENT NO. : xxx,xxxx
APPLICATION NO. : 13/xxx,xxx
ISSUE DATE : 04/04/2011
INVENTOR(S) : YAMADA, Taro

It is certified that an error appears or errors appear in the above-identified patent and that said Letters Patent is hereby corrected as shown below:

Column 12, line 34, "on" should be --of--;
Column 13, lines 3, 4, replace "101" with --102-- (both occurrences)

(修正したい事項を記入)

MAILING ADDRESS OF SENDER (Please do not use customer number below):

This collection of information is required by 37 CFR 1.322; 1.323, and 1.324. The information is required to obtain or retain a benefit by the public which is to file (and by the USPTO to process) an application. Confidentiality is governed by 35 U.S.C. 122 and 37 CFR 1.14. This collection is estimated to take 1.0 hour to complete, including gathering, preparing, and submitting the completed application form to the USPTO. Time will vary depending upon the individual case. Any comments on the amount of time you require to complete this form and/or suggestions for reducing this burden, should be sent to the Chief Information Officer, U.S. Patent and Trademark Office, U.S. Department of Commerce, P.O. Box 1450, Alexandria, VA 22313-1450. DO NOT SEND FEES OR COMPLETED FORMS TO THIS ADDRESS. SEND TO: **Attention Certificate of Corrections Branch, Commissioner for Patents, P.O. Box 1450, Alexandria, VA 22313-1450.**

If you need assistance in completing the form, call 1-800-PTO-9199 and select option 2.

第9章　特許の修正

再発行特許制度（Reissue Patent）

再発行特許制度とは

　詐欺的意図のない錯誤があったために、明細書若しくは図面の瑕疵を理由として、又は特許権者が特許においてクレームする権利を有していたものより多く又は少なくクレームしていることを理由として、特許がその全部若しくは一部において効力を生じない若しくは無効とみなされる場合に、再発行特許出願をすることができます（35U.S.C.271）。

　請求主体：特許権者

　請求時期：特許発行日から2年以内に再発行特許出願を行う場合にはクレームの拡大も認められます。ただし、選択/限定指令で非選択になったクレームセットを分割出願し忘れた場合や、審査中に放棄されたクレームについては、再発行特許で取り戻すこと（Recapture）はできません。

　修正内容（よくある事例）：
- 特許の明細書、図面の記載が不正確だった
- 発明者の記載に不備があった
- クレームの範囲が広すぎた、または狭すぎた
- 優先権主張をしていなかった、または誤って主張していた
- 先の出願の優先権を主張する旨の記載を含めていなかった

　提出時期：特許が有効な期間に随時（但し、クレームの範囲を拡張する場合は、特許日から2年以内）

再発行特許出願の提出書類

- 送付状（PTO/AIA/50）
- 再発行出願用の宣誓書（発明者：PTO/AIA/05、または譲受されている場合：PTO/AIA/06）
- 総ての譲受人の同意書/無譲渡の陳述書（PTO/AIA/53）
- 特許権者である旨の陳述書（PTO/AIA/96）
- 明細書（特許証の写しをそのまま使用する；2コラムのレイアウトのもの）
- 図面（特許証の写しをそのまま使用する）

再発行特許制度 (Reissue Patent)

- 自発補正書（クレーム、明細書、図面における補正する内容を記載）

再発行特許出願手数料（37C.F.R.1.16(e)(h)(i)(s)）

出願料金は、基本料金、サーチ料金、審査料金が含まれます。また、明細書中の独立クレーム、複数従属クレームの有無、クレーム全体数（独立クレームと従属クレームの総数）が一定数を超えると超過料金が発生します。

再発行特許出願の手続

特許権者は再発行特許出願時に一旦特許を放棄します。再発行特許出願後は、通常の特許出願と同様に審査されますが、審査は早期審査の特別扱いになります（M.P.E.P.1442）。再発行特許の特許証には、親特許から削除された部分は［　］で示され、追加部分はイタリック体で記載されます。

第9章 特許の修正

再発行特許の送付状（PTO/AIA/50）

（代理人整理番号、筆頭発明者、特許番号等の記入）

（提出書類をチェック）

再発行特許制度（Reissue Patent）

再発行特許の発明者宣誓書（PTO/AIA/05）

Doc Code: REIS.DECL
Document Description: Reissue Declaration Filed In Accordance With MPEP 1414

PTO/AIA/05 (06-12)
Approved for use through 08/31/2013. OMB 0651-0033
U.S. Patent and Trademark Office; U.S. DEPARTMENT OF COMMERCE
Under the Paperwork Reduction Act of 1995, no persons are required to respond to a collection of information unless it displays a valid OMB

| REISSUE APPLICATION DECLARATION BY THE INVENTOR | Docket Number (Optional) |

（明細書を添付する場合にチェック）

（新法下の3つの宣誓文）

that:
...sidence and mailing address are stated below next to their name.
...riginal inventor or an original joint inventor of the subject matter which is described and claimed
_____, granted _____ and for which a
...sought on the invention titled _____

th_ _ecification of which
☐ is attached hereto.
☐ was filed on _____ as reissue application number _____

（後充の場合にはこちらをチェック）

（発明者は特許が全部、一部において効力を生じないもしくは無効であると信じる旨を宣誓する必要有）

_d application was made or authorized to be made by me.
...dge that any willful false statement made in this declaration is punishable under 18 U.S.C. 1001 by fine _____ of not more than five (5) years, or both.

I believe the original patent to be wholly or partly inoperative or invalid, for the reasons described below. (Check all boxes that apply.)

☐ by reason of a defective specification or drawing.

☐ by reason of the patentee claiming more or less than he had the right to claim in the patent.

☐ by reason of other errors.

At least one error upon which reissue is based is described below. If the reissue is a broad_ reissue, a claim that the application seeks to broaden must be identified:

（特許の瑕疵を記入　クレームを拡大する場合には、その旨を記載）

[Page 1 of 2]
This collection of information is required by 37 CFR 1.175. The information is required to obtain or retain a benefit by the public which is to file (and by the USPTO to process) an application. Confidentiality is governed by 35 U.S.C. 122 and 37 CFR 1.11 and 1.14. This collection is estimated to take 30 minutes to complete, including gathering, preparing, and submitting the completed application form to the USPTO. Time will vary depending upon the individual case. Any comments on the amount of time you require to complete this form and/or suggestions for reducing this burden, should be sent to the Chief Information Officer, U.S. Patent and Trademark Office, U.S. Department of Commerce, P.O. Box 1450, Alexandria, VA 22313-1450. DO NOT SEND FEES OR COMPLETED FORMS TO THIS ADDRESS. SEND TO: **Commissioner for Patents, P.O. Box 1450, Alexandria, VA 22313-1450.**

If you need assistance in completing the form, call 1-800-PTO-9199 and select option 2.

第9章　特許の修正

査定系再審査制度(Ex Parte-Reexamination)

査定系再審査制度とは
　特許が発行された後に当事者または第三者が審査中に審査官によって考慮されなかった先行技術文献を発見した場合、それを引用してクレームの再審査を請求することができます。再審査は訴訟中によく利用される手続きです。再審査の結果、特許が無効になったり、補正によってクレームの範囲が縮小されたりします。

　請求主体：一定の例外（35U.S.C.315(e), 325(e)）を除いて何人も可能（37C.F.R.1.510）

　請求時期：特許権に基づく損害賠償請求が可能な期間に随時

査定系再審査の提出書類
- 再審査請求書（PTO/SB/57）
- 引用した先行技術文献が特許性に関して実質的に新しい疑問を呈することを述べる陳述書
- 引用した先行技術文献における、クレームに対応する箇所の表示
- 先行技術文献（一般発行物、特許文書）の写しとそれを列挙したPTO/SB/08、文献が英語以外の言語であれば英訳文
- 特許権者以外の第三者による請求の場合は、特許権者に提出物の写しを送付したことを示す証明書
- 補正案（請求人が特許権者の場合）
- 再審査の対象となる特許証の写し

査定系再審査請求料（37C.F.R.1.20(c)）
　査定系再審査請求の料金は、請求料の他、当該特許のクレーム数が基本料金（独立クレーム3個、合計クレーム20個）を超える場合、追加料金が発生します。

査定系再審査制度(Ex Parte-Reexamination)

査定系再審査の手続

再審査請求書の提出後、3月以内に再審査が行われる否かの決定が下ります。この決定は、その請求によって、特許の有効性に対して実質的に新たな問題(Substantial New Question of Patentability:SNQ)が提起されたか否か、を基準に判断されます(35U.S.C.303)。特許権者は2月以内にクレームと引例の差異を論じる陳述書と、必要であれば補正書を提出します(37C.F.R. 1.530)。再審査請求人は、その陳述書の提出から2月以内に答弁書を提出します(37C.F.R.1.535)。この答弁書提出以降は再審査請求人は審査に関与することができません。その後、通常の出願手続きのように、特許権者にOAが送達され、それに対して特許権者は2月以内に応答書を提出します。この査定系審査によって、特許に変動があった場合には、その手続きが確定した後に特許の変動に関する証明証が発行され公開されます(35U.S.C.307)。

ワンポイント解説:特許が無効(Invalid)と行使不能(Unenforceable)とはどこが違う?

訴訟などで、"特許は有効"しかし"行使不能"なことから、特許権を行使できず侵害行為を阻止できない、という結論に至ることが時々あります。これは、特許の新規性や非自明性の特許性が認められて特許自体は法的に成立しているにも関わらず、出願人の不衡平行為(Inequitable Conduct)やターミナルディスクレーマなどによって特許権の法的強制力が喪失している場合に起こります。一方、"特許が無効"とは、特許に特許性がないと裁判所に判断されたか、有効期限切れになった状態を意味します。

第9章　特許の修正

補充審査（Supplemental Examination）

補充審査とは
　情報開示義務の下、審査段階で引用例をうっかり提出し損なった等の事実があった場合に、特許権利者は情報開示義務違反の抗弁を恐れて権利活用を躊躇するケースがありました。また、審査手続き時の情報開示義務違反は、後に治癒することができないため、出願人は情報開示義務に対して多大な労力を費やしていました。そこで、今回の法改正では補充審査制度を新設し、特許権者は、特許に関連すると考えられる情報を提出し、U.S.P.T.O.に補充の審査を請求することができるようにしました（35U.S.C.257）。
　請求主体：特許権者（37C.F.R.1.601(a)）
　請求時期：特許発行から特許行使可能な期間（一般には特許期間満了から6年まで）に随時（37C.F.R.1.601(c)）

補充審査の提出物
　補充審査の請求には、主として下記の提出物が必要です（37C.F.R.1.610(a)(b)）。出願人は同一の特許に対して複数の請求を行うことができますが、1回の補充審査請求で提出できる情報は12個までです（37C.F.R.1.605(a)）。
- カバーシート（PTO/SB/59）
- 対象となる特許公報
- 提出する情報及びなぜその情報を提出したかの説明
- ミーンズプラスファンクションクレームの場合には、明細書中の対応する構造等に関する説明
- 提出した情報によって生じる問題
- 非英語文献の場合には翻訳文
- 文献が50ページ以上の場合には関連部分の要約

補充審査請求手数料（37C.F.R.1.20(k)）
　補充審査請求の料金は、基本請求料の他、提出する非特許文献が21ページ以上の場合には所定の追加手数料が発生します。また、補充審査請求時に査定系

補充審査 (Supplemental Examination)

再審査手数料も併せて支払う必要があります。補充審査手続きにて査定系再審査請求命令が発せられなかった場合には、査定系再審査手数料は全額返金されます。

補充審査の手続き及び効果

　U.S.P.T.O.は3月以内に提出された情報が実質的に特許性に関する新たな問題 (Substantial New Question of Patentability：SNQ) か否かを判断します。新た問題が無いと判断された場合には、補充審査証書が発行され、以前の審査過程で考慮されなかった等の理由では権利行使不能とはなりません (35U.S.C. 257(c)(1))。

　ただし、補充審査の請求前の、民事訴訟若しくは連邦FDC法 (Federal Food, Drug and Cosmetic Act) での主張、及び関税法若しくは民事訴訟の抗弁には上記効果の適用がありません (35U.S.C.257(c)(2))。即ち、相手方から再審査請求や、確認訴訟等を起こされた後には補充審査は認められないことになります。従って、権利活用を行う前に補充審査請求を行い、必要に応じて再審査請求を行い、特許に関する問題を解消した上で、警告状の送付等のアクションを開始することが望ましいと言えます。

　一方、新た問題があると判断された場合には、U.S.P.T.O.は補充審査証書を発行し、どの情報が新たな問題があるかと指摘します。1つ以上の情報によって特許性に関する新たな問題が生じた場合には、再審査請求するように特許権者に命令が発せられます (37C.F.R.1.625(a)(b))。従って、補充審査は、再審査の予備的なテストとしての位置づけとも言えます。

ワンポイント解説：詐欺の意図と認められる場合
　補充審査制度にて審査段階での先行技術の未提出行為を治癒することができます。しかし、詐欺行為が認められた場合には、クレームがキャンセルされる可能性があります (35U.S.C.257(e))。

第9章 特許の修正

補充審査請求送付状の記入例（PTO／SB／59）

補充審査（Supplemental Examination）

補充審査請求送付状記入例（PTO/SB/59）の続き

（提出する情報のコピーと非英語であれば翻訳文）

（50ページ以上の場合には、サマリの提出）

第9章 特許の修正

補充審査請求送付状記入例（PTO/SB/59）の続き

```
                                                              PTO/SB/59 (07-12)
                                        Approved for use through 07/31/2015. OMB 0651-0064
                                        U.S. Patent and Trademark Office; U.S. DEPARTMENT OF COMMERCE
Under the Paperwork Reduction Act of 1995, no persons are required to respond to a collection of information unless it displays a valid OMB control number.
                                              (Also referred to as FORM PTO-XXXX)
```

REQUEST FOR SUPPLEMENTAL EXAMINATION TRANSMITTAL FORM
PART B – LIST OF ITEMS OF INFORMATION – Page 1

Patent number for which supplemental examination is requested **X,XXX,XXX**   Issue Date **MM/DD/yyyy**

All items of information (no more than 12) submitted herewith as part of this request for supplemental examination of the above-identified patent are included in the following list:

U. S. PATENT DOCUMENTS

Cite No.[1]	Document Number Number-Kind Code[2][3] (if known)	Publication Date MM-DD-YYYY	Name of Patentee or Applicant of Cited Document	Pages, Columns, Lines, Where Relevant Passages or Relevant Figures Appear
	US- x,xxx,xxx	MM-DD-YYY	SMITH, John	
	US-			
	US-			
	US-			
	US-			
	US-			
	US-			
	US-			
	US-			
	US-			
	US-			
	US-			

（吹き出し）米国特許、米国公開公報の場合には願番等のみ

FOREIGN PATENT DOCUMENTS

Cite No.[1]	Foreign Patent Document Country Code[4]-Number[3]-Kind Code[5] (if known)	Publication Date MM-DD-YYYY	Name of Patentee or Applicant of Cited Document	Pages, Columns, Lines, Where Relevant Passages or Relevant Figures Appear	T[6]
	JP-2008-xxx,xxx	MM-DD-YYY	YAMADA, Taro		X

（吹き出し）外国特許文献の場合には願番等の情報の他、文献のコピーも添付

[1] Applicant's unique citation designation number (optional). [2] See Kinds Codes of USPTO Patent Documents at www.uspto.gov or MPEP ... the document, by the two-letter code (WIPO Standard ST.3). [4] For Japanese patent documents, the indication of the year of the reign of the Emperor ... number of the patent document. [5] Kind of document by the appropriate symbols as indicated on the document under WIPO Standard ST.16 if possible. [6] Applicant is to place a check mark here if English language Translation is attached.

Page 1 of 2

補充審査 (Supplemental Examination)

補充審査請求送付状記入例 (PTO/SB/59) の続き

吹き出し注釈:
- 非特許文献を特定
- 文献の著者名、題名、学会誌名、出版日、掲載ページ、掲載巻、出版会社、出版された場所、国名等で文献を特定し、文献のコピーを添付する。

第10章

特許の攻撃

　自社の製品を米国で販売等する場合に他社の特許や特許出願がビジネス上の阻害になる場合があります。また、他社から警告状を受取った際に当該特許に対して無効を主張したい場合があります。本章では、他人の特許出願や特許を攻撃し、特許出願の権利化の阻止や特許を無効にする制度について説明します。この特許の攻撃に関する規定は、今回の法改正において大きな変化がありました。

　特許の攻撃には以下の4つの制度があります。
- 第三者文献提出制度（Preissurance Submissions by Third Parties）
- 付与後レビュー制度（Post Grant Review：PGR）
- 当事者系レビュー制度（Inter Partes Review：IPR）
- 金融系ビジネス方法特許レビュー（Covered Business Method Patent Review：CBMPR）

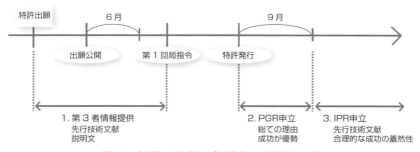

図14　特許の攻撃の各制度の時期的要件

第10章　特許の攻撃

第三者文献提出（Preissurance Submissions by Third Parties）

第三者文献提出制度とは

　第三者文献提出制度とは、出願人以外の第三者が、特許出願に対して関連する先行技術文献を提出できる制度です（35U.S.C.122(e)、37C.F.R.1.290）。特徴は下記の通りです。
- 他の特許の攻撃に対して低コストです。
- 匿名での提出が可能です。（ただし代理人の名前は示す必要があります。）
- 提出期間は、出願公開から6月以内、若しくは、第1回目の局指令の何れか遅い方までです。
- 審査の初期段階で提出物が審査に供されるため、良い結果に結びつきやすいと考えられます。
- 提出文献に基づく新規性、及び非自明性欠如に関する理由のみに限られます。
- 文献提出後に、提出者に意見の機会は与えられません。
- 提出文献が考慮された上で特許になった場合、当該文献は次の攻撃で使いにくくなる、と言えます。

時期的要件

- 基本的に特許出願から公開公報発行後6月または第1回の実体的OAのいずれか遅いときまでに提出します。
- 希ですが、上記期間満了に前に許可通知が発せられた場合には、提出をすることができません。一方、「特許出願」が放棄されたとしても上記期間内であれば、提出することができます。
- 「公開公報発行」は米国の公開公報の発行日であり、外国公報や国際公開公報の発行日は含まれません。
- 「第1回目」のOAですので、再発行特許出願や、再審査特許出願についてはすることができません。分割出願や継続出願は、当該出願の第1回目のOAまでに提出することができます。
- 「実体的OA」とは、発明の新規性や非自明性に関する審査の後に発せら

第三者文献提出（Preissurance Submissions by Third Parties）

れるOAであり、たとえば、選択/限定要求は含まれません。

第三者文献提出の要件

　第三者文献提出時に必要物は下記の通りです（37C.F.R.1.290(d)）。提出はU.S.P.T.O.が提供するEFS-Webのフォームに必要事項を入力することで行うことができます。書面で提出する際には、PTO/SB/429に必要事項を記入します。提出書類は以下の通りです。
- 先行技術文献（37C.F.R.1.290(e)）
  - 米国特許公報
  - 米国特許公開公報
  - 外国特許または公開公報
  - 非特許文献（提出者に公開日付を立証する責任有）

　米国特許公報及び米国特許公開公報は、特許番号、公開公報番号のみをフォームに記入すればよく、実際の書類のコピーを提出する必要はありません。外国特許等の場合には、その書類も提出する必要があります。非英語文献の場合には翻訳文も提出します。非特許文献には、著者、文献名、公開日、出版社等、分かる範囲で文献を特定します。日付の証明が必要な場合には、その証明も添付します。この証明には宣誓書の提出が必要になる場合があります。宣誓書の提出には宣誓者の氏名等を特定する必要がありますので、匿名性を担保したい場合には問題になることが考えられます。
- 提出文献の関連性の説明

　現行法にて提出文献との関連性に関する説明書を提出することができるようになりました。この説明書では、各提出文献の記載とクレームの構成要素とを比較してクレームの構成要素は当該提出文献に開示されている旨を含めます。
- 提出文献が非英語の場合には、必要な部分の翻訳文

　提出文献が非英語文献の場合には、その翻訳文を添付します。必ずしも全文訳が要求されている訳ではありませんので、重要な部分のみの翻訳文でも提出は認められます。また、IDSでの手続きと同様に翻訳文にはその翻訳が正しい旨のステートメントは提出する必要はありません。
- 陳述書

　提出者は、1）IDS義務を有していない、2）提出物は規則に則っている、3）当該特許出願に関して最初かつ唯一提出し、3つ以内の提出物である旨を

第10章　特許の攻撃

陳述する必要があります。
- 費用（37C.F.R.1.17(o)）

1人につき3文献まで無料で提出が可能です。以降、合計10文献につき庁費用が必要です。

提出された文献はIDSと同じように取り扱われる

提出された文献は、審査に供されます。ここで、提出文献はIDSで提出された文献と同様に扱われます。すなわち、提出されたリストの文献に対し、審査官が考慮した旨のサインがなされます。この特許出願が許可された場合には、リストの文献を考慮した上で特許になった、ということになります。従って、後の手続きで同文献を用いて特許の無効の主張をした場合、先に第三者文献提出したことが不利に働く可能性があることに留意する必要があります。

旧法の第三者文献提出は、出願公開から2月以内に行う必要がありました。また、提出文献との関連性が説明を含められなかったため、あまり利用されない制度でした。現行法では、上述の問題点が解消され、最初の実体的OAまで提出が可能になり、また、提出文献との関連性に関する意見を提出することができるようになりました。現行法によって、より利用しやすい制度となりました。

第三者文献提出（Preissurance Submissions by Third Parties）

第三者文献提出の記入例（PTO/SB/429）

第10章　特許の攻撃

第三者文献提出の記入例（PTO/SB/429）の続き

当事者系審判の規則体系

今回の現行法では、当事者系審判として、1）付与後レビュー制度、2）当事者系レビュー制度、3）金融系ビジネス方法特許レビュー、そして、4）発明者決定手続きが創設されました。

これらは準司法的手続きで進められ、その詳細な手続きは規則（37C.F.R.）で規定されます。これら当事者系審判の1）付与後レビュー制度、2）当事者系レビュー制度、3）金融系ビジネス方法特許レビュー、そして、4）発明者決定手続きに関する共通する審判規則については37C.F.R.42.1～42.80に規定されています。そして、それぞれの制度特有な規則については、1）付与後レビュー制度（37C.F.R.42.200～42.224）、2）当事者系レビュー制度（37C.F.R.42.100～42.123）、3）金融系ビジネス方法特許レビュー（37C.F.R.42.300～42.304）、そして、4）発明者決定手続き（37C.F.R.42.400～42.412）に個別に規定がされています。

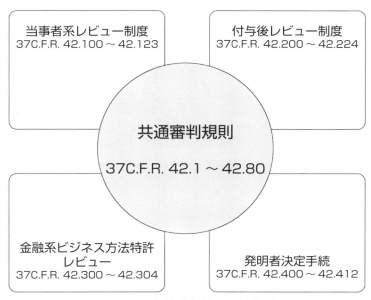

図15 当事者系審判の規則体系

第10章　特許の攻撃

付与後レビュー(Post Grant Review：PGR)制度

付与後レビュー制度とは

付与後レビュー（PGR）は、特許権者以外の第三者からの申立に基づき、U.S.P.T.O.のPTABによる準司法的な審理手続により、1つ以上のクレームの特許の有効性に関する判断をするものです。PGR制度の特徴は以下の通りです。

- 申立ては利害関係人に限られ、匿名で行うことはできません。
- 提出期間は、特許発行後9月以内に行う必要があります。
- 申立理由は、新規性、非自明性違反の他、記載要件や主題適格違反も含まれます。
- 一定の基準を満たした申立てのみ審理されます。従って、総ての申立てが審理される訳ではありません。
- 審理はPTAB：Patent Trial and Appeal Boardが行います。
- 審理は準司法的手続きで行われ、ディスカバリ手続き等も可能です。
- 審理中に一定の範囲でクレームの補正が可能です。
- 審理開始決定から審決まで通常一年以内です。延長するに足りる理由がある場合にはその後6月間延長されます。

PGR申立要件

PGR申立は、利害関係人（Real party-in-interest）のみが行うことができ、匿名での申立てを行うことはできません。PGR申立理由は102条（新規性）、103条（非自明性）の他、101条（法定要件）や112条（記載要件）も認められます。この点が、第三者文献提出や当事者系レビューとは異なる点です。ただし、記載要件中のベストモード違反はPGR申立理由ではありません（(35U.S.C.282(c)(3))）。

PGR申立ができる出願（経過措置）

PGR申立は、2013年3月16日以降になされた出願に係る特許に対して行う事ができます（H.R.1249 SEC.6(f)(2)）。

PGR申立の手続き

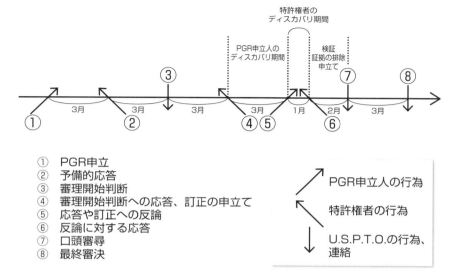

図16　PGRの手続き

PGR申立人によるPGR申立書の提出（35U.S.C.322、37C.F.R.42.204）

PGR申立書は、申立費用と共に以下の内容を含めて提出します。

- 利害関係人である旨の特定
- PGR申立を行うクレーム
- PGR申立理由及びその理由を補強するような証拠（公開公報、特許公報、宣誓書等）

PGR申立書が提出された後は、速やかに公衆の閲覧に供されます。申立の庁費用（37C.F.R.42.15(b)(1)）（クレーム数20個まで、それ以上は1クレーム追加ごとに追加費用）です。審理決定となった場合には追加費用（37C.F.R.42.15(b)(2)）（クレーム数15個まで、それ以上は追加費用）がかかります。PGR申立人は、PGR申立書及びその付属書類を特許権者に送付する必要あります（37C.F.R.42.205）。

特許権者による予備的応答（35U.S.C.323、37C.F.R.42.207）

PGR申立書が提出された後、特許権者は申立てに対して3月以内に予備的応答をする事ができます。この予備的応答には、当該PGR申立が要件を満たして

いないので、審理が開始されるべきではない旨を主張することができます。この予備的応答には、新たな証拠やクレーム等の補正を含めることはできませんが、ターミナルディスクレーマの提出は可能です。

U.S.P.T.O.による審理開始判断（35U.S.C.324、37C.F.R.42.208）

上記予備的応答がなされなかった場合であっても、総てのPGR申立がPTABにて審理される訳ではありません。審理開始前にPGR申立書及び特許権者が提出した予備的応答書が考慮され、「PGR申立理由の有りか無しかで言うと、理由有りが優勢（more likely than not）」との心証を得たか、他の特許や特許出願にとって重要な新規または未解決の法律問題を提起するケースのみ、審理が開始されます。この審理開始の決定は、予備的応答書の提出日、予備的応答書が提出されなかった場合には予備的応答書の提出可能な最終日の何れか遅い日から3月以内になされます。上記決定は、PGR申立人及び権利者に送達され、その内容は公開されます。上記決定自体には不服を申し立てることができません。

他の訴訟との関係（35U.S.C.325）

PGR申立書の提出日前に、当該PGR申立人若しくは利害関係人が当該特許の有効性に関する民事訴訟を提起した場合には審理は開始されません。

また、PGR申立書の提出日後に、当該PGR申立人若しくは利害関係人が当該特許の有効性に関する民事訴訟を提起した場合には、当該民事訴訟は下記の何れかの日まで中断されます。

A）特許権者が中断解除の申立てをした場合
B）特許権者が、PGR申立人若しくは利害関係人を権利侵害として民事訴訟若しくは反訴した場合
C）PGR申立人若しくは利害関係人が、民事訴訟を却下するように裁判所に申立てた場合

特許侵害訴訟が特許発行から3月以内に提起された場合には、裁判所は、PGR申立て若しくはその審理開始に基づき特許権者による予備的差止請求の審理を中断することができません。また、同一の特許について複数のPGR申立があった場合には、中断、併合等される場合があります。

PGR申立人、利害関係人、若しくは当事者関係人は、PGR申立手続き中に提起した、若しくは提起可能であったいかなる理由に基づいて、U.S.P.T.O.での手続きの請求若しくは維持を行うことができません。また、民事訴訟、ITC（International Trade Committee）手続きにおいても、同様の理由に基づい

付与後レビュー（Post Grant Review：PGR）制度

てクレーム無効の主張を行うことができません。

特許権者の応答（35U.S.C.326、37C.F.R.42.220、221）

　審理開始が決定されたPGR申立は、PTABによる審理に供されます。特許権者は、審理開始の決定に対して意見を述べることができます。また、特許権者は、PTABに対してクレームの訂正の申立てを行うことができます。訂正はPTABが認めた場合に限り行うことができます。補正の申立てを行う際には、補正により追加部分の明細書中のサポートを示します。ここで、本申立の非特許性の理由と関係ない訂正や、クレーム範囲を拡大する訂正は認められません。

審理中のディスカバリ等（35U.S.C.326、37C.F.R.42.51、42.70）

　審理は、37C.F.R.42.1以降に規定される準司法的手続きで行われ、ディスカバリ（37C.F.R.42.51、42.224）や口頭審理（37C.F.R.42.70）の機会が与えられます。審理は、原則として、上記図のような手続きで進められます。ここで、各手続きの進め方については、審理開始決定から約1月後に双方どのような申立を行うか等を話し合い、上記スケジュールの調整が行われる場合があります。

和解（35U.S.C.327、37C.F.R.42.74）

　終了請求前にU.S.P.T.O.が結審した場合は除いて、複数のPGR申立人がいる場合には総てのPGR申立人、及び、特許権者からの終了請求により、当該PGR申立の審理は終了します。ここで、1人のPGR申立人が単独で終了請求をした場合には、当該PGR申立人及びその関係者のみ上記禁反言の規定（35U.S.C.325(e)）から除外されます。もしPGR申立人が誰も残らなかった場合には、当該PGR申立審理の終了／審決に進むかはU.S.P.T.O.に委ねられます。

PTABによる最終審決（35U.S.C.328、37C.F.R.42.71）

　審決は最終判断書面にて、申立のあった総てのクレームについて判断がなされます。この書面は、控訴可能期間満了後、若しくは、控訴取下げの時に公衆の閲覧に供されます。これには、審理中にキャンセルされたクレーム、特許性が確認されたクレーム、特許性が確認された追加クレームが記載されます。一定の要件の下に第三者にいわゆる中用権が認められます。最終判断に不服の場合には、控訴することができます。この控訴は、PGR申立人、権利者双方行うことができます（35U.S.C.329）。

第10章 特許の攻撃

> ワンポイント解説：WANTED ― 先行文献！
> 　技術競争も多額の利益や損害が絡んでくると、何が何でも他社の特許を無効にしたいといった場合が出てきます。その究極的手段として、対象特許に賞金が掛かることもあります。特許は新規性・非自明性が覆されれば無効となりますので、そうした先行技術を探し出した者に賞金が与えられるのです。例えば、パテント・トロールに訴えられている場合や、他社に独占されている市場に新規参入したい場合などが、守る側でも攻める側でもたった１つの先行文献で形勢が逆転することもあるのです。

当事者系レビュー
(Inter Partes Review：IPR) 制度

当事者系レビュー制度とは (35U.S.C.311)

　旧法の当事者系再審査制度（Inter Partes Reexamination）は廃止され、これに代わり当事者系レビュー制度が新設されました。特徴は以下の通りです。
- 申立ては利害関係人に限られ、匿名で行うことはできません。
- 提出期間は、特許発行後9月以降であって、PGR申立がなされた場合にはその手続きが完了した後行う必要があります。
　　ここで、旧法適用の特許(2013年3月16日以前の出願)については、PGR申立を行う事ができません。また、35U.S.C.311(c)の規定上、旧法現行法適用の別を問わず、特許についても特許から9月以前は当事者系レビューの申立てできない、という条文の構成になっていました。従って、旧法適用の特許は、特許から9月間は，PGR申立ても当事者系レビューの申立ても行えない空白の期間が存在していました。そこで、この言わば「デッドゾーン」を解消すべく、旧法適用の特許については、特許から9月を待つ事なく当事者系レビューの申立てを行えるように改正されました（H.R. 6621）。
- 申立理由は、特許公報や刊行物に基づいた新規性、若しくは非自明性違反のみです。
- 一定の基準を満たした請求のみ審理されます。従って、総ての申立てが審理される訳ではありません。
- 審理はPTAB：Patent Trial and Appeal Boardが行います。
- 審理は準司法的手続きで行われ、ディスカバリ手続き等も可能です。
- 審理中に一定の範囲でクレームの補正が可能です。
- 審理開始決定から審決まで通常一年以内です。延長するに足りる理由がある場合にはその後6月間延長されます。

IPR申立要件 (35U.S.C.312)

　IPR申立は、利害関係人（Real party-in-interest）のみが行うことができ、匿名で行うことはできません。IPR申立の理由としては、特許公報、公開公

第10章　特許の攻撃

報、または刊行物に基づく102条（新規性）、103条（非自明性）のみ認められます。従って、特許公報や刊行物以外の新規性、非自明性違反や、法定要件、記載要件違反の理由は認められません。

IPR申立の手続き
IPR申立人による申立書の提出（35U.S.C.312、37C.F.R.42.104）
　IPR申立書には、利害関係人である旨、対象クレームと、その理由及びその理由を補強するような証拠（特許公報、刊行物等）、申立費用（37C.F.R.42.15(a)(1)、クレーム数が20を超える場合には、追加料金（37C.F.R.42.15(a)(3)）を付する必要があります。申立書が提出された後は、速やかに公衆の閲覧に供されます。審理開始決定となった場合には更に費用（37C.F.R.42.15(a)(2)、クレーム数が20を超える場合には、追加料金（37C.F.R.42.15(a)(4)）を支払います。申立人は、IPR申立書及びその付属書類を特許権者に送付する必要があります（37C.F.R.42.105）。

特許権者による予備的応答（35U.S.C.313、37C.F.R.42.107）
　IPR申立書が提出された後、特許権者は申立に対して3月以内に予備的応答を行う事ができます。この予備的応答には、IPR申立が要件を満たしていないので、審理が開始されるべきではない旨を主張することができます。この予備的応答には、新たな証拠やクレーム等の補正を含めることはできませんが、ターミナルディスクレーマの提出は可能です。

U.S.P.T.O.による審理開始判断（35U.S.C.314、37C.F.R.42.108）
　上記予備的応答がなされなかった場合であっても、総てのIPRケースがPTABにて審理される訳ではありません。審理開始前にIPR申立書及び特許権者が提出した予備的応答書が考慮され、「IPRの申立人の主張が優勢であるとする合理的な蓋然性がある（reasonable likelihood）」との心証を得たケースのみ審理が開始されます。この審理開始の決定は、予備的応答書の提出日、予備的応答書が提出されなかった場合には予備的最終日の何れか遅い日から3月以内になされます。上記決定は、IPRの申立人及び権利者に通知され、公開されます。上記決定自体には不服を申し立てることができません。

他の訴訟との関係（35U.S.C.315）
　IPR申立日前に、当該申立者若しくは利害関係人が当該特許の有効性に関する民事訴訟を提起した場合には審理は開始されません。また、IPR申立日後

当事者系レビュー（Inter Partes Review：IPR）制度

に、当該請願人若しくは利害関係人が当該特許の有効性に関する民事訴訟を提起した場合には、当該民事訴訟は下記の何れかの日まで中断されます。

A）特許権者が中断解除の申立てをした場合
B）特許権者が、IPR申立人若しくは利害関係人を権利侵害として民事訴訟若しくは反訴した場合
C）申立人若しくは利害関係人が、民事訴訟を却下するように裁判所に申立てた場合

IPR申立人若しくは利害関係人が訴状を受取った日から1年以上後にIPRの申立をした場合には、当該IPRは開始されません。ただし、共同申立人としてIPRに参加した場合には、例外適用があります。また、同一の特許について複数のPGR申立があった場合には、中断や併合等される場合があります。

IPR申立人、利害関係人、若しくは当事者関係人は、PGR申立手続き中に提起した、若しくは提起可能であったいかなる理由に基づいて、U.S.P.T.O.での手続きの請求若しくは維持を行うことができません。また、民事訴訟、ITC（International Trade Committee）手続きにおいても、同様の理由に基づいてクレーム無効の主張を行うことができません。

特許権者の応答（35U.S.C.316、37C.F.R.42.120、121）

審理開始が決定された当事者系レビュー申立は、PTABによる審理に供されます。特許権者は、審理開始の決定に対して意見を述べることができます。また、特許権者は、PTABに対してクレームの訂正の申立てを行うことができます。訂正はPTABが認めた場合に限り行うことができます。訂正の申立てを行う際には、補正により追加部分の明細書中のサポートを示します。ここで、本申立の非特許性の理由と関係ない訂正や、クレーム範囲を拡大する訂正は認められません。

審理中のディスカバリ等（35U.S.C.316、37C.F.R.42.51、42.70）

審理は、37C.F.R.42.1以降に規定される準司法的手続きで行われ、ディスカバリ（37C.F.R.42.51）や口頭審理（37C.F.R.42.70）の機会が与えられます。審理は、原則として前述のPGR申立と同様な手続きで進められます。ここで、各手続きの進め方については、審理決定から約1月後に双方どのような申立を行うか等を話し合い、上記スケジュールの調整が行われる場合があります。

第10章　特許の攻撃

和解（35U.S.C.317、37C.F.R.42.74）

終了請求前にU.S.P.T.O.が結審した場合は除いて、複数のIPR申立人がいる場合には総ての申立人、及び、特許権者からの終了請求により、当該IPRの審理は終了します（35U.S.C.317(a)）。ここで、一人のPGR申立人が単独で終了請求をした場合には、当該PGR申立人及びその関係者のみ上記禁反言の規定（35U.S.C.315(e)）から除外されます。もしPGR申立人が誰も残らなかった場合には、当該PGR申立審理の終了／審決に進むかはU.S.P.T.O.に委ねられます。

PTABによる最終審決（35U.S.C.318、37C.F.R.42.71）

審決は最終判断書面にて、請願のあった総てのクレームについて判断がなされます。この書面は、控訴可能期間満了後、若しくは、控訴取下げの時に公衆の閲覧に供されます。これには、審理中にキャンセルされたクレーム、特許性が確認されたクレーム、特許性が確認された追加クレームが記載されます（35U.S.C.318(a)(b)）。一定の要件の下に第三者にいわゆる中用権が認められます（35U.S.C.318(c)）。

審決に不服の場合

最終判断に不服の場合には、控訴することができます。この控訴は、IPR申立人、権利者双方行うことができます。（35U.S.C.319）

PGRとIPRとの主な相違点

費用

審理に係るクレームが15個以内と仮定した場合、PGRの庁費用は＄30,000であり、IPRは＄23,000です（2017年10月現在）。IPRはPGRに比して約25％安価になっています。PGRはより広範な申立理由を認めていることから、審理が複雑になると予想され、また、安易な申立の乱立を抑制するという趣旨で、PGRはIPRに比して費用が高くなっていると考えられます。

申立の時期

PGRは、特許付与日から9月以内にする必要があります。その一方、IPRは、PGRの手続き、または特許付与日から9月を過ぎた後に行う必要があります。ただし旧法適用の特許に関しては、特許付与後から9月を待たずに申立を行うことができます。

申立の理由

PGRの申立理由は特許無効に関する規定（282(b)または(c)条）に係る理由、即ち、101条、102条、103条、及び112条（ただし、ベストモード要件は除く）が含まれます。一方、IPRの申立理由は、特許公報や公知文献に基づく102条、103条のみが含まれます。

審理手続きに進むための基準

前述の通り、PGR、IPR共に、総ての申立が審理されるのではなく、ある一定の基準を満たした申立のみが審理手続きに進みます。ここで、PGRの審理手続きに進むための判断基準である"more likely than not"と、IPRの審理手続きに進むための判断基準である"reasonable likelihood"との相違について説明します。"more likely than not"は、申立の内容から当該特許が取り消される可能性が、取り消されない可能性よりも高い、ということですので、取り消される可能性が50％よりも高い必要があると解されます。一方、"reasonable likelihood"は、取り消される可能性が50％であっても審理に進むと解されます。従って、可能性がどちらとも言えない、すなわち、50/50のような場合も審理に進むと解されます。また、IPRの審理手続きに進むための基準には、PGRと異なり、他の特許や特許出願にとって重要な新規または未解決の法律問題を提起する申立と判断された場合が含まれていません。

ディスカバリ

ディスカバリ手続きにおけるPGRとIPRとの相違点としては、追加ディスカバリを認めるか否かの判断基準があります。PGRの追加ディスカバリ認否の判断基準は、審理中のいずれかの当事者によって進められ事実的主張に直接関連する証拠か否かである点で、法的公正さの観点から判断がなされるIPRとは異なります（§316(a)(5), §326(a)(5), C.F.R. 42.51(b)(2)(i)）。PGRの追加ディスカバリ認否の判断基準は言わば正当理由があるか否かの観点から判断がなされ（37C.F.R.42.224）、IPRは法的公正さの観点から判断がなされると規定されます。IPRの法的公正さの判断の方が若干高い基準であると考えられます。

一事不再理

PGR、IPRともに、一旦最終審決が発せられた場合には、PGR申立人やその関係者は、同一のクレームについて、申立に含まれる理由、または合理的な範囲でPGR手続き中に提出できたと考えられる如何なる理由に基づいて、手続きの請求を行うことはできません。ここで、PGRの申立理由は、282条(b)(2) or

(3)規定された総ての理由が含まれます。一方、IPRは、特許、刊行物に関する102条及び103条のみに限られます。従って、一事不再理の範囲としては、PGRの方が広いと言えます。

金融系ビジネス方法特許レビュー（Covered Business Method Patent Review：CBMPR）

　ビジネス方法特許は引用例が少ないため、無効にしにくい一方、法定主題（35U.S.C.101）や記載要件（35U.S.C.112）違反であるとの主張が有効な場合があります。また、金融系の特許訴訟は高額になる傾向にある分、銀行等の金融系企業は狙われやすいと言えます。そこで、金融系ビジネス方法特許に限り、法定主題（35U.S.C.101）や記載要件（35U.S.C.112）違反もPGR理由となるPGRをベースとしつつ、申立の時期的制限を撤廃した金融系ビジネス方法特許レビュー制度が創設されました。本制度は金融業界からの強い要望により認められたものであります。

　金融系ビジネス方法特許レビューは付与後レビュー申立制度（PGR）に似ていますが、下記の点で異なります。
- 対象となる特許は金融系のビジネス方法に限られます。
- 申立に時期的制限がありません。(37C.F.R.42.304)（付与後レビュー制度は特許発行後9月までに要申立）
- 申立人は、当該特許を侵害するとして提訴されているか、実質的に論争（DJアクション等）になっている者であることを要します。(37C.F.R.42.302)。
- 現段階では2020年9月16日までの時限立法（8年）となっています。

特許の攻撃はU.S.P.T.O.か裁判所か

　以上説明した通り、法改正によってU.S.P.T.O.でもより司法的な手続きにより、第三者が特許の有効性を争い易くなりました。一方、旧法下からも裁判所において特許の有効性を争う事もできました。特許の攻撃に関し、U.S.P.T.O.と裁判所の手続を比較すると以下のような事がいえます。

クレーム解釈における相違

　U.S.P.T.O.においては、クレームは「合理的な範囲で最広義」に解釈されます。裁判所においては概ね「通常の意味」に解釈される傾向にあります。従って、攻撃される特許を比較的広く解釈するU.S.P.T.O.の方が攻撃し易いと考えられます。

時間的な相違

　U.S.P.T.O.では、PTABは原則審理開始決定から1年以内に結審します。その一方、裁判所では、数年かかる場合もあります。もちろん裁判所によっては、早く結審する所もあります。

費用的な相違

　PGRで30,000ドル、IPRで23,000ドルのU.S.P.T.O.の手数料（2017年10月現在）に加え、代理人費用が掛かります。裁判所では、さらに多くの費用が掛かることが予想されますので、U.S.P.T.O.での手続きが安価と言えます。

判断の相違

　U.S.P.T.O.では専門性の高い審判官による判断で特許の有効性が判断されます。一方、裁判所では、一般には、裁判官によるクレーム解釈に基づいて陪審員による事実認定が行われます。場合によっては陪審員の感情等でクレームの有効性が左右されてしまう事も考えられます。裁判所による特許の有効性の判断はU.S.P.T.O.に比較すると判断の安定性に欠ける場合があると考えられます。

第10章　特許の攻撃

補正の可能性の相違

　U.S.P.T.O.でのPGRやIPRの各手続きにおいては、特許権者に訂正の機会が認められる場合があります。その一方、裁判所での手続きでは、特許権者に訂正の機会は認められません。U.S.P.T.O.でのPGRやIPRの各手続きは、特許を攻撃する側からみると、特許権者の権利をより強くする訂正を行う機会を与えてしまう事にもなります。すなわち、これら各手続き中での補正によってクレームの範囲を減縮することにより、先行技術文献等を回避したより強固なクレームにしてしまう可能性があるということです。訂正後のクレームであっても、なお特許攻撃者の事業を妨げるようであれば、せっかく行ったU.S.P.T.O.での手続きは無意味なものになってしまいます。従って、特許攻撃者は、特許権者がどのような訂正を行うか、を様々な角度から検討する必要があります。この検討によって想定された仮想クレームが自己の事業を妨げないかを次に検討する必要があるでしょう。

審理開始可能性の相違

　U.S.P.T.O.でのPGRやIPRの各手続きにおいては、総ての申立が審理されるのではなく、一定の判断基準で成功の見込みがある申立のみ審理が開始されます。ここで、特許攻撃者が用いた証拠によって審理開始されなかったという専門官庁たるU.S.P.T.O.での判断の事実は、一時不再理効等、後になって特許攻撃者にとって不利に作用する事が考えられます。従って、明白に特許無効を主張できる証拠がある場合に上記各手続きの申立てをする方がよいと考えられます。

ワンポイント解説："ロケット・ドケット"裁判所とは？

　特許案件に限らず事件処理手続きのスピードが速く、起訴から判決までの期間が非常に短い裁判所のことを言います。特許事件が特に集中しているロケット・ドケットの裁判所としては、テキサス州東区連邦地方裁判所とバージニア州東区連邦地方裁判所が著名です。近年ではウィスコンシン州西区連邦地方裁判所、フロリダ州中区連邦地方裁判所、ワシントン州西区連邦地方裁判所もロケット・ドケット化してきております。

資 料

PTO/AIA/01

PTO/AIA/01 (06-12)
Approved for use through 01/31/2014. OMB 0651-0032
U.S. Patent and Trademark Office; U.S. DEPARTMENT OF COMMERCE
Under the Paperwork Reduction Act of 1995, no persons are required to respond to a collection of information unless it displays a valid OMB control number.

DECLARATION (37 CFR 1.63) FOR UTILITY OR DESIGN APPLICATION USING AN APPLICATION DATA SHEET (37 CFR 1.76)

Title of Invention

As the below named inventor, I hereby declare that:

This declaration is directed to:
☐ The attached application, or
☐ United States application or PCT international application number _____
filed on _____.

The above-identified application was made or authorized to be made by me.

I believe that I am the original inventor or an original joint inventor of a claimed invention in the application.

I hereby acknowledge that any willful false statement made in this declaration is punishable under 18 U.S.C. 1001 by fine or imprisonment of not more than five (5) years, or both.

WARNING:

Petitioner/applicant is cautioned to avoid submitting personal information in documents filed in a patent application that may contribute to identity theft. Personal information such as social security numbers, bank account numbers, or credit card numbers (other than a check or credit card authorization form PTO-2038 submitted for payment purposes) is never required by the USPTO to support a petition or an application. If this type of personal information is included in documents submitted to the USPTO, petitioners/applicants should consider redacting such personal information from the documents before submitting them to the USPTO. Petitioner/applicant is advised that the record of a patent application is available to the public after publication of the application (unless a non-publication request in compliance with 37 CFR 1.213(a) is made in the application) or issuance of a patent. Furthermore, the record from an abandoned application may also be available to the public if the application is referenced in a published application or an issued patent (see 37 CFR 1.14). Checks and credit card authorization forms PTO-2038 submitted for payment purposes are not retained in the application file and therefore are not publicly available.

LEGAL NAME OF INVENTOR

Inventor: _____   Date (Optional): _____

Signature: _____

Note: An application data sheet (PTO/SB/14 or equivalent), including naming the entire inventive entity, must accompany this form or must have been previously filed. Use an additional PTO/AIA/01 form for each additional inventor.

This collection of information is required by 35 U.S.C. 115 and 37 CFR 1.63. The information is required to obtain or retain a benefit by the public which is to file (and by the USPTO to process) an application. Confidentiality is governed by 35 U.S.C. 122 and 37 CFR 1.11 and 1.14. This collection is estimated to take 1 minute to complete, including gathering, preparing, and submitting the completed application form to the USPTO. Time will vary depending upon the individual case. Any comments on the amount of time you require to complete this form and/or suggestions for reducing this burden, should be sent to the Chief Information Officer, U.S. Patent and Trademark Office, U.S. Department of Commerce, P.O. Box 1450, Alexandria, VA 22313-1450. DO NOT SEND FEES OR COMPLETED FORMS TO THIS ADDRESS. **SEND TO: Commissioner for Patents, P.O. Box 1450, Alexandria, VA 22313-1450.**

If you need assistance in completing the form, call 1-800-PTO-9199 and select option 2.

資 料

PTO/AIA/02

Doc code: Oath
Document Description: Oath or declaration filed

PTO/AIA/02 (07-13)
Approved for use through 04/30/2017. OMB 0651-0032
U.S. Patent and Trademark Office; U.S. DEPARTMENT OF COMMERCE
Under the Paperwork Reduction Act of 1995, no persons are required to respond to a collection of information unless it displays a valid OMB control number.

SUBSTITUTE STATEMENT IN LIEU OF AN OATH OR DECLARATION FOR UTILITY OR DESIGN PATENT APPLICATION (35 U.S.C. 115(d) AND 37 CFR 1.64)

Title of Invention	

This statement is directed to:

☐ The attached application,

OR

☐ United States application or PCT international application number _____ filed on _____.

LEGAL NAME of inventor to whom this substitute statement applies:

(*E.g.*, Given Name (first and middle (if any)) and Family Name or Surname)

Residence (except for a deceased or legally incapacitated inventor):

City	State	Country

Mailing Address (except for a deceased or legally incapacitated inventor):

City	State	Zip	Country

I believe the above-named inventor or joint inventor to be the original inventor or an original joint inventor of a claimed invention in the application.

The above-identified application was made or authorized to be made by me.

I hereby acknowledge that any willful false statement made in this statement is punishable under 18 U.S.C. 1001 by fine or imprisonment of not more than five (5) years, or both.

Relationship to the inventor to whom this substitute statement applies:

☐ Legal Representative (for deceased or legally incapacitated inventor only),

☐ Assignee,

☐ Person to whom the inventor is under an obligation to assign,

☐ Person who otherwise shows a sufficient proprietary interest in the matter (petition under 37 CFR 1.46 is required), or

☐ Joint Inventor.

[Page 1 of 2]

This collection of information is required by 35 U.S.C. 115 and 37 CFR 1.63. The information is required to obtain or retain a benefit by the public which is to file (and by the USPTO to process) an application. Confidentiality is governed by 35 U.S.C. 122 and 37 CFR 1.11 and 1.14. This collection is estimated to take 1 minute to complete, including gathering, preparing, and submitting the completed application form to the USPTO. Time will vary depending upon the individual case. Any comments on the amount of time you require to complete this form and/or suggestions for reducing this burden, should be sent to the Chief Information Officer, U.S. Patent and Trademark Office, U.S. Department of Commerce, P.O. Box 1450, Alexandria, VA 22313-1450. DO NOT SEND FEES OR COMPLETED FORMS TO THIS ADDRESS. **SEND TO: Commissioner for Patents, P.O. Box 1450, Alexandria, VA 22313-1450.**

If you need assistance in completing the form, call 1-800-PTO-9199 and select option 2.

PTO/AIA/02の続き

PTO/SB/AIA02 (07-13)
Approved for use through 01/31/2014. OMB 0651-0032
U.S. Patent and Trademark Office; U.S. DEPARTMENT OF COMMERCE
Under the Paperwork Reduction Act of 1995, no persons are required to respond to a collection of information unless it displays a valid OMB control number.

SUBSTITUTE STATEMENT

Circumstances permitting execution of this substitute statement:

- [ ] Inventor is deceased,
- [ ] Inventor is under legal incapacity,
- [ ] Inventor cannot be found or reached after diligent effort, or
- [ ] Inventor has refused to execute the oath or declaration under 37 CFR 1.63.

If there are joint inventors, please check the appropriate box below:

- [ ] An application data sheet under 37 CFR 1.76 (PTO/AIA/14 or equivalent) naming the entire inventive entity has been or is currently submitted.

OR

- [ ] An application data sheet under 37 CFR 1.76 (PTO/AIA/14 or equivalent) has not been submitted. Thus, a Substitute Statement Supplemental Sheet (PTO/AIA/11 or equivalent) naming the entire inventive entity and providing inventor information is attached. See 37 CFR 1.64(b).

WARNING:

Petitioner/applicant is cautioned to avoid submitting personal information in documents filed in a patent application that may contribute to identity theft. Personal information such as social security numbers, bank account numbers, or credit card numbers (other than a check or credit card authorization form PTO-2038 submitted for payment purposes) is never required by the USPTO to support a petition or an application. If this type of personal information is included in documents submitted to the USPTO, petitioners/applicants should consider redacting such personal information from the documents before submitting them to the USPTO. Petitioner/applicant is advised that the record of a patent application is available to the public after publication of the application (unless a non-publication request in compliance with 37 CFR 1.213(a) is made in the application) or issuance of a patent. Furthermore, the record from an abandoned application may also be available to the public if the application is referenced in a published application or an issued patent (see 37 CFR 1.14). Checks and credit card authorization forms PTO-2038 submitted for payment purposes are not retained in the application file and therefore are not publicly available.

PERSON EXECUTING THIS SUBSTITUTE STATEMENT:

Name:	Date (Optional):
Signature:	

APPLICANT NAME AND TITLE OF PERSON EXECUTING THIS SUBSTITUTE STATEMENT:

If the applicant is a juristic entity, list the applicant name and the title of the signer:

Applicant Name:

Title of Person Executing
This Substitute Statement:

The signer, whose title is supplied above, is authorized to act on behalf of the applicant.

Residence of the signer (unless provided in an application data sheet, PTO/AIA/14 or equivalent):

City	State	Country

Mailing Address of the signer (unless provided in an application data sheet, PTO/AIA/14 or equivalent)

City	State	Zip	Country

Note: Use an additional PTO/AIA/02 form for each inventor who is deceased, legally incapacitated, cannot be found or reached after diligent effort, or has refused to execute the oath or declaration under 37 CFR 1.63.

PTO/AIA/05

Doc Code: REIS.DECL
Document Description: Reissue Declaration Filed In Accordance With MPEP 1414

PTO/AIA/05 (06-12)
Approved for use through 01/31/2020. OMB 0651-0033
U.S. Patent and Trademark Office; U.S. DEPARTMENT OF COMMERCE
Under the Paperwork Reduction Act of 1995, no persons are required to respond to a collection of information unless it displays a valid OMB control number.

REISSUE APPLICATION DECLARATION BY THE INVENTOR	Docket Number (Optional)

I hereby declare that:
Each inventor's residence and mailing address are stated below next to their name.
I believe I am the original inventor or an original joint inventor of the subject matter which is described and claimed in patent number _____, granted _____ and for which a reissue patent is sought on the invention titled _____,

the specification of which

☐ is attached hereto.

☐ was filed on _____ as reissue application number _____.

The above-identified application was made or authorized to be made by me.

I hereby acknowledge that any willful false statement made in this declaration is punishable under 18 U.S.C. 1001 by fine or imprisonment of not more than five (5) years, or both.

I believe the original patent to be wholly or partly inoperative or invalid, for the reasons described below. (Check all boxes that apply.)

☐ by reason of a defective specification or drawing.

☐ by reason of the patentee claiming more or less than he had the right to claim in the patent.

☐ by reason of other errors.

At least one error upon which reissue is based is described below. If the reissue is a broadening reissue, a claim that the application seeks to broaden must be identified:

[Page 1 of 2]

This collection of information is required by 37 CFR 1.175. The information is required to obtain or retain a benefit by the public which is to file (and by the USPTO to process) an application. Confidentiality is governed by 35 U.S.C. 122 and 37 CFR 1.11 and 1.14. This collection is estimated to take 30 minutes to complete, including gathering, preparing, and submitting the completed application form to the USPTO. Time will vary depending upon the individual case. Any comments on the amount of time you require to complete this form and/or suggestions for reducing this burden, should be sent to the Chief Information Officer, U.S. Patent and Trademark Office, U.S. Department of Commerce, P.O. Box 1450, Alexandria, VA 22313-1450. DO NOT SEND FEES OR COMPLETED FORMS TO THIS ADDRESS. **SEND TO: Commissioner for Patents, P.O. Box 1450, Alexandria, VA 22313-1450.**

If you need assistance in completing the form, call 1-800-PTO-9199 and select option 2.

PTO/AIA/05の続き

PTO/AIA/05 (06-12)
Approved for use through 01/31/2020. OMB 0651-0033
U.S. Patent and Trademark Office; U.S. DEPARTMENT OF COMMERCE
Under the Paperwork Reduction Act of 1995, no persons are required to respond to a collection of information unless it displays a valid OMB control number.

(REISSUE APPLICATION DECLARATION BY THE INVENTOR, page 2)	Docket Number (Optional)

Note: To appoint a power of attorney, use form PTO/AIA/81.

Correspondence Address: Direct all communications about the application to:

☐ The address associated with Customer Number: _____

OR

☐ Firm or Individual Name: _____

Address	
City	State	Zip
Country	
Telephone	Email

WARNING:

Petitioner/applicant is cautioned to avoid submitting personal information in documents filed in a patent application that may contribute to identity theft. Personal information such as social security numbers, bank account numbers, or credit card numbers (other than a check or credit card authorization form PTO-2038 submitted for payment purposes) is never required by the USPTO to support a petition or an application. If this type of personal information is included in documents submitted to the USPTO, petitioners/applicants should consider redacting such personal information from the documents before submitting them to the USPTO. Petitioner/applicant is advised that the record of a patent application is available to the public after publication of the application (unless a non-publication request in compliance with 37 CFR 1.213(a) is made in the application) or issuance of a patent. Furthermore, the record from an abandoned application may also be available to the public if the application is referenced in a published application or an issued patent (see 37 CFR 1.14). Checks and credit card authorization forms PTO-2038 submitted for payment purposes are not retained in the application file and therefore are not publicly available.

Legal name of sole or first inventor (*E.g.*, Given Name (first and middle (if any) and Family Name or Surname)

Inventor's Signature	Date (Optional)
Residence: City	State	Country
Mailing Address		
City	State	Zip	Country

☐ Additional joint inventors are named on the _____ supplemental sheet(s) PTO/AIA/10 attached hereto.

[Page 2 of 2]

261

資　料

PTO/AIA/08

Doc Code: Oath
Document Description: Oath or declaration filed

PTO/AIA/08 (11-15)
Approved for use through 4/30/2017. OMB 0651-0032
U.S. Patent and Trademark Office; U.S. DEPARTMENT OF COMMERCE
Under the Paperwork Reduction Act of 1995, no persons are required to respond to a collection of information unless it contains a valid OMB control number.

DECLARATION FOR UTILITY OR DESIGN PATENT APPLICATION (37 CFR 1.63)		Attorney Docket Number	
		First Named Inventor	
		COMPLETE IF KNOWN	
		Application Number	
☐ Declaration Submitted With Initial Filing	OR ☐ Declaration Submitted After Initial Filing (surcharge (37 CFR 1.16(f)) required)	Filing Date	
		Art Unit	
		Examiner Name	

_____
(Title of the Invention)

As a below named inventor, I hereby declare that:

This declaration is directed to:

☐ The attached application,

OR

☐ United States Application Number or PCT International application number _____

filed on _____.

The above-identified application was made or authorized to be made by me.

I believe I am the original inventor or an original joint inventor of a claimed invention in the application.

I hereby acknowledge that any willful false statement made in this declaration is punishable under 18 U.S.C. 1001 by fine or imprisonment of not more than five (5) years, or both.

Direct all correspondence to:	☐ The address associated with Customer Number:		OR	☐ Correspondence address below
Name				
Address				
City		State		Zip
Country		Telephone		Email

[Page 1 of 2]

This collection of information is required by 35 U.S.C. 115 and 37 CFR 1.63. The information is required to obtain or retain a benefit by the public which is to file (and by the USPTO to process) an application. Confidentiality is governed by 35 U.S.C. 122 and 37 CFR 1.11 and 1.14. This collection is estimated to take 21 minutes to complete, including gathering, preparing, and submitting the completed application form to the USPTO. Time will vary depending upon the individual case. Any comments on the amount of time you require to complete this form and/or suggestions for reducing this burden, should be sent to the Chief Information Officer, U.S. Patent and Trademark Office, U.S. Department of Commerce, P.O. Box 1450, Alexandria, VA 22313-1450. DO NOT SEND FEES OR COMPLETED FORMS TO THIS ADDRESS. **SEND TO: Commissioner for Patents, P.O. Box 1450, Alexandria, VA 22313-1450.**

If you need assistance in completing the form, call 1-800-PTO-9199 and select option 2.

PTO/AIA/08の続き

PTO/AIA/08 (11-15)
Approved for use through 4/30/2017. OMB 0651-0032
U.S. Patent and Trademark Office; U.S. DEPARTMENT OF COMMERCE
Under the Paperwork Reduction Act of 1995, no persons are required to respond to a collection of information unless it contains a valid OMB control number.

DECLARATION — Utility or Design Patent Application

WARNING:

Petitioner/applicant is cautioned to avoid submitting personal information in documents filed in a patent application that may contribute to identity theft. Personal information such as social security numbers, bank account numbers, or credit card numbers (other than a check or credit card authorization form PTO-2038 submitted for payment purposes) is never required by the USPTO to support a petition or an application. If this type of personal information is included in documents submitted to the USPTO, petitioners/applicants should consider redacting such personal information from the documents before submitting them to the USPTO. Petitioner/applicant is advised that the record of a patent application is available to the public after publication of the application (unless a non-publication request in compliance with 37 CFR 1.213(a) is made in the application) or issuance of a patent. Furthermore, the record from an abandoned application may also be available to the public if the application is referenced in a published application or an issued patent (see 37 CFR 1.14). Checks and credit card authorization forms PTO-2038 submitted for payment purposes are not retained in the application file and therefore are not publicly available. Petitioner/applicant is advised that documents which form the record of a patent application (such as the PTO/SB/01) are placed into the Privacy Act system of records DEPARTMENT OF COMMERCE, COMMERCE-PAT-7, System name: *Patent Application Files*. Documents not retained in an application file (such as the PTO-2038) are placed into the Privacy Act system of COMMERCE/PAT-TM-10, System name: *Deposit Accounts and Electronic Funds Transfer Profiles*.

LEGAL NAME OF SOLE OR FIRST INVENTOR:
(*E.g.*, Given Name (first and middle if any) and Family Name or Surname)

Inventor's Signature		Date (Optional)	
Residence: City	State	Country	
Mailing Address			
City	State	Zip	Country

☐ Additional inventors are being named on the _____ Supplemental sheet(s) PTO/AIA/10 attached hereto

資 料

PTO/AIA/14

PTO/AIA/14 (11-15)
Approved for use through 04/30/2017. OMB 0651-0032
U.S. Patent and Trademark Office; U.S. DEPARTMENT OF COMMERCE
Under the Paperwork Reduction Act of 1995, no persons are required to respond to a collection of information unless it contains a valid OMB control number.

Application Data Sheet 37 CFR 1.76	Attorney Docket Number	
	Application Number	
Title of Invention		

The application data sheet is part of the provisional or nonprovisional application for which it is being submitted. The following form contains the bibliographic data arranged in a format specified by the United States Patent and Trademark Office as outlined in 37 CFR 1.76.
This document may be completed electronically and submitted to the Office in electronic format using the Electronic Filing System (EFS) or the document may be printed and included in a paper filed application.

Secrecy Order 37 CFR 5.2:

☐ Portions or all of the application associated with this Application Data Sheet may fall under a Secrecy Order pursuant to 37 CFR 5.2 (Paper filers only. Applications that fall under Secrecy Order may not be filed electronically.)

Inventor Information:

Inventor 1						[Remove]
Legal Name						
Prefix	Given Name		Middle Name		Family Name	Suffix
Residence Information (Select One)		● US Residency	○ Non US Residency		○ Active US Military Service	
City			State/Province		Country of Residence	

Mailing Address of Inventor:				
Address 1				
Address 2				
City			State/Province	
Postal Code			Country i	
All Inventors Must Be Listed - Additional Inventor Information blocks may be generated within this form by selecting the **Add** button.				[Add]

Correspondence Information:

Enter either Customer Number or complete the Correspondence Information section below. For further information see 37 CFR 1.33(a).			
☐ An Address is being provided for the correspondence Information of this application.			
Customer Number			
Email Address		[Add Email]	[Remove Email]

Application Information:

Title of the Invention			
Attorney Docket Number		Small Entity Status Claimed ☐	
Application Type			
Subject Matter			
Total Number of Drawing Sheets (if any)		Suggested Figure for Publication (if any)	

EFS Web 2.2.12

264

PTO/AIA/14の続き

PTO/AIA/14 (11-15)
Approved for use through 04/30/2017. OMB 0651-0032
U.S. Patent and Trademark Office; U.S. DEPARTMENT OF COMMERCE
Under the Paperwork Reduction Act of 1995, no persons are required to respond to a collection of information unless it contains a valid OMB control number.

Application Data Sheet 37 CFR 1.76	Attorney Docket Number	
	Application Number	
Title of Invention		

Filing By Reference:

Only complete this section when filing an application by reference under 35 U.S.C. 111(c) and 37 CFR 1.57(a). Do not complete this section if application papers including a specification and any drawings are being filed. Any domestic benefit or foreign priority information must be provided in the appropriate section(s) below (i.e., "Domestic Benefit/National Stage Information" and "Foreign Priority Information").

For the purposes of a filing date under 37 CFR 1.53(b), the description and any drawings of the present application are replaced by this reference to the previously filed application, subject to conditions and requirements of 37 CFR 1.57(a).

Application number of the previously filed application	Filing date (YYYY-MM-DD)	Intellectual Property Authority or Country

Publication Information:

☐ Request Early Publication (Fee required at time of Request 37 CFR 1.219)

☐ **Request Not to Publish.** I hereby request that the attached application not be published under 35 U.S.C. 122(b) and certify that the invention disclosed in the attached application **has not and will not** be the subject of an application filed in another country, or under a multilateral international agreement, that requires publication at eighteen months after filing.

Representative Information:

Representative information should be provided for all practitioners having a power of attorney in the application. Providing this information in the Application Data Sheet does not constitute a power of attorney in the application (see 37 CFR 1.32). Either enter Customer Number or complete the Representative Name section below. If both sections are completed the customer Number will be used for the Representative Information during processing.

Please Select One:	● Customer Number	○ US Patent Practitioner	○ Limited Recognition (37 CFR 11.9)
Customer Number			

Domestic Benefit/National Stage Information:

This section allows for the applicant to either claim benefit under 35 U.S.C. 119(e), 120, 121, 365(c), or 386(c) or indicate National Stage entry from a PCT application. Providing benefit claim information in the Application Data Sheet constitutes the specific reference required by 35 U.S.C. 119(e) or 120, and 37 CFR 1.78.
When referring to the current application, please leave the "Application Number" field blank.

Prior Application Status			Remove
Application Number	Continuity Type	Prior Application Number	Filing or 371(c) Date (YYYY-MM-DD)

Additional Domestic Benefit/National Stage Data may be generated within this form by selecting the **Add** button.

EFS Web 2.2.12

資　料

PTO/AIA/14の続き

PTO/AIA/14 (11-15)
Approved for use through 04/30/2017. OMB 0651-0032
U.S. Patent and Trademark Office; U.S. DEPARTMENT OF COMMERCE
Under the Paperwork Reduction Act of 1995, no persons are required to respond to a collection of information unless it contains a valid OMB control number.

Application Data Sheet 37 CFR 1.76	Attorney Docket Number	
	Application Number	
Title of Invention		

Foreign Priority Information:

This section allows for the applicant to claim priority to a foreign application. Providing this information in the application data sheet constitutes the claim for priority as required by 35 U.S.C. 119(b) and 37 CFR 1.55. When priority is claimed to a foreign application that is eligible for retrieval under the priority document exchange program (PDX)[i] the information will be used by the Office to automatically attempt retrieval pursuant to 37 CFR 1.55(i)(1) and (2). Under the PDX program, applicant bears the ultimate responsibility for ensuring that a copy of the foreign application is received by the Office from the participating foreign intellectual property office, or a certified copy of the foreign priority application is filed, within the time period specified in 37 CFR 1.55(g)(1).

Remove

Application Number	Country[i]	Filing Date (YYYY-MM-DD)	Access Code[i] (if applicable)

Additional Foreign Priority Data may be generated within this form by selecting the **Add** button.

Statement under 37 CFR 1.55 or 1.78 for AIA (First Inventor to File) Transition Applications

☐ This application (1) claims priority to or the benefit of an application filed before March 16, 2013 and (2) also contains, or contained at any time, a claim to a claimed invention that has an effective filing date on or after March 16, 2013.
NOTE: By providing this statement under 37 CFR 1.55 or 1.78, this application, with a filing date on or after March 16, 2013, will be examined under the first inventor to file provisions of the AIA.

EFS Web 2.2.12

PTO/AIA/14の続き

PTO/AIA/14 (11-15)
Approved for use through 04/30/2017. OMB 0651-0032
U.S. Patent and Trademark Office; U.S. DEPARTMENT OF COMMERCE
Under the Paperwork Reduction Act of 1995, no persons are required to respond to a collection of information unless it contains a valid OMB control number.

Application Data Sheet 37 CFR 1.76	Attorney Docket Number	
	Application Number	
Title of Invention		

Authorization or Opt-Out of Authorization to Permit Access:

When this Application Data Sheet is properly signed and filed with the application, applicant has provided written authority to permit a participating foreign intellectual property (IP) office access to the instant application-as-filed (see paragraph A in subsection 1 below) and the European Patent Office (EPO) access to any search results from the instant application (see paragraph B in subsection 1 below).

Should applicant choose not to provide an authorization identified in subsection 1 below, applicant **must opt-out** of the authorization by checking the corresponding box A or B or both in subsection 2 below.

NOTE: This section of the Application Data Sheet is **ONLY** reviewed and processed with the **INITIAL** filing of an application. After the initial filing of an application, an Application Data Sheet cannot be used to provide or rescind authorization for access by a foreign IP office(s). Instead, Form PTO/SB/39 or PTO/SB/69 must be used as appropriate.

1. Authorization to Permit Access by a Foreign Intellectual Property Office(s)

A. **Priority Document Exchange (PDX)** - Unless box A in subsection 2 (opt-out of authorization) is checked, the undersigned hereby **grants the USPTO authority** to provide the European Patent Office (EPO), the Japan Patent Office (JPO), the Korean Intellectual Property Office (KIPO), the State Intellectual Property Office of the People's Republic of China (SIPO), the World Intellectual Property Organization (WIPO), and any other foreign intellectual property office participating with the USPTO in a bilateral or multilateral priority document exchange agreement in which a foreign application claiming priority to the instant patent application is filed, access to: (1) the instant patent application-as-filed and its related bibliographic data, (2) any foreign or domestic application to which priority or benefit is claimed by the instant application and its related bibliographic data, and (3) the date of filing of this Authorization. See 37 CFR 1.14(h)(1).

B. **Search Results from U.S. Application to EPO** - Unless box B in subsection 2 (opt-out of authorization) is checked, the undersigned hereby **grants the USPTO authority** to provide the EPO access to the bibliographic data and search results from the instant patent application when a European patent application claiming priority to the instant patent application is filed. See 37 CFR 1.14(h)(2).

The applicant is reminded that the EPO's Rule 141(1) EPC (European Patent Convention) requires applicants to submit a copy of search results from the instant application without delay in a European patent application that claims priority to the instant application.

2. Opt-Out of Authorizations to Permit Access by a Foreign Intellectual Property Office(s)

☐ A. Applicant **DOES NOT** authorize the USPTO to permit a participating foreign IP office access to the instant application-as-filed. If this box is checked, the USPTO will not be providing a participating foreign IP office with any documents and information identified in subsection 1A above.

☐ B. Applicant **DOES NOT** authorize the USPTO to transmit to the EPO any search results from the instant patent application. If this box is checked, the USPTO will not be providing the EPO with search results from the instant application.

NOTE: Once the application has published or is otherwise publicly available, the USPTO may provide access to the application in accordance with 37 CFR 1.14.

資　料

PTO/AIA/14の続き

PTO/AIA/14 (11-15)
Approved for use through 04/30/2017. OMB 0651-0032
U.S. Patent and Trademark Office; U.S. DEPARTMENT OF COMMERCE
Under the Paperwork Reduction Act of 1995, no persons are required to respond to a collection of information unless it contains a valid OMB control number.

Application Data Sheet 37 CFR 1.76	Attorney Docket Number	
	Application Number	
Title of Invention		

Applicant Information:

Providing assignment information in this section does not substitute for compliance with any requirement of part 3 of Title 37 of CFR to have an assignment recorded by the Office.

Applicant 1

If the applicant is the inventor (or the remaining joint inventor or inventors under 37 CFR 1.45), this section should not be completed. The information to be provided in this section is the name and address of the legal representative who is the applicant under 37 CFR 1.43; or the name and address of the assignee, person to whom the inventor is under an obligation to assign the invention, or person who otherwise shows sufficient proprietary interest in the matter who is the applicant under 37 CFR 1.46. If the applicant is an applicant under 37 CFR 1.46 (assignee, person to whom the inventor is obligated to assign, or person who otherwise shows sufficient proprietary interest) together with one or more joint inventors, then the joint inventor or inventors who are also the applicant should be identified in this section.

[Clear]

○ Assignee ○ Legal Representative under 35 U.S.C. 117 ○ Joint Inventor

○ Person to whom the inventor is obligated to assign. ○ Person who shows sufficient proprietary interest

If applicant is the legal representative, indicate the authority to file the patent application, the inventor is:

Name of the Deceased or Legally Incapacitated Inventor:

If the Applicant is an Organization check here. ☐

Prefix	Given Name	Middle Name	Family Name	Suffix

Mailing Address Information For Applicant:	
Address 1	
Address 2	
City	
Country	
Phone Number	
Email Address	

State/Province	
Postal Code	
Fax Number	

Additional Applicant Data may be generated within this form by selecting the Add button.

Assignee Information including Non-Applicant Assignee Information:

Providing assignment information in this section does not substitute for compliance with any requirement of part 3 of Title 37 of CFR to have an assignment recorded by the Office.

EFS Web 2.2.12

PTO/AIA/14の続き

PTO/AIA/14 (11-15)
Approved for use through 04/30/2017. OMB 0651-0032
U.S. Patent and Trademark Office; U.S. DEPARTMENT OF COMMERCE
Under the Paperwork Reduction Act of 1995, no persons are required to respond to a collection of information unless it contains a valid OMB control number.

Application Data Sheet 37 CFR 1.76	Attorney Docket Number	
	Application Number	

Title of Invention	

Assignee 1

Complete this section if assignee information, including non-applicant assignee information, is desired to be included on the patent application publication. An assignee-applicant identified in the "Applicant Information" section will appear on the patent application publication as an applicant. For an assignee-applicant, complete this section only if identification as an assignee is also desired on the patent application publication.

If the Assignee or Non-Applicant Assignee is an Organization check here.					☐
Prefix	Given Name	Middle Name	Family Name		Suffix

Mailing Address Information For Assignee including Non-Applicant Assignee:

Address 1			
Address 2			
City		State/Province	
Country i		Postal Code	
Phone Number		Fax Number	
Email Address			

Additional Assignee or Non-Applicant Assignee Data may be generated within this form by selecting the Add button.

Signature:

NOTE: This Application Data Sheet must be signed in accordance with 37 CFR 1.33(b). **However, if this Application Data Sheet is submitted with the INITIAL filing of the application and either box A or B is not checked in subsection 2 of the "Authorization or Opt-Out of Authorization to Permit Access" section, then this form must also be signed in accordance with 37 CFR 1.14(c).**

  This Application Data Sheet **must** be signed by a patent practitioner if one or more of the applicants is a **juristic entity** (e.g., corporation or association). If the applicant is two or more joint inventors, this form must be signed by a patent practitioner, **all** joint inventors who are the applicant, or one or more joint inventor-applicants who have been given power of attorney (e.g., see USPTO Form PTO/AIA/81) on behalf of **all** joint inventor-applicants.
  See 37 CFR 1.4(d) for the manner of making signatures and certifications.

Signature		Date (YYYY-MM-DD)	
First Name		Last Name		Registration Number	

Additional Signature may be generated within this form by selecting the Add button.

EFS Web 2.2.12

資　料

PTO/AIA/14の続き

PTO/AIA/14 (11-15)
Approved for use through 04/30/2017. OMB 0651-0032
U.S. Patent and Trademark Office; U.S. DEPARTMENT OF COMMERCE
Under the Paperwork Reduction Act of 1995, no persons are required to respond to a collection of information unless it contains a valid OMB control number.

Application Data Sheet 37 CFR 1.76	Attorney Docket Number	
	Application Number	
Title of Invention		

This collection of information is required by 37 CFR 1.76. The information is required to obtain or retain a benefit by the public which is to file (and by the USPTO to process) an application. Confidentiality is governed by 35 U.S.C. 122 and 37 CFR 1.14. This collection is estimated to take 23 minutes to complete, including gathering, preparing, and submitting the completed application data sheet form to the USPTO. Time will vary depending upon the individual case. Any comments on the amount of time you require to complete this form and/or suggestions for reducing this burden, should be sent to the Chief Information Officer, U.S. Patent and Trademark Office, U.S. Department of Commerce, P.O. Box 1450, Alexandria, VA 22313-1450. DO NOT SEND FEES OR COMPLETED FORMS TO THIS ADDRESS. **SEND TO: Commissioner for Patents, P.O. Box 1450, Alexandria, VA 22313-1450.**

EFS Web 2.2.12

PTO/AIA/15

PTO/AIA/15 (03-13)
Approved for use through 01/31/2014. OMB 0651-0032
U.S. Patent and Trademark Office; U.S. DEPARTMENT OF COMMERCE
Under the Paperwork Reduction Act of 1995 no persons are required to respond to a collection of information unless it displays a valid OMB control number

UTILITY PATENT APPLICATION TRANSMITTAL

(Only for new nonprovisional applications under 37 CFR 1.53(b))

Attorney Docket No.	
First Named Inventor	
Title	
Express Mail Label No.	

APPLICATION ELEMENTS
See MPEP chapter 600 concerning utility patent application contents.

ADDRESS TO: Commissioner for Patents
P.O. Box 1450
Alexandria, VA 22313-1450

1. ☐ **Fee Transmittal Form** (PTO/SB/17 or equivalent)
2. ☐ **Applicant asserts small entity status.** See 37 CFR 1.27
3. ☐ **Applicant certifies micro entity status.** See 37 CFR 1.29. Applicant must attach form PTO/SB/15A or B or equivalent.
4. ☐ **Specification** [Total Pages _____]
   Both the claims and abstract must start on a new page.
   (See MPEP § 608.01(a) for information on the preferred arrangement)
5. ☐ **Drawing(s)** (35 U.S.C. 113) [Total Sheets _____]
6. ☐ **Inventor's Oath or Declaration** [Total Pages _____]
   (including substitute statements under 37 CFR 1.64 and assignments serving as an oath or declaration under 37 CFR 1.63(e))
   a. ☐ Newly executed (original or copy)
   b. ☐ A copy from a prior application (37 CFR 1.63(d))
7. ☐ **Application Data Sheet** * See note below.
   See 37 CFR 1.76 (PTO/AIA/14 or equivalent)
8. ☐ **CD-ROM or CD-R** in duplicate, large table, or Computer Program (Appendix)
   ☐ Landscape Table on CD
9. **Nucleotide and/or Amino Acid Sequence Submission**
   (if applicable, items a. – c. are required)
   a. ☐ Computer Readable Form (CRF)
   b. ☐ Specification Sequence Listing on:
      i. ☐ CD-ROM or CD-R (2 copies); or
      ii. ☐ Paper
   c. ☐ Statements verifying identity of above copies

ACCOMPANYING APPLICATION PAPERS

10. ☐ **Assignment Papers** (cover sheet & document(s))
    Name of Assignee _____
    _____
11. ☐ **37 CFR 3.73(c) Statement** (when there is an assignee)   ☐ **Power of Attorney**
12. ☐ **English Translation Document** (if applicable)
13. ☐ **Information Disclosure Statement** (PTO/SB/08 or PTO-1449)
    ☐ Copies of citations attached
14. ☐ **Preliminary Amendment**
15. ☐ **Return Receipt Postcard** (MPEP § 503) (Should be specifically itemized)
16. ☐ **Certified Copy of Priority Document(s)** (if foreign priority is claimed)
17. ☐ **Nonpublication Request**
    Under 35 U.S.C. 122(b)(2)(B)(i). Applicant must attach form PTO/SB/35 or equivalent.
18. ☐ **Other:** _____
    _____
    _____
    _____

*** Note:** (1) Benefit claims under 37 CFR 1.78 and foreign priority claims under 1.55 **must** be included in an Application Data Sheet (ADS).
(2) For applications filed under 35 U.S.C. 111, the application must contain an ADS specifying the applicant if the applicant is an assignee, person to whom the inventor is under an obligation to assign, or person who otherwise shows sufficient proprietary interest in the matter. See 37 CFR 1.46(b).

19. CORRESPONDENCE ADDRESS

☐ The address associated with Customer Number: _____   **OR**   ☐ Correspondence address below

Name	
Address	
City		State		Zip Code	
Country		Telephone		Email	
Signature		Date	
Name (Print/Type)		Registration No. (Attorney/Agent)	

This collection of information is required by 37 CFR 1.53(b). The information is required to obtain or retain a benefit by the public which is to file (and by the USPTO to process) an application. Confidentiality is governed by 35 U.S.C. 122 and 37 CFR 1.11 and 1.14. This collection is estimated to take 12 minutes to complete, including gathering, preparing, and submitting the completed application form to the USPTO. Time will vary depending upon the individual case. Any comments on the amount of time you require to complete this form and/or suggestions for reducing this burden, should be sent to the Chief Information Officer, U.S. Patent and Trademark Office, U.S. Department of Commerce, P.O. Box 1450, Alexandria, VA 22313-1450. DO NOT SEND FEES OR COMPLETED FORMS TO THIS ADDRESS. **SEND TO: Commissioner for Patents, P.O. Box 1450, Alexandria, VA 22313-1450.**

If you need assistance in completing the form, call 1-800-PTO-9199 and select option 2.

資　　料

PTO/AIA/18

PTO/AIA/18 (03-13)
Approved for use through 01/31/2014. OMB 0651-0032
U.S. Patent and Trademark Office; U.S. DEPARTMENT OF COMMERCE
Under the Paperwork Reduction Act of 1995 no persons are required to respond to a collection of information unless it displays a valid OMB control number

DESIGN PATENT APPLICATION TRANSMITTAL

(Only for new nonprovisional applications under 37 CFR 1.53(b))

Attorney Docket No.	
First Named Inventor	
Title	
Express Mail Label No.	

ADDRESS TO:
Commissioner for Patents
P.O. Box 1450
Alexandria, VA 22313-1450

DESIGN V. UTILITY: A "design patent" protects an article's ornamental appearance (e.g., the way an article looks) (35 U.S.C. 171), while a "utility patent" protects the way an article is used and works (35 U.S.C. 101). The ornamental appearance of an article includes its shape/configuration or surface ornamentation upon the article, or both. Both a design and a utility patent may be obtained on an article if invention resides both in its ornamental appearance and its utility. For more information, see MPEP § 1502.01.

APPLICATION ELEMENTS
See MPEP chapter 1500 concerning design patent application contents.

1. [ ] **Fee Transmittal Form**
   (PTO/SB/17 or equivalent)
2. [ ] **Applicant asserts small entity status.**
   See 37 CFR 1.27
3. [ ] **Applicant certifies micro entity status.** See 37 CFR 1.29.
   Applicant must attach form PTO/SB/15A or B or equivalent.
4. [ ] **Specification**   [Total Pages _____]
   (preferred arrangement set forth below, MPEP § 1503.01)
   - Preamble
   - Cross References to Related Applications
   - Statement Regarding Fed sponsored R & D
   - Description of the figure(s) of the drawings
   - Feature description
   - Claim (only one (1) claim permitted, MPEP § 1503.03)
5. [ ] **Drawing(s)**   [Total Sheets _____]
   See 37 CFR 1.152
6. **Inventor's Oath or Declaration**   [Total Pages _____]
   (including substitute statements under 37 CFR 1.64 and assignments serving as an oath or declaration under 37 CFR 1.63(e))
   a. [ ] Newly executed (original or copy)
   b. [ ] A copy from a prior application (37 CFR 1.63(d))
7. [ ] **Application Data Sheet**   * See note below.
   See 37 CFR 1.76 (PTO/AIA/14 or equivalent)

ACCOMPANYING APPLICATION PARTS

8. [ ] **Assignment Papers**
   (cover sheet & document(s))
9. [ ] **37 CFR 3.73(c) Statement**   [ ] **Power of Attorney**
   (when there is an assignee)
10. [ ] **English Translation Document**
    (if applicable)
11. [ ] **Information Disclosure Statement (IDS)**
    (PTO/SB/08 or PTO-1449)
    [ ] Copies of foreign patent documents, publications, and other information
12. [ ] **Preliminary Amendment**
13. [ ] **Return Receipt Postcard**
    (MPEP § 503) (Should be specifically itemized)
14. [ ] **Certified Copy of Priority Document(s)**
    (if foreign priority is claimed)
15. [ ] **Request for Expedited Examination of a Design Application**
    (37 CFR 1.155) (NOTE: Use "Mail Stop Expedited Design")
16. [ ] **Other:** _____

*Note: (1) Benefit claims under 37 CFR 1.78 and foreign priority claims under 1.55 **must** be included in an Application Data Sheet (ADS).
(2) For applications filed under 35 U.S.C. 111, the application must contain an ADS specifying the applicant if the applicant is an assignee, person to whom the inventor is under an obligation to assign, or person who otherwise shows sufficient proprietary interest in the matter. See 37 CFR 1.46(b).*

17. CORRESPONDENCE ADDRESS

[ ] The address associated with Customer Number: _____   **OR**   [ ] Correspondence address below

Name	
Address	
City	State	Zip Code
Country	Telephone	Email
Signature		Date
Name (Print/Type)		Registration No. (Attorney/Agent)

This collection of information is required by 37 CFR 1.53(b). The information is required to obtain or retain a benefit by the public which is to file (and by the USPTO to process) an application. Confidentiality is governed by 35 U.S.C. 122 and 37 CFR 1.11 and 1.14. This collection is estimated to take 12 minutes to complete, including gathering, preparing, and submitting the completed application form to the USPTO. Time will vary depending upon the individual case. Any comments on the amount of time you require to complete this form and/or suggestions for reducing this burden, should be sent to the Chief Information Officer, U.S. Patent and Trademark Office, U.S. Department of Commerce, P.O. Box 1450, Alexandria, VA 22313-1450. DO NOT SEND FEES OR COMPLETED FORMS TO THIS ADDRESS. **SEND TO: Commissioner for Patents, P.O. Box 1450, Alexandria, VA 22313-1450.**

If you need assistance in completing the form, call 1-800-PTO-9199 and select option 2.

PTO/AIA/24

Doc Code: EABN
Document Description: Letter Express Abandonment of the application

PTO/AIA/24 (07-17)
Approved for use through 07/31/2017. OMB 0651-0031
U.S. Patent and Trademark Office; U.S. DEPARTMENT OF COMMERCE
Under the Paperwork Reduction Act of 1995, no persons are required to respond to a collection of information unless it displays a valid OMB control number.

EXPRESS ABANDONMENT UNDER 37 CFR 1.138

File the petition electronically using EFS-Web
Or **Mail** the petition to:
Mail Stop Express Abandonment
Commissioner for Patents
P.O. Box 1450, Alexandria, VA 22313-1450

Application Number	
Filing Date	
First Named Inventor	
Art Unit	
Examiner Name	
Attorney Docket Number	

Please **check only one** of boxes 1 or 2 below:
(If no box is checked, this paper will be treated as a request for express abandonment as if box 1 is checked.)

1. ☐ **Express Abandonment**
   I request that the above-identified application be expressly abandoned as of the filing date of this paper.

2. ☐ **Express Abandonment in Favor of a Continuing Application**
   I request that the above-identified application be expressly abandoned as of the filing date accorded the continuing application filed previously or herewith.

NOTE: A paper requesting express abandonment of an application is not effective unless and until an appropriate USPTO official recognizes and acts on the paper. See the Manual of Patent Examining Procedure (MPEP), section 711.01.

TO AVOID PUBLICATION, USE FORM PTO/AIA/24A INSTEAD OF THIS FORM.

TO REQUEST A REFUND OF SEARCH FEE AND EXCESS CLAIMS FEE (IF ELIGIBLE), USE FORM PTO/AIA/24B INSTEAD OF THIS FORM.

I am the:

☐ applicant.

☐ attorney or agent of record. Attorney or agent registration number is _____

☐ attorney or agent acting under 37 CFR 1.34, who is authorized under 37 CFR 1.138(b) because the application is expressly abandoned in favor of a continuing application (box 2 above must be checked). Attorney or agent registration number is _____.

_____   _____
Signature   Date

_____   _____
Typed or printed name   Telephone Number

Note: This form must be signed in accordance with 37 CFR 1.33. See 37 CFR 1.4(d) for signature requirements and certifications. Submit multiple forms if more than one signature is required, see below.

☐ Total of _____ forms are submitted.

This collection of information is required by 37 CFR 1.138. The information is required to obtain or retain a benefit by the public which is to file (and by the USPTO to process an application). Confidentiality is governed by 35 U.S.C. 122 and 37 CFR 1.11 and 1.14. This collection is estimated to take 12 minutes to complete, including gathering, preparing, and submitting the completed application form to the USPTO. Time will vary depending upon the individual case. Any comments on the amount of time you require to complete this form and/or suggestions for reducing this burden, should be sent to the Chief Information Officer, U.S. Patent and Trademark Office, U.S. Department of Commerce, P.O. Box 1450, Alexandria, VA 22313-1450. DO NOT SEND FEES OR COMPLETED FORMS TO THIS ADDRESS. **SEND TO: Mail Stop Express Abandonment, Commissioner for Patents, P.O. Box 1450, Alexandria, VA 22313-1450.**

If you need assistance in completing the form, call 1-800-PTO-9199 and select option 2.

資　料

PTO/AIA/25

PTO/AIA/25 (04-13)
Approved for use through 04/30/2013. OMB 0651-0031
U.S. Patent and Trademark Office; U.S. DEPARTMENT OF COMMERCE
Under the Paperwork Reduction Act of 1995, no persons are required to respond to a collection of information unless it displays a valid OMB control number.

TERMINAL DISCLAIMER TO OBVIATE A PROVISIONAL DOUBLE PATENTING REJECTION OVER A PENDING "REFERENCE" APPLICATION	Docket Number (Optional)

In re Application of:

Application No.:

Filed:

For:

The applicant, _____, owner of _____ percent interest in the instant application hereby disclaims, except as provided below, the terminal part of the statutory term of any patent granted on the instant application which would extend beyond the expiration date of the full statutory term of any patent granted on pending **reference** Application Number _____ filed, _____, as the term of any patent granted on said **reference** application may be shortened by any terminal disclaimer filed prior to the grant of any patent on the pending **reference** application. The applicant hereby agrees that any patent so granted on the instant application shall be enforceable only for and during such period that it and any patent granted on the **reference** application are commonly owned. This agreement runs with any patent granted on the instant application and is binding upon the grantee, its successors or assigns.

In making the above disclaimer, the applicant does not disclaim the terminal part of any patent granted on the instant application that would extend to the expiration date of the full statutory term of any patent granted on said **reference** application, "as the term of any patent granted on said **reference** application may be shortened by any terminal disclaimer filed prior to the grant of any patent on the pending **reference** application," in the event that: any such patent granted on the pending **reference** application expires for failure to pay a maintenance fee, is held unenforceable, is found invalid by a court of competent jurisdiction, is statutorily disclaimed in whole or terminally disclaimed under 37 CFR 1.321, has all claims canceled by a reexamination certificate, is reissued, or is in any manner terminated prior to the expiration of its full statutory term as shortened by any terminal disclaimer filed prior to its grant.

Check either box 1 or 2 below, if appropriate.

1. ☐ The undersigned is the applicant. If the applicant is an assignee, the undersigned is authorized to act on behalf of the assignee.

I hereby acknowledge that any willful false statements made are punishable under 18 U.S.C. 1001 by fine or imprisonment of not more than five (5) years, or both.

2. ☐ The undersigned is an attorney or agent of record. Reg. No. _____

_____   _____
Signature   Date

_____
Typed or printed name

_____   _____
Title   Telephone Number

☐ Terminal disclaimer fee under 37 CFR 1.20(d) is included.

WARNING: Information on this form may become public. Credit card information should not be included on this form. Provide credit card information and authorization on PTO-2038.

This collection of information is required by 37 CFR 1.321. The information is required to obtain or retain a benefit by the public which is to file (and by the USPTO to process) an application. Confidentiality is governed by 35 U.S.C. 122 and 37 CFR 1.11 and 1.14. This collection is estimated to take 12 minutes to complete, including gathering, preparing, and submitting the completed application form to the USPTO. Time will vary depending upon the individual case. Any comments on the amount of time you require to complete this form and/or suggestions for reducing this burden, should be sent to the Chief Information Officer, U.S. Patent and Trademark Office, U.S. Department of Commerce, P.O. Box 1450, Alexandria, VA 22313-1450. DO NOT SEND FEES OR COMPLETED FORMS TO THIS ADDRESS. **SEND TO: Commissioner for Patents, P.O. Box 1450, Alexandria, VA 22313-1450.**

If you need assistance in completing the form, call 1-800-PTO-9199 and select option 2.

PTO/AIA/26

PTO/AIA/26 (04-14)
Approved for use through 07/31/2016. OMB 0651-0031
U.S. Patent and Trademark Office; U.S. DEPARTMENT OF COMMERCE
Under the Paperwork Reduction Act of 1995, no persons are required to respond to a collection of information unless it displays a valid OMB control number.

TERMINAL DISCLAIMER TO OBVIATE A DOUBLE PATENTING REJECTION OVER A "PRIOR" PATENT	Docket Number (Optional)

In re Application of:

Application No.:

Filed:

For:

The applicant, _____, owner of _____ percent interest in the instant application hereby disclaims, except as provided below, the terminal part of the statutory term of any patent granted on the instant application which would extend beyond the expiration date of the full statutory term of **prior patent** No. _____ as the term of said **prior patent** is presently shortened by any terminal disclaimer. The applicant hereby agrees that any patent so granted on the instant application shall be enforceable only for and during such period that it and the **prior patent** are commonly owned. This agreement runs with any patent granted on the instant application and is binding upon the grantee, its successors or assigns.

In making the above disclaimer, the applicant does not disclaim the terminal part of the term of any patent granted on the instant application that would extend to the expiration date of the full statutory term of the **prior patent**, "as the term of said **prior patent** is presently shortened by any terminal disclaimer," in the event that said **prior patent** later:
    expires for failure to pay a maintenance fee;
    is held unenforceable;
    is found invalid by a court of competent jurisdiction;
    is statutorily disclaimed in whole or terminally disclaimed under 37 CFR 1.321;
    has all claims canceled by a reexamination certificate;
    is reissued; or
    is in any manner terminated prior to the expiration of its full statutory term as presently shortened by any terminal disclaimer.

Check either box 1 or 2 below, if appropriate.

1. ☐ The undersigned is the applicant. If the applicant is an assignee, the undersigned is authorized to act on behalf of the assignee.

I hereby acknowledge that any willful false statements made are punishable under 18 U.S.C. 1001 by fine or imprisonment of not more than five (5) years, or both.

2. ☐ The undersigned is an attorney or agent of record. Reg. No. _____

_____   _____
Signature   Date

_____
Typed or printed name

_____   _____
Title   Telephone Number

☐ Terminal disclaimer fee under 37 CFR 1.20(d) included.

WARNING: Information on this form may become public. Credit card information should not be included on this form. Provide credit card information and authorization on PTO-2038.

This collection of information is required by 37 CFR 1.321. The information is required to obtain or retain a benefit by the public which is to file (and by the USPTO to process) an application. Confidentiality is governed by 35 U.S.C. 122 and 37 CFR 1.11 and 1.14. This collection is estimated to take 12 minutes to complete, including gathering, preparing, and submitting the completed application form to the USPTO. Time will vary depending upon the individual case. Any comments on the amount of time you require to complete this form and/or suggestions for reducing this burden, should be sent to the Chief Information Officer, U.S. Patent and Trademark Office, U.S. Department of Commerce, P.O. Box 1450, Alexandria, VA 22313-1450. DO NOT SEND FEES OR COMPLETED FORMS TO THIS ADDRESS. **SEND TO: Commissioner for Patents, P.O. Box 1450, Alexandria, VA 22313-1450.**

If you need assistance in completing the form, call 1-800-PTO-9199 and select option 2.

資料

PTO/AIA/31

PTO/AIA/31 (03-14)
Approved for use through 07/31/2016. OMB 0651-0031
U.S. Patent and Trademark Office; U.S. DEPARTMENT OF COMMERCE
Under the Paperwork Reduction Act of 1995, no persons are required to respond to a collection of information unless it displays a valid OMB control number.

NOTICE OF APPEAL FROM THE EXAMINER TO THE PATENT TRIAL AND APPEAL BOARD

Docket Number (Optional)

I hereby certify that this correspondence is being facsimile transmitted to the USPTO, EFS-Web transmitted to the USPTO, or deposited with the United States Postal Service with sufficient postage in an envelope addressed to "Commissioner for Patents, P.O. Box 1450, Alexandria, on Alexandria, VA 22313-1450" [37 CFR 1.8(a)] on _____. Signature _____ Typed or printed name _____	In re Application of	
	Application Number	Filed
	For	
	Art Unit	Examiner

Applicant hereby **appeals** to the Patent Trial and Appeal Board from the last decision of the examiner.

The fee for this Notice of Appeal is (37 CFR 41.20(b)(1)) $ _____

☐ Applicant asserts small entity status. See 37 CFR 1.27. Therefore, the fee shown above is reduced by 50%, and the resulting fee is: $ _____

☐ Applicant certifies micro entity status. See 37 CFR 1.29. Therefore, the fee shown above is reduced by 75%, and the resulting fee is: $ _____
Form PTO/SB/15A or B or equivalent must either be enclosed or have been submitted previously.

☐ A check in the amount of the fee is enclosed.

☐ Payment by credit card. Form PTO-2038 is attached.

☐ The Director is hereby authorized to charge any fees which may be required, or credit any overpayment to Deposit Account No. _____.

☐ Payment made via EFS-Web.

☐ A petition for an extension of time under 37 CFR 1.136(a) (PTO/AIA/22 or equivalent) is enclosed.
For extensions of time in reexamination proceedings, see 37 CFR 1.550.

WARNING: Information on this form may become public. Credit card information should not be included on this form. Provide credit card information and authorization on PTO-2038.

I am the

☐ applicant   ☐ attorney or agent of record   ☐ attorney or agent acting under 37 CFR 1.34
                    Registration number _____   Registration number _____

Signature _____
Typed or printed name _____
Telephone Number _____
Date _____

NOTE: This form must be signed in accordance with 37 CFR 1.33. See 37 CFR 1.4 for signature requirements and certifications. Submit multiple forms if more than one signature is required, see below*.

☐ * Total of _____ forms are submitted.

This collection of information is required by 37 CFR 41.20(b)(1) and 41.31. The information is required to obtain or retain a benefit by the public which is to file (and by the USPTO to process) an application. Confidentiality is governed by 35 U.S.C. 122 and 37 CFR 1.11, 1.14 and 41.6. This collection is estimated to take 12 minutes to complete, including gathering, preparing, and submitting the completed application form to the USPTO. Time will vary depending upon the individual case. Any comments on the amount of time you require to complete this form and/or suggestions for reducing this burden, should be sent to the Chief Information Officer, U.S. Patent and Trademark Office, U.S. Department of Commerce, P.O. Box 1450, Alexandria, VA 22313-1450. DO NOT SEND FEES OR COMPLETED FORMS TO THIS ADDRESS. **SEND TO: Commissioner for Patents, P.O. Box 1450, Alexandria, VA 22313-1450.**

If you need assistance in completing the form, call 1-800-PTO-9199 and select option 2.

PTO/AIA/32

PTO/AIA/32 (03-13)
Approved for use through 03/31/2013. OMB 0651-0031
U.S. Patent and Trademark Office; U.S. DEPARTMENT OF COMMERCE
Under the Paperwork Reduction Act of 1995, no persons are required to respond to a collection of information unless it displays a valid OMB control number.

REQUEST FOR ORAL HEARING BEFORE THE PATENT TRIAL AND APPEAL BOARD

Docket Number (Optional)

I hereby certify that this correspondence is being facsimile transmitted to the USPTO, EFS-Web transmitted to the USPTO, or deposited with the United States Postal Service with sufficient postage in an envelope addressed to "Commissioner for Patents, P.O. Box 1450, Alexandria, VA 22313-1450" [37 CFR 1.8(a)] on _____. Signature _____ Typed or printed name _____	In re Application of
	Application Number / Filed
	For
	Art Unit / Examiner

Applicant hereby **requests an oral hearing** before the Patent Trial and Appeal Board in the appeal of the above-identified application.

The fee for this Request for Oral Hearing is (37 CFR 41.20(b)(3)) $ _____

☐ Applicant asserts small entity status. See 37 CFR 1.27. Therefore, the fee shown above is reduced by 50%, and the resulting fee is: $ _____

☐ Applicant certifies micro entity status. See 37 CFR 1.29. Therefore, the fee shown above is reduced by 75%, and the resulting fee is: $ _____
Form PTO/SB/15A or B or equivalent must either be enclosed or have been submitted previously

☐ A check in the amount of the fee is enclosed.

☐ Payment by credit card. Form PTO-2038 is attached.

☐ The Director has already been authorized to charge fees in this application to a Deposit Account.

☐ The Director is hereby authorized to charge any fees which may be required, or credit any overpayment to Deposit Account No. _____.

☐ Payment made via EFS-Web.

☐ A petition for an extension of time under 37 CFR 1.136(b) (PTO/SB/23 or equivalent) is enclosed.
For extensions of time in reexamination proceedings, see 37 CFR 1.550.

WARNING: Information on this form may become public. Credit card information should not be included on this form. Provide credit card information and authorization on PTO-2038.

I am the

☐ applicant   ☐ attorney or agent of record   ☐ attorney or agent acting under 37 CFR 1.34
                    Registration number _____   Registration number _____

Signature _____
Typed or printed name _____
Telephone Number _____
Date _____

NOTE: This form must be signed in accordance with 37 CFR 1.33. See 37 CFR 1.4 for signature requirements and certifications. Submit multiple forms if more than one signature is required, see below*.

☐ * Total of _____ forms are submitted.

This collection of information is required by 37 CFR 41.20(b)(3). The information is required to obtain or retain a benefit by the public which is to file (and by the USPTO to process) an application. Confidentiality is governed by 35 U.S.C. 122 and 37 CFR 1.11, 1.14 and 41.6. This collection is estimated to take 12 minutes to complete, including gathering, preparing, and submitting the completed application form to the USPTO. Time will vary depending upon the individual case. Any comments on the amount of time you require to complete this form and/or suggestions for reducing this burden, should be sent to the Chief Information Officer, U.S. Patent and Trademark Office, U.S. Department of Commerce, P.O. Box 1450, Alexandria, VA 22313-1450. DO NOT SEND FEES OR COMPLETED FORMS TO THIS ADDRESS. **SEND TO: Commissioner for Patents, P.O. Box 1450, Alexandria, VA 22313-1450.**

If you need assistance in completing the form, call 1-800-PTO-9199 and select option 2.

資　料

PTO/AIA/33

Doc Code: AP.PRE.REQ

PTO/AIA/33 (03-13)
Approved for use through 07/31/2013. OMB 0651-0031
U.S. Patent and Trademark Office; U.S. DEPARTMENT OF COMMERCE
Under the Paperwork Reduction Act of 1995, no persons are required to respond to a collection of information unless it displays a valid OMB control number.

PRE-APPEAL BRIEF REQUEST FOR REVIEW	Docket Number (Optional)	
I hereby certify that this correspondence is being facsimile transmitted to the USPTO, EFS-Web transmitted to the USPTO, or deposited with the United States Postal Service with sufficient postage as first class mail in an envelope addressed to "Mail Stop AF, Commissioner for Patents, P.O. Box 1450, Alexandria, VA 22313-1450" [37 CFR 1.8(a)] on _____	Application Number	Filed
	First Named Inventor	
Signature _____	Art Unit	Examiner
Typed or printed name _____		

Applicant requests review of the final rejection in the above-identified application. No amendments are being filed with this request.

This request is being filed with a notice of appeal.

The review is requested for the reason(s) stated on the attached sheet(s).
    Note: No more than five (5) pages may be provided.

I am the

☐ applicant.

☐ attorney or agent of record.
    Registration number _____

☐ attorney or agent acting under 37 CFR 1.34.
    Registration number if acting under 37 CFR 1.34 _____

_____
Signature

_____
Typed or printed name

_____
Telephone number

_____
Date

NOTE: This form must be signed in accordance with 37 CFR 1.33. See 37 CFR 1.4 for signature requirements and certifications. Submit multiple forms if more than one signature is required, see below*.

☐ *Total of _____ forms are submitted.

This collection of information is required by 35 U.S.C. 132. The information is required to obtain or retain a benefit by the public which is to file (and by the USPTO to process) an application. Confidentiality is governed by 35 U.S.C. 122 and 37 CFR 1.11, 1.14 and 41.6. This collection is estimated to take 12 minutes to complete, including gathering, preparing, and submitting the completed application form to the USPTO. Time will vary depending upon the individual case. Any comments on the amount of time you require to complete this form and/or suggestions for reducing this burden, should be sent to the Chief Information Officer, U.S. Patent and Trademark Office, U.S. Department of Commerce, P.O. Box 1450, Alexandria, VA 22313-1450. DO NOT SEND FEES OR COMPLETED FORMS TO THIS ADDRESS. **SEND TO: Mail Stop AF, Commissioner for Patents, P.O. Box 1450, Alexandria, VA 22313-1450.**

If you need assistance in completing the form, call 1-800-PTO-9199 and select option 2.

PTO/AIA/50

PTO/AIA/50 (09-14)
Approved for use through 01/31/2020. OMB 0651-0033
U.S. Patent and Trademark Office; U.S. DEPARTMENT OF COMMERCE
Under the Paperwork Reduction Act of 1995 no persons are required to respond to a collection of information unless it displays a valid OMB control number

REISSUE PATENT APPLICATION TRANSMITTAL

Address to:		
Mail Stop Reissue Commissioner for Patents P.O. Box 1450 Alexandria, VA 22313-1450	Attorney Docket No.	
	First Named Inventor	
	Original Patent Number	
	Original Patent Issue Date (Month/Day/Year)	
	Express Mail Label No.	

APPLICATION FOR REISSUE OF:
(Check applicable box) ☐ Utility Patent ☐ Design Patent ☐ Plant Patent

APPLICATION ELEMENTS (37 CFR 1.173)

1. ☐ **Fee Transmittal Form** (PTO/SB/56)
2. ☐ **Applicant asserts small entity status.** See 37 CFR 1.27
3. ☐ **Applicant certifies micro entity status.** See 37 CFR 1.29.
   Applicant must attach form PTO/SB/15A or B or equivalent.
4. ☐ **Specification and Claims** in double column copy of patent format *(amended, if appropriate)*
5. ☐ **Drawing(s)** *(proposed amendments, if appropriate)*
6. ☐ **Reissue Oath/Declaration or Substitute Statement** (37 CFR 1.175) (PTO/AIA/05, 06, or 07)
7. ☐ **Application Data Sheet** NOTE: Benefit claims under 37 CFR 1.78 and foreign priority claims under 37 CFR 1.55 MUST be set forth in an Application Data Sheet (ADS).
8. ☐ **Original U.S. Patent currently assigned?** ☐ Yes ☐ No
   (If Yes, check applicable box(es))
   ☐ Written Consent of all Assignees (PTO/AIA/53)
   ☐ 37 CFR 3.73(c) Statement (PTO/AIA/96)
9. ☐ **CD-ROM or CD-R** in duplicate, Computer Program *(Appendix)* or large table
   ☐ Landscape Table on CD
10. **Nucleotide and/or Amino Acid Sequence Submission**
    (if applicable, items a. – c. are required)
    a. ☐ Computer Readable Form (CRF)
    b. ☐ Specification Sequence Listing on:
       i. ☐ CD-ROM (2 copies) or CD-R (2 copies); **or**
       ii. ☐ Paper
    c. ☐ Statements verifying identity of above copies

ACCOMPANYING APPLICATION PARTS

11. ☐ **Statement of status and support for all changes to the claims.** See 37 CFR 1.173(c).
12. ☐ **Power of Attorney**
13. ☐ **Information Disclosure Statement (IDS)**
    PTOSB/08 or PTO-1449
    ☐ Copies of citations attached
14. ☐ **English translation of Reissue Oath/Declaration** *(if applicable)*
15. ☐ **Return Receipt Postcard** (MPEP § 503)
    (Should be specifically itemized)
16. ☐ **Preliminary Amendment** (37 CFR 1.173; MPEP § 1453)
17. ☐ **Other:** _____
    _____
    _____
    _____
    _____

☐ This is a continuation reissue or divisional reissue application *(i.e., a second or subsequent reissue application for the same issued patent).* *(Check box if applicable.)*

18. CORRESPONDENCE ADDRESS

☐ The address associated with Customer Number: _____ **OR** ☐ Correspondence address below

Name	
Address	
City		State		Zip Code	
Country		Telephone	
Email	
Signature		Date	
Name (Print/Type)		Registration No.	

This collection of information is required by 37 CFR 1.173. The information is required to obtain or retain a benefit by the public which is to file (and by the USPTO to process) an application. Confidentiality is governed by 35 U.S.C. 122 and 37 CFR 1.11 and 1.14. This collection is estimated to take 12 minutes to complete, including gathering, preparing, and submitting the completed application form to the USPTO. Time will vary depending upon the individual case. Any comments on the amount of time you require to complete this form and/or suggestions for reducing this burden, should be sent to the Chief Information Officer, U.S. Patent and Trademark Office, U.S. Department of Commerce, P.O. Box 1450, Alexandria, VA 22313-1450. DO NOT SEND FEES OR COMPLETED FORMS TO THIS ADDRESS. **SEND TO: Mail Stop Reissue, Commissioner for Patents, P.O. Box 1450, Alexandria, VA 22313-1450.**
If you need assistance in completing the form, call 1-800-PTO-9199 and select option 2.

資 料

PTO/AIA/82A

Doc Code: PA..
Document Description: Power of Attorney

PTO/AIA/82A (07-13)
Approved for use through 01/31/2018. OMB 0651-0035
U.S. Patent and Trademark Office; U.S. DEPARTMENT OF COMMERCE
Under the Paperwork Reduction Act of 1995, no persons are required to respond to a collection of information unless it displays a valid OMB control number.

TRANSMITTAL FOR POWER OF ATTORNEY TO ONE OR MORE REGISTERED PRACTITIONERS

NOTE: This form is to be submitted with the Power of Attorney by Applicant form (PTO/AIA/82B) to identify the application to which the Power of Attorney is directed, in accordance with 37 CFR 1.5, unless the application number and filing date are identified in the Power of Attorney by Applicant form. If neither form PTO/AIA/82A nor form PTO/AIA82B identifies the application to which the Power of Attorney is directed, the Power of Attorney will not be recognized in the application.

Application Number	
Filing Date	
First Named Inventor	
Title	
Art Unit	
Examiner Name	
Attorney Docket Number	

SIGNATURE of Applicant or Patent Practitioner

Signature		Date (Optional)	
Name		Registration Number	
Title (if Applicant is a juristic entity)			
Applicant Name (if Applicant is a juristic entity)			

NOTE: This form must be signed in accordance with 37 CFR 1.33. See 37 CFR 1.4(d) for signature requirements and certifications. If more than one applicant, use multiple forms.

☐ *Total of _____ forms are submitted.

This collection of information is required by 37 CFR 1.131, 1.32, and 1.33. The information is required to obtain or retain a benefit by the public which is to file (and by the USPTO to process) an application. Confidentiality is governed by 35 U.S.C. 122 and 37 CFR 1.11 and 1.14. This collection is estimated to take 3 minutes to complete, including gathering, preparing, and submitting the completed application form to the USPTO. Time will vary depending upon the individual case. Any comments on the amount of time you require to complete this form and/or suggestions for reducing this burden, should be sent to the Chief Information Officer, U.S. Patent and Trademark Office, U.S. Department of Commerce, P.O. Box 1450, Alexandria, VA 22313-1450. DO NOT SEND FEES OR COMPLETED FORMS TO THIS ADDRESS. **SEND TO: Commissioner for Patents, P.O. Box 1450, Alexandria, VA 22313-1450.**

If you need assistance in completing the form, call 1-800-PTO-9199 and select option 2.

PTO/AIA/82B

Doc Code: PA..
Document Description: Power of Attorney

PTO/AIA/82B (07-13)
Approved for use through 01/31/2018. OMB 0651-0035
U.S. Patent and Trademark Office; U.S. DEPARTMENT OF COMMERCE
Under the Paperwork Reduction Act of 1995, no persons are required to respond to a collection of information unless it displays a valid OMB control number

POWER OF ATTORNEY BY APPLICANT

I hereby revoke all previous powers of attorney given in the application identified in <u>either</u> the attached transmittal letter or the boxes below.

Application Number	Filing Date

(Note: The boxes above may be left blank if information is provided on form PTO/AIA/82A.)

☐ I hereby appoint the Patent Practitioner(s) associated with the following Customer Number as my/our attorney(s) or agent(s), and to transact all business in the United States Patent and Trademark Office connected therewith for the application referenced in the attached transmittal letter (form PTO/AIA/82A) or identified above: [____]

OR

☐ I hereby appoint Practitioner(s) named in the attached list (form PTO/AIA/82C) as my/our attorney(s) or agent(s), and to transact all business in the United States Patent and Trademark Office connected therewith for the patent application referenced in the attached transmittal letter (form PTO/AIA/82A) or identified above. (Note: Complete form PTO/AIA/82C.)

Please recognize or change the correspondence address for the application identified in the attached transmittal letter or the boxes above to:

☐ The address associated with the above-mentioned Customer Number

OR

☐ The address associated with Customer Number: [____]

OR

☐
Firm or Individual Name	
Address	
City	State	Zip
Country	
Telephone	Email

I am the Applicant (if the Applicant is a juristic entity, list the Applicant name in the box):

[____]

☐ Inventor or Joint Inventor (title not required below)

☐ Legal Representative of a Deceased or Legally Incapacitated Inventor (title not required below)

☐ Assignee or Person to Whom the Inventor is Under an Obligation to Assign (provide signer's title if applicant is a juristic entity)

☐ Person Who Otherwise Shows Sufficient Proprietary Interest (e.g., a petition under 37 CFR 1.46(b)(2) was granted in the application or is concurrently being filed with this document) (provide signer's title if applicant is a juristic entity)

SIGNATURE of Applicant for Patent

The undersigned (whose title is supplied below) is authorized to act on behalf of the applicant (e.g., where the applicant is a juristic entity).

Signature		Date (Optional)	
Name			
Title			

NOTE: Signature - This form must be signed by the applicant in accordance with 37 CFR 1.33. See 37 CFR 1.4 for signature requirements and certifications. If more than one applicant, use multiple forms.

☐ Total of [____] forms are submitted.

This collection of information is required by 37 CFR 1.131, 1.32, and 1.33. The information is required to obtain or retain a benefit by the public which is to file (and by the USPTO to process) an application. Confidentiality is governed by 35 U.S.C. 122 and 37 CFR 1.11 and 1.14. This collection is estimated to take 3 minutes to complete, including gathering, preparing, and submitting the completed application form to the USPTO. Time will vary depending upon the individual case. Any comments on the amount of time you require to complete this form and/or suggestions for reducing this burden, should be sent to the Chief Information Officer, U.S. Patent and Trademark Office, U.S. Department of Commerce, P.O. Box 1450, Alexandria, VA 22313-1450. DO NOT SEND FEES OR COMPLETED FORMS TO THIS ADDRESS. **SEND TO: Commissioner for Patents, P.O. Box 1450, Alexandria, VA 22313-1450.**

If you need assistance in completing the form, call 1-800-PTO-9199 and select option 2.

資 料

PTO/AIA/82C

PTO/AIA/82C (07-13)
Approved for use through 01/31/2018. OMB 0651-0035
U.S. Patent and Trademark Office; U.S. DEPARTMENT OF COMMERCE
Under the Paperwork Reduction Act of 1995, no persons are required to respond to a collection of information unless it displays a valid OMB control number

POWER OF ATTORNEY BY APPLICANT

No more than ten (10) patent practitioners total may be appointed as set forth below by name and registration number. This page need not be submitted if appointing the Patent Practitioner(s) associated with a Customer Number (see form PTO/AIA/82B):

Name	Registration Number

PTO/AIA/96

PTO/AIA/96 (08-12)
Approved for use through 01/31/2013. OMB 0651-0031
U.S. Patent and Trademark Office; U.S. DEPARTMENT OF COMMERCE
Under the Paperwork Reduction Act of 1995, no persons are required to respond to a collection of information unless it displays a valid OMB control number.

STATEMENT UNDER 37 CFR 3.73(c)

Applicant/Patent Owner: _____

Application No./Patent No.: _____ Filed/Issue Date: _____

Titled: _____

_____, a _____
(Name of Assignee)   (Type of Assignee, e.g., corporation, partnership, university, government agency, etc.)

states that, for the patent application/patent identified above, it is (choose **one** of options 1, 2, 3 or 4 below):

1. ☐ The assignee of the entire right, title, and interest.

2. ☐ An assignee of less than the entire right, title, and interest (check applicable box):

   ☐ The extent (by percentage) of its ownership interest is _____%. Additional Statement(s) by the owners holding the balance of the interest <u>must be submitted</u> to account for 100% of the ownership interest.

   ☐ There are unspecified percentages of ownership. The other parties, including inventors, who together own the entire right, title and interest are:

   [   ]

   Additional Statement(s) by the owner(s) holding the balance of the interest <u>must be submitted</u> to account for the entire right, title, and interest.

3. ☐ The assignee of an undivided interest in the entirety (a complete assignment from one of the joint inventors was made). The other parties, including inventors, who together own the entire right, title, and interest are:

   [   ]

   Additional Statement(s) by the owner(s) holding the balance of the interest <u>must be submitted</u> to account for the entire right, title, and interest.

4. ☐ The recipient, via a court proceeding or the like (*e.g.*, bankruptcy, probate), of an undivided interest in the entirety (a complete transfer of ownership interest was made). The certified document(s) showing the transfer is attached.

The interest identified in option 1, 2 or 3 above (not option 4) is evidenced by either (choose **one** of options A or B below):

A. ☐ An assignment from the inventor(s) of the patent application/patent identified above. The assignment was recorded in the United States Patent and Trademark Office at Reel _____, Frame _____, or for which a copy thereof is attached.

B. ☐ A chain of title from the inventor(s), of the patent application/patent identified above, to the current assignee as follows:

   1. From: _____ To: _____
      The document was recorded in the United States Patent and Trademark Office at
      Reel _____, Frame _____, or for which a copy thereof is attached.

   2. From: _____ To: _____
      The document was recorded in the United States Patent and Trademark Office at
      Reel _____, Frame _____, or for which a copy thereof is attached.

[Page 1 of 2]

This collection of information is required by 37 CFR 3.73(b). The information is required to obtain or retain a benefit by the public which is to file (and by the USPTO to process) an application. Confidentiality is governed by 35 U.S.C. 122 and 37 CFR 1.11 and 1.14. This collection is estimated to take 12 minutes to complete, including gathering, preparing, and submitting the completed application form to the USPTO. Time will vary depending upon the individual case. Any comments on the amount of time you require to complete this form and/or suggestions for reducing this burden, should be sent to the Chief Information Officer, U.S. Patent and Trademark Office, U.S. Department of Commerce, P.O. Box 1450, Alexandria, VA 22313-1450. DO NOT SEND FEES OR COMPLETED FORMS TO THIS ADDRESS. **SEND TO: Commissioner for Patents, P.O. Box 1450, Alexandria, VA 22313-1450.**

If you need assistance in completing the form, call 1-800-PTO-9199 and select option 2.

資　料

PTO/AIA/96の続き

PTO/AIA/96 (08-12)
Approved for use through 01/31/2013. OMB 0651-0031
U.S. Patent and Trademark Office; U.S. DEPARTMENT OF COMMERCE
Under the Paperwork Reduction Act of 1995, no persons are required to respond to a collection of information unless it displays a valid OMB control number.

STATEMENT UNDER 37 CFR 3.73(c)

3. From: _____ To: _____
   The document was recorded in the United States Patent and Trademark Office at
   Reel _____, Frame _____, or for which a copy thereof is attached.

4. From: _____ To: _____
   The document was recorded in the United States Patent and Trademark Office at
   Reel _____, Frame _____, or for which a copy thereof is attached.

5. From: _____ To: _____
   The document was recorded in the United States Patent and Trademark Office at
   Reel _____, Frame _____, or for which a copy thereof is attached.

6. From: _____ To: _____
   The document was recorded in the United States Patent and Trademark Office at
   Reel _____, Frame _____, or for which a copy thereof is attached.

☐ Additional documents in the chain of title are listed on a supplemental sheet(s).

☐ As required by 37 CFR 3.73(c)(1)(i), the documentary evidence of the chain of title from the original owner to the assignee was, or concurrently is being, submitted for recordation pursuant to 37 CFR 3.11.

[NOTE: A separate copy (i.e., a true copy of the original assignment document(s)) must be submitted to Assignment Division in accordance with 37 CFR Part 3, to record the assignment in the records of the USPTO. See MPEP 302.08]

The undersigned (whose title is supplied below) is authorized to act on behalf of the assignee.

_____   _____
Signature   Date

_____   _____
Printed or Typed Name   Title or Registration Number

[Page 2 of 2]

PTO/AIA/424
Doc Code: TRACK1.REQ
Document Description: TrackOne Request

PTO/AIA/424 (04-14)

CERTIFICATION AND REQUEST FOR PRIORITIZED EXAMINATION
UNDER 37 CFR 1.102(e) (Page 1 of 1)

First Named Inventor:		Nonprovisional Application Number (if known):	
Title of Invention:			

APPLICANT HEREBY CERTIFIES THE FOLLOWING AND REQUESTS PRIORITIZED EXAMINATION FOR THE ABOVE-IDENTIFIED APPLICATION.

1. The processing fee set forth in 37 CFR 1.17(i)(1) and the prioritized examination fee set forth in 37 CFR 1.17(c) have been filed with the request. The publication fee requirement is met because that fee, set forth in 37 CFR 1.18(d), is currently $0. The basic filing fee, search fee, and examination fee are filed with the request or have been already been paid. I understand that any required excess claims fees or application size fee must be paid for the application.

2. I understand that the application may not contain, or be amended to contain, more than four independent claims, more than thirty total claims, or any multiple dependent claims, and that any request for an extension of time will cause an outstanding Track I request to be dismissed.

3. The applicable box is checked below:

   I. ☐ **Original Application (Track One) - Prioritized Examination under § 1.102(e)(1)**

   i. (a) The application is an original nonprovisional utility application filed under 35 U.S.C. 111(a). This certification and request is being filed with the utility application via EFS-Web.
   ---OR---
   (b) The application is an original nonprovisional plant application filed under 35 U.S.C. 111(a). This certification and request is being filed with the plant application in paper.

   ii. An executed inventor's oath or declaration under 37 CFR 1.63 or 37 CFR 1.64 for each inventor, **or** the application data sheet meeting the conditions specified in 37 CFR 1.53(f)(3)(i) is filed with the application.

   II. ☐ **Request for Continued Examination - Prioritized Examination under § 1.102(e)(2)**

   i. A request for continued examination has been filed with, or prior to, this form.
   ii. If the application is a utility application, this certification and request is being filed via EFS-Web.
   iii. The application is an original nonprovisional utility application filed under 35 U.S.C. 111(a), or is a national stage entry under 35 U.S.C. 371.
   iv. This certification and request is being filed prior to the mailing of a first Office action responsive to the request for continued examination.
   v. No prior request for continued examination has been granted prioritized examination status under 37 CFR 1.102(e)(2).

Signature		Date	
Name (Print/Typed)		Practitioner Registration Number	

Note: This form must be signed in accordance with 37 CFR 1.33. See 37 CFR 1.4(d) for signature requirements and certifications. Submit multiple forms if more than one signature is required.*

☐ *Total of _____ forms are submitted.

資 料

PTO-1390

PTO-1390 (01-17)
Approved for use through 8/31/2019. OMB 0651-0021
U.S. Patent and Trademark Office; U.S. DEPARTMENT OF COMMERCE
Under the Paperwork Reduction Act of 1995, no persons are required to respond to a collection of information unless it displays a valid OMB control number.

TRANSMITTAL LETTER TO THE UNITED STATES DESIGNATED/ELECTED OFFICE (DO/EO/US) CONCERNING A SUBMISSION UNDER 35 U.S.C. 371

Attorney Docket No.	
U.S. Application No. (if known, see 37 CFR 1.5)	

International Application No.	International Filing Date	Priority Date Claimed

Title of Invention

First Named Inventor

Applicant herewith submits to the United States Designated/Elected Office (DO/EO/US) the following items and other information.

1. ☐ This is an express request to begin national examination procedures (35 U.S.C. 371(f)). NOTE: The express request under 35 U.S.C. 371(f) will not be effective unless the requirements under 35 U.S.C. 371(c)(1), (2), and (4) for payment of the basic national fee, copy of the International Application and English translation thereof (if required), and the oath or declaration of the inventor(s) have been received.

2. ☐ A copy of the International Application (35 U.S.C. 371(c)(2)) is attached hereto (not required if the International Application was previously communicated by the International Bureau or was filed in the United States Receiving Office (RO/US)).

3. An English language translation of the International Application (35 U.S.C. 371(c)(2))
   a. ☐ is attached hereto.
   b. ☐ has been previously submitted under 35 U.S.C. 154(d)(4).

4. An oath or declaration of the inventor(s) (35 U.S.C. 371(c)(4))
   a. ☐ is attached.
   b. ☐ was previously filed in the international phase under PCT Rule 4.17(iv).

Items 5 to 8 below concern amendments made in the international phase.

PCT Article 19 and 34 amendments

5. ☐ Amendments to the claims under PCT Article 19 are attached (not required if communicated by the International Bureau) (35 U.S.C. 371(c)(3)).

6. ☐ English translation of the PCT Article 19 amendment is attached (35 U.S.C. 371(c)(3)).

7. ☐ English translation of annexes (Article 19 and/or 34 amendments only) of the International Preliminary Examination Report is attached (35 U.S.C. 371(c)(5)).

Cancellation of amendments made in the international phase

8a. ☐ Do not enter the amendment made in the international phase under PCT Article 19.

8b. ☐ Do not enter the amendment made in the international phase under PCT Article 34.

NOTE: A proper amendment made in English under Article 19 or 34 will be entered in the U.S. national phase application absent a clear instruction from applicant not to enter the amendment(s).

The following items 9 to 17 concern a document(s) or information included.

9. ☐ An Information Disclosure Statement under 37 CFR 1.97 and 1.98.

10. ☐ A preliminary amendment.

11. ☐ An Application Data Sheet under 37 CFR 1.76.

12. ☐ A substitute specification. NOTE: A substitute specification cannot include claims. See 37 CFR 1.125(b).

13. ☐ A power of attorney and/or change of address letter.

14. ☐ A computer-readable form of the sequence listing in accordance with PCT Rule 13*ter*.3 and 37 CFR 1.821-1.825.

15. ☐ Assignment papers *(cover sheet and document(s))*. Name of Assignee: _____

16. ☐ 37 CFR 3.73(c) Statement *(when there is an Assignee)*.

This collection of information is required by 37 CFR 1.414 and 1.491-1.492. The information is required to obtain or retain a benefit by the public, which is to file (and by the USPTO to process) an application. Confidentiality is governed by 35 U.S.C. 122 and 37 CFR 1.11 and 1.14. This collection is estimated to take 15 minutes to complete, including gathering, preparing, and submitting the completed application form to the USPTO. Time will vary depending upon the individual case. Any comments on the amount of time you require to complete this form and/or suggestions for reducing this burden should be sent to the Chief Information Officer, U.S. Patent and Trademark Office, U.S. Department of Commerce, P.O. Box 1450, Alexandria, VA 22313-1450. DO NOT SEND FEES OR COMPLETED FORMS TO THIS ADDRESS. SEND TO: Mail Stop PCT, Commissioner for Patents, P.O. Box 1450, Alexandria, VA 22313-1450.

286

PTO-1390の続き

PTO-1390 (01-17)
Approved for use through 8/31/2019. OMB 0651-0021
U.S. Patent and Trademark Office; U.S. DEPARTMENT OF COMMERCE
Under the Paperwork Reduction Act of 1995, no persons are required to respond to a collection of information unless it displays a valid OMB control number.

U.S. APPLN. No. (if known – see 37 CFR 1.5)	INTERNATIONAL APPLICATION No.	ATTORNEY DOCKET No.

17. ☐ Other items or information:

The following fees have been submitted.		CALCULATIONS	PTO USE ONLY
18. ☐ Basic national fee (37 CFR 1.492(a)) $280		$	
19. ☐ Examination fee (37 CFR 1.492(c)) If the written opinion prepared by ISA/US or the international preliminary examination report prepared by IPEA/US indicates all claims satisfy provisions of PCT Article 33(1)-(4) .... $0 All other situations $720		$	
20. ☐ Search fee (37 CFR 1.492(b)) If the written opinion prepared by ISA/US or the international preliminary examination report prepared by IPEA/US indicates all claims satisfy provisions of PCT Article 33(1)-(4) .... $0 Search fee (37 CFR 1.445(a)(2)) has been paid on the international application to the USPTO as an International Searching Authority .... $120 International Search Report prepared by an ISA other than the US and provided to the Office or previously communicated to the US by the IB .... $480 All other situations $600		$	
TOTAL OF 18, 19, and 20 =		$	
☐ Additional fee for specification and drawings filed in paper over 100 sheets (excluding sequence listing in compliance with 37 CFR 1.821(c) or (e) in an electronic medium or computer program listing in an electronic medium) (37 CFR 1.492(j)). Fee for each additional 50 sheets of paper or fraction thereof $400			

Total Sheets	Extra Sheets	Number of each addition 50 or fraction thereof (round **up** to a whole number)	RATE		
- 100 =	/ 50 =		x $400	$	

Surcharge of **$140.00** for furnishing any of the search fee, examination fee, or the oath or declaration after the date of commencement of the national stage (37 CFR 1.492(h)).	$	

CLAIMS	NUMBER FILED	NUMBER EXTRA	RATE		
Total claims	- 20 =		x $80	$	
Independent claims	- 3 =		x $420	$	
MULTIPLE DEPENDENT CLAIM(S) (if applicable)			+ $780	$	

Processing fee of **$140.00** for furnishing the English translation later than 30 months from the earliest claimed priority date (37 CFR 1.492(i)). +	$	
TOTAL OF ABOVE CALCULATIONS =	$	
☐ Applicant asserts small entity status. See 37 CFR 1.27. Fees above are reduced by ½.		
☐ Applicant certifies micro entity status. See 37 CFR 1.29. Fees above are reduced by ¾. Applicant must attach form PTO/SB/15A or B or equivalent.		
TOTAL NATIONAL FEE =	$	
Fee for recording the enclosed assignment (37 CFR 1.21(h)). The assignment must be accompanied by an appropriate cover sheet (37 CFR 3.28, 3.31). **$40.00** per property. +	$	
TOTAL FEES ENCLOSED =	$	
	Amount to be refunded:	$
	Amount to be charged:	$

[Page 2 of 3]

287

資料

PTO-1390の続き

PTO-1390 (01-17)
Approved for use through 8/31/2019. OMB 0651-0021
U.S. Patent and Trademark Office; U.S. DEPARTMENT OF COMMERCE
Under the Paperwork Reduction Act of 1995, no persons are required to respond to a collection of information unless it displays a valid OMB control number.

a.	☐	A check in the amount of $_____ to cover the above fees is enclosed.
b.	☐	Please charge my Deposit Account No. _____ in the amount of $_____ to cover the above fees.
c.	☐	The Director is hereby authorized to charge additional fees which may be required, or credit any overpayment, to Deposit Account No. _____ as follows:
	i. ☐	any required fee.
	ii. ☐	any required fee except for excess claims fees required under 37 CFR 1.492(d) and (e) and multiple dependent claim fee required under 37 CFR 1.492(f).
d.	☐	Fees are to be charged to a credit card. **WARNING:** Information on this form may become public. Credit card information should not be included on this form. Provide credit card information and authorization on PTO-2038. The PTO-2038 should only be mailed or faxed to the USPTO. However, when paying the basic national fee, the PTO-2038 may NOT be faxed to the USPTO.
		ADVISORY: If filing by EFS-Web, do **NOT** attach the PTO-2038 form as a PDF along with your EFS-Web submission. Please be advised that this is **not** recommended and by doing so your **credit card information may be displayed via PAIR**. To protect your information, it is recommended to pay fees online by using the electronic payment method.

NOTE: Where an appropriate time limit under 37 CFR 1.495 has not been met, a petition to revive (37 CFR 1.137(a) or (b)) must be filed and granted to restore the International Application to pending status.

Statement under 37 CFR 1.55 or 1.78 for AIA (First Inventor to File)Transition Applications

☐ This application (1) claims priority to or the benefit of an application filed before March 16, 2013, and (2) also contains, or contained at any time, a claim to a claimed invention that has an effective filing date on or after March 16, 2013.

NOTE 1: By providing this statement under 37 CFR 1.55 or 1.78, **this application, with a filing date on or after March 16, 2013, will be examined under the first inventor to file provisions of the AIA.**

NOTE 2: A U.S. national stage application may not claim priority to the international application of which it is the national phase. The filing date of a U.S. national stage application is the international filing date. See 35 U.S.C. 363.

Correspondence Address

☐ The address associated with Customer Number: _____ OR ☐ Correspondence address below

Name	
Address	

City		State		Zip Code	
Country			Telephone		
Email					

Signature		Date	
Name (Print/Type)		Registration No. (Attorney/Agent)	

[Page 3 of 3]

PTO/SB/08a

Doc code: IDS
Doc description: Information Disclosure Statement (IDS) Filed

PTO/SB/08a (03-15)
Approved for use through 07/31/2016. OMB 0651-0031
U.S. Patent and Trademark Office; U.S. DEPARTMENT OF COMMERCE

Under the Paperwork Reduction Act of 1995, no persons are required to respond to a collection of information unless it contains a valid OMB control number.

INFORMATION DISCLOSURE STATEMENT BY APPLICANT (Not for submission under 37 CFR 1.99)	Application Number
	Filing Date
	First Named Inventor
	Art Unit
	Examiner Name
	Attorney Docket Number

U.S. PATENTS

Examiner Initial*	Cite No	Patent Number	Kind Code[1]	Issue Date	Name of Patentee or Applicant of cited Document	Pages, Columns, Lines where Relevant Passages or Relevant Figures Appear
	1					

If you wish to add additional U.S. Patent citation information please click the Add button.

U.S. PATENT APPLICATION PUBLICATIONS

Examiner Initial*	Cite No	Publication Number	Kind Code[1]	Publication Date	Name of Patentee or Applicant of cited Document	Pages, Columns, Lines where Relevant Passages or Relevant Figures Appear
	1					

If you wish to add additional U.S. Published Application citation information please click the Add button.

FOREIGN PATENT DOCUMENTS

Examiner Initial*	Cite No	Foreign Document Number[3]	Country Code[2] i	Kind Code[4]	Publication Date	Name of Patentee or Applicant of cited Document	Pages, Columns, Lines where Relevant Passages or Relevant Figures Appear	T[5]
	1							☐

If you wish to add additional Foreign Patent Document citation information please click the Add button

NON-PATENT LITERATURE DOCUMENTS

Examiner Initials*	Cite No	Include name of the author (in CAPITAL LETTERS), title of the article (when appropriate), title of the item (book, magazine, journal, serial, symposium, catalog, etc), date, pages(s), volume-issue number(s), publisher, city and/or country where published.	T[5]

EFS Web 2.1.17

資 料

PTO/SB/08aの続き

INFORMATION DISCLOSURE STATEMENT BY APPLICANT (Not for submission under 37 CFR 1.99)	Application Number
	Filing Date
	First Named Inventor
	Art Unit
	Examiner Name
	Attorney Docket Number

	1		☐

If you wish to add additional non-patent literature document citation information please click the Add button

EXAMINER SIGNATURE

Examiner Signature		Date Considered	

*EXAMINER: Initial if reference considered, whether or not citation is in conformance with MPEP 609. Draw line through a citation if not in conformance and not considered. Include copy of this form with next communication to applicant.

[1] See Kind Codes of USPTO Patent Documents at www.USPTO.GOV or MPEP 901.04. [2] Enter office that issued the document, by the two-letter code (WIPO Standard ST.3). [3] For Japanese patent documents, the indication of the year of the reign of the Emperor must precede the serial number of the patent document. [4] Kind of document by the appropriate symbols as indicated on the document under WIPO Standard ST.16 if possible. [5] Applicant is to place a check mark here if English language translation is attached.

EFS Web 2.1.17

PTO/SB/08aの続き

INFORMATION DISCLOSURE STATEMENT BY APPLICANT (Not for submission under 37 CFR 1.99)	Application Number	
	Filing Date	
	First Named Inventor	
	Art Unit	
	Examiner Name	
	Attorney Docket Number	

CERTIFICATION STATEMENT

Please see 37 CFR 1.97 and 1.98 to make the appropriate selection(s):

☐ That each item of information contained in the information disclosure statement was first cited in any communication from a foreign patent office in a counterpart foreign application not more than three months prior to the filing of the information disclosure statement. See 37 CFR 1.97(e)(1).

OR

☐ That no item of information contained in the information disclosure statement was cited in a communication from a foreign patent office in a counterpart foreign application, and, to the knowledge of the person signing the certification after making reasonable inquiry, no item of information contained in the information disclosure statement was known to any individual designated in 37 CFR 1.56(c) more than three months prior to the filing of the information disclosure statement. See 37 CFR 1.97(e)(2).

☐ See attached certification statement.

☐ The fee set forth in 37 CFR 1.17 (p) has been submitted herewith.

☐ A certification statement is not submitted herewith.

SIGNATURE

A signature of the applicant or representative is required in accordance with CFR 1.33, 10.18. Please see CFR 1.4(d) for the form of the signature.

Signature		Date (YYYY-MM-DD)	
Name/Print		Registration Number	

This collection of information is required by 37 CFR 1.97 and 1.98. The information is required to obtain or retain a benefit by the public which is to file (and by the USPTO to process) an application. Confidentiality is governed by 35 U.S.C. 122 and 37 CFR 1.14. This collection is estimated to take 1 hour to complete, including gathering, preparing and submitting the completed application form to the USPTO. Time will vary depending upon the individual case. Any comments on the amount of time you require to complete this form and/or suggestions for reducing this burden, should be sent to the Chief Information Officer, U.S. Patent and Trademark Office, U.S. Department of Commerce, P.O. Box 1450, Alexandria, VA 22313-1450. DO NOT SEND FEES OR COMPLETED FORMS TO THIS ADDRESS. **SEND TO: Commissioner for Patents, P.O. Box 1450, Alexandria, VA 22313-1450.**

EFS Web 2.1.17

資 料

PTO/SB/09

Doc Code: QPIDS.REQ
Document Description: Quick Path Information Disclosure Statement

PTO/SB/09 (12-16)

CERTIFICATION AND REQUEST FOR CONSIDERATION OF AN INFORMATION DISCLOSURE STATEMENT FILED AFTER PAYMENT OF THE ISSUE FEE UNDER THE QPIDS PILOT PROGRAM	
Non-Provisional Application Number:	Filing Date:
First Named Inventor:	Title of Invention:

THE UNDERSIGNED HEREBY CERTIFIES AND REQUESTS THE FOLLOWING FOR THE ABOVE-IDENTIFIED APPLICATION.

1. Consideration is requested of the information disclosure statement (IDS) submitted herewith, which is being filed after payment of the issue fee.

2. Check the box next to the appropriate selection:

    ☐ Each item of information contained in the IDS was first cited in any communication from a foreign patent office in a counterpart foreign application not more than three months prior to the filing of the IDS. See 37 CFR 1.97(e)(1).

    OR

    ☐ No item of information contained in the IDS was cited in a communication from a foreign patent office in a counterpart foreign application, and, to the knowledge of the person signing the certification after making reasonable inquiry, no item of information contained in the IDS was known to any individual designated in 37 CFR 1.56(c) more than three months prior to the filing of the IDS. See 37 CFR 1.97(e)(2).

    OR

    ☐ See attached certification statement in compliance with 37 CFR 1.97(e).

3. Please charge the IDS fee set forth in 37 CFR 1.17(p) to Deposit Account No. _____.

4. A Petition to Withdraw from Issue After Payment of the Issue Fee (37 CFR 1.313(c)(2)), including the petition fee set forth in 37 CFR 1.17(h), is submitted herewith as a **Web-based ePetition**.
    WARNING: Do not submit the petition as a follow-on paper via EFS-Web. Submit the petition as a Web-based ePetition by signing on to EFS-Web as a registered user, selecting the radio button next to "Existing application/patent," and then selecting the radio button next to "ePetition (for automatic processing and immediate grant, if all petitions requirements are met)." Failure to use the Web-based ePetition interface will result in automatic entry of the RCE.

5. A request for continued examination (RCE) under 37 CFR 1.114 and the RCE fee under 37 CFR 1.17(e) are submitted herewith.

6. The RCE will be treated as a "conditional" RCE. In the event the examiner determines that any item of information contained in the IDS necessitates the reopening of prosecution in the application, the undersigned understands that (i) the RCE will be processed and treated as an RCE under 37 CFR 1.114 and therefore (ii) the IDS fee under 37 CFR 1.17(p) will be returned in accordance with 37 CFR 1.97(b)(4). In the event that no item of information in the IDS necessitates reopening prosecution, the undersigned understands that the RCE will not be processed and the RCE fee under 37 CFR 1.17(e) will be returned.

7. This certification and request is being filed as a **Web-based ePetition** and is not accompanied by an amendment to the application. Inclusion of an amendment will result in automatic entry of the RCE.

Signature	Date
Name (Print/Typed)	Practitioner Registration Number (If applicable)

Note: Signatures of all the inventors or assignees of record of the entire interest or their representative(s) are required in accordance with 37 CFR 1.33 and 11.18. Please see 37 CFR 1.4(d) for the form of the signature. If necessary, submit multiple forms for more than one signature, see below.*

☐ *Total of _____ forms are submitted.

If you need assistance in completing the form, call 1-800-PTO-9199 and select option 2.

PTO/SB/16

PTO/SB/16 (03-13)
Approved for use through 01/31/2014. OMB 0651-0032
U.S. Patent and Trademark Office; U.S. DEPARTMENT OF COMMERCE
Under the Paperwork Reduction Act of 1995 no persons are required to respond to a collection of information unless it displays a valid OMB control number

PROVISIONAL APPLICATION FOR PATENT COVER SHEET – Page 1 of 2
This is a request for filing a PROVISIONAL APPLICATION FOR PATENT under 37 CFR 1.53(c).

Express Mail Label No. _____

INVENTOR(S)		
Given Name (first and middle [if any])	Family Name or Surname	Residence (City and either State or Foreign Country)

Additional inventors are being named on the _____ separately numbered sheets attached hereto.

TITLE OF THE INVENTION (500 characters max):

Direct all correspondence to: **CORRESPONDENCE ADDRESS**

☐ The address corresponding to Customer Number: _____

OR

☐ Firm or Individual Name

Address

City	State	Zip
Country	Telephone	Email

ENCLOSED APPLICATION PARTS (check all that apply)

☐ Application Data Sheet. See 37 CFR 1.76.   ☐ CD(s), Number of CDs _____
☐ Drawing(s) Number of Sheets _____   ☐ Other (specify) _____
☐ Specification (e.g., description of the invention) Number of Pages _____

Fees Due: Filing Fee of $260 ($130 for small entity) ($65 for micro entity). If the specification and drawings exceed 100 sheets of paper, an application size fee is also due, which is $400 ($200 for small entity) ($100 for micro entity) for each additional 50 sheets or fraction thereof. See 35 U.S.C. 41(a)(1)(G) and 37 CFR 1.16(s).

METHOD OF PAYMENT OF THE FILING FEE AND APPLICATION SIZE FEE FOR THIS PROVISIONAL APPLICATION FOR PATENT

☐ Applicant asserts small entity status. See 37 CFR 1.27.
☐ Applicant certifies micro entity status. See 37 CFR 1.29. Applicant must attach form PTO/SB/15A or B or equivalent.
☐ A check or money order made payable to the *Director of the United States Patent and Trademark Office* is enclosed to cover the filing fee and application size fee (if applicable).   **TOTAL FEE AMOUNT ($)**
☐ Payment by credit card. Form PTO-2038 is attached.
☐ The Director is hereby authorized to charge the filing fee and application size fee (if applicable) or credit any overpayment to Deposit Account Number: _____.

USE ONLY FOR FILING A PROVISIONAL APPLICATION FOR PATENT

This collection of information is required by 37 CFR 1.51. The information is required to obtain or retain a benefit by the public which is to file (and by the USPTO to process) an application. Confidentiality is governed by 35 U.S.C. 122 and 37 CFR 1.11 and 1.14. This collection is estimated to take 10 hours to complete, including gathering, preparing, and submitting the completed application form to the USPTO. Time will vary depending upon the individual case. Any comments on the amount of time you require to complete this form and/or suggestions for reducing this burden, should be sent to the Chief Information Officer, U.S. Patent and Trademark Office, U.S. Department of Commerce, P.O. Box 1450, Alexandria, VA 22313-1450. DO NOT SEND FEES OR COMPLETED FORMS TO THIS ADDRESS. **SEND TO: Commissioner for Patents, P.O. Box 1450, Alexandria, VA 22313-1450.**

If you need assistance in completing the form, call 1-800-PTO-9199 and select option 2.

資　料

PTO/SB/16

PTO/SB/16 (03-13)
Approved for use through 01/31/2014. OMB 0651-0032
U.S. Patent and Trademark Office; U.S. DEPARTMENT OF COMMERCE
Under the Paperwork Reduction Act of 1995 no persons are required to respond to a collection of information unless it displays a valid OMB control number

PROVISIONAL APPLICATION FOR PATENT COVER SHEET – Page 2 of 2

The invention was made by an agency of the United States Government or under a contract with an agency of the United States Government.

☐ No.

☐ Yes, the invention was made by an agency of the U.S. Government. The U.S. Government agency name is: _____

☐ Yes, the invention was made under a contract with an agency of the U.S. Government. The name of the U.S. Government agency and Government contract number are: _____

WARNING:

Petitioner/applicant is cautioned to avoid submitting personal information in documents filed in a patent application that may contribute to identity theft. Personal information such as social security numbers, bank account numbers, or credit card numbers (other than a check or credit card authorization form PTO-2038 submitted for payment purposes) is never required by the USPTO to support a petition or an application. If this type of personal information is included in documents submitted to the USPTO, petitioners/applicants should consider redacting such personal information from the documents before submitting them to the USPTO. Petitioner/applicant is advised that the record of a patent application is available to the public after publication of the application (unless a non-publication request in compliance with 37 CFR 1.213(a) is made in the application) or issuance of a patent. Furthermore, the record from an abandoned application may also be available to the public if the application is referenced in a published application or an issued patent (see 37 CFR 1.14). Checks and credit card authorization forms PTO-2038 submitted for payment purposes are not retained in the application file and therefore are not publicly available.

SIGNATURE _____ DATE _____

TYPED OR PRINTED NAME _____ REGISTRATION NO. _____
(*if appropriate*)

TELEPHONE _____ DOCKET NUMBER _____

PTO/SB/20GLBL

Doc Code: PPH.PET.652
Document Description: Petition to make special under Patent Pros Hwy

PTO/SB/20GLBL (12-16)
Approved for use through 04/30/2018. OMB 0651-0058
U.S. Patent and Trademark Office; U.S DEPARTMENT OF COMMERCE

Under the Paperwork Reduction Act of 1995, no persons are required to respond to a collection of information unless it displays a valid OMB control number.

REQUEST FOR PARTICIPATION IN THE GLOBAL/IP5 PATENT PROSECUTION HIGHWAY (PPH) PILOT PROGRAM IN THE USPTO

Application No.:		First Named Inventor:	
Filing Date:		Attorney Docket No.:	
Title of the Invention:			

THIS REQUEST FOR PARTICIPATION IN THE PPH PILOT PROGRAM ALONG WITH THE REQUIRED DOCUMENTS MUST BE SUBMITTED VIA EFS-WEB. INFORMATION REGARDING EFS-WEB IS AVAILABLE AT
HTTP://WWW.USPTO.GOV/PATENTS-APPLICATION-PROCESS/APPLYING-ONLINE/ABOUT-EFS-WEB

APPLICANT HEREBY REQUESTS PARTICIPATION IN THE PATENT PROSECUTION HIGHWAY (PPH) PILOT PROGRAM AND PETITIONS TO MAKE THE ABOVE-IDENTIFIED APPLICATION SPECIAL UNDER THE PPH PILOT PROGRAM.

Office of earlier examination (OEE):

OEE application number: _____

Both the OEE application and the above-identified U.S. application
have the following earliest date (filing or priority date): _____

Type of OEE work product relied upon:

Mailing date of OEE work product: _____

Supporting Documents

1. OEE Work Product and Translation

   A copy of the OEE work product and translation if not already in English:

   ☐ Attached   ☐ Previously submitted   ☐ Not required because the decision to grant a patent was the first office action

   ☐ Applicant requests the USPTO to attempt to obtain the OEE work product from the Dossier Access System or PATENTSCOPE

   NOTE: If the applicant requests the USPTO to obtain the OEE work product electronically and such attempt is unsuccessful, the applicant will be required to supply the document. Accordingly, to avoid dismissal of the initial PPH request and potential denial of participation in the PPH program, the applicant should verify that the OEE work product is actually available via the Dossier Access System or PATENTSCOPE before requesting retrieval. If the applicant is unable to verify availability, then the applicant should submit the document with the PPH request.

2. References Cited in OEE Work Product

   An information disclosure statement (IDS) listing the references cited in the OEE work product and document copies (except U.S. patents and U.S. published patent applications):

   ☐ Attached   ☐ Previously Submitted   ☐ Not required because no references were cited in the OEE work product

[Page 1 of 2]

This collection of information is required by 35 U.S.C. 119, 37 CFR 1.55, and 37 CFR 1.102(d). The information is required to obtain or retain a benefit by the public, which is to file (and by the USPTO to process) an application. Confidentiality is governed by 35 U.S.C. 122 and 37 CFR 1.11 and 1.14. This collection is estimated to take 2 hours to complete, including gathering, preparing, and submitting the completed application form to the USPTO. Time will vary depending upon the individual case. Any comments on the amount of time you require to complete this form and/or suggestions for reducing this burden should be sent to the Chief Information Officer, U.S. Patent and Trademark Office, U.S. Department of Commerce, P.O. Box 1450, Alexandria, VA 22313-1450. DO NOT SEND FEES OR COMPLETED FORMS TO THIS ADDRESS.

資　　料

PTO/SB/20GLBLの続き

PTO/SB/20GLBL (05-16)
Approved for use through 04/30/2018. OMB 0651-0058
U.S. Patent and Trademark Office; U.S DEPARTMENT OF COMMERCE

Under the Paperwork Reduction Act of 1995, no persons are required to respond to a collection of information unless it displays a valid OMB control number.

REQUEST FOR PARTICIPATION IN THE GLOBAL/IP5 PPH PILOT PROGRAM IN THE USPTO
(continued)

Application No.:		First Named Inventor:	

3. Claims Correspondence Certification Statement

All of the claims in this application sufficiently correspond to the patentable/allowable claims in the OEE application.

4. Claims Correspondence Table

Claims in U.S. Application	Patentable Claims in OEE Application	Explanation Regarding the Correspondence

Signature		Date	
Name (print or type)		Registration Number	

PTO/SB/25

PTO/SB/25 (08-11)
Approved for use through 07/31/2012. OMB 0651-0031
U.S. Patent and Trademark Office; U.S. DEPARTMENT OF COMMERCE
Under the Paperwork Reduction Act of 1995, no persons are required to respond to a collection of information unless it displays a valid OMB control number.

TERMINAL DISCLAIMER TO OBVIATE A PROVISIONAL DOUBLE PATENTING REJECTION OVER A PENDING "REFERENCE" APPLICATION	Docket Number (Optional)

In re Application of:

Application No.:

Filed:

For:

The owner*, _____, of _____ percent interest in the instant application hereby disclaims, except as provided below, the terminal part of the statutory term of any patent granted on the instant application which would extend beyond the expiration date of the full statutory term of any patent granted on pending **reference** Application Number _____, filed _____, as the term of any patent granted on said **reference** application may be shortened by any terminal disclaimer filed prior to the grant of any patent on the pending **reference** application. The owner hereby agrees that any patent so granted on the instant application shall be enforceable only for and during such period that it and any patent granted on the **reference** application are commonly owned. This agreement runs with any patent granted on the instant application and is binding upon the grantee, its successors or assigns.

In making the above disclaimer, the owner does not disclaim the terminal part of any patent granted on the instant application that would extend to the expiration date of the full statutory term of any patent granted on said **reference** application, "as the term of any patent granted on said **reference** application may be shortened by any terminal disclaimer filed prior to the grant of any patent on the pending **reference** application," in the event that: any such patent: granted on the pending **reference** application: expires for failure to pay a maintenance fee, is held unenforceable, is found invalid by a court of competent jurisdiction, is statutorily disclaimed in whole or terminally disclaimed under 37 CFR 1.321, has all claims canceled by a reexamination certificate, is reissued, or is in any manner terminated prior to the expiration of its full statutory term as shortened by any terminal disclaimer filed prior to its grant.

Check either box 1 or 2 below, if appropriate.

1. ☐ For submissions on behalf of a business/organization (e.g., corporation, partnership, university, government agency, etc.), the undersigned is empowered to act on behalf of the business/organization.

   I hereby declare that all statements made herein of my own knowledge are true and that all statements made on information and belief are believed to be true; and further that these statements were made with the knowledge that willful false statements and the like so made are punishable by fine or imprisonment, or both, under Section 1001 of Title 18 of the United States Code and that such willful false statements may jeopardize the validity of the application or any patent issued thereon.

2. ☐ The undersigned is an attorney or agent of record. Reg. No. _____

_____   _____
Signature   Date

_____
Typed or printed name

_____
Telephone Number

☐ Terminal disclaimer fee under 37 CFR 1.20(d) is included.

WARNING: Information on this form may become public. Credit card information should not be included on this form. Provide credit card information and authorization on PTO-2038.

*Statement under 37 CFR 3.73(b) is required if terminal disclaimer is signed by the assignee (owner). Form PTO/SB/96 may be used for making this statement. See MPEP § 324.

This collection of information is required by 37 CFR 1.321. The information is required to obtain or retain a benefit by the public which is to file (and by the USPTO to process) an application. Confidentiality is governed by 35 U.S.C. 122 and 37 CFR 1.11 and 1.14. This collection is estimated to take 12 minutes to complete, including gathering, preparing, and submitting the completed application form to the USPTO. Time will vary depending upon the individual case. Any comments on the amount of time you require to complete this form and/or suggestions for reducing this burden, should be sent to the Chief Information Officer, U.S. Patent and Trademark Office, U.S. Department of Commerce, P.O. Box 1450, Alexandria, VA 22313-1450. DO NOT SEND FEES OR COMPLETED FORMS TO THIS ADDRESS. **SEND TO: Commissioner for Patents, P.O. Box 1450, Alexandria, VA 22313-1450.**

If you need assistance in completing the form, call 1-800-PTO-9199 and select option 2.

資　料

PTO/SB/26

PTO/SB/26 (08-11)
Approved for use through 07/31/2012. OMB 0651-0031
U.S. Patent and Trademark Office; U.S. DEPARTMENT OF COMMERCE
Under the Paperwork Reduction Act of 1995, no persons are required to respond to a collection of information unless it displays a valid OMB control number.

TERMINAL DISCLAIMER TO OBVIATE A DOUBLE PATENTING REJECTION OVER A "PRIOR" PATENT	Docket Number (Optional)

In re Application of:

Application No.:

Filed:

For:

The owner*, _____, of _____ percent interest in the instant application hereby disclaims, except as provided below, the terminal part of the statutory term of any patent granted on the instant application which would extend beyond the expiration date of the full statutory term of **prior patent** No. _____ as the term of said **prior patent** is presently shortened by any terminal disclaimer. The owner hereby agrees that any patent so granted on the instant application shall be enforceable only for and during such period that it and the **prior patent** are commonly owned. This agreement runs with any patent granted on the instant application and is binding upon the grantee, its successors or assigns.

In making the above disclaimer, the owner does not disclaim the terminal part of the term of any patent granted on the instant application that would extend to the expiration date of the full statutory term of the **prior patent**, "as the term of said **prior patent** is presently shortened by any terminal disclaimer," in the event that said **prior patent** later:
- expires for failure to pay a maintenance fee;
- is held unenforceable;
- is found invalid by a court of competent jurisdiction;
- is statutorily disclaimed in whole or terminally disclaimed under 37 CFR 1.321;
- has all claims canceled by a reexamination certificate;
- is reissued; or
- is in any manner terminated prior to the expiration of its full statutory term as presently shortened by any terminal disclaimer.

Check either box 1 or 2 below, if appropriate.

1. ☐ For submissions on behalf of a business/organization (e.g., corporation, partnership, university, government agency, etc.), the undersigned is empowered to act on behalf of the business/organization.

   I hereby declare that all statements made herein of my own knowledge are true and that all statements made on information and belief are believed to be true; and further that these statements were made with the knowledge that willful false statements and the like so made are punishable by fine or imprisonment, or both, under Section 1001 of Title 18 of the United States Code and that such willful false statements may jeopardize the validity of the application or any patent issued thereon.

2. ☐ The undersigned is an attorney or agent of record. Reg. No._____

_____   _____
Signature   Date

_____
Typed or printed name

                                                                                _____
                                                                                Telephone Number

☐ Terminal disclaimer fee under 37 CFR 1.20(d) included.

WARNING: Information on this form may become public. Credit card information should not be included on this form. Provide credit card information and authorization on PTO-2038.

*Statement under 37 CFR 3.73(b) is required if terminal disclaimer is signed by the assignee (owner). Form PTO/SB/96 may be used for making this certification. See MPEP § 324.

This collection of information is required by 37 CFR 1.321. The information is required to obtain or retain a benefit by the public which is to file (and by the USPTO to process) an application. Confidentiality is governed by 35 U.S.C. 122 and 37 CFR 1.11 and 1.14. This collection is estimated to take 12 minutes to complete, including gathering, preparing, and submitting the completed application form to the USPTO. Time will vary depending upon the individual case. Any comments on the amount of time you require to complete this form and/or suggestions for reducing this burden, should be sent to the Chief Information Officer, U.S. Patent and Trademark Office, U.S. Department of Commerce, P.O. Box 1450, Alexandria, VA 22313-1450. DO NOT SEND FEES OR COMPLETED FORMS TO THIS ADDRESS. **SEND TO: Commissioner for Patents, P.O. Box 1450, Alexandria, VA 22313-1450.**

If you need assistance in completing the form, call 1-800-PTO-9199 and select option 2.

PTO/SB/27

Doc Code: ROCKET
Document Description: Req for Expedited Processing, Design Rocket Docket

PTO/SB/27 (05-15)
Approved for use through 07/31/2016. OMB 0651-0031
U.S. Patent and Trademark Office, U.S. DEPARTMENT OF COMMERCE
Under the Paperwork Reduction Act of 1995, no persons are required to respond to a collection of information unless it displays a valid OMB control number.

REQUEST FOR EXPEDITED EXAMINATION OF A DESIGN APPLICATION (37 CFR 1.155)	Application Number	
	Filing Date	
	First Named Inventor	
	Title	
	Atty Docket Number	

ADDRESS TO:
MAIL STOP EXPEDITED DESIGN
COMMISSIONER OF PATENTS
P.O. Box 1450
Alexandria, VA 22313-1450

This is a request for expedited examination of a design application under 37 CFR 1.155.

NOTE: If the present form (PTO/SB/27) accompanies a new nonprovisional design application under 37 CFR 1.53(b), include form PTO/SB/18 "Design Patent Application Transmittal" or its equivalent. Do not include the present form (PTO/SB/27) on the date of filing a new international design application. For an international design application to qualify for expedited examination, 37 CFR 1.155(a)(1) provides that the international design application first must have been published by WIPO pursuant to Hague Agreement Article 10(3).

A preexamination search was conducted. The field of search was:
_____
_____
_____

Related applications: _____

The following items are required under 37 CFR 1.155:

- Drawings in compliance with 37 CFR 1.84, unless the design application is an international design application that designates the United States and was published by WIPO pursuant to Hague Agreement Article 10(3).
- The fee set forth in 37 CFR 1.17(k).
- An information disclosure statement in compliance with 37 CFR 1.98.

Note: The Office will not grant a request for expedited examination if all of the requirements of 37 CFR 1.155 are not satisfied. In addition, the Office will not examine an application that is not in a condition for examination (e.g., missing basic filing fee) even if the applicant files a request for expedited examination under 37 CFR 1.155.

_____   _____
Signature   Date

_____   _____
Typed or printed name   Registration Number, if applicable

_____
Telephone Number

Warning: Information on this form may become public. Credit card information should not be included on this form. Provide credit card information and authorization on PTO-2038.

This collection of information is required by 37 CFR 1.48. The information is required to obtain or retain a benefit by the public which is to file (and by the USPTO to process) an application. Confidentiality is governed by 35 U.S.C. 122 and 37 CFR 1.11 and 1.14. This collection is estimated to take 1 hour to complete, including gathering, preparing, and submitting the completed application form to the USPTO. Time will vary depending upon the individual case. Any comments on the amount of time you require to complete this form and/or suggestions for reducing this burden, should be sent to the Chief Information Officer, U.S. Patent and Trademark Office, U.S. Department of Commerce, P.O. Box 1450, Alexandria, VA 22313-1450. DO NOT SEND FEES OR COMPLETED FORMS TO THIS ADDRESS. **SEND TO: Commissioner for Patents, P.O. Box 1450, Alexandria, VA 22313-1450.**

If you need assistance in completing the form, call 1-800-PTO-9199 and select option 2.

PTO/SB/28

Doc Code: PET.SPRE.ACX
Doc Description: Petition for 12-month Accelerated Exam

PTO/SB/28 (07-09)
Approved for use through 09/30/2017. OMB 0651-0059
U.S. Patent and Trademark Office; U. S. DEPARTMENT OF COMMERCE
Under the Paperwork Reduction Act of 1995, no persons are required to respond to a collection of information unless it displays a valid OMB control number.

PETITION TO MAKE SPECIAL UNDER ACCELERATED EXAMINATION PROGRAM

Attorney Docket Number		First Named Inventor	
Application Number (if Known)			
Title of Invention			

APPLICANT HEREBY PETITIONS TO MAKE THE ABOVE-IDENTIFIED APPLICATION SPECIAL UNDER THE REVISED ACCELERATED EXAMINATION PROGRAM. See Instruction sheet on page 3.

1. **Claims of the application:**
   a. The application must contain three (3) or fewer independent claims and twenty (20) or fewer total claims. The application may not contain any multiple dependent claims.

   b. **Applicant hereby agrees not to separately argue the patentability of any dependent claim during any appeal** in the application. Specifically, the applicant agrees that the dependent claims will be grouped together with and not argued separately from the independent claim from which they depend in any appeal brief filed in the application (37 CFR 41.37(c)(1)(vii)).

   c. The claims must be directed to **a single invention**.

2. **Interviews:**
   Applicant hereby agrees to have (if requested by examiner):
   a. An interview (including an interview before a first Office action) to discuss the prior art and any potential rejections or objections with the intention of clarifying and possibly resolving all issues with respect to patentability at that time, and

   b. A telephonic interview to make an election without traverse if the Office determines that the claims are not obviously directed to a single invention.

3. **Preexamination Search Statement and Accelerated Examination Support Document:**
   With this petition, applicant is providing: a **preexamination search statement**, in compliance with the requirements set forth in item 8 of the instruction sheet, and an **"accelerated examination support document"** that includes:
   a. An **information disclosure statement** in compliance with 37 CFR 1.98 citing each reference deemed most closely related to the subject matter of each of the claims;

   b. For each reference cited, **an identification of all the limitations of the claims** that are disclosed by the reference specifying where the limitation is disclosed in the cited reference;

   c. A **detailed explanation of how each of the claims are patentable** over the references cited with the particularity required by 37 CFR 1.111(b) and (c);

   d. A concise **statement of the utility** of the invention as defined in each of the independent claims (unless the application is a design application);

   e. An identification of any cited references that may be disqualified as prior art under 35 U.S.C. 103(c) as amended by the CREATE act; and

   f. **A showing of where each limitation of the claims finds support under the first paragraph of 35 U.S.C. 112** in the written description of the specification. If applicable, the showing must also identify: (1) each means- (or step-) plus-function claim element that invokes consideration under 35 U.S.C. 112, ¶6; and (2) the structure, material, or acts that correspond to any means- (or step-) plus-function claim element that invokes consideration under 35 U.S.C. 112, ¶6. If the application claims the benefit of one or more applications under title 35, United St ates Code, the showing must also include where each limitation of the claims finds support under the first paragraph of 35 U.S.C. 112 in each such application in which such support exists.

The information is required to obtain or retain a benefit by the public which is to file (and by the USPTO to process) an application. Confidentiality is governed by 35 U.S.C. 122 and 37 CFR 1.11 and 1.14. This form is estimated to take 12 hours to complete, including gathering, preparing, and submitting the completed application form to the USPTO. Time will vary depending upon the individual case. Any comments on the amount of time you require to complete this form and/or suggestions for reducing this burden, should be sent to the Chief Information Officer, U.S. Patent and Trademark Office, U.S. Department of Commerce, P.O. Box 1450, Alexandria, VA 22313-1450. DO NOT SEND FEES OR COMPLETED FORMS TO THIS ADDRESS. *If you need assistance in completing the form, call 1-800-PTO-9199 and select option 2.*
EFS Web 2.2.20

PTO/SB/28の続き

Doc Code: PET.SPRE.ACX
Doc Description: Petition for 12-month Accelerated Exam

PTO/SB/28 (07-09)
Approved for use through 09/30/2017. OMB 0651-0059
U.S. Patent and Trademark Office; U. S. DEPARTMENT OF COMMERCE
Under the Paperwork Reduction Act of 1995, no persons are required to respond to a collection of information unless it displays a valid OMB control number.

PETITION TO MAKE SPECIAL UNDER ACCELERATED EXAMINATION PROGRAM
(Continued)

Attorney Docket Number		First Named Inventor	

Attachments:

a.		Accelerated Examination Support Document (see item 3 above).
b.		A statement, in compliance with the requirements set forth in item 8 of the instruction sheet, detailing the preexamination search which was conducted.
c.		Information Disclosure Statement.
d.	☐	Other (*e.g.*, a statement that the claimed subject matter is directed to environmental quality, energy, or countering terrorism (37 CFR 1.102(c)(2)).

Fees: The following fees must be filed electronically via EFS or EFS-Web:

a.	The basic filing fee, search fee, examination fee, and application size fee (if required) under 37 CFR 1.16.
b.	Petition fee under 37 CFR 1.17(h) - unless the petition is filed with a showing under 37 CFR 1.102(c)(2).

Signature:

Click Remove if you wish to remove this signatory [Remove]

Signature		Date	
Name (Print/Typed)		Registration Number	

Click Add if you wish to add additional signatory [Add]

Note: Signatures of all the inventors or assignees of record of the entire interest or their representative(s) are required in accordance with 37 CFR 1.33 and 10.18. Please see 37 CFR 1.4(d) for the form of the signature.

EFS Web 2.2.20

301

資　料

PTO/SB/28の続き

Doc Code: PET.SPRE.ACX
Doc Description: Petition for 12-month Accelerated Exam

PTO/SB/28 (07-09)
Approved for use through 09/30/2017. OMB 0651-0059
U.S. Patent and Trademark Office; U. S. DEPARTMENT OF COMMERCE
Under the Paperwork Reduction Act of 1995, no persons are required to respond to a collection of information unless it displays a valid OMB control number.

Instruction Sheet Petition to Make Special Under the Accelerated Examination

A grantable petition must meet the following conditions:

1. The petition to make special under the accelerated examination program must be filed with the application and accompanied by the fee set forth in 37 CFR 1.17(h) or a statement that the claimed subject matter is directed to environmental quality, energy, or countering terrorism.

2. The application must be a non-reissue utility or design application filed under 35 U.S.C. 111(a).

3. The application must be **filed electronically** using the Office electronic filing system (EFS) or EFS-Web.

4. The application must be complete under 37 CFR 1.51 and in condition for examination on filing. For example, the application must be filed together with the basic filing fee, search fee, examination fee, and application size fee (if applicable), and an oath or declaration under 37 CFR 1.63.

5. The application must contain three (3) or fewer independent claims and twenty (20) or fewer total claims. The application may not contain any multiple dependent claims. The petition must include a statement that **applicant will agree not to separately argue the patentability of any dependent claim during any appeal** in the application. Specifically, the applicant is agreeing that the dependent claims will be grouped together with and not argued separately from the independent claim from which they depend in any appeal brief filed in the application (37 CFR 41.37(c)(1)(vii)).

6. The claims must be directed to a **single invention**. The petition must include a statement that applicant will agree to have a telephonic interview to make an election without traverse in a telephonic interview if the Office determines that all the claims are not directed to a single invention.

7. The petition must include a statement that **applicant will agree** to have an interview (including an interview before a first Office action) to discuss the prior art and any potential rejections or objections with the intention of clarifying and possibly resolving all issues with respect to patentability at that time.

8. At the time of filing, applicant must provide a statement that a **preexamination search was conducted**, including an identification of the field of search by United States class and subclass and the date of the search, where applicable, and, for database searches, the search logic or chemical structure or sequence used as a query, the name of the file or files searched and the database service, and the date of the search.
   a. This preexamination search must involve U.S. patents and patent application publications, foreign patent documents, and nonpatent literature, unless the applicant can justify with reasonable certainty that no references more pertinent than those already identified are likely to be found in the eliminated source and includes such a justification with this statement.
   b. This preexamination search must be directed to the claimed invention and encompass all of the features of the independent claims, giving the claims the broadest reasonable interpretation.
   c. The preexamination search must also encompass the disclosed features that may be claimed, in that an amendment to the claims (including any new claim) that is not encompassed by the preexamination search will be treated as non-responsive and will not be entered.
   d. A search report from a foreign patent office will not be accepted unless the search report satisfies the requirements set forth above.
   e. Any statement in support of a petition to make special must be based on a good faith belief that the preexamination search was conducted in compliance with these requirement. See 37 CFR 1.56 and 10.18.

9. At the time of filing, applicant must provide in support of the petition an **accelerated examination support document that includes:**
   a. An **information disclosure statement** in compliance with 37 CFR 1.98 citing each reference deemed most closely related to the subject matter of each of the claims;
   b. For each reference cited, **an identification of all the limitations of the claims** that are disclosed by the reference specifying where the limitation is disclosed in the cited reference;
   c. A **detailed explanation of how each of the claims are patentable** over the references cited with the particularity required by 37 CFR 1.111(b) and (c);
   d. A concise **statement of the utility** of the invention as defined in each of the independent claims (unless the application is a design application);
   e. An identification of any cited references that may be disqualified as prior art under 35 U.S.C. 103(c) as am ende d by the CREATE act; and
   f. A **showing of where each limitation of the claims finds support under the first paragraph of 35 U.S.C. 112** in the written description of the specification. If applicable, the showing must also identify: (1) each means- (or step-) plus-function claim element that invokes consideration under 35 U.S.C. 112, ¶6; and (2) the structure, material, or acts that correspond to any means- (or step-) plus-function claim element that invokes consideration under 35 U.S.C. 112, ¶6. If the application claims the benefit of one or more applications under title 35, United States Code, the showing must also indicate where each limitation of the claims finds support under the first paragraph of 35 U.S.C. 112 in each such application in which such support exists.
   For more information, see notice "Changes to Practice for Petitions in Patent Applications to Make Special and for Accelerated Examination" available on the USPTO web site at http://www.uspto.gov/web/office s/pac/dapp/ogsheet.html

EFS Web 2.2.20

PTO/SB/30EFS

Doc code: RCEX
Doc description: Request for Continued Examination (RCE)

PTO/SB/30EFS (07-14)
Approved for use through 07/31/2016. OMB 0651-0031
U.S. Patent and Trademark Office; U.S. DEPARTMENT OF COMMERCE
Under the Paperwork Reduction Act of 1995, no persons are required to respond to a collection of information unless it contains a valid OMB control number.

REQUEST FOR CONTINUED EXAMINATION(RCE)TRANSMITTAL
(Submitted Only via EFS-Web)

Application Number		Filing Date		Docket Number (if applicable)		Art Unit	
First Named Inventor				Examiner Name			

This is a Request for Continued Examination (RCE) under 37 CFR 1.114 of the above-identified application.
Request for Continued Examination (RCE) practice under 37 CFR 1.114 does not apply to any utility or plant application filed prior to June 8, 1995, to any international application that does not comply with the requirements of 35 U.S.C. 371, or to any design application. The Instruction Sheet for this form is located at WWW.USPTO.GOV.

SUBMISSION REQUIRED UNDER 37 CFR 1.114

Note: If the RCE is proper, any previously filed unentered amendments and amendments enclosed with the RCE will be entered in the order in which they were filed unless applicant instructs otherwise. If applicant does not wish to have any previously filed unentered amendment(s) entered, applicant must request non-entry of such amendment(s).

☐ Previously submitted. If a final Office action is outstanding, any amendments filed after the final Office action may be considered as a submission even if this box is not checked.

  ☐ Consider the arguments in the Appeal Brief or Reply Brief previously filed on _____

  ☐ Other _____

☐ Enclosed

  ☐ Amendment/Reply

  ☐ Information Disclosure Statement (IDS)

  ☐ Affidavit(s)/ Declaration(s)

  ☐ Other _____

MISCELLANEOUS

☐ Suspension of action on the above-identified application is requested under 37 CFR 1.103(c) for a period of months (Period of suspension shall not exceed 3 months; Fee under 37 CFR 1.17(i) required)

☐ Other _____

FEES

☐ The RCE fee under 37 CFR 1.17(e) is required by 37 CFR 1.114 when the RCE is filed.
The Director is hereby authorized to charge any underpayment of fees, or credit any overpayments, to Deposit Account No _____

SIGNATURE OF APPLICANT, ATTORNEY, OR AGENT REQUIRED

☒ Patent Practitioner Signature
☐ Applicant Signature

EFS - Web 2.1.15

資　料

PTO/SB/30EFSの続き

Doc code: RCEX
Doc description: Request for Continued Examination (RCE)

PTO/SB/30EFS (07-14)
Approved for use through 07/31/2016. OMB 0651-0031
U.S. Patent and Trademark Office; U.S. DEPARTMENT OF COMMERCE
Under the Paperwork Reduction Act of 1995, no persons are required to respond to a collection of information unless it contains a valid OMB control number.

Signature of Registered U.S. Patent Practitioner			
Signature		Date (YYYY-MM-DD)	
Name		Registration Number	

This collection of information is required by 37 CFR 1.114. The information is required to obtain or retain a benefit by the public which is to file (and by the USPTO to process) an application. Confidentiality is governed by 35 U.S.C. 122 and 37 CFR 1.11 and 1.14. This collection is estimated to take 12 minutes to complete, including gathering, preparing, and submitting the completed application form to the USPTO. Time will vary depending upon the individual case. Any comments on the amount of time you require to complete this form and/or suggestions for reducing this burden, should be sent to the Chief Information Officer, U.S. Patent and Trademark Office, U.S. Department of Commerce, P.O. Box 1450, Alexandria, VA 22313-1450.
If you need assistance in completing the form, call 1-800-PTO-9199 and select option 2.

EFS - Web 2.1.15

PTO/SB/38

Doc Code: PD.REQ.RETR
Document Description: Request for USPTO to retrieve priority docs

PTO/SB/38 (10-17)
Approved for use through 10/31/2017. OMB 0651-0031
U.S. Patent and Trademark Office; U.S. DEPARTMENT OF COMMERCE
Under the Paperwork Reduction Act of 1995, no persons are required to respond to a collection of information unless it displays a valid OMB control number.

Request to Retrieve Electronic Priority Application(s)

Send completed form to: Commissioner for Patents
P.O. Box 1450, Alexandria, VA 22313-1450

COMPLETE IF KNOWN	
Application Number	
Filing Date	
First Named Inventor	
Art Unit	
Examiner Name	
Attorney Docket Number	

Pursuant to 37 CFR 1.55(i), the undersigned hereby requests that the USPTO retrieve an electronic copy of each of the following foreign applications for which priority has been claimed under 35 U.S.C. 119(a)-(d) from a foreign intellectual property office participating with the USPTO in a bilateral or multilateral priority document exchange agreement. This Request must be submitted:
- within the later of sixteen months from the filing date of the prior foreign application or four months from the actual filing date of an application under 35 U.S.C. 111(a),
- within four months from the later of the date of commencement (37 CFR 1.491(a)) or the date of the initial submission under 35 U.S.C. 371 of an application entering the national stage under 35 U.S.C. 371, or
- with a petition under 37 CFR 1.55(e) or (f).

☐ **OPTION A**

Please retrieve the priority application identified in **Column C**, a certified copy of which is contained in the EP or JP application identified in Columns A and B:

A	B			C	
Code for Participating Office (EP or JP only)	Application containing the non-participating priority application			Non-participating priority application to be retrieved	
	App. No.	Filing Date	Access Code (for JP only)	Country Code	App. No.
1					

☐ **OPTION B**

This Request may be used for the infrequent circumstance when a claim for priority to an application filed in a participating foreign intellectual property office was made prior to that foreign intellectual property office becoming a participating foreign intellectual property office.

Please retrieve the priority application identified in Columns A and B:

A	B		
Code for Participating Office (e.g., EP, KR, CN) or WIPO DAS Depositing Office (e.g., AU, DK, EE, ES, FI, GB, IB, JP, MA, NZ, SE)	Application to be retrieved		
	App. No.	Filing Date	Access Code (for WIPO DAS Depositing Office)
1			
2			

The USPTO will not attempt to retrieve the identified priority application(s) unless an identical claim for foreign priority to the application identified above is made pursuant to 37 CFR 1.55(d) or a petition is granted under 37 CFR 1.55(e) or (f). Applicants are advised to consult Private PAIR (accessed through www.uspto.gov) to assure that the retrieval has been successful. The applicant bears the ultimate responsibility for ensuring that a copy of the foreign application is received by the Office from the participating foreign intellectual property office, or a certified copy of the foreign priority application is filed, within the time period set forth in 37 CFR 1.55(g)(1).

I hereby declare that I have the authority to grant access to the above-identified foreign application(s).

Signature	Date
Printed or Typed Name	Telephone Number
Title	Registration Number, if applicable

This collection of information is required by 37 CFR 1.55(d). The information is required to obtain or retain a benefit by the public which is to file (and by the USPTO to process) an application. Confidentiality is governed by 35 U.S.C. 122 and 37 CFR 1.11 and 1.14. This collection is estimated to take 8 minutes to complete, including gathering, preparing, and submitting the completed application form to the USPTO. Time will vary depending upon the individual case. Any comments on the amount of time you require to complete this form and/or suggestions for reducing this burden, should be sent to the Chief Information Officer, U.S. Patent and Trademark Office, U.S. Department of Commerce, P.O. Box 1450, Alexandria, VA 22313-1450. DO NOT SEND FEES OR COMPLETED FORMS TO THIS ADDRESS. **SEND TO: Commissioner for Patents, P.O. Box 1450, Alexandria, VA 22313-1450.**

If you need assistance in completing the form, call 1-800-PTO-9199 and select option 2.

資 料

PTO/SB/44

PTO/SB/44 (09-07)
Approved for use through 01/31/2020. OMB 0651-0033
U.S. Patent and Trademark Office; U.S. DEPARTMENT OF COMMERCE
Under the Paperwork Reduction Act of 1995, no persons are required to respond to a collection of information unless it displays a valid OMB control number.
(Also Form PTO-1050)

UNITED STATES PATENT AND TRADEMARK OFFICE
CERTIFICATE OF CORRECTION

Page _____ of _____

PATENT NO. :
APPLICATION NO.:
ISSUE DATE :
INVENTOR(S) :

It is certified that an error appears or errors appear in the above-identified patent and that said Letters Patent is hereby corrected as shown below:

MAILING ADDRESS OF SENDER (Please do not use Customer Number below):

This collection of information is required by 37 CFR 1.322, 1.323, and 1.324. The information is required to obtain or retain a benefit by the public which is to file (and by the USPTO to process) an application. Confidentiality is governed by 35 U.S.C. 122 and 37 CFR 1.14. This collection is estimated to take 1.0 hour to complete, including gathering, preparing, and submitting the completed application form to the USPTO. Time will vary depending upon the individual case. Any comments on the amount of time you require to complete this form and/or suggestions for reducing this burden, should be sent to the Chief Information Officer, U.S. Patent and Trademark Office, U.S. Department of Commerce, P.O. Box 1450, Alexandria, VA 22313-1450. DO NOT SEND FEES OR COMPLETED FORMS TO THIS ADDRESS. **SEND TO: Attention Certificate of Corrections Branch, Commissioner for Patents, P.O. Box 1450, Alexandria, VA 22313-1450.**

If you need assistance in completing the form, call 1-800-PTO-9199 and select option 2.

PTO/SB/51

PTO/SB/51 (09-12)
Approved for use through 01/31/2020. OMB 0651-0033
U.S. Patent and Trademark Office; U.S. DEPARTMENT OF COMMERCE
Under the Paperwork Reduction Act of 1995, no persons are required to respond to a collection of information unless it displays a valid OMB control number.

REISSUE APPLICATION DECLARATION BY THE INVENTOR	Docket Number (Optional)

I hereby declare that:
Each inventor's residence, mailing address and citizenship are stated below next to their name.
I believe the inventors named below to be the original and first inventor(s) of the subject matter which is described and claimed in patent number _____, granted _____ and for which a reissue patent is sought on the invention entitled _____,

the specification of which

☐ is attached hereto.

☐ was filed on _____ as reissue application number _____

and was amended on _____ .
(If applicable)

I have reviewed and understand the contents of the above-identified specification, including the claims, as amended by any amendment referred to above. This application was made or was authorized to be made by me.
I acknowledge the duty to disclose information which is material to patentability as defined in 37 CFR 1.56.

☐ I hereby claim foreign priority benefits under 35 U.S.C. 119(a)-(d) or (f), or 365(b). Attached is form PTO/SB/02B (or equivalent) listing the foreign applications.

I verily believe the original patent to be wholly or partly inoperative or invalid, for the reasons described below. (Check all boxes that apply.)

☐ by reason of a defective specification or drawing.

☐ by reason of the patentee claiming more or less than he had the right to claim in the patent.

☐ by reason of other errors.

At least one error upon which reissue is based is described below. If the reissue is a broadening reissue, such must be stated with an explanation as to the nature of the broadening:

[Page 1 of 2]

This collection of information is required by 37 CFR 1.175. The information is required to obtain or retain a benefit by the public which is to file (and by the USPTO to process) an application. Confidentiality is governed by 35 U.S.C. 122 and 37 CFR 1.11 and 1.14. This collection is estimated to take 30 minutes to complete, including gathering, preparing, and submitting the completed application form to the USPTO. Time will vary depending upon the individual case. Any comments on the amount of time you require to complete this form and/or suggestions for reducing this burden, should be sent to the Chief Information Officer, U.S. Patent and Trademark Office, U.S. Department of Commerce, P.O. Box 1450, Alexandria, VA 22313-1450. DO NOT SEND FEES OR COMPLETED FORMS TO THIS ADDRESS. **SEND TO: Commissioner for Patents, P.O. Box 1450, Alexandria, VA 22313-1450.**

If you need assistance in completing the form, call 1-800-PTO-9199 and select option 2.

資　料

PTO/SB/51の続き

PTO/SB/51 (09-12)
Approved for use through 01/31/2020. OMB 0651-0033
U.S. Patent and Trademark Office; U.S. DEPARTMENT OF COMMERCE
Under the Paperwork Reduction Act of 1995, no persons are required to respond to a collection of information unless it displays a valid OMB control number.

(REISSUE APPLICATION DECLARATION BY THE INVENTOR, page 2)	Docket Number (Optional)

All errors corrected in this reissue application arose without any deceptive intention on the part of the applicant.

Note: To appoint a power of attorney, use form PTO/SB/81.

Correspondence Address: Direct all communications about the application to:

☐ The address associated with Customer Number: [   ]

OR

☐ Firm or Individual Name	
Address	
City	State / Zip
Country	
Telephone	Email

WARNING:

Petitioner/applicant is cautioned to avoid submitting personal information in documents filed in a patent application that may contribute to identity theft. Personal information such as social security numbers, bank account numbers, or credit card numbers (other than a check or credit card authorization form PTO-2038 submitted for payment purposes) is never required by the USPTO to support a petition or an application. If this type of personal information is included in documents submitted to the USPTO, petitioners/applicants should consider redacting such personal information from the documents before submitting them to the USPTO. Petitioner/applicant is advised that the record of a patent application is available to the public after publication of the application (unless a non-publication request in compliance with 37 CFR 1.213(a) is made in the application) or issuance of a patent. Furthermore, the record from an abandoned application may also be available to the public if the application is referenced in a published application or an issued patent (see 37 CFR 1.14). Checks and credit card authorization forms PTO-2038 submitted for payment purposes are not retained in the application file and therefore are not publicly available.

I hereby declare that all statements made herein of my own knowledge are true and that all statements made on information and belief are believed to be true; and further that these statements were made with the knowledge that willful false statements and the like so made are punishable by fine or imprisonment, or both, under 18 U.S.C. 1001, and that such willful false statements may jeopardize the validity of the application, any patent issuing thereon, or any patent to which this declaration is directed. I hereby acknowledge that any willful false statement made in this declaration is punishable under 18 35 U.S.C. 1001 by fine or imprisonment of not more than five (5) years, or both.

Full name of sole or first inventor (given name, family name)	
Inventor's signature	Date
Residence	Citizenship
Mailing Address	

Full name of second joint inventor (given name, family name)	
Inventor's signature	Date
Residence	Citizenship
Mailing Address	

☐ Additional joint inventors or legal representative(s) are named on separately numbered sheets forms PTO/SB/02A or 02LR attached hereto.

[Page 2 of 2]

PTO/SB/52

PTO/SB/52 (09-12)
Approved for use through 01/31/2020. OMB 0651-0033
U.S. Patent and Trademark Office; U.S. DEPARTMENT OF COMMERCE
Under the Paperwork Reduction Act of 1995, no persons are required to respond to a collection of information unless it displays a valid OMB control number.

REISSUE APPLICATION DECLARATION BY THE ASSIGNEE	Docket Number (optional)

I hereby declare that:

The residence, mailing address and citizenship of the inventors are stated below.

I am authorized to act on behalf of the following assignee: _____

and the title of my position with said assignee is: _____

The entire title to the patent identified below is vested in said assignee.

Inventor	Citizenship
Residence/Mailing Address	
Inventor	Citizenship
Residence/Mailing Address	

☐ Additional Inventors are named on separately numbered sheets attached hereto.

Patent Number	Date of Patent Issued

I believe said inventor(s) to be the original and first inventor(s) of the subject matter which is described and claimed in said patent, for which a reissue patent is sought on the invention entitled:

the specification of which

☐ is attached hereto.

☐ was filed on _____ as reissue application number _____ / _____

and was amended on _____
(If applicable)

I have reviewed and understand the contents of the above identified specification, including the claims, as amended by any amendment referred to above. This application was made or was authorized to be made by me.

I acknowledge the duty to disclose information which is material to patentability as defined in 37 CFR 1.56.

☐ I hereby claim foreign priority benefits under 35 U.S.C. 119(a)-(d) or (f), or 365(b). Attached is form PTO/SB/02B (or equivalent) listing the foreign applications.

I verily believe the original patent to be wholly or partly inoperative or invalid, for the reasons described below. (Check all boxes that apply.)

☐ by reason of a defective specification or drawing.

☐ by reason of the patentee claiming more or less than he had the right to claim in the patent.

☐ by reason of other errors.

[Page 1 of 2]

This collection of information is required by 37 CFR 1.175. The information is required to obtain or retain a benefit by the public which is to file (and by the USPTO to process) an application. Confidentiality is governed by 35 U.S.C. 122 and 37 CFR 1.11 and 1.14. This collection is estimated to take 30 minutes to complete, including gathering, preparing, and submitting the completed application form to the USPTO. Time will vary depending upon the individual case. Any comments on the amount of time you require to complete this form and/or suggestions for reducing this burden, should be sent to the Chief Information Officer, U.S. Patent and Trademark Office, U.S. Department of Commerce, P.O. Box 1450, Alexandria, VA 22313-1450. DO NOT SEND FEES OR COMPLETED FORMS TO THIS ADDRESS. **SEND TO: Commissioner for Patents, P.O. Box 1450, Alexandria, VA 22313-1450.**

If you need assistance in completing the form, call 1-800-PTO-9199 and select option 2.

資料

PTO/SB/52の続き

PTO/SB/52 (09-12)
Approved for use through 01/31/2020. OMB 0651-0033
U.S. Patent and Trademark Office; U.S. DEPARTMENT OF COMMERCE
Under the Paperwork Reduction Act of 1995, no persons are required to respond to a collection of information unless it displays a valid OMB control number.

REISSUE APPLICATION DECLARATION BY THE ASSIGNEE	Docket Number (Optional)

At least one error upon which reissue is based is described as follows:

[Attach additional sheets, if needed.]

All errors corrected in this reissue application arose without any deceptive intention on the part of the applicant.

I hereby appoint:
☐ Practitioners associated with Customer Number: _____
OR
☐ Practitioner(s) named below:

Name	Registration Number

as my/our attorney(s) or agent(s) to prosecute the application identified above, and to transact all business in the United States Patent and Trademark Office connected therewith.

Correspondence Address: Direct all communications about the application to:

☐ The address associated with Customer Number: _____
OR
☐ Firm or Individual Name

Address	
City		State		Zip	
Country	
Telephone		Email	

WARNING:

Petitioner/applicant is cautioned to avoid submitting personal information in documents filed in a patent application that may contribute to identity theft. Personal information such as social security numbers, bank account numbers, or credit card numbers (other than a check or credit card authorization form PTO-2038 submitted for payment purposes) is never required by the USPTO to support a petition or an application. If this type of personal information is included in documents submitted to the USPTO, petitioners/applicants should consider redacting such personal information from the documents before submitting them to the USPTO. Petitioner/applicant is advised that the record of a patent application is available to the public after publication of the application (unless a non-publication request in compliance with 37 CFR 1.213(a) is made in the application) or issuance of a patent. Furthermore, the record from an abandoned application may also be available to the public if the application is referenced in a published application or an issued patent (see 37 CFR 1.14). Checks and credit card authorization forms PTO-2038 submitted for payment purposes are not retained in the application file and therefore are not publicly available.

I hereby declare that all statements made herein of my own knowledge are true and that all statements made on information and belief are believed to be true; and further that these statements were made with the knowledge that willful false statements and the like so made are punishable by fine or imprisonment, or both, under 18 U.S.C. 1001 and that such false statements may jeopardize the validity of the application, any patent issuing thereon, or any patent to which this declaration is directed. I hereby acknowledge that any willful false statement made in this declaration is punishable under 18 U.S.C. 1001 by fine or imprisonment of not more than five (5) years, or both.

Signature		Date	
Full name of person signing (given name, family name)			
Address of Assignee			

PTO/SB/53

PTO/SB/53 (09-07)
Approved for use through 01/31/2020. OMB 0651-0033
U.S. Patent and Trademark Office; U.S. DEPARTMENT OF COMMERCE
Under the Paperwork Reduction Act of 1995, no persons are required to respond to a collection of information unless it displays a valid OMB control number.

REISSUE APPLICATION: CONSENT OF ASSIGNEE; STATEMENT OF NON-ASSIGNMENT	Docket Number (Optional)

This is part of the application for a reissue patent based on the original patent identified below.

Name of Patentee(s)

Patent Number	Date Patent Issued

Title of Invention

1. ☐ Filed herein is a statement under 37 CFR 3.73(b). (Form PTO/SB/96)

2. ☐ Ownership of the patent is in the inventor(s), and no assignment of the patent is in effect.

One of boxes 1 or 2 above must be checked. If multiple assignees, complete this form for each assignee. If box 2 is checked, skip the next entry and go directly to "Name of Assignee".

The written consent of all assignees and inventors owning an undivided interest in the original patent is included in this application for reissue.

The assignee(s) owning an undivided interest in said original patent is/are _____, and the assignee(s) consents to the accompanying application for reissue.

Name of assignee/inventor (if not assigned)

Signature	Date

Typed or printed name and title of person signing for assignee (if assigned)

This collection of information is required by 37 CFR 1.172. The information is required to obtain or retain a benefit by the public which is to file (and by the USPTO to process) an application. Confidentiality is governed by 35 U.S.C. 122 and 37 CFR 1.14. This collection is estimated to take 6 minutes to complete, including gathering, preparing, and submitting the completed application form to the USPTO. Time will vary depending upon the individual case. Any comments on the amount of time you require to complete this form and/or suggestions for reducing this burden, should be sent to the Chief Information Officer, U.S. Patent and Trademark Office, U.S. Department of Commerce, P.O. Box 1450, Alexandria, VA 22313-1450. DO NOT SEND FEES OR COMPLETED FORMS TO THIS ADDRESS. **SEND TO: Commissioner for Patents, P.O. Box 1450, Alexandria, VA 22313-1450.**

If you need assistance in completing the form, call 1-800-PTO-9199 and select option 2.

資 料

PTO/SB/57

PTO/SB/57 (09-16)
Approved for use through 09/30/2018. OMB 0651-0064
U.S. Patent and Trademark Office; U.S. DEPARTMENT OF COMMERCE
Under the Paperwork Reduction Act of 1995, no persons are required to respond to a collection of information unless it displays a valid OMB control number.

(Also referred to as FORM PTO-1465)

REQUEST FOR *EX PARTE* REEXAMINATION TRANSMITTAL FORM

Address to:
**Mail Stop *Ex Parte* Reexam
Commissioner for Patents
P.O. Box 1450
Alexandria, VA 22313-1450**

Attorney Docket No.:_____

Date:_____

1. ☐ This is a request for *ex parte* reexamination pursuant to 37 CFR 1.510 of patent number _____ issued _____. The request is made by:

   ☐ patent owner.   ☐ third party requester.

2. ☐ The name and address of the person requesting reexamination is:
   _____
   _____
   _____

3. Requester asserts ☐ small entity status (37 CFR 1.27) or ☐ certifies micro entity status (37 CFR 1.29). Only a patent owner requester can certify micro entity status. Form PTO/SB/15A or B must be attached to certify micro entity status.

4. ☐ a. A check in the amount of $_____ is enclosed to cover the reexamination fee, 37 CFR 1.20(c)(1);

   ☐ b. The Director is hereby authorized to charge the fee as set forth in 37 CFR 1.20(c)(1) to Deposit Account No. _____;

   ☐ c. Payment by credit card. Form PTO-2038 is attached; **or**

   ☐ d. Payment made via EFS-Web.

5. ☐ Any refund should be made by ☐ check or ☐ credit to Deposit Account No._____.
   37 CFR 1.26(c). If payment is made by credit card, refund must be to credit card account.

6. ☐ A copy of the patent to be reexamined having a double column format on one side of a separate paper is enclosed. 37 CFR 1.510(b)(4).

7. ☐ CD-ROM or CD-R in duplicate, Computer Program (Appendix) or large table
   ☐ Landscape Table on CD

8. ☐ Nucleotide and/or Amino Acid Sequence Submission
   If applicable, items a. – c. are required.

   a. ☐ Computer Readable Form (CRF)

   b. Specification Sequence Listing on:

      i. ☐ CD-ROM (2 copies) or CD-R (2 copies); **or**

      ii. ☐ paper

   c. ☐ Statements verifying identity of above copies

9. ☐ A copy of any disclaimer, certificate of correction or reexamination certificate issued in the patent is included.

10. ☐ Reexamination of claim(s) _____ is requested.

11. ☐ A copy of every patent or printed publication relied upon is submitted herewith including a listing thereof on Form PTO/SB/08, PTO-1449, or equivalent.

12. ☐ An English language translation of all necessary and pertinent non-English language patents and/or printed publications is included.

[Page 1 of 2]

This collection of information is required by 37 CFR 1.510. The information is required to obtain or retain a benefit by the public which is to file (and by the USPTO to process) a request for reexamination. Confidentiality is governed by 35 U.S.C. 122 and 37 CFR 1.11 and 1.14. This collection is estimated to take 18 minutes to complete, including gathering, preparing, and submitting the completed application form to the USPTO. Time will vary depending upon the individual case. Any comments on the amount of time you require to complete this form and/or suggestions for reducing this burden, should be sent to the Chief Information Officer, U.S. Patent and Trademark Office, U.S. Department of Commerce, P.O. Box 1450, Alexandria, VA 22313-1450. DO NOT SEND FEES OR COMPLETED FORMS TO THIS ADDRESS. **SEND TO: Mail Stop *Ex Parte* Reexam, Commissioner for Patents, P.O. Box 1450, Alexandria, VA 22313-1450.**
If you need assistance in completing the form, call 1-800-PTO-9199 and select option 2.

PTO/SB/57の続き

PTO/SB/57 (09-16)
Approved for use through 09/30/2018. OMB 0651-0064
U.S. Patent and Trademark Office; U.S. DEPARTMENT OF COMMERCE
Under the Paperwork Reduction Act of 1995, no persons are required to respond to a collection of information unless it displays a valid OMB control number.

13. ☐ The attached detailed request includes at least the following items:

    a. A statement identifying each substantial new question of patentability based on prior patents and printed publications. 37 CFR 1.510(b)(1).

    b. An identification of every claim for which reexamination is requested, and a detailed explanation of the pertinency and manner of applying the cited art to every claim for which reexamination is requested. 37 CFR 1.510(b)(2).

14. ☐ A proposed amendment is included (only where the patent owner is the requester). 37 CFR 1.510(e).

15. ☐ It is certified that the statutory estoppel provisions of 35 U.S.C. 315(e)(1) or 35 U.S.C. 325(e)(1) do not prohibit requester from filing this *ex parte* reexamination request. 37 CFR 1.510(b)(6).

16. ☐ a. It is certified that a copy of this request (if filed by other than the patent owner) has been served in its entirety on the patent owner as provided in 37 CFR 1.33(c).
    The name and address of the party served and the date of service are:
    _____
    _____
    Date of Service: _____ ; or

    ☐ b. A duplicate copy is enclosed since service on patent owner was not possible. An explanation of the efforts made to serve patent owner **is attached**. See MPEP 2220.

17. Correspondence Address: Direct all communication about the reexamination to:

☐ The address associated with Customer Number: _____

OR

☐ Firm or Individual Name _____

Address

City	State	Zip
Country		
Telephone	Email	

18. ☐ The patent is currently the subject of the following concurrent proceeding(s):

    ☐ a. Copending reissue Application No. _____
    ☐ b. Copending reexamination Control No. _____
    ☐ c. Copending Interference No. _____
    ☐ d. Copending litigation styled: _____
    _____

WARNING: Information on this form may become public. Credit card information should not be included on this form. Provide credit card information and authorization on PTO-2038.

Authorized Signature	Date
Typed/Printed Name	Registration No.

☐ For Patent Owner Requester
☐ For Third Party Requester

資料

PTO/SB/59

PTO/SB/59 (09-16)
Approved for use through 09/30/2018. OMB 0651-0064
U.S. Patent and Trademark Office; U.S. DEPARTMENT OF COMMERCE
Under the Paperwork Reduction Act of 1995, no persons are required to respond to a collection of information unless it displays a valid OMB control number.

REQUEST FOR SUPPLEMENTAL EXAMINATION TRANSMITTAL FORM

Address to:
Commissioner for Patents
P.O. Box 1450
Alexandria, VA 22313-1450

Attorney Docket No.:

Date:

1. ☐ This is a request for supplemental examination pursuant to 37 CFR 1.610 of patent number _____ issued _____. 37 CFR 1.610(b)(1).

2. Supplemental examination of claim(s) _____ is requested. 37 CFR 1.610(b)(4).

3. ☐ a. The name(s) of the patent owner(s) (**not** the patent practitioner(s)) is (are):

   _____
   _____
   _____
   _____

   ☐ b. A submission by the patent owner(s) in compliance with 37 CFR 3.73(c), which establishes that the patent owner(s) has (have) the entirety of the ownership in the patent for which supplemental examination is requested, is included. 37 CFR 1.610(b)(9).

4. ☐ a. A check in the amount of $_____ is enclosed to cover the fee for processing and treating a request for supplemental examination, the fee for reexamination ordered under 35 USC 257, and the fee for processing and treating each non-patent document over 20 sheets in length (37 CFR 1.20(k)(1 - 3));

   ☐ b. The Director is hereby authorized to charge all applicable fees as set forth in 37 CFR 1.20(k)(1 - 3) to Deposit Account No. _____; or

   ☐ c. Payment by credit card. Form PTO-2038 is attached. 37 CFR 1.610(a).

5. ☐ Any refund should be made by ☐ check or ☐ credit to Deposit Account No. _____.
   37 CFR 1.26(c). If payment is made by credit card, refund must be to the credit card account.

6. ☐ A copy of the patent for which supplemental examination is requested, and a copy of any disclaimer or certificate issued for the patent are included. 37 CFR 1.610(b)(6).

7. ☐ CD-ROM or CD-R in duplicate, Computer Program (Appendix) or large table
   ☐ Landscape Table on CD

8. ☐ Nucleotide and/or Amino Acid Sequence Submission
   If applicable, items a. – c. are required.

   a. ☐ Computer Readable Form (CRF)
   b. Specification Sequence Listing on:

       i. ☐ CD-ROM (2 copies) or CD-R (2 copies); **or**
       ii. ☐ paper

   c. ☐ Statements verifying the identity of above copies

9. ☐ A list of no more than 12 items of information submitted as part of this request is provided in Part B of this form. Where appropriate, the list must meet the requirements of 37 CFR 1.98(b). 37 CFR 1.605(a), 1.610(b)(2).

[Page 1 of 2]
This collection of information is required by 37 CFR 1.610. The information is required to obtain or retain a benefit by the public which is to file (and by the USPTO to process) an application. Confidentiality is governed by 35 U.S.C. 122 and 37 CFR 1.11 and 1.14. This collection is estimated to take 0.3 hours to complete, including gathering, preparing, and submitting the completed application form to the USPTO. Time will vary depending upon the individual case. Any comments on the amount of time you require to complete this form and/or suggestions for reducing this burden, should be sent to the Chief Information Officer, U.S. Patent and Trademark Office, U.S. Department of Commerce, P.O. Box 1450, Alexandria, VA 22313-1450. DO NOT SEND FEES OR COMPLETED FORMS TO THIS ADDRESS.

PTO/SB/59の続き

Patent No. _____

PTO/SB/59 (09-16)
Approved for use through 09/30/2018. OMB 0651-0064
U.S. Patent and Trademark Office; U.S. DEPARTMENT OF COMMERCE
Under the Paperwork Reduction Act of 1995, no persons are required to respond to a collection of information unless it displays a valid OMB control number.

10. ☐ A legible copy of each item of information listed in Part B of this form, and an English language translation of all necessary and pertinent parts of each non-English language item of information are included.

Copies of items of information that form part of the discussion within the body of the request (see 37 CFR 1.605(b)), and copies of U.S. patents and patent application publications, are not required. 37 CFR 1.610(b)(7).

11. ☐ A summary of the relevant portions of each non-patent document that is over 50 pages in length (other than the request) is included. The summary includes the required citations to the particular pages containing the relevant portions. 37 CFR 1.610(b)(8).

12. ☐ A separate, detailed explanation of the relevance and manner of applying each item of information to each claim of the patent for which supplemental examination is requested, is included. 37 CFR 1.610(b)(5).

13. ☐ The below list includes all prior or concurrent post-patent Office proceedings (*ex parte* or *inter partes* reexamination, reissue, supplemental examination, post grant review, or *inter partes* review) involving the patent for which supplemental examination is being requested. 37 CFR 1.610(b)(3). An identifying number may be, e.g., a control no. or reissue application no. Any prior or concurrent post-patent Office proceedings not listed below are listed on a separate paper accompanying the request.

Type of Proceeding	Identifying Number	Filing Date

☐ See accompanying paper for a list of additional prior or concurrent post-patent Office proceedings involving the patent for which supplemental examination is requested. The paper should be a separate sheet titled "List of Prior or Concurrent Post-Patent Office Proceedings" and must provide the type, identifying number, and filing date of the post-patent Office proceeding.

14. Correspondence Address: Please recognize, or change, the correspondence address for the file of the patent for which supplemental examination is requested **and** for the supplemental examination proceeding to be:

☐ The address associated with Customer Number: [_____] **OR**

☐ Firm or Individual Name

Address

City	State	Zip

Country

Telephone	Email

15. **WARNING: Information on this form may become public. Credit card information should not be included on this form. Provide credit card information and authorization on PTO-2038.**

_____   _____
Authorized Signature   Date

_____   _____
Typed/Printed Name   Registration No.

資 料

PTO/SB/59の続き

PTO/SB/59 (09-16)
Approved for use through 09/30/2018. OMB 0651-0064
U.S. Patent and Trademark Office; U.S. DEPARTMENT OF COMMERCE
Under the Paperwork Reduction Act of 1995, no persons are required to respond to a collection of information unless it displays a valid OMB control number.

(Also referred to as FORM PTO-XXXX)

REQUEST FOR SUPPLEMENTAL EXAMINATION TRANSMITTAL FORM
PART B – LIST OF ITEMS OF INFORMATION – Page 1

Patent number for which supplemental examination is requested _____ Issue Date _____

All items of information (no more than 12) submitted herewith as part of this request for supplemental examination of the above-identified patent are included in the following list:

U. S. PATENT DOCUMENTS

Cite No.[1]	Document Number Number-Kind Code[2] (if known)	Publication Date MM-DD-YYYY	Name of Patentee or Applicant of Cited Document	Pages, Columns, Lines, Where Relevant Passages or Relevant Figures Appear
	US-			
	US-			
	US-			
	US-			
	US-			
	US-			
	US-			
	US-			
	US-			
	US-			
	US-			
	US-			

FOREIGN PATENT DOCUMENTS

Cite No.[1]	Foreign Patent Document Country Code[3]-Number[4]-Kind Code[5] (if known)	Publication Date MM-DD-YYYY	Name of Patentee or Applicant of Cited Document	Pages, Columns, Lines, Where Relevant Passages or Relevant Figures Appear	T[2]

[1] Applicant's unique citation designation number (optional). [2] See Kinds Codes of USPTO Patent Documents at www.uspto.gov or MPEP 901.04. [3] Enter Office that issued the document, by the two-letter code (WIPO Standard ST.3). [4] For Japanese patent documents, the indication of the year of the reign of the Emperor must precede the serial number of the patent document. [5] Kind of document by the appropriate symbols as indicated on the document under WIPO Standard ST.16 if possible. [6] Applicant is to place a check mark here if English language Translation is attached.

Page 1 of 2

PTO/SB/59の続き

PTO/SB/59 (09-16)
Approved for use through 09/30/2018. OMB 0651-0064
U.S. Patent and Trademark Office; U.S. DEPARTMENT OF COMMERCE
Under the Paperwork Reduction Act of 1995, no persons are required to respond to a collection of information unless it displays a valid OMB control number.

(Also referred to as FORM PTO-XXXX)

REQUEST FOR SUPPLEMENTAL EXAMINATION TRANSMITTAL FORM
PART B – LIST OF ITEMS OF INFORMATION – Page 2

Patent number for which supplemental examination is requested _____ Issue Date _____

All items of information (no more than 12) submitted herewith as part of this request for supplemental examination of the above- identified patent are included in the following list:

OTHER DOCUMENTS

Cite No.[1]	Document Information (include, where appropriate, name of the author, title of the article, book, magazine, journal, serial, symposium, catalog, etc., publication date, page(s), volume-issue number(s), publisher, city and/or country where published. If a court document, identify the specific court, the designation (case citation or numeric designation), the title of the document, and the date submitted in court. If a declaration, include the type (e.g., 37 CFR 1.132 or 1.131), name of declarant, and the date of declaration. If an invoice or sales receipt, include the date issued and the name of the issuer (e.g., the name of the corporation or other place of business). If a discussion within the body of the request, include the pages of the request on which the discussion appears, and a description of the discussion (e.g., "discussion in request of why the claims are patentable under 35 U.S.C. 101, pages 7-11.") For all other materials, include, where appropriate, the title, author, date, and any descriptive information that would describe the document.)	T[2]

[1] Applicant's unique citation designation number (optional). [2] Applicant is to place a check mark here if English language Translation is attached.

資　　料

PTO/SB/130

Doc code : PET.OP.AGE
Description : Petition to make special based on Age/Health

PTO/SB/130 (07-09)
Approved for use through 01/31/2013. OMB 0651-0031
U.S. Patent and Trademark Office, U.S. DEPARTMENT OF COMMERCE
Under the Paperwork Reduction Act of 1995, no persons are required to respond to a collection of information unless it contains a valid OMB control number

PETITION TO MAKE SPECIAL BASED ON AGE FOR ADVANCEMENT OF EXAMINATION UNDER 37 CFR 1.102(c)(1)

Application Information

Application Number		Confirmation Number		Filing Date	
Attorney Docket Number (optional)		Art Unit		Examiner	
First Named Inventor					
Title of Invention					

Attention: Office of Petitions

An application may be made special for advancement of examination upon filing of a petition showing that the applicant is 65 years of age, or more. No fee is required with such a petition. See 37 CFR 1.102(c)(1) and MPEP 708.02 (IV).

APPLICANT HEREBY PETITIONS TO MAKE SPECIAL FOR ADVANCEMENT OF EXAMINATION IN THIS APPLICATION UNDER 37 CFR 1.102(c)(1) and MPEP 708.02 (IV) ON THE BASIS OF THE APPLICANT'S AGE.

A grantable petition requires one of the following items:
(1) Statement by one named inventor in the application that he/she is 65 years of age, or more; or
(2) Certification by a registered attorney/agent having evidence such as a birth certificate, passport, driver's license, etc. showing one named inventor in the application is 65 years of age, or more.

Name of Inventor who is 65 years of age, or older

Given Name	Middle Name	Family Name	Suffix

A signature of the applicant or representative is required in accordance with 37 CFR 1.33 and 10.18.
Please see 37 CFR 1.4(d) for the format of the signature.

Select (1) or (2) :

○ (1) I am an inventor in this application and I am 65 years of age, or more.

● (2) I am an attorney or agent registered to practice before the Patent and Trademark Office, and I certify that I am in possession of evidence, and will retain such in the application file record, showing that the inventor listed above is 65 years of age, or more.

Signature		Date (YYYY-MM-DD)	
Name		Registration Number	

EFSWeb 1.0.18

PTO/SB/429

Doc Code: IDS.3P
Document Description: Information Disclosure Statement Filed

PTO/SB/429 (06-15)
Approved for use through 07/31/2018. OMB 0651-0062
U.S. Patent and Trademark Office; U.S. DEPARTMENT OF COMMERCE
Under the Paperwork Reduction Act of 1995 no persons are required to respond to a collection of information unless it displays a valid OMB control number

THIRD-PARTY SUBMISSION UNDER 37 CFR 1.290	Application Number (required):
(Do **not** submit this form electronically via EFS-Web)	

U.S. PATENTS AND U.S. PATENT APPLICATION PUBLICATIONS

Cite No.	Document Number Number-Kind Code[1]	Issue Date or Publication Date MM/DD/YYYY	First Named Inventor
	US-		
	US-		
	US-		
	US-		
	US-		
	US-		
	US-		
	US-		
	US-		

FOREIGN PATENTS AND PUBLISHED FOREIGN PATENT APPLICATIONS

Cite No.	Country or Patent Office and Document Number Country Code[2]-Number[3]-Kind Code[4]	Publication Date MM/DD/YYYY	Applicant, Patentee or First Named Inventor	Translation Attached
				☐
				☐
				☐
				☐
				☐
				☐
				☐
				☐
				☐

1. If known, enter kind of document by the appropriate symbols indicated on the document under WIPO Standard ST.16. See MPEP 901.04(a). 2. Enter the country or patent office that issued the document by two-letter country code under WIPO Standard ST.3. See MPEP 1851. 3. For Japanese patent documents, the indication of the year of the reign of the Emperor must precede the serial number of the patent document. 4. If known, enter kind of document by the appropriate symbols indicated on the document under WIPO Standard ST.16. See MPEP 901.04(a).

This collection of information is required by 35 U.S.C. 122(e) and 37 CFR 1.290. The information is required to obtain or retain a benefit by the public, which is to update (and by the USPTO to process) the file of a patent or reexamination proceeding. Confidentiality is governed by 35 U.S.C. 122 and 37 CFR 1.14. This collection is estimated to take 10 hours to complete, including gathering, preparing, and submitting the completed application form to the USPTO. Time will vary depending upon the individual case. Any comments on the amount of time you require to complete this form and/or suggestions for reducing this burden, should be sent to the Chief Information Officer, U.S. Patent and Trademark Office, U.S. Department of Commerce, P.O. Box 1450, Alexandria, VA 22313-1450. DO NOT SEND FEES OR COMPLETED FORMS TO THIS ADDRESS. **SEND TO: Commissioner for Patents, P.O. Box 1450, Alexandria, VA 22313-1450.**

資 料

PTO/SB/429の続き

Doc Code: IDS.3P
Document Description: Information Disclosure Statement Filed

PTO/SB/429 (06-15)
Approved for use through 07/31/2018. OMB 0651-0062
U.S. Patent and Trademark Office; U.S. DEPARTMENT OF COMMERCE

Under the Paperwork Reduction Act of 1995 no persons are required to respond to a collection of information unless it displays a valid OMB control number

THIRD-PARTY SUBMISSION UNDER 37 CFR 1.290 (Page 2 of 2)	Application Number (required):

NON-PATENT PUBLICATIONS (e.g., journal article, Office action)

Cite No.	Author (if any), title of the publication, page(s) being submitted, publication date, publisher (where available), and place of publication (where available)	Translation Attached	Evidence of Publication Attached
		☐	☐
		☐	☐
		☐	☐
		☐	☐
		☐	☐
		☐	☐
		☐	☐
		☐	☐
		☐	☐
		☐	☐

STATEMENTS

The party making the submission is not an individual who has a duty to disclose information with respect to the above-identified application under 37 CFR 1.56.

This submission complies with the requirements of 35 U.S.C. 122(e) and 37 CFR 1.290.

☐ The following fee set forth in 37 CFR 1.290(f) is submitted herewith: ☐ regular undiscounted ☐ small entity*

☐ The fee set forth in 37 CFR 1.290(f) is not required because this submission lists three or fewer total items and, to the knowledge of the person signing the statement after making reasonable inquiry, this submission is the first and only submission under 35 U.S.C. 122(e) filed in the above-identified application by the party making the submission or by a party in privity with the party.

☐ This resubmission is being made responsive to a notification of non-compliance issued for an earlier filed third-party submission. The corrections in this resubmission are limited to addressing the non-compliance. As such, the party making this resubmission: (1) requests that the Office apply the previously-paid fee set forth in 37 CFR 1.290(f), or (2) states that no fee is required to accompany this resubmission as the undersigned is again making the fee exemption statement set forth in 37 CFR 1.290(g).

Signature		Date	
Name (Printed/Typed)		Reg. No., if applicable	

Examiner Signature**		Date Considered	

*SUBMITTER: By selecting the "small entity" box and paying the applicable small entity fee, the party making the submission asserts that the party qualifies as a small entity. A third party is not eligible for the micro entity discount.

**EXAMINER: Signature indicates all items listed have been considered, except for citations through which a line is drawn. Draw line through citation if not considered. Include a copy of this form with next communication to applicant.

U.S.P.T.O.料金表

(2018年1月16日改定)

参考URL：https://www.uspto.gov/learning-and-resources/fees-and-payment/uspto-fee-schedule

USPTO Fee Schedule

Effective January 16, 2018

The fee schedule provides information and fee rates for USPTO's products and services. All payments must be paid in U.S. dollars for the full amount of the fee required. View the Accepted Payment Methods page or call the USPTO Contact Center at 571-272-1000 or 800-786-9199 for assistance.

Warning about non-USPTO solicitations requesting payments that are sent by numerous companies unaffiliated with the USPTO.

Patent Fees

The fees subject to reduction upon establishment of small entity status (37 CFR 1.27) or micro entity status (37 CFR 1.29) are shown in separate columns. Except for provisional applications, each application for a patent requires the appropriate search fee and examination fee in addition to the appropriate fees in the "Patent Application Filing Fees" section below. This means each fee listed as a "Basic filing fee" in the "Patent Application Filing Fee" section should be accompanied by the appropriate search fee listed in the "Patent Search Fees" section as well as the appropriate examination fee listed in the "Patent Examination Fees" section. The $400/$200 non-electronic filing fee (fee codes 1090/2090/3090 or 1690/2690/3690) must be paid in addition to the filing, search and examination fees, in each original nonprovisional utility application filed in paper with the USPTO. The only way to avoid payment of the non-electronic filing fee is by filing your nonprovisional utility application via EFS-Web. The non-electronic filing fee does not apply to reissue, design, plant, or provisional applications.

Patent Application Filing Fees

Fee Code	37 CFR	Description	Fee	Small Entity Fee	Micro Entity Fee
1011/2011/3011	1.16(a)	Basic filing fee - Utility (paper filing also requires non-electronic filing fee under 1.16(t))	300	150	75
4011†	1.16(a)	Basic filing fee - Utility (electronic filing for small entities)	n/a	75	n/a
1012/2012/3012	1.16(b)	Basic filing fee - Design	200	100	50
1017/2017/3017	1.16(b)	Basic filing fee - Design (CPA)	200	100	50
1013/2013/3013	1.16(c)	Basic filing fee - Plant	200	100	50
1005/2005/3005	1.16(d)	Provisional application filing fee	280	140	70
1014/2014/3014	1.16(e)	Basic filing fee - Reissue	300	150	75
1019/2019/3019	1.16(e)	Basic filing fee - Reissue (CPA)	300	150	75
1051/2051/3051	1.16(f)	Surcharge - Late filing fee, search fee, examination fee, inventor's oath or declaration, or application filed without at least one claim or by reference	160	80	40
1052/2052/3052	1.16(g)	Surcharge - Late provisional filing fee or cover sheet	60	30	15
1201/2201/3201	1.16(h)	Each independent claim in excess of three	460	230	115
1204/2204/3204	1.16(h)	Each reissue independent claim in excess of three	460	230	115
1202/2202/3202	1.16(i)	Each claim in excess of 20	100	50	25
1205/2205/3205	1.16(i)	Each reissue claim in excess of 20	100	50	25
1203/2203/3203	1.16(j)	Multiple dependent claim	820	410	205

庁 費 用

Fee Code	37 CFR	Description	Fee	Small Entity Fee	Micro Entity Fee
1081/2081/3081	1.16(s)	Utility Application Size Fee - for each additional 50 sheets that exceeds 100 sheets	400	200	100
1082/2082/3082	1.16(s)	Design Application Size Fee - for each additional 50 sheets that exceeds 100 sheets	400	200	100
1083/2083/3083	1.16(s)	Plant Application Size Fee - for each additional 50 sheets that exceeds 100 sheets	400	200	100
1084/2084/3084	1.16(s)	Reissue Application Size Fee - for each additional 50 sheets that exceeds 100 sheets	400	200	100
1085/2085/3085	1.16(s)	Provisional Application Size Fee - for each additional 50 sheets that exceeds 100 sheets	400	200	100
1090/2090/3090	1.16(t)	Non-electronic filing fee — Utility (additional fee for applications filed in paper)	400	200	200
1053/2053/3053	1.17(i)(1)	Non-English translation	140	70	35
1091/2091/3091	1.21(o)(1)	Submission of sequence listings of 300MB to 800MB	1,000.00	500	250
1092/2092/3092	1.21(o)(2)	Submission of sequence listings of more than 800MB	10,000.00	5,000.00	2,500.00

† The 4000 series fee code may be used via EFS-Web

Patent Search Fees

Fee Code	Fee Code	Description	Fee	Small Entity Fee	Micro Entity Fee
1111/2111/3111	1.16(k)	Utility Search Fee	660	330	165
1112/2112/3112	1.16(l)	Design Search Fee	160	80	40
1113/2113/3113	1.16(m)	Plant Search Fee	420	210	105
1114/2114/3114	1.16(n)	Reissue Search Fee	660	330	165

Patent Examination Fees

Fee Code	37 CFR	Description	Fee	Small Entity Fee	Micro Entity Fee
1311/2311/3311	1.16(o)	Utility Examination Fee	760	380	190
1312/2312/3312	1.16(p)	Design Examination Fee	600	300	150
1313/2313/3313	1.16(q)	Plant Examination Fee	620	310	155
1314/2314/3314	1.16(r)	Reissue Examination Fee	2,200.00	1,100.00	550

Patent Post-Allowance Fees

Fee Code	37 CFR	Description	Fee	Small Entity Fee	Micro Entity Fee
1501/2501/3501	1.18(a)(1)	Utility issue fee	1,000.00	500	250
1511/2511/3511	1.18(a)(1)	Reissue issue fee	1,000.00	500	250
1502/2502/3502	1.18(b)(1)	Design issue fee	700	350	175
1503/2503/3503	1.18(c)(1)	Plant issue fee	800	400	200
n/a	1.18(d)(1)	Publication fee for early, voluntary, or normal publication	0	0	0
1505/2505/3505	1.18(d)(3)	Publication fee for republication	300	300	300.00*

* Third-party filers are not eligible for the micro entity fee.

Patent Extension of Time Fees

Fee Code	37 CFR	Description	Fee	Small Entity Fee	Micro Entity Fee
1251/2251/3251	1.17(a)(1)	Extension for response within first month	200	100	50
1252/2252/3252	1.17(a)(2)	Extension for response within second month	600	300	150
1253/2253/3253	1.17(a)(3)	Extension for response within third month	1,400.00	700	350

322

1254/2254/3254	1.17(a)(4)	Extension for response within fourth month	2,200.00	1,100.00	550
1255/2255/3255	1.17(a)(5)	Extension for response within fifth month	3,000.00	1,500.00	750

Patent Maintenance Fees

Fee Code	37 CFR	Description	Fee	Small Entity Fee	Micro Entity Fee
1551/2551/3551	1.20(e)	For maintaining an original or any reissue patent, due at 3.5 years	1,600.00	800	400
1552/2552/3552	1.20(f)	For maintaining an original or any reissue patent, due at 7.5 years	3,600.00	1,800.00	900
1553/2553/3553	1.20(g)	For maintaining an original or any reissue patent, due at 11.5 years	7,400.00	3,700.00	1,850.00
1554/2554/3554	1.20(h)	Surcharge - 3.5 year - Late payment within 6 months	160	80	40
1555/2555/3555	1.20(h)	Surcharge - 7.5 year - Late payment within 6 months	160	80	40
1556/2556/3556	1.20(h)	Surcharge - 11.5 year - Late payment within 6 months	160	80	40
1558/2558/3558	1.17(m)	Petition for the delayed payment of the fee for maintaining a patent in force	2,000.00	1,000.00	500

Miscellaneous Patent Fees

Fee Code	37 CFR	Description	Fee	Small Entity Fee	Micro Entity Fee
1817/2817/3817	1.17(c)	Request for prioritized examination	4,000.00	2,000.00	1,000.00
1819/2819/3819	1.17(d)	Correction of inventorship after first action on merits	600	300	150
1801/2801/3801	1.17(e)(1)	Request for continued examination (RCE) - 1st request (see 37 CFR 1.114)	1,300.00	650	325
1820/2820/3820	1.17(e)(2)	Request for continued examination (RCE) - 2nd and subsequent request (see 37 CFR 1.114)	1,900.00	950	475
1830/2830/3830	1.17(i)(1)	Processing fee, except in provisional applications	140	70	35
1808/2808/3808	1.17(i)(2)	Other publication processing fee	130	130	130
1803/2803/3803	1.17(i)(2)	Request for voluntary publication or republication	130	130	130.00*
1802/2802/3802	1.17(k)	Request for expedited examination of a design application	900	450	225
1806/2806/3806	1.17(p)	Submission of an Information Disclosure Statement	240	120	60
1818/2818	1.17(o)	Document fee for third-party submissions (see 37 CFR 1.290(f))	180	90	n/a*
1807/2807/3807	1.17(q)	Processing fee for provisional applications	50	50	50
1809/2809/3809	1.17(r)	Filing a submission after final rejection (see 37 CFR 1.129(a))	840	420	210
1810/2810/3810	1.17(s)	For each additional invention to be examined (see 37 CFR 1.129(b))	840	420	210

* Third-party filers are not eligible for the micro entity fee.

庁 費 用

Post Issuance Fees

Fee Code	37 CFR	Description	Fee	Small Entity Fee	Micro Entity Fee
1811/2811/3811	1.20(a)	Certificate of correction	150	150	150
1816/2816/3816	1.20(b)	Processing fee for correcting inventorship in a patent	150	150	150
1831/2831/3831	1.20(c)(1)	Ex parte reexamination (§1.510(a)) Streamlined	6,000.00	3,000.00	1,500.00*
1812/2812/3812	1.20(c)(2)	Ex parte reexamination (§1.510(a)) Non-streamlined	12,000.00	6,000.00	3,000.00*
1821/2821/3821	1.20(c)(3)	Each reexamination independent claim in excess of three and also in excess of the number of such claims in the patent under reexamination	460	230	115
1822/2822/3822	1.20(c)(4)	Each reexamination claim in excess of 20 and also in excess of the number of claims in the patent under reexamination	100	50	25
1814/2814/3814	1.20(d)	Statutory disclaimer, including terminal disclaimer	160	160	160
1826/2826/3826	1.20(k)(1)	Request for supplemental examination	4,400.00	2,200.00	1,100.00
1827/2827/3827	1.20(k)(2)	Reexamination ordered as a result of supplemental examination	12,100.00	6,050.00	3,025.00
1828/2828/3828	1.20(k)(3)(i)	Supplemental Examination Document Size Fee - for nonpatent document having between 21 and 50 sheets	180	90	45
1829/2829/3829	1.20(k)(3)(ii)	Supplemental Examination Document Size Fee - for each additional 50 sheets or a fraction thereof in a nonpatent document	280	140	70

* Third-party filers are not eligible for the micro entity fee.

Patent Trial and Appeal Fees

Fee Code	37 CFR	Description	Fee	Small Entity Fee	Micro Entity Fee
1405/2405/3405	41.20(a)	Petitions to the Chief Administrative Patent Judge under 37 CFR 41.3	400	400	400
1401/2401/3401	41.20(b)(1)	Notice of appeal	800	400	200.00*
n/a	41.20(b)(2)(i)	Filing a brief in support of an appeal	0	0	0
1404/2404/3404	41.20(b)(2)(ii)	Filing a brief in support of an appeal in an inter partes reexamination proceeding	2,000.00	1,000.00	500.00*
1403/2403/3403	41.20(b)(3)	Request for oral hearing	1,300.00	650	325.00*
1413/2413/3413	41.20(b)(4)	Forwarding an appeal in an application or ex parte reexamination proceeding to the Board	2,240.00	1,120.00	560.00*
1406/2406/3406	42.15(a)(1)	Inter partes review request fee - Up to 20 claims	15,500.00	15,500.00	15,500.00
1414/2414/3414	42.15(a)(2)	Inter partes review post-institution fee - Up to 15 claims	15,000.00	15,000.00	15,000.00
1407/2407/3407	42.15(a)(3)	Inter partes review request of each claim in excess of 20	300	300	300
1415/2415/3415	42.15(a)(4)	Inter partes post-institution request of each claim in excess of 15	600	600	600
1408/2408/3408	42.15(b)(1)	Post-grant or covered business method review request fee - Up to 20 claims	16,000.00	16,000.00	16,000.00

324

Fee Code	37 CFR	Description	Fee	Small Entity Fee	Micro Entity Fee
1416/2416/3416	42.15(b)(2)	Post-grant or covered business method review post-institution fee - Up to 15 claims	22,000.00	22,000.00	22,000.00
1409/2409/3409	42.15(b)(3)	Post-grant or covered business method review request of each claim in excess of 20	375	375	375
1417/2417/3417	42.15(b)(4)	Post-grant or covered business method review post-institution request of each claim in excess of 15	825	825	825
1412/2412/3412	42.15(c)(1)	Petition for a derivation proceeding	400	400	400
1411/2411/3411	42.15(d)	Request to make a settlement agreement available and other requests filed in a patent trial proceeding	400	400	400

* Third-party filers are not eligible for the micro entity fee.

Patent Petition Fees

Fee Code	37 CFR	Description	Fee	Small Entity Fee	Micro Entity Fee
1462/2462/3462	1.17(f)	Petitions requiring the petition fee set forth in 37 CFR 1.17(f) (Group I)	400	200	100
1463/2463/3463	1.17(g)	Petitions requiring the petition fee set forth in 37 CFR 1.17(g) (Group II)	200	100	50
1464/2464/3464	1.17(h)	Petitions requiring the petition fee set forth in 37 CFR 1.17(h) (Group III)	140	70	35
1453/2453/3453	1.17(m)	Petition for revival of an abandoned application for a patent, for the delayed payment of the fee for issuing each patent, or for the delayed response by the patent owner in any reexamination proceeding	2,000.00	1,000.00	500
1454/2454/3454	1.17(m)	Petition for the delayed submission of a priority or benefit claim	2,000.00	1,000.00	500
1784/2784/3784	1.17(m)	Petition to excuse applicant's failure to act within prescribed time limits in an international design application	2,000.00	1,000.00	500
1783/2783/3783	1.17(t)	Petition to convert an international design application to a design application under 35 U.S.C. chapter 16	180	90	45
1455/2455/3455	1.18(e)	Filing an application for patent term adjustment	200	200	200
1456/2456/3456	1.18(f)	Request for reinstatement of term reduced	400	400	400
1824/2824/3824	1.20(c)(6)	Petitions in a reexamination proceeding, except for those specifically enumerated in 37 CFR 1.550(i) and 1.937(d)	1,940.00	970	485.00*
1457/2457/3457	1.20(j)(1)	Extension of term of patent	1,120.00	1,120.00	1,120.00
1458/2458/3458	1.20(j)(2)	Initial application for interim extension (see 37 CFR 1.790)	420	420	420
1459/2459/3459	1.20(j)(3)	Subsequent application for interim extension (see 37 CFR 1.790)	220	220	220

* Third-party filers are not eligible for the micro entity fee.

庁 費 用

PCT Fees - National Stage

Fee Code	37 CFR	Description	Fee	Small Entity Fee	Micro Entity Fee
1631/2631/3631	1.492(a)	Basic National Stage Fee	300	150	75
n/a	1.492(b)(1)	National Stage Search Fee - U.S. was the ISA or IPEA and all claims satisfy PCT Article 33(1)-(4)	0	0	0
1641/2641/3641	1.492(b)(2)	National Stage Search Fee - U.S. was the ISA	140	70	35
1642/2642/3642	1.492(b)(3)	National Stage Search Fee - search report prepared and provided to USPTO	520	260	130
1632/2632/3632	1.492(b)(4)	National Stage Search Fee - all other situations	660	330	165
n/a	1.492(c)(1)	National Stage Examination Fee - U.S. was the ISA or IPEA and all claims satisfy PCT Article 33(1)-(4)	0	0	0
1633/2633/3633	1.492(c)(2)	National Stage Examination Fee - all other situations	760	380	190
1614/2614/3614	1.492(d)	Each independent claim in excess of three	460	230	115
1615/2615/3615	1.492(e)	Each claim in excess of 20	100	50	25
1616/2616/3616	1.492(f)	Multiple dependent claim	820	410	205
1617/2617/3617	1.492(h)	Search fee, examination fee or oath or declaration after the date of commencement of the national stage	140	70	35
1618/2618/3618	1.492(i)	English translation after thirty months from priority date	140	70	35
1681/2681/3681	1.492(j)	National Stage Application Size Fee - for each additional 50 sheets that exceeds 100 sheets	400	200	100

PCT Fees - International Stage

Fee Code	37 CFR	Description	Fee	Small Entity Fee	Micro Entity Fee
1601/2601/3601	1.445(a)(1)(i)(A)	Transmittal fee	240	120	60
1690/2690/3690	1.445(a)(1)(ii)	Non-electronic filing fee (additional fee for applications filed in paper)	400	200	200
1602/2602/3602	1.445(a)(2)(i)	Search fee - regardless of whether there is a corresponding application (see 35 U.S.C. 361(d) and PCT Rule 16)	2,080.00	1,040.00	520
1604/2604/3604	1.445(a)(3)(i)	Supplemental search fee when required, per additional invention	2,080.00	1,040.00	520
1621/2621/3621	1.445(a)(4)(i)	Transmitting application to Intl. Bureau to act as receiving office	240	120	60
1605/2605/3605	1.482(a)(1)(i)(A)	Preliminary examination fee - U.S. was the ISA	600	300	150
1606/2606/3606	1.482(a)(1)(ii)(A)	Preliminary examination fee - U.S. was not the ISA	760	380	190
1607/2607/3607	1.482(a)(2)(i)	Supplemental examination fee per additional invention	600	300	150
1619/2619/3619		Late payment fee	variable	variable	variable
1627/2627/3627	1.445(a)(5) and 1.482(c)	Late furnishing fee for providing a sequence listing in response to an invitation under PCT rule 13*ter*	300	150	75

PCT Fees to Foreign Offices

Fee Code	37 CFR	Description	Fee	Small Entity Fee	Micro Entity Fee
1701		International filing fee (first 30 pages - filed electronically without ePCT or PCT-EASY .zip file)	1,263.00	1,263.00	1,263.00
1710		International filing fee (first 30 pages - filed electronically with ePCT or PCT-EASY .zip file)	1,161.00	1,161.00	1,161.00
1702		International filing fee (first 30 pages)	1,366.00	1,366.00	1,366.00
1703		Supplemental fee (for each page over 30)	15	15	15
1704		International search (EPO)	2,202.00	2,202.00	2,202.00
1715		International search (ILPO)	995	995	995
1712		International search (IPAU)	1,722.00	1,722.00	1,722.00
1717		International search (IPOS)	1,646.00	1,646.00	1,646.00
1716		International search (JPO)	1,385.00	1,385.00	1,385.00
1709		International search (KIPO)	1,134.00	1,134.00	1,134.00
1714		International search (Rospatent)	691	691	691
1705		Handling fee	205	205	205
1706		Handling Fee - 90% reduction, if applicant meets criteria specified at: http://www.wipo.int/export/sites/www/pct/en/fees/fee_reductio n.pdf	20.5	20.5	20.5

** PCT Fees to Foreign Offices subject to periodic change due to fluctuations in exchange rate.

Hague - International Design Application Fees

Fee Code	37 CFR	Description	Fee	Small Entity Fee	Micro Entity Fee
1781/2781/3781	1.1031(a)	Hague International Design Application - Transmittal fee	120	60	30
1782	1.1031(c)	International design application fees payable to WIPO	variable	variable	variable

Patent Service Fees

Fee Code	37 CFR	Description	Fee	Small Entity Fee	Micro Entity Fee
8001	1.19(a)(1)	Printed copy of patent w/o color, delivery by USPS, USPTO Box, or electronic means	3	3	3
8005	1.19(a)(1)	Patent Application Publication (PAP)	3	3	3
8003	1.19(a)(2)	Printed copy of plant patent in color	15	15	15
8004	1.19(a)(3)	Color copy of patent (other than plant patent) containing a color drawing	25	25	25
8007	1.19(b)(1)(i)(A) and (ii)(A)	Copy of patent application as filed	35	35	35
8010	1.19(b)(1)(i)(D)	Individual application documents, other than application as filed, per document	25	25	25
8051	1.19(b)(1)(i)(B)	Copy patent file wrapper, paper medium, any number of sheets	280	280	280

庁費用

Fee Code	37 CFR	Description			
8052	1.19(b)(1)(ii)(B)	Copy patent file wrapper, electronic medium, any size or provided electronically	55	55	55
8013	1.19(b)(3)	Copy of office records, except copies of applications as filed	25	25	25
8014	1.19(b)(4)	For assignment records, abstract of title and certification, per patent	35	35	35
8904	1.19(c)	Library service	50	50	50
8017	1.19(f)	Copy of non-U.S. document	25	25	25
8020	1.21(e)	International type search report	40	40	40
n/a	1.21(h)(1)	Recording each patent assignment, agreement or other paper, per property – if submitted electronically	0	0	0
8021	1.21(h)(2)	Recording each patent assignment, agreement or other paper, per property – if not submitted electronically	50	50	50
8022	1.21(i)	Publication in Official Gazette	25	25	25
8026	1.21(n)	Handling fee for incomplete or improper application	130	130	130
8053	1.21(p)	Additional fee for overnight delivery	40	40	40
8054	1.21(q)	Additional fee for expedited service	160	160	160

Patent Enrollment Fees

Fee Code	37 CFR	Description	Fee
9001	1.21(a)(1)(i)	Application fee (non-refundable)	100
9010	1.21(a)(1)(ii)(A)	For test administration by commercial entity	200
9011	1.21(a)(1)(ii)(B)	For test administration by the USPTO	450
9003	1.21(a)(2)(i)	On registration to practice under §11.6	200
9026	1.21(a)(2)(ii)	On grant of limited recognition under §11.9(b)	200
9025	1.21(a)(2)(iii)	On change of registration from agent to attorney	100
9005	1.21(a)(4)(i)	Certificate of good standing as an attorney or agent, standard	40
9006	1.21(a)(4)(ii)	Certificate of good standing as an attorney or agent, suitable for framing	50
9012	1.21(a)(5)(i)	Review of decision by the Director of Enrollment and Discipline under §11.2(c)	400
9013	1.21(a)(5)(ii)	Review of decision of the Director of Enrollment and Discipline under §11.2(d)	400
9020	1.21(a)(9)(i)	Delinquency fee	50
9004	1.21(a)(9)(ii)	Administrative reinstatement fee	200
9014	1.21(a)(10)	On petition for reinstatement by a person excluded or suspended on ethical grounds, or excluded on consent from practice before the Office	1,600.00
9024	1.21(k)	Unspecified other services, excluding labor	AT COST
9027	1.21(a)(6)(i)	For USPTO-assisted recovery of ID or reset of password for the Office of Enrollment and Discipline Information System	70
9028	1.21(a)(6)(ii)	For USPTO-assisted change of address within the Office of Enrollment and Discipline Information System	70
9029	1.21(a)(1)(iii)	For USPTO-administered review of registration examination	450

索　引

あ行

アドバイザリ・アクション（Advisory Action：AA） …………………148
新たな争点の提起（Substantial New Question：SNQ）…………………152
意見書（Remarks）…………………………………………………………138
維持費（Maintenance fee）…………………………………………………216
意匠出願（Design Patent Application）……………………………………15
意匠出願の早期審査 ………………………………………………………194
一部継続出願（Continuation-In-Part）……………………………………155
委任状…………………………………………………………………………65
延長費用 ……………………………………………………………………125
応答書（Response to the Office Action）…………………………………138

か行

外国出願ライセンス ………………………………………………………121
仮出願（U.S. Provisional Application）……………………………………12
関連出願の表示（Cross Reference to Related Applications）……………30
記載要件 ……………………………………………………………………107
共通審判規則 ………………………………………………………………241
共同研究契約…………………………………………………………………99
許可可能通知（Notice of Allowability）…………………………………201
許可通知（Notice of Allowance）…………………………………………201
許可理由（Reasons for Allowance）………………………………………201
金融系ビジネス方法特許レビュー ………………………………………252
グラハム判決 ………………………………………………………………105
クレーム（Claims）…………………………………………………………30
クレーム数の計算 …………………………………………………………33
形式審査 ……………………………………………………………………124
継続出願（Continuation Application）……………………………………155
継続審査請求（Request for Continued Examination：RCE）……………152

索　引

継続的出願（Continuing Application）……………………………144
欠落部分提出通知（Notice to File Missing Parts）………………124
限定要求（Restriction Requirement）………………………………130
行使不能（Unenforceable）……………………………………………227
口頭審尋（Oral Hearing）………………………………………………177
口頭審尋期日指定通知書………………………………………………178
口頭審尋請求書…………………………………………………………177
国際出願（International Application）…………………………………4
国際調査機関……………………………………………………………10
国際調査報告書（ISR：International Search Report）……………10
極小規模事業体（Micro Entity）………………………………………83
個人（Person）……………………………………………………………82

さ行

最終局指令（Final Office action）……………………………………143
最終局指令後の期間の計算……………………………………………150
最終審決…………………………………………………………………245
再発行特許（Reissue Patent）………………………………………222
先発明主義…………………………………………………………………91
査定系再審査制度（Ex Parte-Reexamination）……………………226
実施可能要件……………………………………………………………107
実施例（Detailed Description）………………………………………30
実体審査……………………………………………………………………5
自明タイプの二重特許…………………………………………………114
修正書面提出通知（Notice to File Corrected Application Paper）…………127
修正先願主義………………………………………………………………91
従来技術（Background）………………………………………………30
出願公開……………………………………………………………………4
出願受領証………………………………………………………………121
出願データシート…………………………………………………………37
小規模事業体（Small business concern）……………………………82
小規模事業体（Small Entity）…………………………………………82

譲渡証（Assignment）・・59
情報開示陳述書（IDS）・・・68
植物特許出願（Plant Patent Application）・・・・・・・・・・・・・・・・・・・・・・・・9
所有権の連鎖（Chain of Title）・・・・・・・・・・・・・・・・・・・・・・・・・・・・・・・・・・・・59
新規性（Novelty）・・91
審査官による答弁書・・・172
審査官による答弁書（Examiner's Answer）・・・・・・・・・・・・・・・・・・・・・172
審査官補正（Examiner's Amendment）・・・・・・・・・・・・・・・・・・・・・・・・・201
審査官面談（Interview）・・・140
審査の再開（Reopen）・・・180
審判応答書（Reply Brief）・・・・・・・・・・・・・・・・・・・・・・・・・・・・・・・・・・・・・・・175
審判官合議体・・179
審判請求（Notice of Appeal）・・・・・・・・・・・・・・・・・・・・・・・・・・・・・・・・・・・163
審判理由補充書（Appeal Brief）・・・・・・・・・・・・・・・・・・・・・・・・・・・・・・・・・163
審理及び審決（Board Review and Decision）・・・・・・・・・・・・・・・・・・・179
審理開始判断・・244
スーパーバイザ（Supervisor）・・・・・・・・・・・・・・・・・・・・・・・・・・・・・・・・・・・・148
図面（Drawings）・・35
図面の簡単な説明（Brief Description of The Drawings）・・・・・・30
先願未公開出願・・92
宣誓書（Declaration）・・・47
宣誓文が含まれた譲渡証・・57
選択要求（Election Requirement）・・・・・・・・・・・・・・・・・・・・・・・・・・・・・130
早期審査制度・・183
送付状（Transmittal）・・・21
速達郵便（Express Mail）・・・20

た行

ターミナルディスクレーマ（Terminal disclaimer）・・・・・・・・・・・・・114
第三者文献提出制度（Preissuarance Submissions by Third parties）・・・・・・・・236
代用陳述書・・・54
多項従属クレーム（Multiple Dependent Claim）・・・・・・・・・・・・・・・・33

索　引

陳述書（Statement）……………………………………………201
提出物（Submission）……………………………………………152
ディスカバリ……………………………………………………245
訂正証明書の請求（Certificate of Correction）………………219
電子受理証（Electronic Acknowledgement Receipt）…………18
同一タイプの二重特許…………………………………………114
当事者系レビュー制度（Inter Partes Review：IPR）…………247
特許期間調整（Patent Term Adjustment：PTA）………………214
特許協力条約（Patent Cooperation Treaty：PCT）……………10
特許出願（Utility Patent Application）…………………………9
特許証（Letters of Patent）………………………………………213
特許審査マニュアル（Manual of Patent Examining Procedure：M.P.E.P.）…3
特許審判控訴部（Patent Trial and Appeal Board）……………176
特許証発行通知……………………………………………………213
特許発行の延期……………………………………………………215
特許発行の取下げ…………………………………………………215
特許発行料（Issue fee）…………………………………………209

な行
二重特許（Double Patent）………………………………………114
日本語出願…………………………………………………………12

は行
バージニア州東部連邦地方裁判所
　（District Court for Eastern District of Virginia）……………179
発明者決定手続……………………………………………………197
発明の概要（Summary）…………………………………………30
発明の名称（Title of the invention）……………………………30
パリルート出願……………………………………………………10
非営利団体（Nonprofit Organization）…………………………82
非最終局指令（Non-final Office Action）………………………138
非自明性（Unobviousness）………………………………………104

ファクシミリ	20
不意図（Unintentional）	216
不完全出願通知（Notice to Incomplete Application）	129
付与後レビュー制度（Post Grant Review：PGR）	242
プレアピールブリーフ（Preappeal Brief）	180
分割出願（Divisional Application）	155
米国特許規則（37C.F.R.）	2
米国特許法（35U.S.C.）	2
ベストモード要件	107
返金請求	85
放棄（Lapse）	160
放置（Abandonment）	160
法定主題	111
冒認出願	197
補充審査（Supplemental Examination）	228
補正書（Amendment）	138
本出願（Non-provisional Application）	9

ま行

ミーンズプラスファンクション	108
無効（Invalid）	227
明細書（Specification）	30

や行

有効出願日（Effective filing date）	91
優先権書類の電子取寄せ申請書 　（Request to Retrieve Electronic Priority Applications）（PTO/SB/38）	45
優先審査制度（TRACK 1）	192
郵送証明書付郵便（Certificate of Mailing）	20
要約（Abstract）	30
予備的応答	243
予備的補正書（Preliminary Amendment）	46

索　引

ら行
利害関係人 …………………………………………………242
レターサイズ ………………………………………………30
連邦巡回裁判所（Court of Appeals for the Federal Circuit：CAFC）……179

わ行
和解 …………………………………………………………245

A
A 4 サイズ …………………………………………………30

E
EFS-Web ……………………………………………………16
eTDターミナルディスクレーマ電子提出 ………………118
Ex Parte Quayle Action …………………………………142

I
IDS試行プログラム（Quick Path IDS program：QPIDS）………78

K
KSR最高裁判決 ……………………………………………105

P
PCT19条、34条補正 ………………………………………23
PCT審査着手請求（Express Request）…………………23
PCTバイパス出願 …………………………………………10
Private PAIR ………………………………………………87
Public PAIR …………………………………………………87

T
TSMテスト …………………………………………………105

(著者略歴)

大坂　雅浩　（おおさか　まさひろ）
METROLEXIS LAW GROUP創業者　日本国弁理士

法政大学電気工学科卒業後、旧日本デジタルイクイップメント株式会社にシステムエンジニアとして入社。
主として、プロセス系製造業におけるシステム設計やネットワーク構築のコンサルティングに携わる。

1993年〜	三好内外国特許事務所
1996年	弁理士登録
1998年〜	ワシントンD.C.の法律事務所にてトレイニーとして研修後、米国駐在員としてワシントンD.C.に赴任
2007年	ワシントンD.C.で、MOTSLAW, PLLCを共同創立
2017年	事務所創立10周年を迎え、事務所名をMETROLEXIS LAW GROUPに改称
	現在に至る

日本顧客の国際的な知的財産保護業務の傍ら、セミナー講師や著作等を多数努める。趣味は水泳、ゴルフ、テニス、サイクリング。

Metrolexis Law Group, PLLC
ワシントンD.C.オフィス
　202-828-1008
　202-478-2237
　900 17St. N.W. Suite 320
　Washington, D.C. 20006
大阪オフィス
　06-6314-6530
　06-6314-6533
　大阪府大阪市北区南森町2-1-20
　南森町エンシンビル801　〒530-0054
http://www.metrolexis.com/

米国特許手続ハンドブック

平成25年9月17日	初版	第1刷発行
平成30年3月1日	第2版	第1刷発行

著　者	大坂　雅浩 ©2013　OSAKA Masahiro
発　行	一般社団法人　発明推進協会
発行所	一般社団法人　発明推進協会 所在地　〒105-0001 　　　　東京都港区虎ノ門2-9-14 電　話　03(3502)5433(編集) 　　　　03(3502)5491(販売) F A X　03(5512)7567(販売)

乱丁・落丁本はお取替えいたします。
ISBN978-4-8271-1297-9
本書の全部または一部の無断写複製を禁じます(著作権法上の例外を除く)。

発明推進協会ホームページ：http://www.jiii.or.jp/